THE POLITICS OF CC

C000125104

Indonesia is the world's third largest democracy and its courts are an important part of its democratic system of governance. Since the transition from authoritarian rule in 1998, a range of new specialised courts have been established from the Commercial Courts to the Constitutional Court and the Fisheries Courts. In addition, constitutional and legal changes have affirmed the principle of judicial independence and accountability. The growth of Indonesia's economy means that the courts are facing greater demands to resolve an increasing number of disputes. This volume offers an analysis of the politics of court reform through a review of judicial change and legal culture in Indonesia. A key concern is whether the reforms that have taken place have addressed the issues of the decline in professionalism and increase in corruption. This volume will be a vital resource for scholars of law, political science, law and development, and law and society.

MELISSA CROUCH is Associate Professor at the Law Faculty, the University of New South Wales, Sydney. She holds a BA/LLB and PhD from the University of Melbourne. She teaches and researches on law and religion, law and governance, and comparative constitutional law, with a focus on Southeast Asia. Her research has been funded by numerous awards, including the Endeavour Australia Research Fellowship and an Australian Research Council Discovery Grant. She is the author of *Law and Religion in Indonesia* (2014) and *The Constitution of Myanmar* (2019).

THE POLITICS OF COURT REFORM

REFORM

Judicial Change and Legal Culture in Indonesia

Edited by

MELISSA CROUCH

University of New South Wales, Sydney

CAMBRIDGE
UNIVERSITY PRESS

CAMBRIDGE
UNIVERSITY PRESS

University Printing House, Cambridge CB2 8BS, United Kingdom

One Liberty Plaza, 20th Floor, New York, NY 10006, USA

477 Williamstown Road, Port Melbourne, VIC 3207, Australia

314-321, 3rd Floor, Plot 3, Splendor Forum, Jasola District Centre, New Delhi - 110025, India

79 Anson Road, #06-04/06, Singapore 079906

Cambridge University Press is part of the University of Cambridge.

It furthers the University's mission by disseminating knowledge in the pursuit of
education, learning and research at the highest international levels of excellence.

www.cambridge.org
Information on this title: www.cambridge.org/9781108737081
DOI: 10.1017/9781108636131

© Cambridge University Press 2019

First published 2019
First paperback edition 2021

A catalogue record for this publication is available from the British Library

Library of Congress Cataloging in Publication data
Names: Crouch, Melissa, editor.
Title: The politics of court reform : judicial change and legal culture in Indonesia / edited by
Melissa Crouch, University of New South Wales, Sydney.
Description: Cambridge, United Kingdom ; New York, NY, USA : Cambridge University
Press, 2019. | "This volume is the result of numerous collaborations and several academic
workshops and seminars in Indonesia and elsewhere" – ECIP acknowledgements. | Includes
bibliographical references and index.
Identifiers: LCCN 2019010799 | ISBN 9781108493468
Subjects: LCSH: Justice, Administration of – Indonesia – Congresses.
Classification: LCC KNW470.A67 P65 2019 | DDC 347.598/01–dc23
LC record available at https://lccn.loc.gov/2019010799

ISBN 978-1-108-49346-8 Hardback
ISBN 978-1-108-73708-1 Paperback

CONTENTS

FIGURES

TABLES

CONTRIBUTORS

ADRIAAN BEDNER is a professor at the University of Leiden. His research has a particular focus on access to justice, dispute resolution and the judiciary. He is the author of *Administrative Courts in Indonesia* (Kluwer Law, 2001) and *Court Reform* (2008). He has published numerous book chapters and journal articles, including in *Asian Journal of Law and Society, Journal of Legal Pluralism, Hague Journal on the Rule of Law* and *Utrecht Law Review*. Adriaan has undertaken work of a more theoretical and comparative nature on rule of law and access to justice. He has been project leader and/or steering board member of several research projects in Indonesia sponsored by the Royal Dutch Academy of Sciences, the Dutch Research Council and the Dutch Department of Foreign Affairs. At present he oversees a cooperative research project between the Dutch and the Indonesian Ombudsman, as well as the research component of a cooperation project between the Indonesian and the Dutch supreme courts. Furthermore, he has been involved in extracurricular teaching within the framework of the Indonesian-Netherlands' legal cooperation programmes. His consultancy work for the Van Vollenhoven Institute includes giving expert opinions about Indonesian law, as well as advisory work for Indonesian institutions and the Ugandan Judicial Studies Centre.

ARIA SUYUDI is a senior researcher at the Centre for Indonesian Law and Policy Studies. He is a graduate of the Faculty of Law, University of Indonesia, and obtained his master of laws degree from Erasmus University, Rotterdam. He is an expert on bankruptcy and teaches at Jentera School of Law, Jakarta. Aria provides expert advice to the Government of Indonesia through various assignments by the Judicial Reform Team Office, Supreme Court of Indonesia, World Bank Group, The Asia Foundation, the United Nations Development Programme (UNDP) and various domestic and international agencies. For example, he was involved in drafting the regulation on the electronic court, as well as in the implementation of regulation on information technology in the legal sector and working towards improving Indonesia's ranking in the *Ease of Doing Business* Survey.

BINZIAD KADAFI holds degrees from the Faculty of Law, University of Indonesia and the University of Washington School of Law (supported by a Fulbright Scholarship). He is currently a PhD candidate at Tilburg University Law School, the Netherlands. He has held positions as a legal researcher with the Corruption Eradication Commission in Indonesia and the Legal Department of the International Monetary Fund (IMF), Senior Adviser to the Australia Indonesia Partnership for Justice, Lecturer at Jentera Law School and Senior Lawyer at Assegaf Hamzah & Partners in Indonesia. He is the author or co-author of a wide range of articles, book chapters and policy papers on legal reform in Indonesia.

DANIEL PASCOE is an assistant professor at the School of Law, City University of Hong Kong. He received his undergraduate degrees in Law and in Asian Studies (Indonesian) from the Australian National University, and his Master of Philosophy in Criminology and Criminal Justice and Doctor of Philosophy in Law degrees from the University of Oxford, where he was the Keith Murray Graduate Scholar at Lincoln College. Daniel has published on crime and punishment in a number of Southeast Asian jurisdictions, including Indonesia. He is the author of *Last Chance for Life: Clemency in Southeast Asian Death Penalty Cases* (Oxford University Press, 2019). His publications have also appeared in the *International & Comparative Law Quarterly, Australian Journal of Asian Law, International Review of Victimology* and *Vienna Journal on International Constitutional Law*.

FACHRIZAL AFANDI is a lecturer in the law faculty of the University of Brawijaya (UB), Malang, Indonesia, where he teaches courses on Indonesian Criminal Procedure, Criminology and Anthropology of Law. He is now a PhD researcher at the Leiden Law School in the Netherlands. He has been involved in various academic activities in Indonesian criminal justice system and sociolegal issues. He is currently an executive director at the UB Centre for Criminal Justice Research (PERSADA UB). Fachrizal completed his bachelor's and master's degrees in Law at UB. He also received his BA from the Faculty of Psychology, Islamic State University of Malang, Indonesia.

FRANK W. MUNGER is Professor of Law at New York Law School. He is a past president of the Law and Society Association and former General Editor of the *Law & Society Review*, as well as Chair of the section on Sociology of Law of the American Sociological Association and Chair of the Law and Social Sciences section of the American Association of Law Schools. His current research examines foundations for the rule of law in Southeast Asia, and he is completing a book about activist attorneys practising at the margins of Thailand's complex evolving political system. Among other projects related to this research, a 2015 introductory essay compared the prospects for activist lawyers in eleven Asian societies (co-authored with Scott Cummings and Louise Trubek), drawing in part on a three-year collaboration with practising lawyers and scholars who contributed articles for the symposium.

FRITZ EDWARD SIREGAR is an alumnus of the University of New South Wales (UNSW) Law School and in June 2017 was also a visiting fellow there. He was appointed by the President of Indonesia to an important post on the Indonesian Elections Supervisory Board (2017–2022). Fritz completed his bachelor's degree from the Faculty of Law, the University of Indonesia. He holds a master of laws degree from the Erasmus University of Rotterdam and the UNSW. In 2016, he completed his SJD at UNSW on judicial behaviour and judicialisation of Indonesia Constitutional Court. Prior to this, from 2004 to 2009, he was part of the founding generation of staff on the Indonesia Constitutional Court as a justice assistant to Justice Maruarar Siahaan. In 2006, he was selected as the first foreigner to work as an intern as Judicial Associate at the High Court of Australia. He also previously worked at the IMF's project on legal reform in Indonesia. He is the co-investigator, with Melissa Crouch, on a UNSW Indonesia Seed Fund and an ANU Indonesia Research grant to study judicial independence and the courts in Indonesia. Fritz is the author of several journal articles.

GUSTAAF REERINK is a registered foreign lawyer in Jakarta and a regular guest lecturer at several Indonesian universities, including the University of Indonesia. He holds a PhD in Law from the University of Leiden, the Netherlands. He is the author of the book *Tenure Security for Indonesia's Urban Poor: A Socio-legal Study on Land, Decentralization and the Rule of Law in Bandung* (Leiden University Press, 2011). He is also the author of several book chapters and journal articles on Indonesian legal matters. His expertise in legal practice, research and teaching includes foreign investment, mergers and acquisitions, and competition law and other related commercial law topics.

HERLAMBANG PERDANA WIRATRAMAN is Senior Lecturer at the Constitutional Law Department and Director of the Center of Human Rights Law Studies (HRLS), Faculty of Law, University of Airlangga, Indonesia. He is an expert in constitutional law, human rights, law and society and press freedom. He obtained his PhD in Law from the Van Vollenhoven Institute, Leiden Law School. He has held visiting researcher positions at the Graduate School of International Development, Nagoya University (2015), the Centre for Asian Legal Studies, National University of Singapore (2017), Sidney Myer Asia Centre, the University of Melbourne (2017) and the Norwegian Centre for Human Rights, University of Oslo (2018). He has served as the chairperson of the Indonesian Association of Legal Philosophy (AFHI, 2013–2014) and the Indonesian Lecturers Association for Human Rights (SEPAHAM Indonesia, 2014–2017). Currently, he serves as a member of the Steering Committee of Southeast Asian Human Rights Studies Network (SEAHRN).

INDRIASWATI DYAH SAPTANINGRUM is an experienced legal researcher, human rights advocate and PhD candidate at the Law Faculty of the University of New South Wales, Australia. She is the former Director of the Institute for Policy Research and Advocacy (known as ELSAM), a prominent civil society organisation based in Jakarta, Indonesia. She is a recipient of the prestigious Australian Awards Scholarship and the British Chevening Award. She is the author of 'Freedom on the Net Report' in Indonesia chapter published annually by Freedom House (2016–present). She has contributed to numerous research reports, including the *Report on the Performance and Establishment of National Human Rights Institutions in Asia* (2008), *A Gender Responsive Parliament: A Handbook on Gender Mainstreaming in the Legislature* (UNDP Indonesia, 2008), as well as other policy papers.

KEN SETIAWAN is Lecturer in Indonesian and Asian Studies at the Asia Institute, the University of Melbourne. She is also an Associate at the Centre for Indonesian Law, Islam and Society (CILIS) at the

Melbourne Law School. Ken holds an undergraduate degree in Indonesian language, a Master of Arts in Southeast Asian Studies and a PhD in Law from Leiden University, the Netherlands. She has more than ten years of research experience in Asia and her research interests include globalisation and human rights as well as historical violence and transitional justice. Ken has widely published on the politics of human rights in Indonesia, in journals such as the *Journal of the Humanities and Social Sciences of Southeast Asia, Journal of Contemporary Asia* and the *Australian Journal of Asian Law.* Her book *Promoting Human Rights: National Human Rights Commissions in Indonesia and Malaysia* was published by Leiden University Press (2013).

KEVIN OMAR SIDHARTA graduated from the Faculty of Law, University of Indonesia and cum laude from Leiden University with a master of laws degree in International Business Law. His master's thesis compared the Indonesian, Dutch and US bankruptcy regimes. Kevin has worked as a researcher on the Implementation of the Indonesian Bankruptcy Law Monitoring Project, which was part of a Technical Assistance Project funded by the IMF and the Dutch government. This project resulted in a chapter with Marie-Christine Schröeder van-Waes, 'Upholding Indonesian Bankruptcy Legislation', published in *Business in Indonesia: New Challenges, Old Problems* (ISEAS, 2004) and a paper with the same co-author 'Upholding Bankruptcy Legislation: Court Performance Assessment Study' (unpublished 2014) for the IMF. Kevin is a bankruptcy and restructuring partner in Ali Budiardjo, Nugroho, Reksodiputro (ABNR) Counsellors at Law, one of Indonesia's largest and oldest law firms. He has been involved in numerous bankruptcy and cross-border restructuring matters.

MELISSA CROUCH is an Associate Professor at the Law Faculty of the University of New South Wales, Sydney. She obtained her BA/LLB and PhD from the University of Melbourne. She works in the areas of comparative constitutional law, law and governance, and law and religion, with a focus on Southeast Asia. She is the author of *Law and Religion in Indonesia: Conflict and the Courts in West Java* (2014) and *The Constitution of Myanmar* (2019). She is the editor of several volumes, including *The Business of Transition: Law Reform, Development and Economics in Myanmar* (Cambridge University Press, 2017) and *Islam and the State in Myanmar* (Oxford University

Press, 2016). Melissa has published in a range of peer-reviewed journals, including the *International Journal of Constitutional Law, Oxford Journal of Legal Studies* and *Asian Legal Studies*. She has been the recipient of many grants for her research on Indonesia, including an Endeavour Award, the University of Indonesia Visiting Fellowship and the ANU Indonesia Research Grant.

PUTRI K. AMANDA is the Program Manager and Technical Lead for Access to Justice at the Center on Child Protection and Wellbeing (PUSKAPA). She holds an LLM from the University of Washington and in 2015 passed the bar exam. Through her work, she has been involved in reviewing, drafting and advocating policies related to child protection and well-being. Putri has expertise in the issue of juvenile justice and policy reform. She has been involved in working groups with the Supreme Court to establish internal regulations on Legal Services for the Poor and implement the regulation on the Juvenile Justice Law.

RIFQI S. ASSEGAF is an experienced legal researcher from Indonesia and is undertaking his PhD at Melbourne Law School, the University of Melbourne. He previously worked in the President's Delivery Unit (UKP4) and with the Presidential Taskforce to Combat Corruption in the Enforcement System. He established and served as the Executive Director of LeIP (2003–2007) – a non-governmental organisation concentrating on legal and judicial reform. His main research expertise is in the area of judicial reform, anti-corruption and access to information. He is the author of several major legal research initiatives that combine empirical research with policy advocacy and practical application in Indonesia. He is the author of 'Judicial Reform in Indonesia: 1998–2006' in *Reforming Laws and Institutions in Indonesia* (Institute of Developing Economies Japan External Trade Organization, 2007). In 2005, he received The Asia Foundation 50th Anniversary Award in Recognition of Outstanding Contribution to Law Reform in Indonesia.

ROSS TAPSELL is a Senior Lecturer and researcher of Indonesian media and culture at the Australian National University in Canberra. He is also the Director of the ANU Malaysia Institute. He is the author of *Media Power in Indonesia: Oligarchs, Citizens and the Digital Revolution* (2017) and co-editor of *Digital Indonesia: Connectivity and Divergence* (ISEAS Publishing, 2017). Ross has been a visiting fellow at the University of Indonesia (Jakarta), University of

Airlangga (Surabaya) and Indiana University in the United States. He works closely with the ANU Indonesia Project and the academic analysis website New Mandala. He has published journal articles in *South East Asia Research, Indonesia Journal, Journal of Contemporary Asia* and *Asian Studies Review.*

SANTI KUSUMANINGRUM is the founder and Co-Director of the Center on Child Protection and Wellbeing (PUSPAKA), the University of Indonesia, Jakarta. Her research expertise focuses on understanding child well-being and resilience, on overcoming challenges concerning access to legal identity and on turning evidence into policy transformations that affect children and families. Through her previous work with UNICEF, she was involved in the development of Indonesia's Juvenile Justice Law. She is the author of several journal articles and policy papers, including on topics of social exclusion in civil registration and Indonesia's juvenile justice system. In addition, she serves as an advisory board member for the Care and Protection of Children Learning Network.

SHARYN GRAHAM DAVIES is Associate Professor in the School of Social Science and Public Policy at Auckland University of Technology, New Zealand. Sharyn's research focuses on Indonesia, particularly on aspects concerning gender, sexuality and criminology. Sharyn has published three books, including *Sex and Sexualities in Contemporary Indonesia* (2015), and is winner of the 2015 Ruth Benedict Prize for best edited collection. Sharyn has also published on juvenile justice, prisons, policing and LGBT rights. She is the author of *Gender Diversity in Indonesia* (2011) and *Challenging Gender Norms* (2007). She has published in *Asian Studies Review, Journal of Gender Studies* and *Journal of Southeast Asian Studies.*

SHAILA TIEKEN has a bachelor's degree in criminology with a focus on transnational crime from Indonesia's top university, the University of Indonesia. Her primary areas of research interest and expertise are child migration and forced displacement. She has pursued a career in research and advocacy with the PUSKAPA, an initiative of the University of Indonesia, Columbia University and the Indonesian Ministry of National Development Planning. In her free time, she works with a civil society network to advocate for a more accommodating immigration policy for child asylum seekers.

SIMON BUTT is Professor of Indonesian Law and Director of the Centre for Asian and Pacific Law at the University of Sydney Law School. Prior to joining Sydney Law School, Simon worked as a consultant on the Indonesian legal system to the Australian government, the private sector and international organisations, including the UNDP and the International Commission of Jurists (ICJ). He has taught in over seventy law courses in Indonesia on a diverse range of topics, including intellectual property, Indonesian criminal law, Indonesian terrorism law and legislative drafting. He is fluent in Indonesian. Simon is the author of numerous articles and books on Indonesia, most recently *Indonesian Law* (OUP, 2018, with Tim Lindsey) *The Constitutional Court and Democracy in Indonesia* (Brill, 2015), *Climate Change and Forest Governance: Lessons from Indonesia* (2015 with Rosemary Lyster and Tim Stephens), *Corruption and Law in Indonesia* (2012) and *The Constitution of Indonesia* (2012, with Tim Lindsey). Research for this chapter was funded by the Australian Government through Professor Butt's ARC Future Fellowship (FT150100294).

SITA DEWI received her master's degree from the Australian National University. She has extensive expertise as a leading journalist in Indonesia. She is currently a deputy editor for the national desk at Indonesia's leading English-language newspaper *The Jakarta Post*. She is responsible for national affairs covering politics, law, human rights, education, public health and environment. She has reported extensively on high-profile trials, such as those of former Corruption Eradication Commission chief Antasari Azhar and former Bank Indonesia deputy governor Miranda Goeltom at the Jakarta Corruption Court, as well as closed-door trials involving underaged defendants and the trial of serial murderer Baekuni.

SOPHIE HEWITT is a student at the Australian National University, undertaking bachelor degrees in Law (Honours) and Asian Studies. Sofie is a recipient of the Australian government's New Colombo Plan Scholarship, and as part of this programme she interned at ABNR in Jakarta. Sofie was previously Head Research Assistant for the Commonwealth Sentencing Database based at the National Judicial College of Australia. She has also clerked Norton Rose Fulbright in Sydney.

STIJN CORNELIS VAN HUIS is a researcher who has expertise and experience on interdisciplinary research about Islamic courts, Muslim family law and women's access to justice in Southeast Asia, and Indonesia in particular. He holds a PhD from the Leiden Law School of Leiden University, the Netherlands, and is currently based at the Bina Nusantara University in Jakarta. He has published numerous journal articles about divorce and marriage law, and Islamic courts in Indonesia, including in *Utrecht Law Review, Australian Journal of Asian Law* and *Journal of the Humanities and Social Sciences of Southeast Asia*. His most recent studies concern filiation of Muslim children under Indonesian law and the best interest of the child principle in child's custody and child support cases in Indonesia and Malaysia. He is the author of *Islamic Courts and Women's Divorce Rights in Indonesia* (2015).

SURYA TJANDRA is a well-known Indonesian labour academic-activist. He is a lecturer at the Law Faculty of Atma Jaya Catholic University, and for many years he was associated with the Indonesian Legal Aid Institute (LBH) in Jakarta, Indonesia. He is also the founder of the Trade Union Rights Centre, a labour resource NGO based in Jakarta. Surya holds a PhD in Law from Leiden University, the Netherlands, with a thesis concerned with the political economy of labour law reform in Indonesia after the *Reformasi*. He was one of the key figures in the struggle for social security reforms in Indonesia, which led to the enactment of the Law on the Social Security Executing Agency in 2011.

THEUNIS ROUX is Professor of Law at the University of New South Wales in Sydney. His main research interest is in comparative constitutional law, focusing on the politics of judicial review in new democracies. He is the author of *The Politics of Principle: The First South African Constitutional Court, 1995–2005* (Cambridge University Press, 2013) and *The Politico-Legal Dynamics of Judicial Review: A Comparative Analysis* (Cambridge University Press, 2018). His most recent co-edited volume, with Rosalind Dixon, is *Constitutional Triumphs, Constitutional Disappointments: A Critical Assessment of the 1996 South African Constitution's Local and International Influence* (Cambridge University Press, 2018).

ACKNOWLEDGEMENTS

This volume is the result of numerous collaborations and several academic workshops and seminars in Indonesia and elsewhere. In late 2014, the University of New South Wales (UNSW) Law School and the University of Sydney co-hosted a workshop on Indonesia's Constitutional Court, featuring former Chief Justice Jimly Asshiddiqie. In 2017 and 2018, two roundtables were held in Jakarta on judicial independence in collaboration with Dr Fritz Siregar, UNSW alumni, formerly of the University of Indonesia and now of Jentera Law School and Commissioner of the General Election Supervision Body (Bawaslu). In May 2018, I presented at the 'Politics in Action in Southeast Asia Update' at the University of Sydney. In June 2018, a panel discussion on 'The Politics of Courts and Legal Culture: Indonesia's Judiciary and the Legacy of Dan S. Lev' was held at the Law and Society Association conference, Toronto. In July 2018, a workshop on 'Courts, Power and Legal Process in Indonesia' was hosted by the UNSW Law School, and several chapters were also presented at the adjacent event, the Asian Studies Association of Australia biannual conference. In the same month, I spoke at a seminar on 'Judges, Courts and the Politics of Law in Indonesia' hosted at Jentera Law School, Jakarta (physically located next to the Dan S. Lev Law Library in Jakarta). In December 2018, a workshop on 'The Law and Politics of Indonesia's Elections' was also hosted by the UNSW Law School in collaboration with the Indonesian Election Commission, the General Election Supervision Body and International Institute for Democracy and Electoral Assistance. I also gave seminars at the University of Gadjah Mada, Trisakti University and the University of Indonesia. I am grateful to the many contributors, commentators, chairs and participants at these events who helped stimulate discussion and debate on the topic. It is wonderful to see the keen interest in Dan S. Lev's work in Indonesia, as well as overseas. This is a testimony to the great legacy and impression he left on the lives of many scholars, activists and lawyers.

These forums and events would not have been possible without the generous support of several academic institutions. I express my thanks to the following institutions for funding to support these initiatives: the UNSW Indonesia Seed Funds and ANU Indonesia Project and SMERU Research Institute Research Grants (2016–2017, Melissa Crouch and Fritz Siregar); a Faculty Workshop Grant from the UNSW Law School; a Workshop Grant from the Gilbert + Tobin Centre for Public Law at UNSW; and a University of Indonesia Visiting Fellowship (2017, Melissa Crouch). I am grateful to the UNSW Law School for its support of these initiatives and of research collaborations in Indonesia. I would also like to thank Vivien Ngyuen for her assistance at the end stages in the formatting of this volume.

Finally, my thanks to all the contributors to this volume. It is wonderful to have a mix of experts from Indonesia and from further afield, including the Netherlands and Australia. I hope that this is just the beginning of efforts to not only re-engage with the scholarship and activism of Lev but go deeper theoretically and comparatively in exploring the dramatic and significant reforms to Indonesia's judicial system.

The Judicial Reform Landscape in Indonesia

Innovation, Specialisation and the Legacy of Dan S. Lev

MELISSA CROUCH

Indonesia's extensive court system delivers justice for the world's third largest democracy of more than 260 million people. The dramatic end of authoritarian rule under Suharto in 1998 ushered in two decades of law reform. Since then, the constitutional and political system has undergone major changes and legal reform. These innovations and reforms have also affected the courts, which have been restructured and imbued with new powers. The judiciary has changed due to constitutional amendments designed to enhance the independence of the courts from the executive and reinforce the concept of the separation of powers in the Constitution (Indrayana 2008; Horowitz 2013; Crouch forthcoming). At the same time, judges have come under renewed scrutiny with the constitutional establishment of the Judicial Commission and the legislative creation of the Corruption Eradication Commission.

Indonesian courts have expanded in expertise, size and geography, with the introduction of a wide range of specialised courts scattered across the islands. The contemporary judicial landscape features at least thirteen different types of courts in Indonesia. This includes the creation of a specialised Constitutional Court, Tax Courts, Human Rights Courts, Fisheries Courts, Anti-corruption Courts and Commercial Courts. These specialised courts often seek to disrupt existing concerns with the general court system, such as by appointing a majority of non-career judges to the bench in an attempt to circumvent the cycles of corruption inherent in the career judiciary. More generally, these new courts allow judges to focus and develop their expertise in a particularly complex and highly specialised area of law. These specialised institutions are also aimed at reducing the time it takes to handle cases and enhance access to justice. This emphasis on judicial reform, new courts and the trend towards judicial specialisation is not unique to Indonesia and can be found across jurisdictions in Asia (Nicholson and Harding 2010). Nevertheless, the

Indonesian case is remarkable in the number and breadth of topics and areas of specialisation.

Despite sweeping changes to the judicial system, there has not yet been a thorough analysis of how and why Indonesia's courts have changed. There has been little consideration of the politics of either court reform or about the changes and continuities in legal culture in Indonesia. This is with the exception of the Constitutional Court, which is the highest profile specialised court and continues to attract significant public attention because of the political ramifications of its decisions (Butt and Lindsey 2012; Butt 2015a; Crouch, Butt and Dixon 2016; Nardi 2018).

The politics of Indonesia's courts were the subject of sustained scholarly analysis by the late Professor Dan S. Lev. His work was grounded in a socio-legal approach to the study of law, legal actors and legal institutions. In this volume, we seek to reinvigorate and affirm the importance of Lev's work on the politics of courts and legal culture for the study of the judiciary in Indonesia. While we acknowledge that many of Lev's findings were specific to the time and era in which he wrote, at the same time, much of his work on courts points to broader patterns and trends in the courts that are still relevant.

In this volume we consider what Lev's ideas about the politics of courts and the legal culture of judicial institutions might tell us about the recent decades of *reformasi* in Indonesia. What is the role of courts in Indonesia? Where do judges fit? What is the symbolic status and authority of legal institutions and the law? To what extent has the function and influence of the courts changed, or remained the same over time? How do judges interact with other legal actors such as prosecutors or independent agencies? What can we learn from the case of Indonesia more broadly about how to study the politics of court reform?

In this chapter, I begin by offering an overview of the courts in Indonesia. The debate over legal culture is one way of considering the politics of court reform. The judicial landscape has changed over the past thirty years through a combination of increased demands for independence, specialisation and professionalism. I briefly summarise the existing socio-legal debate on the concept of legal culture and the discussion over its usefulness. I then consider the work of Dan S. Lev, a political scientist and Indonesianist, and focus specifically on his work on courts. Lev's work broadly promotes the concept of legal culture as one means of understanding the politics of courts. Lev's work, while primarily focused on the colonial era and the immediate decades following independence in 1945, offers one lens and framework through which to rethink how we study the politics of courts in Indonesia. Lev's work helps us on two levels. The first level of Lev's work is in terms of theory and method. His methodological and theoretical approach to Indonesian law remains critical to the study of the politics of courts. He built theory through practice. His work was deeply empirical. He maintained a particular (and peculiar) geographic commitment to Southeast Asia and to Indonesia, regardless of academic trends. In this way the corpus of his work offers an example of the 'deep research' that he encourages others to undertake. On the second level, Lev's work points us to the uses and misuses of the concept of legal culture for the study of the politics of courts. He exhorts us to interrogate 'grand myths' and in doing so warns us not to use 'culture' as a lazy label or gloss to explain everything. His work demonstrates the utility of legal culture for the purpose of understanding the politics of courts and provides a frame of reference with which to interrogate the role of courts in post-1998 Indonesia. I conclude by reflecting on the common themes of judicial innovation, specialisation and the pervasive issue of corruption that unites the chapters that follow in this volume.

A Timeline of Courts and Judicial Reform in Indonesia

Dan Lev's work charts the emergence of Indonesia's judicial system from its Dutch colonial roots to its postcolonial manifestations. Today, the Indonesian judicial system bears traces of influence from a wide range of sources both domestic and global, from international human rights norms to local understandings of Islamic law and *adat* (customary) law, as well as the persistence of the Dutch legal legacy. The contemporary Indonesian judicial landscape includes both the general courts and specialised courts, as well as various independent accountability agencies. Taken as a whole, we can discern common patterns and trends across what appear to be vastly distinct judicial institutions.

The core of the judicial system since independence in 1945 has been the Supreme Court at the apex of the general court system (Pompe 2005). Below the Supreme Court is a complex network of lower courts spread across Indonesia's thirty-four provinces, hundreds of cities and regencies and thousands of districts. In the 1990s, two additional specialised courts were added – the Administrative Courts based on a Dutch civil law model, and the formalisation of a nationwide system of Religious (Islamic) Courts (which existed in a different form prior to this). The creation of the administrative courts in 1986 marks the beginning of a trend to establish specialised courts. Over a period of sixteen years, from 1998 to 2014, the establishment of new courts took place as part of the *reformasi* agenda. As Table 1.1 demonstrates, the *reformasi* agenda began with the creation of the Commercial Courts in the late 1990s and extends to the establishment of the Small Claims Courts and Fisheries Courts.

Judicial reform is seen as a critical part of the wider *reformasi* call, and has been the motivation for major structural reforms to the Constitution. Judicial independence was reinforced and the separation of powers mandated by the Constitution in an explicit effort to reduce executive influence over the courts. In particular, the long-held demands for judicial independence resulted in what are known as the 'one roof reforms'. In the past, justice was administered under 'two roofs', so to speak, the executive as represented by the Ministry of Law and Human Rights, and the Ministry of Religion, and the judiciary as represented by the Supreme Court and Religious Courts. This meant that matters of budget allocation, appointments, discipline and court administration were subject to the influence and interference of the executive. This was one of the main causes of concern and grievance for the advocates of rule of law over the past few decades.

The post-1998 constitutional and legislative reforms changed all this and gave jurisdiction over all matters of court administration and the lower courts to the Supreme Court (including over the Religious Courts). The 'one roof reform' promised a culture of judicial independence, judicial control over the budget and court administration, the absence of executive interference, and greater efficiency in the execution of justice. There was an attempt to balance this expansion of judicial power with the creation of the Judicial Commission as an accountability mechanism enshrined in the Constitution but whose mandate is explained further in legislation. Within the Supreme Court, major reforms began in 2001 led by Chief Justice Bagir Manan. The Supreme Court continues its long-term reform agenda under the Supreme Court Blueprint 2010–2035 (Supreme Court 2010).

Common challenges and shared legal culture exist across these different judicial institutions. There are two types of specialised courts in Indonesia in terms of institutional status. One is specialised courts that are a separate and independent entity with its own court buildings and procedures, such as the Constitutional Court, the Administrative Courts

Table 1.1 *Legislative reform for the creation of specialised courts and independent agencies in Indonesia*[a]

1986	Administrative Courts (rev 2004, 2009, 2014)
1989	Religious Courts (rev 2006, 2009)
1993	National Human Rights Commission (rev 1999, 2000, 2008)
1997	Military Courts
1997	Juvenile Courts (rev 2012)
1999	Commercial Courts (amended 2004)
2000	National Ombudsman (rev 2008)
2002/2003	Syariah Courts (Mahkamah Syariah) in Aceh (rev 2006)
2000	Human Rights Courts (ad hoc, inactive since 2005)
2002	Tax Courts[b]
2003	Constitutional Court (rev 2011, 2014)
2005	Judicial Commission (commenced 2005, rev 2009)
2004	Industrial Relations Courts[c]
2004–2010	Anti-corruption Court (Jakarta only)
2009	Provincial Anti-corruption Courts (in all 34 provinces)
2009	Fisheries Courts (commenced 2014)
2010	Central Information Commission
2013	Small Claims Courts (commenced 2014)
2015	General Election Supervisory Body (rev 2017)

[a] This table notes the year the court was first established by legislation, and notes in brackets the year the court commenced where its establishment was delayed, and any revisions to the law and jurisdiction of the court. This table begins in the mid-1980s, although there were some specialised courts during colonial rule and under the New Order.
[b] A Tax Review Tribunal had existed prior to this since 1915: Juwana 2014: 308.
[c] Since the 1960s, the Regional Committee for Labour Dispute Settlement (Panitia Penyelesaian Perselisihan Perburuhan Daerah, known as 'P4D') had existed to resolve labour disputes.

and the Religious Courts. I call these 'independent specialised courts'. They operate relatively autonomously from the general court system, although for many of these courts there is still an avenue of appeal to the Supreme Court, as is the case with the Administrative Courts, Military Courts and Religious Courts.

The second type of courts is specialised courts that exist *within* the scope of another court (usually the district or provincial courts). They may use the same buildings, and are often subject to the same legal procedure and bench composed of the same judges as the general courts. I call these 'dependent specialised courts' in the sense that institutionally they are still reliant on the infrastructure, knowledge and personnel of the general court system. They do not have an independent existence separate from the general court structure, but rather remain dependent on it. These dependent specialised courts include the Industrial Relations Courts, the Juvenile Courts, the Commercial Courts, the Anti-corruption Courts, the Fisheries Courts, the Small Claims Courts, the Human Rights Courts and the Tax Courts. All of these are under the general courts with the exception of the Tax Courts, which is within the Administrative Courts. By thinking of these courts as dependent specialised courts, it puts their function and the scope of their mandate in perspective with the rest of the court system.

Specialised courts share other common characteristics. Most specialised courts are permanent institutions, although some have gradually expanded their location over time. Only one, the Human Rights Courts, may function as both permanent and ad hoc. A permanent human rights court for crimes after 2000 has been established in Makassar, and there are provisions for its establishment in Central Jakarta, Surabaya and Medan. Ad hoc human rights courts can be established for crimes prior to 2000 (see Setiawan, this volume).

Most specialised courts are creatures of legislation and are the legacy of the active role of parliament in justice sector reform. This is with the exception of the Constitutional Court, Administrative Courts, Military Courts and the Religious Courts, which all have constitutional recognition. This means that specialised courts are dependent on the goodwill of the legislature for not only the scope of their jurisdiction but also its very existence as an institution. This is important because, as we will see later, specialised courts are not immune to calls to be abolished, as is the potential fate of the Fisheries Court (see Saptaningrum, this volume).

Many courts do have a long legal history in Indonesia or existed in different forms prior to the creation or nationalisation of the court. This is the case, for example, with the Religious Courts (Lev 1972a; Huis 2015), the Tax Courts which was preceded by a tribunal since 1915, and the Industrial Relations Courts that were preceded by an administrative body since the 1960s. It is important to note that Aceh is exceptional because its special autonomy status permits the establishment of the Syariah Courts (Mahkamah Syari'ah). The jurisdiction of these courts is similar to, but more expansive than, the Religious Courts in other provinces and has been covered extensively elsewhere (see Feener 2014).

Geography and location remains of critical importance in Indonesia. With more than 17,000 islands, 34 provinces, 514 cities or regencies, and thousands of districts, the location of a court matters for access to justice. Some courts are centralised and exist only in the capital city, Jakarta, such as the Constitutional Court and Supreme Court. The general court system exists in every province and district. Specialised courts vary in the scope of their geographic coverage. Some, like the Human Rights Court, are intended to exist only in four set locations, while others, like the Anti-corruption Courts, are now required to exist in every district court across Indonesia. Regionalisation stands out as a trend and an important criterion for access to justice. The lack of local coverage has meant that courts such as the Industrial Relations Courts, which exists only at the provincial level and not at the district or township level, are difficult to access (Tjandra 2016: 207).

It is useful to consider what exactly is 'specialised' about specialised courts in Indonesia. Three aspects stand out: the subject matter or jurisdiction of the court; the judicial selection and composition process, often having a majority of non-career or 'expert' judges on the bench; and the investigation and determination procedure, often differing from the general courts and designed to be more efficient. While many of these specialised courts are the result of legal reform, several years on many of these courts have undergone a second stage of reform, and there remain ongoing calls for future reforms. Often debates go back and forth between those who perceive the primary need to be to improve the implementation of the existing law as opposed to the need to amend the law or introduce new laws to amend the court's jurisdiction or role.

An important reform measure that spans both general and specialised courts is the increase in 'non-career', ad hoc or expert judges.[1] Indonesia is a civil law system, and so judges in the general court system are typically career judges selected through a process of closed recruitment (Pompe 2005).[2] By career judge, I mean someone who is recruited as part of the civil service and works their way up the judicial ranks but stays within the court system throughout their career. While there was a history of occasional external appointments to judicial office (Pompe 2005: 25), this practice diminished under the New Order. In contrast, ad hoc judges are usually not civil servants and may enter the judiciary at different stages of their career, generally serving a short term. The

---

[1] The terms 'non-career', 'ad hoc' or 'expert' judge are used interchangeably in this book.
[2] See Shapiro (1981: 150) for a general description of judges as career judges.

appointment of non-career judges occurred with the creation of the Administrative Courts, although this recruitment option was later abolished (Bedner 2001). Then in 2000, non-career judges were appointed to the Supreme Court and Bagir Manan became the first non-career judge to hold the office of Chief Justice. Most specialised courts have a majority of non-career judges, though the ratio of non-career to career-judges varies.

There are common issues and shared problems that have arisen in the establishment of specialised courts. Many issues arise from the broader lack of professionalism, incompetence and corruption that have long been identified with the general court system, first by Lev and then by many others since (e.g. Bell 2017). For example, both the Industrial Relations Courts (Tjandra 2016) and the Human Rights Court (Setiawan, this volume) failed to pay their ad hoc judges in the first few months or years of the court's existence. This forced judges to find other sources of income out of necessity. Many of the problems of establishing specialised courts that exist within the general courts in Indonesia centre around the role and position of ad hoc judges. Given that career judges already receive a wage, payment and recognition of their role is often not an issue. A major issue has emerged due to career judges being exempt from taxation, while non-career judges who are not civil servants must pay 15 per cent tax (Tjandra 2016: 217). This is an immediate financial disincentive to take on the role of a non-career judge. Specialised courts are also beset with the issue of needing capable and competent judges to train and develop specialised expertise. The past two decades have seen significant efforts at judicial training and public education campaigns, or 'socialisation' as it is called in Indonesia, of new laws and legal institutions.

The reasons for the establishment of specialised courts vary although common justifications are evident. Often external donors see the creation of a specialised court as a means to create a body of legal precedent and therefore enhance certainty and consistency in decision-making. But legal culture in Indonesia does not place high value on following court decisions, either in law school (where cases are not read) or in legal or judicial practice (Bedner 2013). The desire to circumvent the corruption endemic to the general court system and to career judges in general is often a prominent reason for the creation of specialised courts. A further reason is the recognition of new and emerging areas of law that require high levels of expertise and judges who are not subject to a rotation system, as are career judges of the general courts. Some specialised courts, such as the Commercial Courts, are the direct result of conditionality loans imposed by external donors such as the IMF (see Reerink et al., this volume), while others such as the Fisheries Courts appear to be more domestically driven initiatives.

The function of all courts in Indonesia, general or specialised, has been affected by the rapid advances in technological innovations. Access to legal information has long been a challenge in Indonesia (Churchill 1992). The Internet has changed how people access information about the courts. All courts in Indonesia have a website, and often a Facebook page, Twitter account and YouTube profile. The Constitutional Court now uploads audio files of all court hearings. Some District Courts have their own profiles on YouTube.[3] The introduction of technology, and new case management and administration procedures has been a core part of the justice sector programmes in Indonesia, undertaken in collaboration with a range of donors, including the Netherlands and Australia in particular (Indrayana 2018). Media coverage of court trials has used these new technologies to enhance their coverage of certain controversial cases (see Tapsell and Dewi, this volume).

There is a system of Military Courts (*Peradilan Militer*) in Indonesia. All members of the armed forces are tried in these courts. However, occasionally, military officers are tried in civilian courts, as has been the case in people smuggling trials (e.g. Crouch and Missbach 2013). There has been significant attention to the withdrawal of the military from an overt political role (Mietzner 2011),[4] but little attention to the Military Courts nor its relationship to the general court system. This remains an area that requires scholarly attention.

This book is focused on courts, but it is important to note the rise of arbitration and the range of non-judicial avenues for dispute resolution from the National Human Rights Commission to the Ombudsman and the Freedom of Information Commission.[5] The main independent accountability institution that is recognised in the Constitution is the Judicial Commission; all other non-judicial dispute resolution mechanisms are subject to the desires of the legislature. There are also new actors

---

[3] See, for example, Profil Pengadilan Negeri Ungaran Klas 1B: www.youtube.com/watch?v=NzhaNtsFVOI.

[4] Contrary to this, the military have often been able to ensure for themselves a role in new legislation, such as the role of the military in situations of 'social conflict' according to the Law on Social Conflict: Crouch 2017b.

[5] On these institutions, see Crouch 2007, Crouch 2008, Crouch 2013; Butt 2013; Setiawan 2013; Setiawan 2016.

such as the General Election Supervisory Body (Badan Pengawas Pemilihan Umum, known as 'Bawaslu') established in 2015 as an ad hoc body that can receive certain complaints about the electoral process (often about the General Election Commission itself). The mandate of Bawaslu was expanded in 2017, and there is the possibility that its role as an independent quasi-judicial investigative body may be upgraded to the status of a court. This is to keep up with the demands for accountability and supervision of elections, although it does create multiple layers in terms of who guards the guardians.

The Study of Courts in Indonesia: The Contribution of Dan S. Lev

Dan S. Lev was a scholar of broad disciplinary orientation, his work engaging with the fields of political science, international relations, Asian studies, legal history, comparative law, legal pluralism and sociology. But above all he was an Indonesianist and unashamedly so (Perry 2006; Pompe 2012). His work was grounded in extended field research and deep in-country knowledge, although he was rarely explicit about this methodology in his writing. This volume is unable to do justice to the full body of Lev's scholarship. Instead, we focus more specifically on his research that relates to the politics of courts in Indonesia. I begin by emphasising the centrality of his *empirical* commitment to his research and the way this method informed his approach to the study of the politics of courts. In many respects, his work fits with the interpretive turn in political science (Yanow and Schwartz-Shea 2006).

Lev's Methodological Approach and Concerns

Lev was writing in the post-colonial era when Indonesia and many other 'new states' (as he called them) from Asia to Africa were struggling with the task of nation-building. In this light, Lev consistently called for 'problem focused research' (Lev 1972a: 224). He argued for the need for 'deep research' in a similar vein to Geertz's (1971) 'thick description'. Lev had little tolerance for research that took legal text literally or divorced from political context. He criticised the 'vacuity of studies of law in new states that take statutory provisions and legal structures at face value' (Lev 1972a: 1). He saw no use for analysis of legal text if that analysis was void of context. His work encouraged empirical inquiry (Lev 2000d: 11). He modelled this deep research approach in his own work, which was based on extended field research, interviews, media analysis, analysis of legal texts, court observation and local academic commentary (e.g. Lev 1965b; Lev 1972a: xi).

Further, he did not shy away from hard research. Much of his research was the first of its kind in English. His pioneering work on the Islamic courts in Indonesia was not only unusual in the field of Islamic studies (with its heavy and almost exclusive focus on the Middle East) but the Islamic Courts were a topic that had never been thoroughly considered in the context of Indonesia (Lev 1972a; see also Crouch 2016a). Likewise, there had been little attention to the courts, the prosecution, the police and the legal profession, as well as the relationship between the two prior to Lev's seminal work. Like other scholars of Asian Studies in the age before the internet, he also took the time to make important documents accessible to a wider audience (Lev 1958).

He was particularly concerned with methods that could capture legal change and continuity in new states, post-colonial Indonesia being his primary focus. Lev argued that:

> In order to understand legal systems in the midst of political transformation, we must examine them from the ground up to find out what sort of political and social space is allotted to them, what kinds of functions they are permitted to serve, encouraged to serve, and forbidden to serve. (Lev 1972a: 2)

Lev was concerned with the Indonesian experience of legal change and the expanding and contracting space for legal institutions (Lev 2000b). Lev's research displayed an ethnographic sensibility and he was particularly concerned with the ethics of research. He sought to illuminate the evolution of local law and legal institutions, but in full consciousness of its political, economic and social settings. He was also acutely aware, and called out, the bias towards European and North American legal experience as the criteria for evaluation of other legal systems. This relates to his concern with the production of power and the 'struggle over the political and ethical dimensions of the Indonesian state' (Lev 2000a: 319). Lev devoted his career to understanding the 'intimate relationship between political and legal authority and structure' (Lev 2000b). Lev advocated for cross-institutional research, that is, to undertake research that understands the courts as one institution in relationship to other institutions, state and non-state. In this way, he eschewed the study of courts in isolation from other political institutions.

Lev maintained a commitment to sustained empirical research as a means of generating theory, in a similar vein to grounded theory (though a field he did not engage with explicitly). His work ranged across genres and wove in stories from his field research, such as the story of the dispute over the broken toilet in his hotel room (which he claims was not his fault) and his failed attempt to have a judge intervene as a means of demonstrating conceptions of justice and the way disputes are resolved in Indonesia (Lev 1972a).

Lev's Approach to the Politics of Courts and Legal Culture

As mentioned earlier, Lev developed his work on legal culture largely in isolation from the more theoretical work in this area. Following Friedman, he argues that there are two key concepts: legal system and legal culture (Lev 1972b: 247). He defines a 'legal system' as formal processes and procedures, which includes formal institutions, such as bureaucracies and the courts, and how they manage conflict. According to Lev, the legal system is legitimated and receives its authority from the political system, and it is used as a tool for social management. He argues that 'legal systems are politically derivative and cannot be understood apart from political structures, interests, ideology and the conflicts they incur' (Lev 2000c: 3). Lev starts with an understanding of a legal system as the 'skeleton of the modern state' (Lev 2000c: 1), and the attendant calls for rule of law as a pillar of modernisation.

Lev goes on to define 'legal culture' as the values that underlie the law and legal process. This includes procedural legal values and substantive legal values, which are often polar opposites and can change over time. Lev argues that law is 'fundamentally dependent upon political reception of legal process – its habits, ideology, principles and controls, and the willing submission, within limits usually, of political leadership to legal constraint' (Lev 2005b: 354). This notion of law is heavily reliant on politics and political process, almost as if law has no autonomy from politics. Lev considers legal culture in the context of studying patterns of change in Indonesia's legal system since the Revolution and in particular explores how judicial institutions relate to political processes and cultural values (Lev 1972b). In terms of courts specifically, Lev saw courts as 'a subsystem of a larger administrative apparatus' (Lev 1972a: 122). Rather than fixate on legislative provisions, he suggests that we should see courts as institutional creatures. He argues that we should 'bypass ... the normal function of judicial institutions and look at them first of all as organisations like any other with group interests to defend and ambitions to pursue' (Lev 1965b: 173). Considering courts as institutions and organisations compels an interdisciplinary approach.

Lev was attentive to the symbolic function of law and its relationship to authority. Lev was concerned with a range of sources of authority, from state authority to religious authority. He notes 'legal systems and law are symbols, and what they are symbolic of, inter alia, is authority, not necessarily coercive authority, but social and political authority, which by its legitimacy, its social rightness, earns loyalty and a measure of compliance' (Lev 1972a: 263). Two symbols of importance reoccur frequently in Lev's writing: the rule of law, or *negara hukum*, and the separation of powers, *trias politika* (Lev 1965b: 184). These were key concepts in post-colonial Indonesia and the decades in which Lev was writing and, they also remain key concepts in post-1998 Indonesia. Lev also tended towards an expansive definition of law: 'law is many things, serves many functions in society, and can be usefully defined in many different ways'. He was clear that his focus was not just on formal legal structures and legal rules, although he includes these in his analysis. Rather, he was concerned with both law and legal institutions in terms of 'how structures and rules are understood, variously used, manipulated, accepted, avoided and so on, along with all the informal structures and modes of action that this kind of definition implies' (Lev 1972a: 263). It is on this basis then that he turns his attention to legal culture.

The Politics of Courts and the Misuses of Culture

Lev articulates his idea of 'grand myths' in an article on 'Conceptual Filters and Obfuscation' (2005b), writing in the context of a debate on Indonesian politics some forty years ago. I seek to re-introduce this idea of grand myths as a useful analytical tool or euphoric couplet.[6] Lev argues that '*Many of us ... remain devoted to grand myths that operate as filters, predisposing us to avoid the empirically obvious in favour of the conceptually obscure*' (Lev 2005b: 345). In fact, this idea of grand myths was present in Lev's earlier work. For example, in 1972, he expresses scepticism at grand theories and cautions against discovering a grand historical trend (Lev 1972a: 224). Instead, he says 'such trends are really conceptual blinders; they inhibit rather than provoke research'. In 2005, more than

---

[6] A euphoric couplet is a term Cribb (2005) defines as an 'adjective-noun combination encapsulating a previously elusive analytical truth'.

thirty years later, Lev returns to and expands upon this idea of grand myths.

Lev employs the concept of grand myths as a way to remind us to be attentive to the empirically obvious, rather than the academically fashionable. Lev was critical of the prior assumptions we bring to our research. He claims that academics sometimes rely on grand myths as a shortcut that simplifies the 'hard work' of research. He warns us to be alert to grand myths and not to fall into their trap. He calls academics to question the origins and implications of such grand myths (Lev 2005b: 347). He goes on to say that we must

> re-examine, as a matter of course, the common myths and explanations we take for granted and, before applying them indiscriminately, to ask whether they make sense among the realities we are trying to understand. (Lev 2005a: 355)

In this regard, Lev understands the work of academics as the hard work of re-examining common grand myths in order to shed new light on present realities. One of the grand myths identified by Lev is that of culture. I first put Lev's work in the broader context of the literature on legal culture, and then turn to show how he employed legal culture in his work, while warning against the dangers of a blanket approach to explain the phenomenon as 'culture'.

The Dimensions of Legal Culture

Legal culture as a concept has received significant scholarly attention over recent decades. The study of legal culture spans several fields including anthropology, comparative law, and law and society (Merry 2010). As many have noted, central to the study of legal culture is the concern over power, authority and equality (e.g. Rosen 2008). Lev's work is primarily empirical rather than theoretical, and so he engages only at a minimal level with the literature on legal culture of his time. Lev cites early work by Laurence Friedman (1969) on legal culture as a 'network of values and attitudes related to law which determines when and why people turn to law, and when they turn away' (see also Friedman 1975). Aside from this early work of Friedman, Lev did not engage with the wider theoretical literature in this area. However, through Lev's methodology, he demonstrates the value of empirical studies for the politics of courts and legal culture.

The debate on legal culture focuses on the meaning of the term and whether the term itself has taken on too many meanings or become essentially meaningless. The work of Susan Silbey is influential in this area.[7] Silbey attributes the rise in legal culture to the shift from the study of law and society to the study of law in society or the cultural turn (see also Riles 2005). Increasingly in the 1980s and 1990s, the focus on legal culture began to overlap with ideas of legal consciousness as the study of public perceptions and use of law and the courts. Silbey is one example of a scholar who initially championed the concept (Ewick and Silbey 1992), like Lev, only later to renege on the term (Silbey 2005). More recently, Sally Engel Merry (2010) and David Engel (Engel 2010; see also Engel and Yngvesson 1984) sought to shift attention away from circular debates about the meaning of the term legal culture, as I do, and instead consider its utility as a key concept in socio-legal research.

Merry (2010) identifies four distinct uses of the term 'legal culture', and this is endorsed as meaningful by others such as Engel (2010). It is particularly helpful because Merry puts Friedman's work and therefore Lev's assumptions in the context of other kinds of studies of legal culture. The first two ways of understanding legal culture, Merry suggests, are the practices and ideologies within the legal system and public attitudes towards the law. She sees these as analogous to Friedman's opposing ideas of internal and external legal culture. Merry's two further categories, legal mobilisation and legal consciousness, capture more recent trends and patterns in scholarship on legal culture. She sees the study of legal mobilisation as one of how people define their problems in legal terms and the related concept of legal consciousness as the way individuals experience the law and understand its relevance to their lives. Examples of this in the context of Indonesia are Juwana Hikmahanto's study of public perceptions of the courts (2014) or The Asia Foundation's preliminary citizen assessment of perceptions of justice (2001) in Indonesia. One of the most outstanding academic studies of judicial perceptions has been conducted by Surya Chandra (2016), whose thesis on the Industrial Relations Courts explores how non-career judges navigate the tensions of deciding cases against the background of being appointed by either the unions or by employers.

Simon Halliday and Bronwyn Morgan (2013) also affirm and find value in inquiries of legal culture. Like Merry, they also maintain the position that legal culture and its cousin, legal consciousness, remain an important field of inquiry. Legal culture can be a useful concept when

---

[7] Another example in the debate over legal culture is the long-standing interchange between Roger Cotterrell (1983; 1995; 2004; 2006) and David Nelken (2001; 2003; 2016).

used with care in socio-legal research. In this volume, the chapters are primarily looking at the *internal* legal culture of the courts and of actors within legal and judicial institutions more broadly. By legal culture we mean the attitudes and opinions of law actors that animate and drive the practice of law in courts and legal institutions. The concept of legal culture is relevant to understanding the politics of court reform. From this basis arises my question: how are we to understand the politics of court reform in Indonesia since 1998?

The Usefulness and Dangers of Legal Culture

In many respects, Lev's entire body of work was committed to exploring and explaining legal culture in Indonesia. His criticism of the broad term 'culture' comes later in his career and after he had spent several decades working on *legal* culture in Indonesia. One reading of Lev's later work is that he repudiates the usefulness of culture entirely, leaving little room for the study of legal culture. I want to suggest that this reading is mistaken, and instead Lev should be read as warning of the dangers and misuses of culture as a grand myth (Lev 2000d: 5). Lev warns of reliance on vague notions of culture, adding that 'culture does not explain much, in fact, and often diverts attention from more critical influences' (Lev 2000b: 74). He puts aside direct engagement with culture, 'in favour of interest, ideology, organisation and power as the primary factors that shape political orders and the legal systems they support' (2005b). His turn to ideology is less explicit, although appears to draw on the work of Geertz (Geertz 1964, cited in Lev 1972b: 309). This should encourage us not to do away with legal culture, but to be more precise and specific in the way that we employ and apply the term.

Lev highlights the tendency of cultural analysis to simplify complexity and therefore present an inadequate and insufficient understanding of concepts of legal change (Lev 2005b: 346). He calls for restraint and sensitivity to the 'weaknesses, shortcomings and dangers of cultural analysis' and avoidance of 'oversimplification inherent' in cultural analysis. He argues that we must not let cultural analysis divert our attention from proximate causes.[8] Lev is arguing that we cannot short-circuit deep research. Serious academics must question the origins and implications of these myths. We must avoid stereotypes, for example, about Javanese

---

[8] Other scholarship on legal culture agrees and endorses this idea; see, for example, Engel 2010.

culture. In this regard, he is critical of Anderson's 'questionable analysis of the Javanese concept of power – now a crutch for academics'. He suggests grand myths are not peculiar to Indonesian studies and that studies of other regions are also 'burdened by assorted descriptor myths'.

Lev was openly critical in his work of the decline in the standards and status of the judiciary. Lev did not hold back his criticisms concerning the increase in corruption within the bureaucracy, and particularly within the judiciary. He went as far as to call them the 'judicial mafia' (Lev 2000a: 310). Lev cautions us to be realistic when it comes to judicial reform. He argues that legal reform is only likely when new political elites take legal process seriously. He also suggests that 'to embark on a program of legal reform before one examines the structure of political power and its conditions is rather dreamy, to put it mildly'. Lev goes on to add that 'uninformed foreign pressure meant to bring about dramatic and quick improvement in legal process has little or no hope of success' (Lev 2005b: 354). He clearly had little patience for developments such as the Commercial Courts, part of a conditionality agreement with the IMF (see Reerink et al., this volume).

Lev argues that fundamental, deep reform can be addressed in two ways: radical and quick (but often shallow) or relatively slow and gradual (which is more expensive and requires more sophisticated strategies over long run). Lev does warn that fundamental reform, deep reform, takes a long time. Lev argues that it is only when the political elite agrees to take certain ideas or processes seriously that these reforms will mean anything. The work of Lev leaves a significant and intellectually formidable legacy for the study of legal culture and the politics of courts. Many of his formative ideas can be built upon and extended in a way that enhances understanding of the role of courts in contemporary Indonesia.

What then of a research agenda for the politics of courts and judicial reform going forward? Lev's focus on grounded research leaves us a ready set of questions with which to consider and assess the last twenty years since the *reformasi*. His work addresses questions of the relationship between judicial institution and broader political and economic processes (How do judicial institutions relate to political and economic processes?); the relationship between courts and social change (To what extent have courts adapted to changing social circumstances? To what extent have courts played a significant role in encouraging social or political change? What sets off efforts at change? What hopes are vested in courts today? (Lev 2000c) Who supports or opposes the role of courts in social change? What conditions and strategies are likely to promote effective change?); and the relative place and importance of law and legal institutions in Indonesia (What is the place of legal institutions in Indonesian state and society? What does the formal legal order look like in post 1998? Given the rise of formal law, has formal law become more important? How important, or insignificant, is written law? When does law count and why?). Lev also urges us to consider the meaning and purpose of the judicial system (What new meanings and purposes has the judicial system been given post 1998? What is the symbolic status of the judiciary in Indonesia today?); the conceptions of justice at work (What are the basic characteristics of Indonesian conceptions of justice? What is the relationship between these conceptions and national law?); and the values of law and its uses as a tool of governance (What kind of value is placed on obedience to law and on the use of law as an instrument of governance?). These are some of the questions that the chapters in this volume begin to consider.

Outline of This Volume

In this volume, experts on Indonesian law and courts reflect on the growth and changes in the role and function of courts in Indonesia. Indonesia's judiciary is a critical part of its democratic system. Lev's work looms large in the study of courts in Indonesia. This volume seeks to revive engagement and debate with his work and its relevance to courts in Indonesia today. This collection of essays on the politics of court reform covers the diverse terrain of judicial and legal reform in Indonesia.

Part I considers continuity and change in the General Court System, with chapters on the Supreme Court, the District Courts and the public prosecution. The Supreme Court has played an important role in leading the judicial reform process since 1998, though, of course, at times it has not been the solution so much as part of the problem. There has not been sustained attention on the Supreme Court since Pompe's seminal work on the Supreme Court (2005). Rifqi Assegaf's chapter, 'The Supreme Court: Reformasi, Independence and the Failure to Ensure Legal Certainty', seeks to reinvigorate discussion and debate on the role of the Supreme Court in Indonesia. The changes to the Supreme Court's role and symbolic power since 1998 have been nothing short of remarkable. The Supreme Court has gained significant authority and status in reformasi Indonesia, enabling it to resist efforts by the House of Representatives (Dewan Perwakilan Rakyat, DPR) or the Judicial

Commission to keep it accountable. Assegaf highlights some of the institutional rivalries that play out in post-1998 Indonesia, in a similar way to Lev's focus on rivalries between the courts, the prosecutor and the lawyers. There are ongoing tensions between the Supreme Court and the Judicial Commission, evident in the blatant refusal of the Supreme Court to enforce recommendations of the Judicial Commission to punish judges found guilty of misconduct. Assegaf also demonstrates the various forms of corruption that exist, such as judges accepting accommodation or transportation services from local companies or local governments. Assegaf highlights the importance of internal reforms in the Supreme Court, such as the introduction of a chambers system to ensure judges can develop specialisation and expertise in particular types of cases consistent with their past expertise. Assegaf's main argument is that because the Supreme Court continues to fail to provide legal certainty and justice, applicants in fact seek out other forums such as the Constitutional Court or other institutions to resolve their disputes. This demonstrates how the inadequacies of one judicial institution have a flow on effect for other institutions.

Below the Supreme Court in the Indonesian court hierarchy are the District Courts and High Courts. This vast network of courts cannot be covered fully in a single chapter, and so Pascoe focuses on sentencing as the lens through which to consider the role and culture of judges in the District Courts. Pascoe's work offers a new methodological approach to study courts in Indonesia, that is, by interviewing judges themselves. As some participants noted at the workshop, this has rarely been done in Indonesia. Pascoe first focuses on the dynamics of internal deliberations among judges and the deciding influence of the most senior judge, although he suggests this is not necessarily inconsistent with decision-making by consensus. Pascoe affirms some of Lev's earlier findings about the nature of the relationship between judges and prosecutors, and shared experience as civil servants, as opposed to defence lawyers. Like Assegaf, Pascoe also highlights the persistence of corruption in the District Courts. Pascoe does emphasise that, at least based on self-perceptions, judges see their role as civil servants rather than as political, contrary to some of Lev's work on the political awareness of judges in the early years of independence and then the New Order period.

Central to the general court system and criminal cases is the public prosecution. Aside from Lev's work, there has been no research on the public prosecution in Indonesia. Fachrizal Afandi's chapter on the public prosecution breaks new ground in beginning not only to rethink Lev's

work on the prosecution, but also to chart a new agenda for understanding the prosecution service in post-1998 Indonesia. Afandi's central
thesis is that the public prosecution is the 'justice system postman', an apt
metaphor that conveys a sense of the relative lack of importance of the
prosecutor compared to other actors in the justice system. He identifies
many factors related to this, such as the loss of power to supervise
investigations in the 1980s. He also identifies a culture within the prosecution that is highly disciplined and military-like in nature. Like Lev,
Afandi maps the tensions between the jurisdiction of the police and the
prosecution, and the relationship between the prosecution and the judiciary. He suggests that although the prosecution is no longer closely
affiliated with the military today, it retains its militarised internal culture.
On corruption, Afandi notes that prosecutors can and do seek permission from the president to investigate corruption cases and in fact
investigate three times as many cases of corruption per year as the police.
But overall, Afandi depicts the prosecution as a conduit, delivering the
dossier prepared by the police to the court. This demonstrates that,
compared to Lev's analysis several decades earlier, the prosecution has
lost the battle for power and status, relative to other justice sector actors.

Part II of the book considers specialised courts established under the
New Order, namely the Religious Courts and Administrative Courts. The
reason it treats these two particular courts as distinct is that they do not
have their *origins* in the judicial reform frenzy of post-1998, although
both have been the subject of reforms since 1998. Building on his earlier
work (Huis 2015), Stijn van Huis' chapter on the Religious Courts is able
to engage with Lev's work in detail, in part because the Religious
(Islamic) Courts are the only specialised court that Lev wrote an entire
book about (1972a).[9] While the Religious Courts are a separate institution, there is a right to appeal to the Supreme Court. In his day, Lev
demonstrated that the Religious Courts were useful as a forum for
responding to the complaints of women on issues of marriage and
divorce. Concerned with this duality between a civil and a religious
judicial system, Huis explains how the Religious Courts have become
incorporated within the state system since the 1970s but that this has not
led to civilian subordination of the Religious Courts.

The volume is enriched by Adriaan Bedner's long-standing expertise
on the administrative courts in Indonesia. In Bedner and Wiratraman's
chapter, 'The Administrative Courts: A Legal Transplant 30 Years On',

---

[9] For a review of the literature on Islamic law and courts in Southeast Asia, see Crouch 2016.

they reflect on some of the major reforms that have taken place in the administrative courts. The Administrative Courts were a specialised court created under Suharto, partly to provide a veneer of accountability of government administration at a time when the New Order was under pressure domestically and abroad. The environment in which the court operates thirty years on is dramatically different, both in terms of the legislative changes that have revised the court's jurisdictional mandate,[10] and broader technological changes that affect all courts such as the digitisation of court decisions, enhancing access to the courts and transparency in decision-making. Even if the Administrative Courts were initially a Dutch legal transplant, its adaptation in the Indonesia context and different interpretation of legal concepts means it has developed its own culture of hearing and deciding administrative disputes. Similar to Assegaf, Bedner and Wiratraman are also concerned with the concept of legal certainty. Through a case study of the general principles of proper administration, they explain the extent to which these principles are applied and show that there remains a need for greater consistency in the application of these principles. The Administrative Courts are also afflicted with the common symptoms of corruption, although given their relatively low caseload this problem is not as pressing as in the general court system.

Part III of the book focuses on specialised courts as a judicial reform strategy of the post-1998 reformasi era. The chapters in this section acknowledge that the turn away from authoritarian rule and the desire to pursue reform to strengthen judicial power has been the reason for the establishment of many new courts. The first chapter, 'The Anti-Corruption Courts and the Persistence of Judicial Culture', by Simon Butt, is crucial to the volume as a whole. Butt directly addresses the issue of corruption, not only in terms of whether specialised courts have been able to punish those found guilty of corruption and have a broader deterrent effect, but whether the institution and its judges have also now fallen prey to corruption itself. Butt builds on his previous research on corruption in Indonesia (e.g. Butt 2012) to explore the implications of the expansion of the Anti-Corruption Courts to the regions. While the Anti-Corruption Courts were initially seen to be distinctive in their internal culture and willingness to convict in corruption cases, the creation of these courts in the regions now means that they are more prone to

---

[10] More recent analysis includes Bedner 2009; and in the context of permit disputes, Crouch 2014: 100–102, 123–129.

corruption internally than ever before and may now be losing some of their original distinctiveness.

While there have been some preliminary assessments of the Commercial Courts (Linnan 2008, 2010; Mahy 2013), Gustaaf Reerink, Kevin Omar Sidharta, Aria Suyudi and Sophie Hewitt offer an updated and contextualised analysis of the Commercial Courts in their chapter. The commercial courts, unlike some other specialised courts such as the Islamic Courts or Administrative Courts, deal with fields of law that are subject to increasing globalisation including company law, intellectual property law (Antons 2011) and competition law. These fields of law also play an increasingly important role in cross-border transactions involving Indonesian and foreign parties. The authors base their research on extended qualitative interviews with judges of the commercial courts, as well as on their experience as commercial lawyers. They consider how the judges, as second-generation lawyers trained and experienced in Indonesia rather than the Netherlands, deal with contemporary legal questions relating to highly globalised fields of law. They find that while the Commercial Courts offer greater certainty than the general courts in terms of procedure and outcome, it is not necessarily a certainty based on globalised norms but is often infused with localised understandings and procedures. The establishment of, and reforms to, the Commercial Courts have been substantial, but the authors suggest there remains significant room for improvement and future reform. Like other chapters in the volume, they admit that the Commercial Courts do not escape Lev's assessment of a pervasive culture of corruption in the courts.

The two newest specialised courts in Indonesia are the Small Claims Courts and the Fisheries Courts. The chapter by Binziad Kadafi covers the Small Claims Courts. It has only been in operation since 2015, so it is still too early to assess its effectiveness. Kadafi, an expert on this new and emerging Small Claims Courts, highlights the potential for this court to resolve small-scale disputes quickly and effectively, circumventing some of the arduous and time-consuming processes that characterise the general courts. The Small Claims Courts will face the same challenges as many other specialised courts – the need to train judges, the challenge of balancing non-career and career judges, and the all-important issue of 'socialisation' as it is known in Indonesia, that is, educating potential users and the broader public.

The second newest court is the Fisheries Courts, as considered by Indri Saptaningrum. This specialised court is a slightly unusual story for two reasons. First, unlike the Commercial Courts or Small Claims Courts, the creation of the Fisheries Court was primarily a local initiative rather than donor-driven initiative (although countries like Australia may have played a part). Second, the future of the court is now under threat due to the rapid rise of an unusual political figure, the outspoken and unconventional Minister for Maritime Affairs and Fisheries, Susi Pudjiastuti (2014–2019). Indonesia's archipelago of 17,000 islands and the waterways in between are both a major asset and a significant challenge to govern. The ocean is under threat from large-scale pollution, said to be second only to China. 'Bu Susi', as she is known by her Twitter fans, has brought the fisheries portfolio into the centre of public attention through dramatic tactics like the destruction of foreign fishing boats in Indonesian waters. But she has also made it her mission to abolish the Fisheries Court and instead give jurisdiction over these matters to District Court judges. Her use of social media makes this campaign a very public affair over what was previously a rather marginal specialised court. This chapter is a story of a fledgling court initiated with sincere intentions but caught in a political battle and with support neither of the Supreme Court nor of the executive ministry that created it.

Finally, turning to a more well-known specialised court, Roux reflects on the role of the Constitutional Court through his comparative research on the law and politics of constitutional courts. Beginning with Lev, he suggests that there is a fundamental tension at the heart of Lev's work. On one hand, Lev as political scientist depicts the authority of law as a function of politics. Yet on the other hand, Lev recognises the importance of law as an autonomous force that lies above politics for the greater good. Turning to constitutionalism in Indonesia, Lev had a particular ambivalence or hesitance about constitutionalism and whether it is able to promote social justice (see Crouch 2018). Roux picks up on this realist, as opposed to romantic, theme and what he refers to as the ideological function of constitutionalism. Roux discerns in Lev's work a concern for those seeking to use constitutionalism for their political interests, such as the legal profession (see also Crouch 2011), academics, students and the middle class. Roux is attentive to the different forms that constitutionalism comes in. Based on his conception of four possible political-legal orders (Roux 2018), he suggests that the Indonesian Constitutional Court has vacillated between a concept of its own authority that is sometimes legalist and at other times more instrumentalist. Roux argues that the Court should seek to stabilise its authority based on a legalist conception. The Court will continue to be an important forum in years to come given the challenges posed by populism, religion, the military and the tendency towards authoritarian rule.

Part IV considers the intersection between rights and courts. The chapters consider children's rights through a study of the Juvenile Courts, the protection of human rights more broadly through the creation of an ad hoc Human Rights Court, the enforcement of labour rights through the Industrial Relations Courts and the role of the media as a means to ensure transparency and accountability of the courts. Surya Tjandra's chapter, 'The Industrial Relations Courts', considers the challenges for labour rights and dispute resolution. The court commenced operation in 2006 but in recent years Tjandra suggests there has been a decline in public confidence. He argues that the poor performance of the Industrial Relations Courts primarily affects employees and trade unions, rather than employers. In outlining the powers and jurisdiction of this court, he points out some of its more unusual features that set it in tension with the need for judicial independence. For example, ad hoc judges can be recommended by unions and employers, but this may lead to conflicted loyalties for judges who may feel a sense of obligation to the side that appointed them. Further in the start-up phase from 2006 to 2008, ad hoc judges effectively went without pay, and this lack of wages most seriously affected judges appointed from the labour unions. With basic operational problems like this, it is no wonder there have been difficulties in attracting suitably qualified ad hoc judges. The issue of hidden costs associated with bringing a case to the court also needs to be addressed. Tjandra illustrates these very real and practical issues with a range of examples drawn from in-depth field research and interviews. Overall, Tjandra points to the need for further reforms to this system of dispute resolution although he acknowledges that the present political environment may not be supportive of such reforms.

In the chapter on the Juvenile Courts, Sharyn Davies, Shaila Tieken, Santi Kusumaningrum and Putri K. Amanda consider how this specialised court is protecting and upholding children's rights in Indonesia. Given that about 25 per cent of the population are below fifteen years old, and more than 3,000 children are imprisoned in Indonesia every year, this is a serious human rights issue. This chapter is an important contribution to broader global debates on juvenile justice (e.g. Langer et al. 2015), which has not sufficiently considered the case of Indonesia. The authors point out that Indonesia has ratified the Convention on the Rights of the Child, and so the law establishing the Juvenile Courts is one example of global legal values influencing Indonesian legal practice.

The authors are particularly concerned with the failure to use imprisonment as an absolute last means of resort in cases involving juvenile offenders. Like many specialised courts, part of the challenge lies in the major task of educating and socialising judges and court users, including prosecutors and police (see Afandi, this volume) to ensure that the new laws are translated into new practices. In relation to Lev's work, the authors concur with the broad emphasis on the need for meaningful change in legal culture and not just in written laws. This means that areas like juvenile justice continue to offer long-term opportunities for civil society organisations and government institutions to support and enhance understanding of the changes to the law.

Aside from children's rights, post-1998 Indonesia saw broader calls for human rights protection and accountability, including the inclusion of a bill of rights in the Constitution that borrows heavily from global norms. As Ken Setiawan explains in her chapter, legislative reforms go further and provide for the establishment of both a permanent and ad hoc human rights court (in addition to a Human Rights Commission, see Crouch 2013). Building on previous research (Cammack 2010), Setiawan reconsiders the strong criticisms aimed at the court for failing to hold perpetrators accountable. Setiawan acknowledges the political embeddedness and dependency of the court, which is reliant on political actors to permit the application and enforcement of human rights norms. Focusing on Lev's procedural and substantive elements of legal culture, Setiawan argues that the overemphasis on procedure corresponds to and masks the lack of emphasis on the substance of human rights cases. By this she means that while human rights have been institutionalised in the formal legal and judicial system, the Human Rights Court has been unable to influence understandings of rights in a way conducive to human rights reform. Alarmingly, it has instead reinforced notions of impunity in the three trials that have been held, and in many ways leaves the atrocities of the past and the perpetrators unaffected. The despair that Lev echoes in his work on New Order Indonesia and the capture of the courts by the authoritarian politics of the day in some respects lives on in the despair human rights advocates have for the Human Rights Court.

Finally, Lev was concerned with a wide range of legal actors and institutions, including the role of the media. Lev considered how legal activists use the media to publicise their case and garner public support for their case (Lev 1978). Similarly, Ross Tapsell and Sita Dewi in their chapter continue this line of thought in a new direction by focusing on 'megaspectacles' or court cases that gain prime time media coverage, and the extent to which this enhances transparency and accountability in the court proceedings. It is not uncommon for judges to permit television cameras in court-rooms, including live-to-air coverage. Tapsell and Dewi point out that Indonesia has a long history of state-sponsored judicial 'megaspectacles', but in the post-New Order period, the media now exploit the range of available technology platforms. This raises difficult questions about the extent to which television coverage provides a greater level of transparency or simply greater populism in decision-making among judges. Tapsell and Dewi offer case studies of several high-profile examples, such as the Schapelle Corby trial of 2004 and the coffee-cyanide murder case of Mirna Salihin in 2016, both of which have regional dimensions given the links to Australia. A more domestic case, though one that gained international profile, is the blasphemy trial of the former governor of Jakarta, Basuki 'Ahok' Tjahaja Purnama, a Chinese Christian and former running mate of the president, Joko Widodo or 'Jokowi' as he is known. Related to Saptaningrum's chapter, there is also the extensive use of Twitter and social media by courts and law actors, such as Bu Susi in relation to the Fisheries Court. Tapsell and Dewi canvass the arguments for and against media coverage of court hearings and consider the impact of first allowing but then later banning cameras in the Ahok case. Tapsell and Dewi suggest that critical media coverage of judicial trials can enhance transparency and potentially go some way to reducing issues such as corruption. But there are real dangers and distorting effects of media coverage, such as the pressures of populism on the court and the potential for media coverage to bias judicial decision-making.

Frank Munger concludes the volume with a broader reflection on Lev and his admirable lifetime of academic activism on Indonesian law. Lev's work has informed Frank's own law and society scholarship in Thailand and his involvement with the Law & Society Association. Similarly, some of the authors of this volume are involved directly or indirectly in key legal advocacy and non-government organisations in contemporary Indonesia, from LBH to ELSAM to Hukumonline. It is this mix of academic scholarship and practical advocacy that informs the chapters in this volume and orients the chapters towards Lev's work as an example of scholarship infused with activism.

Conclusion

This volume has sought to bring together local Indonesian perspectives with that of foreign academics from Australia, the Netherlands and beyond. The chapters share the common goal of looking back over the past few decades to make sense of judicial reforms that have taken place, while at the same time considering to what extent Lev's observations of the courts remain true today. In this chapter, I have offered a broader frame of reference and introduction to the chapters that follow. I have identified some of the broad trends in judicial innovation, specialisation and ongoing shared challenges of dealing with corruption. While acknowledging the differences between general and specialised courts, and the distinction between independent specialised courts and dependent specialist courts, there are similarities in the judicial culture across these legal jurisdictions. This includes the common challenges of establishing a new judicial institution under difficult conditions, the challenge of balancing career judges with non-career judges and the challenge of new judicial institutions finding their way amongst the increasingly crowded judicial and administrative landscape. Across all courts, and therefore across all chapters in this book, strategies to prevent and address corruption, as well as the challenges of building professionalism and competence arise. It remains an ongoing struggle to break away from the New Order legacy of subordinating the courts and allowing them to descend into corruption as the modus operandi, as so aptly described by Lev. In extending Lev's work on courts in Indonesia, this volume collectively suggests the need to reconsider the courts as institutions that are affected by its political, social and economic surroundings. This book will inform and enlighten readers interested in the politics of court reform and seeking to engage – academically, through public policy, advocacy or otherwise – with the intricate system of courts in Indonesia.

PART I

Continuity and Change in the General Court System

2

The Supreme Court

Reformasi, Independence and the Failure to Ensure Legal Certainty

RIFQI S. ASSEGAF[*]

The primary role of the Supreme Court (Mahkamah Agung) is not to correct individual mistakes in lower court decisions but to ensure justice and consistent application of laws (legal certainty), to guarantee individual rights, particularly from abuse by the state (checks and balances), as well as to bridge the gap between law and society (legal development). These are imbedded in the Supreme Court's role in decision-making, judicial review and, to some extent, regulatory and legal-technical supervisory functions. During the Old and New Order periods, due to long-term political pressure and negligence, as well as organisational problems, the Supreme Court failed to perform these crucial roles. Legal certainty and legal development were in many cases absent, while government actions were left unchecked (see generally, Bedner 2001; Lev 2000d; Pompe 2005).

As part of the *reformasi* era (1998–today), we have slowly witnessed some recovery of the functioning of the Supreme Court and the judiciary at large, triggered by political changes that led to the amendment of the Constitution and other statutory modifications as well as internal reform of the Supreme Court. This chapter assesses the reform process and its impact on the Supreme Court's decision-making function, as well as its judicial review and legal development roles. The operation of the Court's new mandate to manage administrative affairs of the lower courts is also discussed. While there are improvements in several areas, such as judicial independence and accountability and, more visibly, case management and legal development, the Supreme Court continually fails to afford

[*] The author would like to thank Melissa Crouch for her input in preparing this chapter and also researchers in LeIP, particularly Arsil, for his thought and help in providing some data.

legal certainty and protection to justice seekers. I argue that the success and failure of reform initiatives can be explained primarily by understanding the historical and continuing political and economic influences over the Court (as suggested by Lev 2005a: 3–6) and the persistent legal culture of judges that often undermines legal certainty.

The Supreme Court: An Overview

The role and powers of the Supreme Court are mentioned in the Constitution and further elaborated in legislation.[1] I begin by explaining the powers of the Supreme Court according to Law 14/1985, unless stated otherwise. As the Court of Cassation, the principal role of the Supreme Court is to ensure legal certainty – the uniform application of the law. The decision of a subordinate court can only be appealed in the following circumstances: if it is made outside jurisdiction, if there is an error in its application or it violates the law, or if it fails to comply with requirements provided by the law (art. 30). Only a few types of cases are outside the Supreme Court's jurisdiction, including decisions concerning pretrial hearings (*praperadilan*), criminal cases involving crimes punishable by one-year or less imprisonment and/or fines (art. 45A) as well as torts and breach of contract cases under 200 million rupiah (approximately US$14,300)[2] with few exceptions.[3] Unlike in some jurisdictions, the Supreme Court does not have authority to choose the cases it wishes to hear and decide upon. The cases are decided based on written submissions alone without the presence of the relevant parties.

The Supreme Court also has power to reconsider, through special review (*peninjauan kembali*),[4] any case that has already been decided upon and which is of conclusive legal effect – including cassation decisions – if, among other grounds, it is made based on falsehood on the part of the opposing party and the deception only comes to light after the case has been decided, there is new important evidence or there is an obvious error in the decision (art. 67). In practice, special review has become a fourth level of appeal since 90 per cent of the applications being lodged were based on the 'obvious error' ground, although most of them were rejected (LeIP 2008: 49).

---

[1] Law 14/1985 on the Supreme Court, as partially amended by Law 5/2004 and Law 3/2009 ('Law 14/1985') and Law 48/2009 on Judicial Power.
[2] This figure uses the early 2018 exchange rate of US$1.00 = Rp. 14,000.
[3] Article 3 of Supreme Court Regulation 2/2015.
[4] Some scholars refer to *peninjauan kembali* in English as 'reconsideration'.

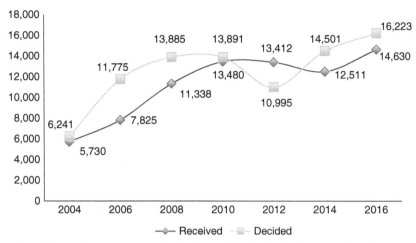

Figure 2.1 Total number of cases lodged to and decided by the Supreme Court between 2004 and 2016

(Source: Supreme Court Yearly Report 2016: 24, 28)

The total number of cases submitted to the Supreme Court has steadily increased over time, as presented in Figure 2.1, with an average of around 11,300 cassation and special review appeals (roughly 1.75 per cent of the decisions of the first instance courts were appealed to the Supreme Court).[5]

The Supreme Court's leadership claims that the relatively high number of cases that are being appealed indicates public trust in the Court (*Aktual* 2017). However, it has also said that these same figures show satisfaction in lower court decisions because they only constitute a minor percentage of the cases being decided by the lower courts (*Hukumonline* 2018a). This demonstrates the Supreme Court's contradictory arguments. On one hand, the Supreme Court claims that the high number of first instance court decisions that are being appealed shows public trust in the court. But on the other, the Court also claims that, because only a small fraction of lower court decisions are appealed, this also shows public trust in the lower court. In 2005, the total number of pending cases on the Supreme Court's docket[6] was approximately 24,300 (Mahkamah Agung 2016: 24).

---

[5] Based on the total cases decided by first instance courts in 2017 (approximately 550,000 cases), not including those that are not within the jurisdiction of the Supreme Court, such as traffic violations and the cassation appeal to the Supreme Court (approximately 9,650 cases).

[6] The pending case here is defined as all cases that remain in the Court's docket by the end of each year.

Table 2.1 *Number and type of cassation and special review cases lodged with the Supreme Court in 2016*

| Case type | Total cases | | Description |
	Cassation	Special review	
Civil	4,942	934	Tort (27.5%), Land (23%), Contract (15%), Labour (15%), Consumer protection (3%), Bankruptcy (1.5%)
Criminal	4,334	353	Drugs (25%), Corruption (16%), Child Protection (11%), Fraud and Embezzlement (9.5%), Theft (3.5%), Assault (3%)
Civil – Religion	822	123	Divorce (56%), Inheritance (19%)
Administrative	575	2,057	Tax (60%)[a], Land (16.5%), Licence (4%) –
Criminal – Military	372	20	Drugs (56%), Sexual-related offence (13%)
Total	11,045	3,487	

[a] The majority of special reviews involve tax cases because Tax Court decisions can only be 'appealed' through special review.
(Source: Mahkamah Agung 2016: 32–78)

Meanwhile, the clearance rates were relatively low (in comparison with the pending cases and incoming cases each year), which cause case delays.

However, the Supreme Court has succeeded in overcoming these issues. Not only has it continued to finalise more appeals than were lodged per year, the Supreme Court has also significantly reduced the case backlog, with only around 2,300 pending cases remaining at the end of 2016. The majority of cases were resolved, with 70 per cent taking between a few months to two years and 20 per cent taking two to three years (Mahkamah Agung 2014: 73, 2015: 27, 2016: 31). If the current productivity is maintained, the disposal time will be shorter.

The majority of appeals involve civil cases, with criminal cases coming second, as shown in Table 2.1.

The Constitution grants the power of reviewing laws to two institutions: the Constitutional Court (*Mahkamah Konstitusi*) and the Supreme Court. The power to review the constitutionality of a statute is in the hands of the Constitutional Court. The Supreme Court has jurisdiction to review laws of a level lower than statutes as against statutes or other higher laws, but it can not review the constitutionality of laws.[7] This includes assessing whether or not the substance of a law is valid and the procedures under which a law was drafted and enacted were complied with. The review can be done by application made directly to the Court or via the district court (art. 31A(1)). The judicial review decision is final.[8] Approximately seventy laws are reviewed by the Supreme Court each year.

Before 2004, the organisational, financial and personnel management of all of the lower courts were the responsibility of the government. The Supreme Court only controlled their 'technical-judicial' function. In the so-called one roof (*satu atap*) system, those affairs were transferred to and are now administered by the Supreme Court. These include managing courts' personnel (e.g. recruitment, transfer, training and supervising of judges and courts' staff), budget and facilities.[9] Across 825 courts there are approximately 7,900 judges, 13,000 clerks and bailiffs and 10,250 staff to manage. This new function significantly increases the Supreme Court's workload.

The Supreme Court is empowered to issue regulations to fill gaps in the law of procedure (art. 79). The regulation of the Supreme Court (*Peraturan Mahkamah Agung*) binds the courts' users. The Supreme Court can also issue a circular letter (*surat edaran*) as a tool to supervise judges in exercising administrative and judicial affairs, including how to administer cases and how to interpret and apply the law (art. 32). Unlike regulations, this circular letter only binds judges, although, in practice, they affect the users of the courts. The law also grants other powers to the Supreme Court, such as to provide legal opinions to state institutions (art. 37) and to advise the president to accept or reject petitions for clemency and restoration of a good name (art. 35). Recently, the Supreme Court has been empowered to decide on the opinion of the local parliament (Dewan Perwakilan Rakyat Daerah (DPRD)) about alleged misconduct or violations of oaths and laws by the head and/or deputy of local government.[10]

---

[7] Article 24A[1] and 24C[1] of the Constitution and Article 31[2] of Law 14/1985.
[8] Article 9 of Supreme Court Regulation 1/2011.
[9] Article 21 of Law 48/2009.
[10] Article 80[1][a] of Law 23/2014 on Local Government, and to decide certain types of election disputes Article 463[5] of Law 7/2017 on Election.

In terms of appointment and tenure, the law allows a maximum of sixty judges in the Court. However, only around fifty posts are usually filled. According to the Judicial Commission, this is because of the limited number of qualified candidates who apply for the post and the Commission's desire to ensure high-quality candidates (*Hukumonline* 2011a, 2017a). Candidates come from two sources: high court judges (career judges) and, to a limited degree, academics and lawyers (non-career),[11] although the latter are not always welcomed by the former. Judicial candidates are selected through a 'fit and proper' test by an independent Judicial Commission (*Komisi Yudisial*), then nominated to the House of Representatives (Dewan Perwakilan Rakyat, DPR) before being formally appointed by the president (art. 8). Since 2013, following a decision of the Constitutional Court,[12] the Judicial Commission only needs to make one nomination, instead of three, for one vacant position to be approved by the DPR. A judge serves until retirement at seventy years old and can only be removed from office by the president upon the recommendation of the Chief Justice and/or the Judicial Commission, among others, with the following reasons: incapable of performing his/her duties, convicted of a criminal offence, violated the code of conduct or consistently neglected his/her duties (arts. 11 and 11A). Prior to being removed from office, they shall be afforded the opportunity to defend themselves in front of a disciplinary committee made up of their fellow judges with or without the involvement of the Judicial Commission, depending on the ground of removal.

The Supreme Court Pre- and Post-*Reformasi*

Pre-Reformasi: *Institutional Collapse*

The autonomy and status of the judiciary, including the Supreme Court, was at its lowest point under the Old Order's 'Guided Democracy' (1959–65). Soekarno dismantled the separation of powers (*trias politika*) and positioned the Chief Justice as a member of the cabinet (Lev 2000d:

---

[11] According to Article 7 of Law 14/1985 on Supreme Court, the appointment system of the Supreme Court judges is a 'closed system', meaning only meant for career judges. However, non-career judges can be appointed among those who have knowledge in certain legal fields. In the New Order, only a handful of non-career judges were appointed, usually as the Chief Justice, to maintain Soeharto's grips to the Court. The number grew in *reformasi* with the intention to ensure the appointment of reformist, clear and capable legal professionals to the Court due to the lack of trust of the career judges. Today, there are less than ten non-career judges in the Supreme Court.

[12] Constitutional Court Decision 27/PUU-XI/2013.

176–7). The independence of the judiciary was further diminished by the enactment of the 1964 Judicial Power Law, which granted power to the president to intervene with the judicial process in the name of the revolution, and this power was used before and after the law was passed (Lev 2000d: 177; Pompe 2005: 43–4). This rendered the Supreme Court's control over the government practically absent. Lev (2000d: 134) argues that the Supreme Court's role in legal development, such as concerning *adat* law (customary law), was minimal because judges had negative perceptions of *adat* principles, there was a deficiency of knowledge about the law and there was a tendency to rely on written law, which is influenced by the civil law traditions.

In the early period of the New Order, the Court tried to rebuild its power and status. It sought the authority to review the constitutionality of a statute and asserted this power by annulling a few colonial laws (Pompe 2005: 90–2). Rejecting the proposal, Suharto's regime intervened and delegitimised the Supreme Court. The executive, while re-establishing the Supreme Court's position as equal to other arms of government, controlled the Court by appointing judges, particularly chief justices, who were loyal to the executive (Pompe 2005: 353–5, 381–2). The DPR played little more than the role of rubber-stamping selected judges. Seniority and bribery contaminated the process. The government's intrusions in lower courts were done through the Supreme Court or with its power to administer their personnel, budget and organisation (Bedner 2001: 230; Pompe 2005: 126–7, 151). The status of the Supreme Court as an institution remained weak. As an illustration, the size and furnishing of the Supreme Court judges' offices as well as other facilities and allowances were inferior to those of middle-rank government officials.

During the Old Order, the Supreme Court was forced to broaden its cassation function due to statutory changes, poor decisions made by unqualified lower court judges (including because of a lack of funding to train and provide legal resources) and also the political pressure to ensure judicial support for the government agenda (Pompe 2005: esp. chapters 6, 8 and 10). The Supreme Court became a third court of appeal, which increased its caseload and further decreased its capability to deliver sound and consistent decisions. The conditions worsened in the Suharto era. The significant growth of new first instance and appellate courts, the distrust of lower courts' decisions, the interest of litigants/lawyers to prolong the trial process and other institutional problems increased the Supreme Court's dockets (Pompe 2005: 280–6). The government then

pushed the Supreme Court to gradually enlarge its organisation and the
number of its judges, which made it harder to maintain consistent
decisions. Attempts to improve coordination between judges to agree
on a unified interpretation of the law, such as through the establishment
of the Supreme Court's Junior Chairperson, and the Court's leadership
meetings (*Rapat Pimpinan*) failed for various reasons (Pompe 2005: 322).

At the same time, the role of *yurispudensi tetap* (a repeated Supreme
Court decision on a particular legal issue) as a tool to ensure consistent
application of the law and legal development was gradually diminished.
One of the reasons was the denial of the Supreme Court's authority by
judges and legal professionals. As a substitute, the Supreme Court issued
circular letters, which, although respected by lower court judges, are not
always effective because of the difficulty in implementation (Pompe 2005:
256–68). From the 1970s onwards, the escalation of corrupt practices
among judges, including the Supreme Court, decreased the quality and
consistency of court decisions (Pompe 2005: 411–17). The paying party
could dictate the outcome of the case, irrespective of the law or case law
(Bedner 2013: 262).

Under these conditions, the Supreme Court failed to perform its vital
functions. It lacked independence and impartiality in deciding cases
against the government or those with financial capacity. After the
1970s, the Supreme Court never challenged the legality of laws (Pompe
2005: 137–41). Legal certainty was absent. As noted by Supreme Court
judges in 1994, '[d]ecisions go in all directions, and for each case you can
find a similar one going exactly the other way. You also get totally
unexpected, sometimes absurd decisions' (Pompe 2005: 324). The institution had practically collapsed.

The Constitution and Institutional Reform

Reformasi brought noteworthy changes to the autonomy, status and
power of the Supreme Court. Constitutional amendments restored the
separation of powers between state organs and provided stronger protection for judicial independence, including by granting power to Supreme
Court judges to appoint the Chief and Deputy Chief Justices (art 24A[4]).
The amendments also instituted a new independent body, the Judicial
Commission, with the mandate to propose candidates for Supreme Court
judges and 'maintain the honor, dignity and behavior of judges' (art.
24B). Changes to the law governing the Supreme Court secured the
appointment, tenure and dismissal of judges. Another important change

was the transfer of the administration of lower courts from the government to the Supreme Court. After decades of struggle, in 1999, the lawmakers passed an amendment of the Judicial Power Law (Law 35/1999). In 2004, this led to the transfer of power to manage administrative affairs of the lower court from the government to the Supreme Court. The Supreme Court also wanted to have a fixed percentage of the state budget each year and the power to review the constitutionality of a statute, but these changes were not part of the amendment.[13]

The budget of the Supreme Court, as well as the remuneration, allowances and facilities of the judges, has been gradually increased. In 2004, the Supreme Court received a total budget of 153 billion rupiah (almost US$11 million), which is greater than five times the 1998 budget.[14] Judicial salaries have also been increased, and today the take-home pay of a Supreme Court judge is approximately 72 million rupiah (US$5,150) per month. The Court also now has more representative offices and improved facilities.

Most of the major constitutional and legal changes in the early *reformasi* were driven by the parliament and the government with support and pressure from the public. The Supreme Court was passive and even opposed a number of reform agendas to enhance accountability and professionalism (e.g. the introduction of the Judicial Commission or the appointment of non-career judges), except in issues that served their interests (Pompe 2005: 472–5). In 2000, the first transparent and merit-based appointment process took place. Several reform-minded career and non-career judges were appointed. In 2001, the 'internal' institutional reform began with the appointment of Bagir Manan as Chief Justice, a former bureaucrat and law professor (Assegaf 2007: 28). By 2003, approximately 60 per cent of Supreme Court judges were new, some also with good track records. With the new leadership and champions from within, as well as the support from donors, NGOs[15] and other

---

[13] For more discussion on the issue of judicial independence and constitutional reform, see, e.g., Lindsey 2008; Hosen 2017: 186–208.

[14] This is before the Supreme Court managed the lower courts' budget; see Supreme Court Blueprint 2003: 76–7.

[15] Donor agencies that did and still support judicial reform programmes include, among others, International Monetary Fund (IMF), AusAID, USAID, Dutch-funded National Legal Reform Program (NLRP), Europa Union (EU), United Nations Development Programme (UNDP), The Asia Foundation and Partnership for Governance Reform in Indonesia (*Kemitraan*). Unlike judicial reform in some other countries, the role of the 'foreign expert' is very minimal. Most of the reform agendas, and particularly their implementations, are prepared and conducted by NGO activists and 'local consultants'.

pro-reform actors inside or outside the government, the Supreme Court prepared a series of reform plans ('blueprints'), instituted judicial reform teams and commenced programmes.

Numerous ongoing reforms have been undertaken in various areas, including judicial transparency and accountability (e.g. mass publication of court decisions and consistent publication of the Court's annual report, improvements in financial and case management, both in the Supreme Court and lower courts); enhancing professionalism (e.g. judicial training and chamber system); enhancing access to justice (e.g. better facilitation of legal aid funding, waiving court fees for the poor); and development of legal policies (e.g. the issuance of regulations and policies to meet current needs). The next section highlights some critical institutional reform programmes in more detail and assesses how these reforms affect the performance of the Supreme Court in its decision-making, judicial review and legal development functions.

Reformasi *and Its Impact on the Performance of the Supreme Court*

Judicial Autonomy and Corruption

As a result of constitutional and political reform, the Supreme Court overall is relatively autonomous from political interference. It is not uncommon for the Supreme Court to decide cases against the interests of the government, political parties and, to some extent, big business. The Supreme Court, for example, has revoked local government licenses in national interest projects involving government limited companies and conglomerates in the case of *Kendeng Farmers* v. *Semen Indonesia*, the *Jakarta Bay Reclamation* case (Kompas 2016b; *Hukumonline* 2017b, 2018a) and numerous others in the environmental sector. In a more politically sensitive case, such as concerning the Golkar Party's internal leadership conflict, the Supreme Court cancelled the government's administrative decision that supported Agung Laksono, the leadership of the government ally, although there was an allegation of improper influence on how the case was handled (*Kompas* 2016a). Also, the Supreme Court now regularly convicts central and local members of

Some NGOs, like Lembaga Kajian dan Advokasi untuk Independensi Peradilan (LeIP), and also Pusat Studi Hukum dan Kebijakan (PSHK) and Masyarakat Pemantau Peradilan (Mappi), work closely with the Court in the reform process, while others, like Indonesian Corruption Watch (ICW), carry out a 'watchdog' role.

parliament and other government and high-ranking public officials for corruption, some of which with severe sentences. Furthermore, many lower court acquittal decisions on corruption were overturned in the cassation or special review appeal (ICW 2014: 16).

There are, however, decisions that raise doubt on the extent to which judges are free from political intervention, such as in the *Akbar Tanjung* case, *Guterres* case or *Time* case (see, e.g. Tahyar 2012: 126–33). Despite the Supreme Court's positive support for press freedom during *reformasi* (Herlambang 2014: 168, 193), a Suharto loyalist with no expertise in hearing press cases was assigned as the head of the panel in the *Suharto* v. *Time* case. In this case, *Time* was found guilty of tort without sound argument, although the decision was later corrected by special review (Tahyar 2012: 212–15; Herlambang 2014: 124, 212–15).

The allegations of political intervention in the Supreme Court are not without cause. Various sources confirmed how members of DPR allegedly traded-off their judicial appointment, budgeting, lawmaking and supervisory power over the Supreme Court to secure cases involving their colleagues, parties and cronies as well as to get their 'share' from the Court's budget projects. Since 2013 until today, for example, the DPR has proposed that judges should be reassessed every five years to determine whether they can continue in office, as set out in the Supreme Court Bill and Judicial Officer Bill (*Surabaya Pagi* 2013; *Hukumonline* 2016b). While proponents claim the proposal ensures professionalism, it is believed that the real agenda is for parliament to exert more control over the judges. In the name of the supervisory function, in 2012 the DPR created a special team to 'examine' problematic Supreme Court decisions (e.g. decided without proper procedure) and enforcement issues. It was suspected that this reform would be used by some DPR members to increase its power over the Court and open an avenue for the DPR to assess cases that concern them (*Gatra* 2012a). Meanwhile the Supreme Court has interests in various amendments of laws discussed and passed by the DPR. This includes laws concerning the extension of judges' tenure, and expansion of the Supreme Court's power and organisation, as well as limiting the Judicial Commission's involvement in judicial affairs and toughening requirements for the selection of non-career judges (Assegaf 2004: 113–14).

Some suggest that the government has used its lawmaking and budgeting power to win the Supreme Court's favour in deciding cases related to its concerns. The government changed its initial rejection and supported the Supreme Court's proposal to recruit approximately 1,600 lower court judges, despite having no justification for the new recruits. The Supreme Court leadership and judges still receive calls from top government officials (and also other political elites) asking for favours or complaining about cases. Aside from these soft interventions, the central and local government ignores Supreme Court decisions that contradict its interests. The government, for instance, issued new decisions or licenses similar to those being annulled by the Court in the cases concerning *Partai Persatuan Pembangunan* internal party's conflict (*Hukumonline* 2016c) and the *Kendeng Farmers* v. *Semen Indonesia.*

The One Roof System has yet to fulfil its promise. Judges still complain about a lack of adequate budget and facilities to support their work, which has resulted in the courts' continuous dependence on the support of local government and sometimes business. Recent examples include cases concerning district court judges receiving free housing from Freeport and car facilities from the Surabaya Local Government (*Hukumonline* 2017d; *Kompas* 2018a). The ingrained practices of nepotism and bribery still colours the promotion process, despite improvements in this area (Irianto *et al.* 2017: 99–123). Now, lower court judges face a more serious threat of intervention from heads of local courts, local government and/or elites (Irianto *et al.* 2017: 168–73) and, in some cases, also Supreme Court judges.

The independence of the district courts in deciding cases and enforcing decisions is also threatened by uncivil elements of Indonesian society, particularly in politically and publicly sensitive cases. This intimidation has meant that their autonomy is further compromised by intimidation when it decides pretrial hearings challenging police investigations or detention (Irianto *et al.* 2017: 173–5). The courts are aware that they need to keep the police onside to ensure they remain willing to safeguard trials – and the judges – in cases that attract public attention. The district courts are threatened physically in some sensitive cases. They need the support from the police to ensure the security of judges and of the trial, but in doing so this may compromise its independence. According to Irianto *et al.*, in 90 per cent of pre-trial hearings, the court rejects the pre-hearing motion brought by the accused.

Much slower progress is shown in the context of judicial impartiality. There are improvements in judicial transparency and accountability, and also enhancement of the Supreme Court (and Judicial Commission's) supervisory functions. But misconduct and corruption practices are still endemic, as evident from the increased number of judges and court staff that are being disciplined (Supreme Court 2016: 361–2). Part of the reason is that the sanctions imposed on those convicted of illegality are very lenient (*Hukumonline* 2009b). For example, the district court judges that were found guilty of receiving bribes were only temporarily released from judicial function duties by the disciplinary committee (*Hukumonline* 2014d). This is also true in the case of Supreme Court judges. Allegations of misconduct or corruption were never processed or 'settled' internally. The only exception is when the allegation was investigated by the Judicial Commission or became public. The *Hengky Gunawan case* is a good example. In this controversial case, the panel of judges reduced the penalty of the drug kingpin from death to fifteen years' imprisonment, grounding the decision in human rights principles against the death penalty,[16] despite the fact that all members had imposed the death sentence in other cases.[17] One member, Justice Ahmad Yamanie, further cut the already discounted sentence to twelve years by forging the verdict. The Supreme Court initially only asked Yamanie to retire, although then decided to remove him from office for 'unprofessional conduct' due to pressure from the Judicial Commission and the public (*Hukumonline* 2012e, 2012f). No further investigation was conducted into the chairperson or another panel member. In another case, Justice Timur Manurung, then the Head of the Supreme Court Supervision Chamber, was handed a 'statement of disapproval' for meeting with an accused involved in corruption cases and his lawyer and was reassigned as the Head of the Military Chamber (*Hukumonline* 2012e).

The Supreme Court tends to resist oversight from other institutions, particularly the Judicial Commission. One example is the Supreme Court's refusal to enforce the recommendations of the Judicial Commission to sanction judges (*Kompas* 2016c). However, this is also caused by different interpretations between the Supreme Court and the Judicial Commission concerning the boundary between monitoring judicial conduct, such as communicating with parties outside the trial – which is the domain of both institutions – and examining 'unprofessional conduct', such as when judges include the testimony of a witness who never appeared in the trials in the decisions – which is beyond the Judicial Commission's mandate (Kompas 2016c). Those conditions have severely damaged the function of the Court, and also weakened public confidence in the institution. In the 2017 survey by *Kompas*, a leading Indonesian newspaper, only 64.3 per cent of respondents view the Supreme Court's

---

[16] Supreme Court Decision 39 PK/Pid.Sus/2011: 52.
[17] Supreme Court Decision 29 PK/Pid/2009; 38 PK/Pid.Sus/2011.

image as positive, which is lower than the Police Force (70 per cent) and the Constitutional Court (69.4 per cent), although higher than the Attorney General's Office (58.8 per cent) (*Kompas* 2017).

Judicial Review

With stronger autonomy, the Supreme Court is also more willing to exercise its judicial review power. There are many cases where it has invalidated laws that contradict higher laws, some of which provide creative judicial reasoning to overcome legal obstacles. In 2011, the Supreme Court finally enacted a new procedure to abolish the time constraint of judicial review applications.[18] Before that, the Supreme Court imposed a 180-day time limit for the applicant to lodge an application, starting from the date that the law was enacted. This significantly limited access to justice because the majority of applications were rejected because they had been filed out of time (Butt and Parsons 2014: 74).

There are several outstanding issues. The new procedure law, for example, still does not recognise oral argument in the review process and the decisions 'lack . . . consistent, principled, and transparent judicial reasoning' (Butt and Parsons 2014; 71). There is also a tendency for the Supreme Court to avoid reviewing sensitive issues that could arouse political and social dissent, such as religion, as shown in the cases of the Tangerang and Bantul local regulations (Crouch 2009: 80; Fauzi 2013) and Ahmadiyah (Crouch 2012b). Also, in a number of cases, the Supreme Court refuses to review the legality of certain legal instruments, such as circular letters (*surat edaran*) or decisions (*keputusan*). Although they could only internally bind the agency that issues them, they also contain abstract 'legal norms' thus impacting the general public (Butt and Parsons 2014: 73–5). This can leave the aggrieved party with no legal remedy. The most striking example is the review concerning Supreme Court Circular Letter 7/2014. This policy requires that a special review (*peninjauan kembali*) application can only be submitted one time[19] and instructs lower courts not to send a second special review application. When this circular letter was challenged, under tort law, the Jakarta District Court rejected it, reasoning that the case should be heard by judicial review proceedings (*Hukumonline* 2015a). However, when judicial review was lodged, the Supreme Court rejected it, arguing that it was

---

[18] Supreme Court Regulation 1/1999.
[19] This is in conflict with Constitutional Court Decision 34/PUU-XI/2013 that allows multiple applications of special review.

outside the jurisdiction of judicial review because a circular letter is not considered a 'regulation' as it is only an 'internal administrative guidance'.[20]

Legal Development and Legal–Technical Supervision

Another transformation that has occurred is the Supreme Court's more active engagement in legal development through its regulatory function. In 2016 alone, the Supreme Court issued fourteen regulations, the same amount as all regulations passed from independence to *reformasi* (Pompe 2005: 253). Many of them were initiated and drafted by the Court itself, while others were responding to and discussed with those who proposed them. Most of the regulations were passed to fill gaps in the law of procedure, for example, the Supreme Court's Regulation 4/2014 and Regulation 3/2017 concern the handling of cases regarding children and women. Other regulations have also dealt with substantive law. In Regulation 2/2012, the Supreme Court altered the amount of loss necessary for an act to constitute a minor property offence in the Penal Code as well as the maximum fines for most offences to adjust them with current values. This regulation was deemed to be necessary because it was last amended in the 1960s. With this adjustment, petty theft offenders stealing equal to or less than Rp. 2.5 million (approximately US$ 178)[21] cannot be detained prior to the trial and face a much lighter penalty. Judges are encouraged to impose fines instead of imprisonment. The Supreme Court has instituted a Small Claim Court so that minor tort and breach of contract cases are processed in a simple, fast and inexpensive manner (see chapter by Binziad Kadafi, this volume).[22] The Supreme Court also stipulates guidance for judges and law enforcers in determining criteria for attributing the *actus reus* to the corporation and elaborates other procedural matters to ensure the consistent application of provisions concerning corporate criminal liability in various statutes.[23] Aside from this regulatory function, the Supreme Court continues, as in *pre-reformasi*, to issue circular letters to advise or instruct lower court judges about how to administer cases and apply laws.

The Supreme Court's efforts have generated public support because many of the regulations being passed respond to a public need for justice

---

[20] Supreme Court Decision 27 P/HUM/2015: 57.
[21] Before the adjustment, the criterion of an act to be considered a minor offence was only ≤Rp. 250 or, approximately, US$ 0.018. 1 US$ equals to Rp. 14,000.
[22] Supreme Court Regulation 2/2015.
[23] Supreme Court Regulation 13/2016.

(*Kompas* 2016d). However, the excessive use of the Supreme Court's regulatory and legal–technical supervisory function is not without issues and risks. Some of the regulations were enacted without proper drafting processes, such as consultation with relevant parties. This issue becomes more troubling in the context of regulations that concern substantive law, which is beyond the Court's mandate. There are also problems concerning the implementation of those initiatives. Four years after the issuance of Regulation 2/2012, for example, many minor theft cases remain to be tried under the old Penal Code provisions, including by Supreme Court judges themselves (Assegaf, forthcoming). More troubling, some of the circular letters issued conflict with the law and public interest. As touched upon, Circular Letter 7/2014, which instructs judges to reject the second application of special review for the same case, is in contradiction with the Constitutional Court decision on the matter.

Decision-making Function

In the context of its decision-making function, the Supreme Court's main concerns are to improve case management, particularly to reduce case backlog. With the instalment of better case tracking and monitoring systems, the Supreme Court can now address the bottleneck in the process of case handling and assess the performance of its judges and staff. Results are circulated among them to improve productivity. The Supreme Court also enacted detailed standards with specific timelines on how cases should be processed in each stage as well as streamlining it (JSSP 2015: 9–12). It cut the time-consuming drafting process, *minutasi*,[24] including by requesting lower courts to submit the electronic version of their decisions so that the Supreme Court can just copy and paste the relevant information. Just recently, the Supreme Court simplified the format of the decisions (*Kompas* 2018a). These efforts have significantly reduced the number of pending cases and case disposal time. It also promises better transparency and services since court users can track the progress of their cases.

Another highlight is the introduction in 2011 of the 'Chamber System' to improve consistency and quality of decisions, as well as to speed up case handling (JSSP 2015: 6). Previously, judges with different areas of expertise, such as the religious or military courts, could hear any type of cases regardless of their professional training

---

[24] *Minutasi* is a process where the clerks – after the case is decided in deliberation meeting – prepare the draft of the decision to be reviewed, corrected – if necessary, and signed by the judges.

(LeIP 2010: 20). In this new system, every Supreme Court judge is assigned to a specific chamber according to their legal expertise and can only decide cases in that chamber – although there are exceptions during the transition periods. Five chambers were established: criminal, civil, religious, administrative and military. Each chamber is headed by a Head of Chamber (*Kepala Kamar*), which replaced the old Junior Chief Justice (*Ketua Muda*) model. Judges in each chamber routinely meet to discuss and agree upon unsettled legal issues and interpretation. The agreements are published in the form of a circular letter to be used as guidance for all judges in deciding cases. There have been at least six circular letters issued up to now. However, as discussed in more detail next, this guidance has not improved the quality of decisions and consistent legal application. More troublingly, the Supreme Court judges themselves have not followed some of the circular letters.

Lastly, the reform agenda has not yet touched the issue of the enforcement of decisions. Many decisions have failed to be executed because of external factors, such as government unwillingness to enforce administrative review decisions or public intimidation in the enforcement process. There are also internal factors, such as an error in the decision regarding the object of the case, or improper influence or intervention from the party or by the Supreme Court itself (Simanjuntak 2009). Occasionally, issues in enforcement of decisions arise because of how the Supreme Court sees its functions. In 2017, for instance, the Vice Chief Justice took the oath of the newly elected head of *Dewan Perwakilan Daerah* (Regional Representatives Council) although just a few days earlier the Court invalided the legal grounds used to elect that council's leadership – making the head ineligible to run for the seat. The Supreme Court argued that the two functions should be seen as independent of each other in this instance (*Hukumonline* 2017c).

The Failure to Ensure Legal Certainty: Case Studies

The Supreme Court's primary functions are to ensure legal certainty and justice, particularly through its decision-making power, by providing sound and consistent judgments to be followed by all courts. Due to the legal and historical setting, the Supreme Court can and continues to use circular letters to achieve these objectives, including enforcing the consensus of chambers' agreements. In the case studies below I show how the Supreme Court fails to perform these vital roles. As a result, this has driven people to seek legal certainty, protection and justice from other institutions, particularly the Constitutional Court and the government.

The Prita Case: Failure to Provide Guidance and Weak Coordination between Panels

The infamous *Prita case* is an excellent example of the multilayered problems concerning cassation and special review. The accused, Prita, faced a civil lawsuit and criminal charges for complaining about her poor experiences in dealing with doctors and hospitals (e.g. misdiagnoses, false lab results, etc.) through a mailing list of twenty friends. Her email was then re-circulated to other mailing lists and came to the attention of the two concerned parties. The doctors, represented by their lawyers, reported her to the police for defamation while the hospital brought a civil action. In the criminal case, the prosecution indicted Prita by alternative charges of defamation or insults under article 45(1) in conjunction with 27(3) of the Law 11/2008 on Information and Electronic Transaction ('ITE Law') or articles 310(2) or 311(1) of the Penal Code. The district court judges rejected the criminal charges due to a lack of clarity. However, in the civil proceedings, she was found guilty and ordered to pay damages. This decision was affirmed by the high court. Both the civil and criminal decisions were challenged in the Supreme Court.

A brief legal explanation is needed to grasp the issues of the case. The Penal Code provides various types of 'off-line' insult/defamation offences, each with different elements of crimes and levels of penalties. To be liable for libel and slander (*pencemaran*), the action must be done deliberately, show the intention to publicise the action (by stating it in public or make the material available to the public) and be done without public interest or necessary defence justification (art. 310). Furthermore, according to the Code and case law, the criminal process can only be started if the victim himself or herself reports the act to law enforcement authorities (they cannot be represented by others, such as a lawyer).[25] There are separate provisions concerning calumny (*fitnah*), minor defamation, defamation against a public official and other related offences. On the other hand, before the 2016 amendment, article 27(3) and 45(1) of

---

[25] Article 319 of the Penal Code and Supreme Court Decision 76 K/Kr/1969.

ITE Law only provided for general prohibition of 'intentionally and unlawfully, distributing ... electronic information and/or documents, that contain libel and/or defamation'. It is not clear whether or not the qualifications regarding intention, complaint procedure, and/or defences in the Penal Code were applicable.

In that context, the Supreme Court had to address several critical legal issues as raised by the criminal defence lawyer including: whether the provisions in the ITE Law should be read in conjunction with the Penal Code provisions, whether the written statement constituted an insult, whether the intention to circulate the statement was *vis-à-vis* the public interest, and the legality of the criminal process since the victims did not report the case to the police.

Since the civil and criminal cases were heard by a different panel of judges and there was no coordination between the two, they arrived at contradictory decisions. The panel on the civil case overturned the appellate court judgment, arguing that the communication was private and the substance of the email was within the realm of freedom of expression.[26] However, on the criminal case, the panel of judges found Prita guilty under the ITE Law by merely stating that (1) 'the statement was an insult in nature' without pointing to the exact statement in question; (2) the statement 'did not intend to be in the interest of the general public because it was made against the doctor' (this is unclear); and (3) she failed to report the matters through the proper channel, the Medical Disciplinary Council.[27] The judges did not respond to any of the defence arguments. Both decisions also failed to refer to a Constitutional Court decision passed a few months earlier which, although declaring that article 27 is constitutional, also stated in the *dicta* that it should be read in accordance with the relevant provisions in the Penal Code as intended by the drafters.[28]

When the criminal case decision was retried on special review, the Supreme Court found her not guilty. However, the court only provided brief reasons, including that there was error in the cassation decision because 'Prita did not have the intention to insult, and the 'unlawful' element was not established'.[29] Again, none of the above legal questions were addressed, as if the judges found it sufficient to fix the error of the cassation decision *per se*.

[26] Supreme Court Decision 300/Pdt/2010; 47–8).
[27] Supreme Court Decision 822 K/Pid.Sus/2010; 42.
[28] Constitutional Court Decision 50/PUU-VI/2008; 110.
[29] Supreme Court Decision 225/PK/Pid.Sus/2011; 39.

The *Prita case* is important because it was the first time that the draconian and vague ITE Law was used to silence critics. The use of the ITE Law has increased. In this case, the Supreme Court had to provide firm guidance to all courts and law enforcement agencies on how the law should be interpreted in light of freedom of expression. It failed to do this, despite sound legal arguments from the defence lawyer. As a result, law enforcers and judges continue to apply the ITE Law inconsistently (Djafar and Abidin 2014). The Supreme Court has also used the ITE Law to convict individuals who sent allegedly insulting private text messages directly to the victim or a few targeted individuals (who were not to the victim).[30]

The *Prita case* also shows that issues in coordination between the panels within the court still exist despite case management reforms.[31] While it did not result in permanent injustice for Prita because of the correction on special review, this is not always the case. In 2013, Marten Apuy and other members of Kutai Kartanegara Local Parliament were charged for breaching Corruption Laws. In the cassation, Apuy was found guilty while other members, who were tried by a separate panel, were discharged. This led him to lodge a special review application on the basis of, among other arguments, the conflicting judgements. However, the judges rejected the argument.[32] Conflict of judgments also occurred in other corruption cases of a similar nature.[33]

Inconsistent Application of Chamber's Guidance on Drugs-User Cases

As with the case of the ITE Law, Law 35/2009 on Narcotics defines several drug offences in a vague manner. Articles 111(1) and 112(1), for instance, provide for a minimum of four years and a maximum of twelve years imprisonment for whoever 'plants', 'grows', 'owns', 'keeps' or 'possesses' certain drugs. The penalty increases for those who 'offer', 'sell', 'buy' or 'receive' them (art. 114[1]). While these tough provisions are aimed at large-quantity drug producers, sellers or traffickers, the police and prosecutors have frequently abused them by charging drug users. This is done regardless of the

---

[30] See, e.g., Supreme Court Decision 340 K/Pid.Sus/2015; Supreme Court Decision 2671 K/Pid.Sus/2015.

[31] In Circular Letter 7 of 2012 [28], the Supreme Court advises heads of all courts (including the Chief Justice) to assign a same panel of judges to hear multi-offenders cases that were charged separately.

[32] Supreme Court Decision 203 PK/Pid.Sus/2013; 83.

[33] Supreme Court Decision 73 PK/Pid.Sus/2013 [85–6]; Decision 138 PK/Pid.Sus/2013 [49].

fact that the law provides separate specific provisions for drug users, such as mere treatment for drug addicts (art. 103) or lower imprisonment penalties without a mandatory minimum sentence and/or treatment for drug users (art. 127) (The Supreme Court defines 'drug users' as those who only possess a small amount of drugs on apprehension, have positive drug test results and show no indication of being drug producers, sellers or traffickers).[34] By doing so, law enforcers can extort offenders for a higher settlement price to stop the case, alter charges or recommend lighter charges. As a consequence, a majority of drug users are charged and sentenced by non-drug use provisions. With approximately 44,000 drug-related cases decided by the lower court each year (Mahkamah Agung 2017: 49), of which many concern drug users, these practices not only create massive injustice but also cause overcrowding of prison populations (*Sindonews* 2017).

Before the establishment of the chambers system, the Supreme Court and the lower courts' response to drug users being charged by other provisions were inconsistent. The Supreme Court criminal chamber tried to unify them by issuing circular letters on the matter as guidance. The 2012 guidance maintained that judges could not depart from the provision used by the prosecutor in the charges, even in the case where drug users, who are supposedly indicted with article 127 or 103, were charged under harsher provisions.[35] Nevertheless, many Supreme Court judges ignore this guideline. Some punish drug users with article 127 although they were not charged under that provision.[36] Others, while agreeing to the charges, sentence the offenders below the mandatory minimum penalties.[37]

As a response, in 2015, the Supreme Court reinforced the 2012 policy but allowed judges to depart from the mandatory minimum penalty.[38] However, some Supreme Court judges disregard it. For example, in 2017, district and high court judges, following the new guidance, convicted a drug user with article 112(1), but sentenced him below the mandatory minimum penalty. Nonetheless, the Supreme Court overturned the decision and sentenced the man with article 127(1).[39] In other legal issues, the

---

[34] Supreme Court Circular Letter 7/2009 and 4/2010.

[35] Supreme Court Circular Letter 7/2012; 31–2.

[36] See, e.g., Supreme Court Decision 750 K/Pid.Sus/2014; 8–9 and 1127 K/Pid.Sus/2014; 15–6.

[37] E.g., Supreme Court Decision 2303 K/Pid.Sus/2013; 11–2.

[38] Supreme Court Circular Letter 3/2015. This also has been found to occur in people smuggling trials: Crouch and Missbach 2013.

[39] Supreme Court Decision 942 K/Pid.Sus/2017; [7–10]. See also similar judgments in Supreme Court Decision 2184 K/Pid.Sus/2016 [16–8] and Supreme Court Decision 712 K/Pid.Sus/2016 [10].

Supreme Court arrived at a different conclusion on whether or not offenders who only possess a small amount of drugs, showed no indication of being drug producers/sellers/traffickers *but* had a negative drug test (or were not tested) can be considered as drug users (Arsil 2018).

The above cases show how the chamber system and the guidance that was issued have not successfully ensured consistent interpretation of law, at least on drug user–related offences. None of the above-cited decisions mentioned the guidance. Furthermore, the policies that were introduced also show how the Supreme Court tolerates abuse of power by law enforcers by not compelling judges to simply free drug users who are mischarged.

The Response of the Public to the Court's Failures

The Supreme Court's failure in ensuring legal certainty diminishes public trust in the Court, which is already low due to corruption and other issues. This had pushed the public to seek protection from other institutions. The common strategy used is to lodge a request for constitutional review with the Constitutional Court. The Constitutional Court can declare a particular provision of a statute 'conditionally constitutional', meaning that it is only constitutional when interpreted in certain ways to ensure consistency in its application. Some lawyers admit to frequently lodging reviews in the Constitutional Court merely to get 'statutory interpretation' to push the consistent application of the law of the general courts. Alternatively, the interested parties request the Constitutional Court to annul provisions that are commonly being interpreted in a different manner on the ground of violation of the 'right to a legal certainty' in article 28D(1) of the Constitution, as in the review of the ITE Law. Some applications even quote examples of inconsistent court decisions as one of the grounds for constitutional review, such as in the case of the review on Narcotics Law[40] or that of the Penal Code provision on special review.[41] Another recourse is to request lawmakers to amend provisions in the law, as, for example, tried in the cases of the Narcotic Law and ITE Law.

However, there are limits to this approach. Although the Constitutional Court can fill the gap neglected by the Supreme Court, there are cases in which the Constitutional Court still leaves the general courts to interpret problematic laws on a case-by-case basis.[42] The

---

[40] Constitutional Court Decision 48/PUU-IX/2011; 16.
[41] Constitutional Court Decision 33/PUU-XIV/2016; 5–7.
[42] See the Narcotic Law review Decisions 31/PUU-XV/2017; 30–2.

Supreme Court can ignore Constitutional Court decisions, as has happened on several occasions. Amendment of laws is not always an ultimate solution. Amendment requires time, thus the 'harm' may already have occurred, or may not have fully addressed the issue. At the end of the day, it is the court that has the power to interpret and apply these matters.

The Reasons for the Lack of Reform

Why have some reforms occurred but not others? Why have there been improvements in case management, enhancing the Court's involvement in legal development and, to a lesser degree, its autonomy in deciding cases against the power holder, but not in other areas such as ensuring legal certainty? The success, or the failure, of judicial reform depends on the existence of various conditions, among others (see, e.g., World Bank 2002: 11–14; Dacolias 1995: 225–9): an interest and desire for change from members of the judiciary, particularly its leadership; and effective support and pressure from political authority and relevant stakeholders – such as law enforcers, lawyers, civil society and academics. It also requires an adequate legal framework and budget; and appropriate reform plans and strategies as well as capacity to implement them, including monitoring (e.g. effective, motivated and capable organisation). Furthermore, some reform agendas are more technical/procedural in nature and may be more in line with the Court's internal interests, thus more attainable and desirable to be addressed. Other reforms are more complex and challenge the political and economic interest of the status quo or concern deep-rooted problems (Lev 2005a: 3–7; Hammergren 2007).

Many of the reforms that have been achieved are those that are linked to the Supreme Court's leadership concerns and interests, supported by many stakeholders including political authorities, and are also more technical or procedural in nature, with some exceptions. The presence of these political support, or at least minimal resistance, is vital, while the strong aspirations and ownership of the reform agenda from the agency, in this case the Supreme Court's leadership and the Chief Justice, are crucial to reform outcomes, due to the paternalistic culture of the institution.

Progress on judicial independence, for example, is a direct result of the strong demand for checks and balances between branches of government in early *reformasi*, manifested by the enactment of other supporting constitutional and legal frameworks. During this time many independent and reform-minded judges and staff within the Court's leadership were appointed due to a better selection system, which was sustained by the Judicial Commission and strengthened by the Constitutional Court. Moreover, as in the case of the Constitutional Court (Mietzner 2010: 412–13), with the dispersal of power between government, parliament and other actors post-New Order, no single political actor has enough power to effectively control the Court. However, as a consequence of the unfinished political reform, political elites and the government still exercise their lawmaking, supervisory or budgeting power to influence the Court. The persistence of corruption in the legal process has further weakened the Supreme Court. This shows that political and economic approaches, as suggested by Lev (2005a: 2–4), are still relevant to understand the Court's role.

The Supreme Court's achievement in case management reform, including the reduction of backlog and the publication of court decisions, is directly related to the keen interest of the Supreme Court's leadership in these agendas. This started with Chief Justice Bagir Manan and his Vice, Marianna Sutadi, and was sustained by Chief Justice Harifin Tumpa and Hatta Ali. Case backlog and long case disposal time has always been considered a crucial issue for almost every Chief Justice in Supreme Court's history because it undermines justice and damages the image of the Court. Addressing them serves the institutional and individual's desire for political and popular recognition. The success of more efficient and transparent case management reform and backlog reduction, for example, has been highlighted by the Supreme Court in its yearly reports and has received acknowledgements from the public, the *DPR* and the president (*dpr.go.id*, 15 March 2016; *Hukumonline* 2016a). Without undermining the Supreme Court's efforts and achievement, those types of reform programmes are less sensitive and more attainable than, for instance, eradication of corruption. The more transparent case process and publication of judgments, for example, mainly impacts the financial interest of the court staff, who can still receive bribes. Judges and courts staff can always keep certain decisions out of the public eye, as many court decisions, especially of the lower courts, are not published. Programmes like the establishment of the Small Claims Court or the alterations of minor property offences provisions, while showing the Court's responsiveness to the aspiration of justice, have also been done with the expectation of reducing incoming cassation cases to the Supreme Court.

Similarly, the introduction of the chamber system is in line with agendas to reduce case backlog and speed up the case process. This initiative also attracted support from general court judges, the 'elite group' in the Supreme Court, as opposed to those from other jurisdictions (such as religious, administrative and military courts). This is because, understanding the case compositions, it means more seats available for judges with civil and criminal law expertise. However, for the new system to attain its other objectives, increasing consistency and quality of decisions, is a different story because they are concerned with more sensitive and deeply rooted multilayer issues. The broadening of the Supreme Court's cassation function pre-*reformasi* (as a result of statutory change and political pressure) has made the Supreme Court become a third instance for appeal and increased incoming cases, which has led to the backlog. The conditions declined due to the increase in size of the Supreme Court organisation and its judges, which has made it harder for the Court to maintain consistent decisions. The Supreme Court has failed to develop a system to respond to these issues and is merely concerned to empty its slate, regardless of the quality or consistency of the decisions (Pompe 2005: 320). At the same time, corruption has gradually become the norm while professionalism is declining within the judicial apparatus and other legal professions. Also, the role of *yurispundensi* as sources of law and assurance of legal certainty has been progressively diminished.

The combination of these long-term political pressures, organisational dysfunction and decline in professionalism has affected the legal culture of the institution and its judges. The term 'legal culture' used here refers to 'the practice of legal institutions' (Merry 2010: 48) or 'internal legal culture' (Friedman 1977: 76), which includes beliefs, norms, values and practices of courts and judges as well as other legal institutions and actors. One of the serious effects is that the Supreme Court has lost its role as the Court of Cassation. It construes its decision-making function as merely to settle individual disputes (who should win – regardless the future impact of the decisions) and also to decide cases promptly. Chief Justice Harifin Tumpa, when welcoming the newly appointed Supreme Court judges, hoped that 'the productivity of the Supreme Court in settling disputes will increase (because) [t]hat is the main function of the Supreme Court' (*Hukumonline* 2010b). This clearly shows the focus is on the case management and backlog reduction agenda, not to ensure consistency in decisions which will face intense challenges and opposition.

The judges' failure to see case law as an important source of law and a tool to ensure consistent legal interpretation has not improved and may even have declined. While many lower court judges maintain that *yurisprudensi* is a 'persuasive precedent', the dominant understanding is that lower court judges are not bound by *yurisprudensi* and may only follow them if they agree with them (Supreme Court's R & D 2010: 38). This view is common among the Supreme Court leadership and judges. Many of them are also of the view that judicial independence means that judges are accountable and bound not to the case law, but to the Constitution, statutes and God. This misconception of judicial independence was used, for example, to reject the *Apuy case* and other similar cases mentioned earlier. Responding to Apuy's appeal for the Supreme Court to review his decisions so that they were consistent with other decisions received by his colleague that committed the same corruption offence, the judges maintained that[43]

> [T]he different judgments between panels of Judges, as expressed in the legal reasoning of each panel's decision ... is a manifestation of Judges' responsibility in exercising their independence in decision-making [power], thus [Judges] are not bound by the reasoning of the decisions in other cases.

With similar reasoning, some Supreme Court judges also challenge the authority of circular letters issued as the result of chambers' agreements. They view them as a form of interference with judicial autonomy (Rahmadi 2016).

The reluctance to follow previous decisions and chamber's decisions is also because of the distrust between judges and other legal professionals on the motive behind a charge or a decision (Bedner 2013: 263). This is not without cause. The *Hengky Gunawan case*, for instance, shows how judges can make contradictory legal interpretations depending on the 'request' of the parties. The main reason some judges ignore Circular Letter 7/2012 that forbids judges to depart from the prosecutors' charge in dealing with drug cases was because they know that law enforcers frequently abuse the law to extort money from offenders.

The complexity of the issue surrounding quality and consistency of judgments means that merely introducing a new system, such as the chamber system, or offering guidance, is insufficient. The Court needs to deal with more fundamental issues, such as judicial corruption and incompetence as well as change how the institution and its judges perceive the role as the Court of Cassation, the case law or other guidance, as well as the meaning of judicial independence principles.

---

[43] Supreme Court Decision 203 PK/Pid.Sus/2013; 83.

Conclusion

Whatever doubts there are about improvements to the Supreme Court, it would be unfair to contend that significant judicial reforms have not taken place. There are noteworthy signs of progress such as in the areas of judicial transparency and case management system, including backlog reduction, and, to a lesser degree, judicial accountability and independence. However, as pointed out by Lev (2005a: 3–4), the judicial reform process has not been a 'deep reform' involving 'getting rid of old institutions, replacing them with new ones, and inventing new rules'. Deep reform is gradual and will involve resistance from power holders and its institutional base. As a consequence, while many changes have been achieved in less complex and insensitive areas of interest to the judges and the Court's leadership, in other areas, there is much to be accomplished.

To some degree, constitutional and political reform has given the Supreme Court greater autonomy and status. The Court's budget and the judges' salary and facilities have significantly increased. In a number of cases, the Supreme Court did not hesitate to decide against the interest of political authorities or review the laws. However, the government, and particularly the DPR, has continued trying to influence the Court through their appointment, budgeting, lawmaking and supervisory power.

The decision-making function of the Supreme Court is severely impeded by immense incompetence and corruption in the institution as well as in the lower courts and other legal professionals. The case studies examined in this chapter show that Supreme Court decisions remain inconsistent, lack sound arguments and have minimal authority as guidance for future cases. The efforts to improve these conditions, such as through circulation of chambers' agreements on particular legal interpretation, have not succeeded as even Supreme Court judges themselves ignore them. This situation is caused not only by incompetence and corruption, but by neglect as well as organisational dysfunction. The Supreme Court perceives its function as one of deciding individual cases in a timely manner and to resolve backlog regardless of the future effect of the decisions and their qualities. The conditions have declined due to judges' misconception of judicial independence *vis-à-vis* the role of case law to ensure consistent legal interpretation and application. As the result, the public have sought legal protection and justice from other institutions, particularly the Constitutional Court.

As Lev argues (2005a), meaningful judicial reform relies on change in many other institutions – the legislature, the police, the Attorney

General's Office, and among the legal profession and law faculties. Today these institutions show less appetite for reform. Nevertheless, the energy of young, reform-minded judges does offer hope. For the reform process to be more meaningful, it will require stamina, smarter strategies and broader support including from the public.

3

The District Courts

Sentencing Decisions as Evolving Legal Culture?

DANIEL PASCOE[*]

'In any country, when the [political] system changes, the decision of the judge also changes'.[1] Does this principle hold true without exception? As part of the present edited collection, aimed at evaluating and extending the work of the late Daniel S. Lev on Indonesian legal culture,[2] in this chapter I aim to determine the extent to which Lev's academic legacy remains relevant in the District Courts of greater Jakarta during Indonesia's 'Reform' (*reformasi*) era from 1998 onwards. In other words, is modern Jakarta's District Court 'culture' recognisable from Lev's early works? The regency or municipality-level District Courts (*Pengadilan Negeri*) try both civil and criminal cases across the Indonesian archipelago,[3] including all private disputes not falling within the jurisdiction of special courts (Juwana 2014: 306).[4] However, this chapter's case study focuses exclusively on sentencing decisions in criminal cases at first instance, which tend to dominate the case dockets of the District Courts (Mahkamah Agung 2018). Criminal punishment, as a subject attracting strong views and even cultural fascination, and unconstrained in Indonesia's predominantly civil law criminal justice system by formal case law precedents or sentencing guidelines (Lindsey & Nicholson 2016: 91; Assegaf 2018b: 1, 15),

[*] Assistant Professor, City University of Hong Kong. Email: dcpascoe@cityu.edu.hk. My thanks go to the School of Law Research Committee for funding this research through a Strategic Research Grant, to Indonesia Jentera School of Law for hosting me in Jakarta, and to Mulki Shader for his help with the interviews. Also thank you to Toni Tong Yihan, Ada Hung Ching, Muhammad Arif Hidayah and Cherry Chow for their research assistance.
[1] Interview with District Court Judge #2, 17 May 2018.
[2] Particularly the following works: Lev (1962); Lev (1976); Lev (1978); Lev (1999); Lev (2000c); Lev (2000d); Lev (2007c); Lev (2011).
[3] Law 48/2009, art. 25(2); Law 8/2004, art. 4(1); Law 2/1986, art. 50.
[4] With the exception of family law disputes between Muslims, for which there exist religious tribunals (*Peradilan Agama*).

forms an ideal vehicle through which to analyse a jurisdiction's 'internal legal culture', as it manifests here in the attitudes and customs of judges.

Legal culture is a famously nebulous concept (Siems 2014: 119). Previous definitions have focused on the law 'in action', rather than the law 'on the books' (Nelken 2004: 2; Siems 2014: 119), the views and behaviours of the public towards laws and the legal system (as 'external legal culture': Friedman 1975: 193, 223–4; Friedman 2006: 189), and informal dispute-resolution processes and methods of social control (Siems 2014: 120). As noted by Crouch in this volume, Merry's understanding of legal culture as having four dimensions is particularly useful (Merry 2010: 43–4). Within this chapter, I focus on 'legal culture' as 'internal legal culture' – namely, repeated beliefs, practices and behaviours on the part of legal professionals. This definition largely accords with Merry's first conception (Friedman 1975: 194, 223; Merry 2010: 43), and importantly, falls within Lev's own use of the term (Lev 2000d: 162).

The courts, as the precise locus of this research, are the central institutional features of modern legal systems and are therefore prominent repositories of local or national legal culture (Lev 2000d: 161, 184). Judges, as the institutional actors who apply law, give the written law colour and meaning through cultural beliefs and practices. And the more than 350 regency- or municipality-level District Courts in Indonesia feature the largest number of criminal trials at first instance, ranging from traffic violations through to murder cases (Lindsey & Nicholson 2016: 65; Mahkamah Agung 2018). Each panel of judges trying a criminal case in the District Courts normally enjoys a wide discretion to impose the appropriate criminal punishment up to a defined maximum, ranging from non-custodial to custodial penalties, even extending to capital punishment in murder, narcotics and terrorism cases (Lindsey & Nicholson 2016: 95). Although newer legislation beyond the 1918 Criminal Code (*Kitab Undang-Undang Hukum Pidada*) has established mandatory minimum fines and mandatory minimum sentences of imprisonment for particular offences,[5] the judicial imposition of such mandatory penalties has proven patchy (Missbach & Crouch 2013: 13–14), and the differences between minimum and maximum sentences remain wide.[6] Whenever such broad discretion exists within the legal

---

[5] See, e.g., Law 5/1997 and Law 35/2009 (narcotics); Law 31/1999 (corruption); Government Regulation in Lieu of Law 1/2002 and Law 15/2003 (terrorism) and Law 6/2011 (people smuggling).

[6] Ibid. For example, Law 35/2009, art. 111(1), penalises the possession of Class 1 narcotics with a minimum four year prison sentence and a minimum Rp. 800,000,000 fine, whereas

system, culture through ingrained habits and belief systems typically operates to 'tame' it (Hawkins 1992: 39), just as has occurred in Indonesia's District Courts.

In short, the present chapter has two aims: first, to distil the common beliefs, attitudes and behaviours exhibited by greater Jakarta District Court judges in considering sentences for convicted offenders, and second, to determine whether modern legal culture in the greater Jakarta District Courts, as reflected in sentencing decision-making, accords with Lev's characterisation of Indonesian legal culture in his seminal essay 'Judicial Institutions and Legal Culture' (Lev 2000d), together with his related work on the subject.[7] If not, which factor(s) explain such differences?

In brief, my findings on Lev's continuing influence are mixed: some of Lev's earlier observations mirror the current attitudes and behaviours of greater Jakarta District Court judges in criminal cases, yet other observations are either no longer relevant after *reformasi*, or at the very least, may not be relevant at the District Court level or within greater Jakarta as a geographical region and cultural space.

Measuring Legal Culture over Time

Most existing scholarship on legal culture tends to be comparative in nature (e.g. He 1994; Ferrarese 1997; Miyazawa 1997; Nelken 2004; Kurkchiyan 2012). This is presumably because a nation-state's legal culture can be somewhat difficult to grasp if considered purely in its own context (Friedman 2006: 189). How is it possible to measure the practices, beliefs and behaviours which bring the written law to life without comparing and contrasting with other jurisdictions? How is legal culture to be assessed as either 'normal' or 'exceptional' without international comparison (Nelken 2011: 393–4)?[8] One solution might be to compare legal culture within a vertical plane (i.e. between different courts in the same jurisdiction) (e.g. Crouch, this volume). However, the

---

the maximum punishment is twelve years plus a Rp. 8,000,000,000 fine. Law 31/1999 punishes individuals who unlawfully enrich themselves with a prison sentence of between four and twenty years (extending to life in the most serious cases), plus a fine of between Rp. 200,000,000 and Rp. 1,000,000,000.

[7] See note 2, above.

[8] Another explanation for the scarcity of longitudinal research on legal culture is that the field is relatively young. Although law has long been associated with societal culture, scholars typically trace the field of legal culture to the late 1960s with Lawrence Friedman himself (Cotterrell 2006: 82; Carrillo 2011: 72).

present case study instead serves to extend academic scholarship on legal culture in a new *longitudinal* direction, by asking whether judicial behaviours, practices and beliefs have changed within the criminal trial courts in Indonesia over time, independently of formal legislative and procedural changes to the Indonesian legal system (Friedman 1975: 234–5).[9] With academic research on legal culture only becoming widespread from the late 1960s onwards,[10] it is a relatively rare privilege to be able to reassess cultural practices in any particular legal system more than fifty years after Lev's pioneering work on the subject.

There are three main reasons to measure changes in Indonesian legal culture over time: first is to gauge the continued theoretical significance of Lev's scholarship for the Indonesian legal system, and for studies on legal culture and legal institutions more generally. Second is to seek more general lessons on the way in which legal culture changes over time. Indonesia offers an ideal opportunity to test the hypothesis that legal culture normally changes incrementally over time (Junquiera 2003: 67; Friedman 2006: 193; Nelken 2014: 270), but can change more rapidly during periods of democratisation, as several Iberian and Latin American examples suggest (e.g. Morn & Toro 1990; Bergoglio 2003; 54–5; Faivovich 2003: 130–1).[11] After all, 2018 marks exactly twenty years since the President Suharto resigned, triggering the *reformasi* era in Indonesian politics. The third, instrumental, reason to mark cultural contrasts is to effect and continue institutional change in a post-authoritarian society such as Indonesia. As Lev (2007c: 250) and Nelken (2014: 262) have both suggested, successful law reform efforts in transitional societies begin with a profound knowledge of local legal culture in a contemporaneous setting, rather than through blindly imposing legal transplants developed in other contexts.

Above, I outlined several disagreements over what is meant by the phrase 'legal culture'. There are also disagreements between legal scholars

---

[9] Nonetheless, the formal legal changes relevant to sentencing in the District Courts have been significant since Lev first began writing about Indonesian legal culture during the late Sukarno period. There have been several new iterations of the Judicial Power Law passed since then (the most recent of which is Law 48/2009). The law governing the general courts has been reformed three times (by Law 13/1965, Law 2/1986 and Law 8/2004). The current Criminal Procedure Code was passed in 1981 (Law 8/1981), supplanting the previous Dutch code (Herziene Inlandsch (Indonesisch) Reglement 1941). There have also been several new criminal offences created (see note 5, above).

[10] See note 8, above.

[11] Compare Dias' research on legal culture in Portugal after the 'Carnation Revolution' of 1974 (Dias 2016).

on how to *measure* 'internal' legal culture at any one point in time (Nelken 2014: 262; Grodeland & Miller 2015: 17–18). Analysing case judgements systematically is one approach (Friedman 1985: 119), albeit with several drawbacks: to obtain a wide sample, this method is time-intensive; moreover, Jakarta District Court judgements have only been widely available since approximately 2010 and are not yet available in full on the Indonesian Supreme Court's website (Mahkamah Agung 2018). Perhaps most importantly, where written judgements *are* available they do not always convey the beliefs, practices and behaviours of the judges in resolving the case. In other words, court judgements have insufficient *validity* as a measure of legal culture.

Another option would have been to observe court proceedings in detail (see Hurst, this volume) – i.e. legal anthropology/ethnography. The major drawbacks of this approach are, again, the time it takes for the researcher; the difficulty in obtaining a large and representative sample of cases when only one proceeding can be observed at a time; and as with the written judgement-based approach, the lack of access to the judge's private thoughts, and to the negotiations conducted in the private conference between the panel of judges in coming to the decision (*musya-warah*). Almost by definition, 'internal' legal culture includes not only what happens in public view, but also what transpires behind closed doors, and within the judges' own thoughts.

Ultimately, I have chosen to adopt an approach I have applied to previous research on decision-making in the context of commutations and pardons by the executive, including in Indonesia (Pascoe 2014, 2017a, 2019). I conducted semi-structured 'elite' interviews with relevant decision-makers (the judges themselves), and with other observants and participants in the courtroom (defence advocates and legal NGO staff), who provide an important outsider's view of judicial customs and behaviour, to counter judges' potentially selective and self-justifying answers.[12] Together with researchers from Indonesia Jentera Law School, I conducted semi-structured interviews with twelve

---

[12] Corruption is a good example of an issue that bears upon judicial customs and behaviour, but nonetheless requires outside viewpoints, as judges will not admit to involvement in corrupt practices and will be loath to implicate their colleagues. As Butt (2012: 22) states:

It is important ... to emphasise that claims about the extent of corruption within [Indonesian] law enforcement agencies are based largely on public perceptions, anecdotal accounts, commonly revealed in the media and *discussions with lawyers and law reform activists*, rather than on firm empirical data [.] [emphasis added]

District Court judges from the greater Jakarta Area over a one-month period in May 2018, together with eight other interviews with legal NGO staff and legal advocates. Semi-structured interviews may possess their own disadvantages as a method of measuring 'internal' legal culture,[13] but for a study of judicial culture in Indonesian courts, they are entirely fit for purpose.

Daniel S. Lev on Culture in the Indonesian Courts

Before he turned away from culture later in his career in favour of 'ideology' (Lev 1992: 1–2; Lev 2005b: 354; Pompe 2012: 201), the foremost Western scholar of the Indonesian legal system during the Sukarno and Suharto administrations (1945–98), the late Daniel S. Lev (1933–2006), described Indonesian 'legal culture' as consisting of several key elements, at least as they relate to the court system and to judicial officers as legal professionals.[14] To reach the following conclusions, Lev's methods included an eclectic mix of historical, legal doctrinal, interview-based and ethnographic approaches. Together, Lev's works provide a multifaceted theory of Indonesian legal culture that the present study seeks to evaluate across a more recent timeframe and a more specific legal context (namely, criminal punishment).

Lev's first set of observations relate to public and judicial attitudes towards the law in Indonesia, invoking both 'internal' and 'external' legal culture (Friedman 1975: 223–4). Here, Lev saw the formal law as a dispute resolution mechanism lessened in importance by 'rules of influence, money, family, social status and military power' (Lev 2000d: 171, 185).[15] Likewise, the role of conciliation and compromise was prominent in resolving legal disputes, both inside and outside the courtroom (Lev 2000d: 179, 186–93). Lev's conception of Indonesian

---

[13] For example, impressionistic, self-aggrandising, or simplistic accounts by the interviewee; answers being affected by the setting (the interview and the interviewer); incomplete 'corporate answers' designed to protect the reputation of the individual or the institution; and inconsistency between different accounts from the same interviewee or different interviewees (e.g. Nelken 2011: 92; Lilleker 2007: 208; Davies 2001: 75; Pascoe 2017b). Note that, wherever possible, I have attempted to provide at least two independent interview sources to support a proposition, or to verify interview data with written sources, in accordance with standard academic practice (Davies 2001: 78).

[14] Here, I attempt to break Indonesian legal culture into several constituent parts for later explanation, rather than using legal culture as an explanatory variable in itself (see Nelken 1997: 71–2).

[15] See also Butt and Parsons (2014: 58–9).

legal culture as involving frequent informal dispute resolution is an account corroborated by more recent publications (e.g. Naibaho 2011: 91; Komisi Yudisial Republik Indonesia 2017a; Mann 2015). As Nicholson (2009: 273) observes, 'Consensually-based forms of dispute resolution (*musyawarah*) have a strong cultural base and a long history in Indonesia'. Lev himself (2000d: 192) labelled conciliation 'as permanent a characteristic of Indonesian legal culture as one can imagine'.

Furthermore, Lev described within Indonesian judges' (and litigants') thinking a pluralistic tension between the supremacy of Dutch-inherited civil law, Islamic Law precepts and customary (*adat*) law, even if each of these sources of law only informs one or more specific legal fields (Lev 1972a: 63–9; Lev 2000d: 167, 194–5). Lev also described a conflict between judicial views favouring local justice to suit local needs, justice to be imposed in a uniform manner across the Indonesian archipelago,[16] and justice to boost Western (particularly European) views of Indonesia's developing legal system (Lev 1962: 210–13, 218; Lev 2000d: 211). In other words, according to Lev, during the Sukarno and Suharto eras, Indonesian judges were conflicted about their geographical audience and the role that religion and custom should play in dispensing justice.

On the interpersonal relationships and personal politics of judges, at least until Suharto's early rule, Lev described keen political consciousness on the part of certain Indonesian judges (Lev 1962: 205; Lev 1965b: 186–7; Lev 2000d: 180–1). Judges also saw themselves as singular, patrimonial arbiters of disputes, in the Javanese village tradition (Lev 1976: 138, 160, 169; Lev 2000d: 171, 199). Given the authoritarian context under Sukarno's 'Guided Democracy' phase (1957–66) and then Suharto's 'New Order' military regime (1967–98), it is perhaps unsurprising that Lev also perceived a close 'connection between judges and prosecutors to the exclusion of [defence] advocates' in criminal cases (Lev 1999: 183, 186; Lev 2000d: 175, 178; Lev 2011: 204, 303), and noted the implicit and explicit influence of the politics of the day over judicial decision-making (Lev 1962: 223; Lev 2000c: 8–9). In Lev's final work, his posthumously released biography of the prominent Indonesian human rights lawyer Yap Thiam Hien, Lev (2011: 303) wrote:

> Indonesian judges have always considered themselves *pegawai negeri*, civil servants, which implies, formally independent or not, a primary obligation to the state and its leadership. Their identity, institutionally and psychologically, is within the state bureaucracy; this establishes a deep

---

[16] See also Pompe (2005: 201–203).

divide between judges, as public lawyers, and professional advocates, as private lawyers.

Legal Culture in the District Courts: Views from the Field

Based explicitly on Lev's characterisation of Indonesia's 'internal legal culture' on the part of judges, as described above, the questions I put to available District Court judges from the five Jakarta District Courts (North, South, East, West, Central), as well as from the satellite town Bekasi in West Java province and to selected courtroom observers focused on three broad topics. First was the power relationship in the courtroom between judges, advocates and prosecutors, and in the judges' conference (*musyawarah*) between the judges themselves. Second were the background cultural influences such as religion, ethnic group and political beliefs on decision-making in the sentencing process; and third was the disparity in sentencing ideology and practice between different courts – whether in Jakarta, Java, or in Indonesia as a whole.

The themes that emerged from the twenty interviews conducted are described below, with interviewees' identities and courts served anonymised, in accordance with ethical stipulations.[17] Indeed, the Chief Justice of one District Court observed that no foreign scholar had ever shown any direct empirical interest in the business of the lowest level criminal courts in Jakarta. Surveying recent scholarship, this is not entirely true (e.g. Lindsey & Nicholson 2016; Nicholson 2009).[18] However, it remains the case that most extensive English-language scholarship on Indonesian courts tends to focus on the apex levels of the court system – the Supreme Court and the Constitutional Court (e.g. Hendrianto 2018; Butt 2015; Butt & Lindsey 2012; Stockmann 2007; Pompe 2005).

Power and Decision-Making in Criminal Cases

To reach a verdict in criminal cases, as with the decision on sentencing quantum, the legislative starting point in Indonesia is the 1981 Criminal Procedure Code (*Kitab Undang-Undang Hukum Acara Pidana*).[19]

---

[17] City University of Hong Kong, Research Committee, Application Number H001634.

[18] See Loebis (1974) and Komisi Yudisial Republik Indonesia (2017b) for similar studies published in Bahasa Indonesian. However, the latter study surveys District Court judges in cities other than Jakarta.

[19] Law 8/1981, art. 182.

Closed-door deliberations (*musyawarah*) between a panel of three (or five) District Court judges determine the verdict and sanction in each case.[20] Within the *musyawarah*, the Chair of the Panel (*Ketua Majelis*) asks questions to each judge from least experienced to most experienced, concluding with him- or herself. Each judge provides his or her decision, along with relevant reasoning. Although the panel should seek to issue a unanimous decision through this process, after reasonable discussions a majority judgement is also possible. Following a guilty verdict, the judicial panel may pass the following sentences, detailed in the Criminal Code (*Kitab Undang-Undang Hukum Pidada*): capital punishment, imprisonment and fines (which are listed as primary penalties); revocation of rights, seizure of property and publicising the court's verdict (which are listed as supplementary penalties).[21] Subject to the maximum sentence prescribed for the offence, imprisonment may be for life, or for a fixed period of between one day and fifteen years, extending up to twenty years if there are significant aggravating circumstances.[22] There is always a written judgement outlining the panel's reasoning (Lindsey & Nicholson 2016: 91), although as noted above, first instance judgements have only recently become available to researchers through the Supreme Court's website.

Importantly, the legislative stipulations on the decision-making process give no indication of the power dynamics among the three (or five) justices, nor do they give any indication as to the relative influence of the prosecutor or the defence advocate on judges' thinking. All that the Criminal Procedure Code provides is that the judges' deliberations must be based upon the prosecutor's indictment and the evidence that has been presented at trial.[23] In theory, all judges have an equal impact on the disposition of the case. Yet, the prevailing legal culture reveals otherwise.

> *It's not like we pressure the youngsters.*
> Interview with District Court Judge (21 May 2018).

> *Experience is an important factor. For the junior judges, the wisdom of the 'Hakim Ketua Majelis' is also significant.*

---

[20] Five judges are only appointed in important cases, at the discretion of the Chief Justice of each District Court (Interview with District Court Judge, 14 May 2018; Interview with District Court Judge, 21 May 2018). See Law 48/2009, art. 11(1), 14(1).

[21] Criminal Code, art. 10. Imprisonment for one year or less may be suspended with a probation period (art. 14a(1)).

[22] Criminal Code, art. 12(1)–(4).

[23] Law 8/1981, art. 182.

Interview with District Court Judge (23 May 2018), describing the
Chair's implicit influence on the panel.

In practice, the Chair of the panel possesses an outsized influence
on each case's outcome by initially asking most of the questions to
the parties in the courtroom, even if the other judges on the panel
later form separate opinions on the verdict.[24] Then, within the
musyawarah itself, the Chair begins by giving a presentation to
the other judges 'about the case, the regulation[s], and about the
mitigating and aggravating factors'.[25] Thereafter, as the Chair's
questioning proceeds in increasing order of seniority, each judge's
opinion is discussed thoroughly by the entire panel, rather than
acting as an isolated and independent 'vote' on the outcome.[26] This
is particularly so in criminal sentencing, where judges on the panel
might reach a consensus position midway between high and low
penalties favoured by different judges.[27] On face value, negotiation
and compromise are therefore major components of judicial decision
-making in the District Courts, albeit conducted in a private rather than
a public setting. As Lev identifies in his own work, replacing direct
conflict with deliberation by consensus is a key Indonesian cultural
tradition with Islamic roots,[28] and is reflected in the version of democracy favoured by *Pancasila* (the Indonesian state ideology).[29] Indeed,
when compared with judicial panels in the common law tradition,
Indonesian District Court judges, with their preference for consensual,
unanimous decision-making behind closed doors, arguably better
resemble a jury of laypersons, rather than a bench which frequently
splits along ideological or evidential grounds in written decisions.

Nevertheless, although the Criminal Procedure Code procedures are
designed to provide a fair opportunity for the two to four less senior
judges to present their opinions without the pressure of having to follow

---

[24] Interview with Defence Advocate #2, 15 May 2018; Interview with Legal NGO Staff,
9 May 2018.
[25] Interview with District Court Judge, 8 May 2018; Interview with District Court Judge,
14 May 2018.
[26] Interview with District Court Judge, 8 May 2018; Interview with Defence Advocate,
3 May 2018.
[27] Interview with District Court Judge, 11 May 2018.
[28] See, e.g., Geertz (1983: 213); Bowen (2003: 89); Tyson (2010: 62).
[29] *Kerakyatan Yang Dipimpin oleh Hikmat Kebijaksanaan, Dalam Permusyawaratan
Perwakilan* (democracy, led by the wisdom of *consensual deliberation* among representatives) (Constitution of Indonesia 1945, preamble). See Bourchier (1999: 235–6) for
further commentary on 'Pancasila Democracy'.

the Chair's lead,[30] in practice, the more experienced Chair's comments and full opinion often prove influential in procuring a unanimous decision from the panel.[31] The Chair's influence is even more pronounced if the Chair of the adjudicatory panel (*Ketua Majelis*) is also the Chair of the entire District court (*Ketua Pengadilan Negeri*).[32] Two interviewees commented that this phenomenon is a reflection of the importance of seniority in Javanese culture.[33] Here, the lesson is that deference to seniority is not necessarily incompatible with decision-making by consensus, especially if the latter provides the means, and the former is typically the end result.

> *They are responsive to each other. Something like 'you have a space in my heart'.*
> Interview with Legal NGO Staff #3 (15 May 2018), mocking District Court judges' amiability towards prosecutors.

As for the role of prosecutors and defence counsel in the courtroom (see also Fachrizal Afandi, this volume), their ultimate influence on judicial decision-making was perceived by several non-judicial interviewees as being minimal, given the heavy judicial intervention through questioning during the trial.[34] To a common law-trained observer of a full bench criminal trial at the Central Jakarta District Court, the judges' total power over proceedings and case disposition was even evident from the layout of the courtroom, with the elevated panel of five judges prominently

---

[30] Interview with District Court Judge, 14 May 2018; Interview with District Court Judge, 23 May 2018; Interview with District Court Judge, 8 May 2018.

[31] Interview with District Court Judge, 11 May 2018; Interview with District Court Judge, 23 May 2018; Interview with District Court Judge, 21 May 2018; Interview with Defence Advocate, 3 May 2018; Interview with Defence Advocate #2, 15 May 2018. Contrast Interview with District Court Judge #2, 8 May 2018; Interview with District Court Judge, 17 May 2018. See also Komisi Yudisial Republik Indonesia (2017b: 217). Two interviewees stated that differing opinions in the *musyawarah* and ultimately via dissenting judgements were more common in Jakarta, given the more senior status of 'junior' judges, who routinely have more than fifteen years' experience as judges in other parts of Indonesia, usually as Chief Justices of regional District Courts (Interview with District Court Judge, 11 May 2018; Interview with District Court Judge #2, 8 May 2018).

[32] Interview with District Court Judge, 23 May 2018; Interview with District Court Judge, 21 May 2018; Interview with Defence Advocate, 3 May 2018. Contrast Interview with District Court Judge #2, 8 May 2018.

[33] Interview with Defence Advocate, 3 May 2018; Interview with District Court Judge, 21 May 2018. See also Fitzpatrick (2008: 503).

[34] Interview with Defence Advocate, 3 May 2018; Interview with Legal NGO Staff #3, 15 May 2018; Interview with Legal NGO Staff #4, 15 May 2018. See generally Strang (2008: 200).

facing the public gallery, and the teams of advocates and prosecutors facing each other across the room, to create an inverse 'U' shape.[35] In this absolutist model of judicial decision-making, there is very little room for negotiation over the final sentencing outcome with either party in the courtroom, other than through corrupt practices (which I elaborate on below). The judicial panel saves its own internal debate for the *musya-warah*, whereas the litigating parties play a more passive role in adducing and testing evidence,[36] unlike the practice of 'negotiated truth' typical in common law systems of justice (Jorg et al. 1995: 47–8; Vriend 2016: 98).

Still, when interviewees directly compared the influence of prosecutors and defence advocates, almost all respondents who addressed this issue saw prosecutors' bearing on case outcomes as far greater than defence advocates'. Echoing Lev's own position (2011: 303), a common explanation given by non-judicial interviewees was that District Court judges possess a 'natural relationship' with prosecutors as fellow civil servants.[37] A second explanation was that judges wish to avoid prosecutorial appeals and the paperwork that goes with them, if they were to impose a sentence grossly divergent from the prosecutor's demand (*tuntutan Jaksa*).[38] After a case is disposed of, occasionally the written judgement will refer to the defence advocate's submissions, but this is merely to 'pay lip service' to defence arguments.[39] It is more common for written judgements to reflect arguments made by prosecutors in court.[40] In sum, the judges' own considerations are of paramount importance, with the prosecutor's arguments secondary and the defence arguments a distant third.

There are also more explicit institutional links between the judiciary and prosecutors. During the Guided Democracy period, the *Panca Tunggal* institution brought together army commanders, police, prosecutors and

---

[35] Contrast a 1971 photo of human rights lawyer and associate of Daniel S. Lev, Yap Thiam Hien, who is pictured sitting directly in front of the justices of a *Pengadilan Negeri* in Jakarta (Lev 2011: 280), and Lev's account of the seating arrangements under Sukarno, where the prosecutor was seated *on* the bench next to the judges (Lev 1965b: 182 n27).

[36] Interview with Legal NGO Staff #4, 15 May 2018; Interview with District Court Judge, 20 May 2018; Interview with District Court Judge, 14 May 2018; Interview with District Court Judge, 8 May 2018.

[37] Interview with Legal NGO Staff #2, 11 May 2018; Interview with Legal NGO Staff, 9 May 2018; Interview with Legal NGO Staff #3, 15 May 2018.

[38] Interview with Legal NGO Staff, 9 May 2018; Interview with Legal NGO Staff #5, 16 May 2018; Interview with Legal NGO Staff #6, 21 May 2018.

[39] Interview with Defence Advocate, 3 May 2018; Interview with Legal NGO Staff #2, 11 May 2018.

[40] Interview with Defence Advocate #2, 15 May 2018; Interview with Legal NGO Staff #2, 11 May 2018; Interview with Legal NGO Staff #4, 15 May 2018.

judges to discuss pressing law and order issues (Lev 2011: 205; Liang 1995: 64). In 1984, during the Suharto era, the *Mahkejapol* forum was established for regular cooperation and coordination between the Indonesian Supreme Court, the Attorney General's Office and the police force, regarding the latest political developments and concerns in criminal justice (Mulya Lubis 1993: 117; Brata 2014: 118).[41] A similar forum at the regency level, incorporating District Court Chief Justices, was called *Muspida* from 1986 onwards (Honna 2010: 141 n8). The cooperative relationship between these state agencies and institutions has even continued to the present day, with a similar *Mahkumjakpol* forum created in 2010, now incorporating the Ministry of Law and Human Rights, despite the purported independence of the judicial branch since *reformasi* (Alim 2010; Hukum Online 2012).[42] Although such cooperation typically involves the judicial tiers above the District Courts, over the years these forums have provided an informal setting whereby the judiciary has developed a closer relationship with the executive branch, rather than with the defence bar (Alim 2010; Lev 2011: 205).[43] At worst, the forums have facilitated outright collusion between state officials (Lev 1999: 183; Alim 2010).[44]

Finally, it is impossible to analyse judicial culture in the District Courts without making reference to judicial corruption. In addition to the institutional factors described above, one further explanation for the apparent close connection between judges and prosecutors is to ensure that defendants' main opportunity for a positive result in their cases is to try to bribe either party (Butt 2012: 23). As with the entire criminal justice system in Indonesia (Pompe 2005: 413–14; Lindsey & Santosa 2008: 10; Butt 2012: 1, 22–4), corruption remains endemic at the District Court level as a key influence on sentencing decision-making in cases involving wealthy and powerful defendants (International Federation for Human Rights et al. 2011: 34). Although, as two non-judicial interviewees made clear, there are certainly competent and impartial judges adjudicating on the District Courts,[45] it is telling that Butt (this volume) has labelled pervasive corruption as the most

---

[41] See also Bourchier (1999: 238) on *Mahkehja*, combining representatives from the Supreme Court, Ministry of Justice and Attorney General's Office.

[42] The Code of Code of Ethics and Code of Conduct for Judges (2006) permits judges to maintain a 'reasonable relationship' with executive and legislative institutions so long as this does not affect current or pending cases before the courts.

[43] See also Interview with Legal NGO Staff, 9 May 2018.

[44] See also Interview with Legal NGO Staff #4, 15 May 2018.

[45] Interview with Legal NGO Staff #2, 11 May 2018; Interview with Legal NGO Staff #4, 15 May 2018. See also Pompe (2005: 414) and Butt (2012: 22–3).

identifiable feature of Indonesian legal culture within the court system. Several non-judicial interviewees blamed judicial corruption in the District Courts on the relatively low salaries of judges,[46] who are still paid modestly as civil servants, despite their purportedly elevated social status (Lev 1978: 65; Bedner 2001: 234). Mirroring Lev's observations during the Suharto era, it remains the case that 'under-the-table money – so common that it is often above the table – has become a standard procedural stratagem, as it were, in both civil and criminal cases' (Lev 1999: 186).

Cultural Influences on Sentencing Practice

On the whole, judicial interviewees were less receptive to questions in this category, possibly because they wished to avoid any perception of bias in favour of defendants of a certain religion, ethnic group, provincial origin, or political ideology. This kind of result is not unique in studies of judicial behaviour (Renteln 1998: 236). In sentencing offenders, most judges interviewed merely affirmed their close reliance on the relevant legislation, and on relevant aggravating and mitigating factors.[47] Nonetheless, judges are human beings, and not judicial robots. Even if they may not be able to recognise it themselves, or may not wish to, background cultural factors undoubtedly influence their decision-making when it comes to the severity of punishment (Freiberg et al. 1996: 237–41).[48] Indeed, one staff member of a legal defence NGO stated that his organisation takes into account particular judges' educational background, religion, previous academic writings and judicial training in developing an advocacy strategy.[49] A minority of judicial (and a majority of non-judicial) interviewees were able to explore the role of culture beyond the archetypal 'corporate' answer – namely, that no cultural factors whatsoever influence criminal verdicts or sentencing.[50] Below, I outline several common responses.

More than one respondent from outside the judiciary mentioned blasphemy cases[51] as a limited example where the *religion* of the judge would

---

[46] Interview with Defence Advocate, 3 May 2018; Interview with Legal NGO Staff #6, 21 May 2018. See also Butt (2012: 24).

[47] Interview with District Court Judge, 8 May 2018; Interview with District Court Judge, 11 May 2018; Interview with District Court Judge, 14 May 2018; Interview with District Court Judge #2, 8 May 2018.

[48] See also Interview with District Court Judge, 23 May 2018.

[49] Interview with Legal NGO Staff #2, 11 May 2018.

[50] See note 13, above.

[51] Criminal Code, art. 156(a); Presidential Decree No 1/PNPS/1965.

affect sentencing outcomes,[52] despite Indonesia's nominally secular criminal justice system.[53] Two judges also mentioned public drunkenness offences in this context,[54] which, anecdotally, Christian judges tend to treat more leniently, for example, in parts of eastern Indonesia and in North Sumatra province.[55] One interviewee stated that religion had a greater bearing on sentencing deliberations since the fall of Suharto;[56] however, that interviewee may have merely been referring to the dramatic increase in blasphemy cases brought by prosecutors during the *reformasi* era (Crouch 2014).

A second example of religious impact on sentencing decision-making is the perception that Muslim judges were more likely to issue death sentences, and were more ideologically comfortable in doing so than were judges of other faiths.[57] Although this makes theoretical sense given Islamic Law's provision for the death penalty for particular *qisas, tazir* and *hudud* crimes (El-Awa 1982), the general proposition that Muslim judges in Indonesia issue proportionally more death sentences than do judges of other faiths requires more detailed empirical verification. By contrast, in non-capital punishment cases, interviewees did not view Muslim judges as any more punitive than judges of Indonesia's minority faiths.[58] They might even be *less* punitive, due to the prominent role of forgiveness in the Islamic religion.[59] Some judges stated that although they and their colleagues cite verses from the Qur'an, Buddhist canon, or from the Bible in their judgements in criminal cases, the verses are mainly included for illustrative purposes, after the fact, rather than constituting evidence of religion influencing the reasoning process.[60]

> *Nope. I hate politics and politician[s].*
> Interview with District Court Judge, 20 May 2018, denying that he ever talks about politics with his colleagues on the bench.

---

[52] Interview with Defence Advocate, 3 May 2018; Interview with Legal NGO Staff, 9 May 2018; Interview with Legal NGO Staff #6, 21 May 2018.

[53] Excluding Aceh. See Salim (2015: 80–2) and Elmont (2017) on Islamic Law in Aceh.

[54] Criminal Code, art. 492, 536.

[55] Interview with District Court Judge, 8 May 2018; Interview with District Court Judge, 17 May 2018.

[56] Interview with Defence Advocate, 3 May 2018. See also Lindsey and Santosa (2008: 8).

[57] Interview with Defence Advocate, 3 May 2018; Interview with Legal NGO Staff, 9 May 2018. See also Joint Standing Committee on Foreign Affairs, Defence and Trade (2016: 71).

[58] Interview with Defence Advocate, 3 May 2018; Interview with District Court Judge #2, 17 May 2018.

[59] Interview with District Court Judge #2, 17 May 2018. See generally Moucarry (2004).

[60] Interview with District Court Judge, 8 May 2018; Interview with District Court Judge #2, 17 May 2018.

Interviewees, both from inside and outside the judiciary, were also sceptical as to whether judges' personal political opinions affected the sentencing process. One hypothesis holds that the more politically conservative the judge, the heavier the average punishment administered, all else being equal (Clancy et al. 1981: 552). However, judges are not permitted to be members of political parties in Indonesia or to openly declare their support for a political party,[61] and in most cases, do not hold strong political opinions anyway.[62] One exception may be for treason (*makar*)[63] committed by separatists, with more politically conservative judges favouring heavier penalties for what is seen as a serious crime against the state.[64] Blasphemy may be another exception,[65] although there the relevant cultural influence on punishment would be better characterised as religious adherence, as above, rather than political ideology.

However, this is not to say that judges are immune from political developments at the national level, or indeed from public opinion. One judge openly acknowledged taking into account statements by then-President Susilo Bambang Yudhoyono in his decision-making on punishment.[66] Several defence advocates and human rights lawyers accused District Court judges of being directly beholden to popular opinion in passing verdicts and sentences in narcotics and corruption cases – crimes that are heavily politicised in modern Indonesia. Defendants accused of these crimes are arguably 'sentenced in the court of public opinion' before their trials even commence, leaving judges with only one option: conviction, followed by severe punishment.[67] Nevertheless,

---

[61] Code of Ethics and Code of Conduct for Judges, 2006; Law 48/2009, art. 5(3).

[62] Interview with District Court Judge, 23 May 2018; Interview with District Court judge, 20 May 2018; Interview with Defence Advocate, 3 May 2018.

[63] Criminal Code, art. 104, 106, 107.

[64] Interview with Legal NGO Staff, 9 May 2018.

[65] See notes 51 and 52 and the associated text, above. One judge observed that if the decision has the potential to cause widespread public dissatisfaction, such as with a blasphemy case, then the *Ketua Pengadilan* will provide appropriate guidance to the judicial panel (Interview with District Court Judge, 23 May 2018).

[66] Interview with District Court Judge #2, 17 May 2018.

[67] Interview with Legal NGO Staff #2, 11 May 2018; Interview with Defence Advocate #2, 15 May 2018; Interview with Legal NGO Staff #3, 15 May 2018. Butt (this volume) argues that an informal 'presumption of guilt' for corruption cases applies more so to cases brought in the Special Courts for Corruption Crimes (initially based within the Central Jakarta District Court), rather than for corruption cases brought within the regular District Court process. Statistics support this contention: from its founding in 2004, through to 2009, the Special Court for Corruption crimes in Jakarta maintained a barely believable 100 per cent conviction rate over approximately 250 cases. Regional Anti-Corruption Courts have recently

respondents perceived this form of judicial bias to be greater within the outer island provinces, as opposed to Jakarta.[68]

> [T]he community is reliant on us, especially the victims ... We feel the responsibility to keep their trust[.]
>> Interview with District Court Judge, 8 May 2018, outlining a heavy judicial responsibility to the community in criminal cases.

> [Serving as a] judge is a noble job. The judge establishes himself as a public figure not to gain respect but to maintain authority.
>> Interview with District Court Judge, 23 May 2018, on judicial motivations.

Are trial judges equivalent to village-level patrimonial leaders of their communities – or, in Bahasa Indonesian, *tokoh-tokoh masyarakat*? Surprisingly, interviewees' reaction to this question was strongly negative.[69] Functionally speaking, *tokoh-tokoh masyarakat* and the District Court judges under study here do share certain similarities. For example, one courtroom observer noted that judges frequently provided moral exhortations to unrepresented defendants, defendants in traffic violation cases and defendants younger than themselves.[70] One judge, although he denied he behaved as a patrimonial community leader as Lev has suggested, nonetheless saw the judiciary's role as one of multifaceted supervision in the community: mediating between aggrieved parties, and bringing police, lawyers and prosecutors together to solve local law enforcement problems.[71] This judge also described how members of the public often approach him out of court to 'ask for a way out of their problem[s]', which involve a mix of legal and non-legal issues.[72] Judges' own perceived prominence in the community even belies their relatively low government salary, compared with the better-remunerated defence advocates.[73]

---

maintained a conviction rate at 81 per cent (Butt & Schutte 2014: 607, 611). By contrast, around 50 per cent of corruption defendants were acquitted across Indonesia before the Special Courts were established (Dick & Butt 2013: 18).

[68] Interview with Defence Advocate #2, 15 May 2018; Interview with Legal NGO Staff #3, 15 May 2018. See note 82 and the associated text, below.

[69] Interview with District Court Judge, 21 May 2018; Interview with District Court Judge, 11 May 2018; Interview with District Court judge, 20 May 2018; Interview with Legal NGO Staff #3, 15 May 2018; Interview with Legal NGO Staff #6, 21 May 2018.

[70] Interview with Legal NGO Staff #3, 15 May 2018.

[71] See also notes 41–2 and associated text, above.

[72] Interview with District Court judge, 20 May 2018.

[73] Interview with District Court Judge, 23 May 2018; Interview with Defence Advocate, 3 May 2018. However, other interviewees argued that the general public's view of judges at all levels is severely compromised by perceptions of corruption (Interview with Legal NGO Staff, 9 May 2018; Interview with Legal NGO Staff #6, 21 May 2018).

Based on such anecdotal evidence at least, greater Jakarta District Court judges do seem to exert moral authority both within and outside of the courtroom. Even though they may not identify directly with *tokoh-tokoh masyarakat*, in essence, greater Jakarta District Court judges still see themselves as community leaders, although the 'patrimonial' analogy may be taking things too far.

Regional and International Dimensions

I think every case has [a] unique pattern and story . . . there will be [a] difference between one case to another case, moreover [differences between] courts.
Interview with District Court Judge, 20 May 2018, claiming indifference to sentencing disparity between courts.

Wherever a judge goes, he must learn the local customs.
Interview with District Court Judge #2, 17 May 2018.

In his own work, Lev did not come to a firm conclusion on judicial attitudes towards disparity of punishment across the Indonesian archipelago. Sentencing disparity between District Courts certainly exists (United Nations Asia and Far East Institute 2002: 14; Ministry of Law and Human Rights, n.d.) and has been recently catalogued in acute detail by the Indonesian Judicial Commission (Komisi Yudisial Republik Indonesia 2014). For some non-judicial interviewees, any sentencing disparity at all reflects poorly on the District Courts' performance.[74]

Most judicial interviewees, on the other hand, did not find disparity in punishment between courts such a major problem. After all, every case is unique, and regional cultural factors tend to influence sentencing.[75] One judge gave the example of the theft of a water buffalo (*kerbau*) in a rural area of South Sulawesi. As a vital and expensive part of villagers' livelihood, the punishment for stealing the animal would be greater in a regional District Court than it would be in a Javanese court.[76] A second judge

---

[74] Interview with Legal NGO Staff, 9 May 2018; Interview with Legal NGO Staff #3, 15 May 2018; Interview with Legal NGO Staff #4, 15 May 2018. See also *Hukum Online* (2013).

[75] Interview with District Court Judge, 20 May 2018; Interview with District Court Judge, 11 May 2018; Interview with District Court Judge, 14 May 2018; Interview with District Court Judge #2, 17 May 2018.

[76] Interview with District Court Judge, 17 May 2018. A second judge from the same court provided a similar example regarding chickens stolen in Ambon (where meat is rare) compared with the equivalent situation in Jakarta (Interview with District Court Judge #2, 17 May 2018).

observed that in a murder case involving *carok* (a Maduranese fighting tradition exercised for self-esteem and pride), a Maduranese Judge would pass a much lighter sentence than a judge in Jakarta.[77] A third judge gave the example of different regional crime rates justifying sentences of differing severity.[78] Non-judicial interviewees perceived heavier sentences for equivalent drug crimes in Tangerang, where Jakarta's international airport is located;[79] heavier sentences for terrorism in West Jakarta, reportedly home to a network of terror cells; and lighter sentences for white-collar crimes in South Jakarta, due to the pervasive influence of corruption within the local court serving Jakarta's business district.[80]

It is difficult, however, to study sentencing disparity on a truly empirical basis, isolating the trial venue as an independent variable contributing to sentencing outcomes. For example, are proportionally more death sentences passed in the Tangerang District Court because more defendants are arrested for drug trafficking there, and Tangerang drug cases evince numerous aggravating factors (such as recidivism, foreign nationality, or trafficking over international borders), or are the judges serving on the Court simply more punitive? Would the equivalent caseload be treated the same way in the Central Jakarta District Court? Of all the Jakarta courts, the Central Jakarta District Court (which Lev (2011: 372) labelled 'the most important district court of the land') was perceived by non-judicial interviewees to be the most fair and consistent in its rulings for defendants, as a result of greater judicial experience and a higher number of journalists to report on irregularities and corruption scandals.[81] Interviewees also perceived Jakarta District Courts, in general, to issue decisions of greater quality than courts in the outer islands.[82]

As to whether judges saw themselves as serving the local community, the city of Jakarta, the island of Java, or Indonesia more broadly, there

---

[77] Interview with District Court Judge, 8 May 2018.

[78] Interview with District Court Judge, 11 May 2018.

[79] Interview with Legal NGO Staff, 9 May 2018; Interview with Legal NGO Staff #5, 16 May 2018.

[80] Interview with Legal NGO Staff, 9 May 2018; Interview with Legal NGO Staff #4, 15 May 2018.

[81] Ibid. Contrast Lev's (2011: 373) account of corruption in the Central Jakarta District Court, during the Suharto period.

[82] Interview with Legal NGO Staff #3, 15 May 2018; Interview with District Court Judge, 8 May 2018. See also ASEAN Law Association (2005: 53) and Pompe (2005: 449).

were a mixture of views, as with Lev's earlier characterisation. Here, interviewees' responses often varied based on the type of offence. Narcotics was seen as a national or even an international problem.[83] In sentencing corruption cases, judges were also performing a service to the nation as a whole, rather than their immediate jurisdiction.[84] Terrorism cases also involved both a national and an international dimension.[85] The pattern is clear: with murder the notable exception, the crimes with the heaviest maximum penalties (death or life imprisonment) are typically seen as a national or international problem requiring diligence by local judges on the 'front lines' in Jakarta.[86] Crimes of lesser seriousness, such as theft, are perceived by Jakartan judges as more of a local concern.[87]

Not one respondent believed that his or her judicial influence simply disappeared at the borders of the court's jurisdiction (for example, the municipality of East Jakarta or West Jakarta), given the fluid movement of people and commerce within Indonesia's sprawling capital city of close to 10 million people. Moreover, judges in the Jakarta District Courts tended to have a much broader national outlook, given their typically lengthy work experience in outer island courts earlier in their careers, their eclectic ethnic background, and, of course, their present service within Indonesia's capital city. Nevertheless, other than for exceptional crimes perceived as a national or international problem (as above), the judicial panel's focus was typically on the offender him or herself, when considering punishment in the name of specific deterrence, incapacitation, rehabilitation and retribution.[88]

By contrast, several interviewees viewed judges *outside of* Jakarta as more concerned with their immediate geographical communities in

---

[83] Interview with District Court Judge, 14 May 2018; Interview with Legal NGO Staff #2, 11 May 2018; Interview with District Court Judge, 21 May 2018; Interview with District Court Judge, 11 May 2018.

[84] Interview with District Court Judge, 8 May 2018; Interview with District Court Judge #2, 21 May 2018.

[85] Interview with Legal NGO Staff #4, 15 May 2018; Topsfield and Rompies (2016).

[86] The judicial interviewees did not discuss the more rarely prosecuted death-eligible offences such as treason, piracy resulting in death, robbery resulting in death, possession and misuse of firearms or explosives, criminal acts aboard aircraft, human rights violations and child rape (Cornell Center on the Death Penalty Worldwide, 2018; *BBC News*, 2016).

[87] Interview with District Court Judge #2, 8 May 2018; Interview with District Court Judge, 21 May 2018.

[88] Interview with District Court Judge, 14 May 2018; Interview with District Court Judge, 8 May 2018; Interview with District Court Judge, 17 May 2018; Interview with District Court Judge #2, 17 May 2018.

sentencing offenders, given Jakarta's status as Indonesia's foremost cultural and ethnic melting pot, compared with other provinces' more homogenous cultures.[89] One interviewee who had served on courts in the outer islands pointed to the Law on Judicial Power,[90] and interpreted the need to apply 'legal values and a sense of justice living in society' as referring to the legal values of his local community, rather than of Indonesian society as a whole.[91]

One area that future research might address, in addition to further empirical study on sentencing disparity in the District Courts across the country, is differing perceptions of the judicial role in criminal cases within Jakarta and Java, as compared with Indonesia's outer island provinces. Certainly, the results of this study suggest an initial hypothesis that serious crimes taking place in Jakarta are seen by Jakarta District Court judges (and perhaps also by the Jakartan public) as a major concern for all of Indonesia. However, the same may not be true in District Courts within Indonesia's outer islands. Aggrandising social and criminal ills on the national stage is a tactic often employed by Indonesian politicians (Aspinall 2016: 78). Might Jakarta District Court judges also have bought into this rhetoric?

Discussion: Vindicating Lev?

Based on the interview data presented above, does Daniel S. Lev's characterisation of Indonesian legal culture during the early Suharto period still hold relevance today, at least when reassessed in relation to criminal cases within the District Courts? Again, there are caveats concerning measurement and sampling to be borne in mind. The interviews conducted as part of this study reveal a series of opinions and practices on the part of District Court judges in greater Jakarta. As described earlier, this is only one possible means of measuring 'internal' legal culture. Moreover, the available sample (twelve different judges plus eight further experts and outside observers) may or may not be representative of all District Court judges in Jakarta and may or may not be representative of all judges in more than 350 District Courts in other parts of Indonesia.

---

[89] Interview with Legal NGO Staff #4, 15 May 2018; Interview with Legal NGO Staff #3, 15 May 2018; Interview with District Court Judge, 11 May 2018.
[90] Law 48/2009, art. 5(1).
[91] Interview with District Court Judge, 20 May 2018. See Yulianti & Ikhwan (2017) for a paper interpreting this provision of the Law on Judicial Power.

The critique of Lev's work outlined below may therefore derive from a reasonably narrow case study, but it also contributes to the theoretical debate over the legacy of Lev's work for *all* contemporary Indonesian District Courts.

There are six main trends evident from the interviews conducted. First, extra-legal factors are still clearly relevant to judicial decision-making on criminal punishment, as in Lev's conception of Indonesian legal culture. With democratisation in the *reformasi* era, *corruption* may have surpassed nepotism and favouritism to the military as a means of doing judicial business (Butt & Parsons 2014: 58–9), but the deleterious impact on the reputation of the District Courts remains the same. As for Lev's emphasis on conciliation and compromise between opposing parties, this may hold true for civil matters, given compulsory mediation by law,[92] and a continuing preference for settlement outside the courtroom (Juwana 2014: 335–6), but for criminal matters the only compromises evident were those made behind closed doors between judges, during the *musyawarah* session. Whatever influence the parties bear on sentencing outcomes is achieved by presenting their evidence and arguments before the court, rather than through direct negotiation.

If anything, the interview data presented here suggests that Lev's theory of negotiation and consensual deliberation as means of resolving legal disputes ought also to be bolstered by emphasis on the influence of *seniority* in Indonesian, and particularly Javanese, culture (e.g. Uhlenbeck 1978: 333; Fitzpatrick 2008: 503, 509). More generally, the results of this study query whether, in the Indonesian context, preference for consensual deliberation in resolving disputes merely serves to entrench existing power structures (here, the authority of the Chair of the Judicial Panel (*Ketua Majelis*), or the Chair of the Court (*Ketua Pengadilan Negeri*)), rather than helping to create a blank slate upon which less powerful actors can shape decisions.[93]

Second, consistent with Lev's writings, greater Jakarta District Court judges still tend to presumptively side with prosecutors over defence lawyers, whether due to their comity as fellow civil servants, long-established institutional links (such as the *Mahkumjakpol*), a desire to avoid prosecutorial appeals, or indeed as a means of soliciting bribes from defendants seeking a favourable outcome. This calls into question

---

[92] E.g. Law 48/2009, art. 58, 60; Supreme Court Circular Letter 1/2002.

[93] Several non-Indonesian scholars have previously noted the shortcomings of consensual deliberation as a method of decision-making, observing that it tends to entrench existing power structures. See Knierbein and Hou (2017: 234), Osei-Kufour (2010: 56) and Rigon (2015).

the effectiveness of the separation of the judiciary from the executive branch after 1998 (Assegaf 2007: 12–13; Juwana 2014: 304–5, 319–20). Although higher-level Indonesian courts are increasingly willing to find against the government in civil cases (Butt & Lindsey 2012: 104; Assegaf 2018a), are District Court judges really neutral arbiters within criminal litigation? Alternatively, is the problem of partiality merely limited to 'extraordinary' crimes considered a threat to the entire nation or the dominant religious grouping – currently narcotics, corruption, terrorism and blasphemy? Pursuant to the 'one roof' administrative system established under the Supreme Court in the *reformasi* era (Assegaf 2007: 12–14), members of the political executive no longer instruct judges to pursue particular policy objectives in their decisions.[94] However, in a system that has long espoused the presumption of innocence for defendants,[95] any conscious or unconscious favouritism towards the prosecution side remains a threat to fair and just decision-making in criminal cases.

Third, both the District Court judges and the non-judicial actors interviewed largely rejected politics as an internalised influence on decision-making in criminal cases, and even as a personal interest of judges. This is a notable divergence from Lev's writings centring on the late Sukarno and early Suharto periods, as well as the accompanying literature covering the same period (Pompe 2005: 36, 111, 411; Lindsey & Santosa 2008: 10). Illuminating is the quote from one judge, provided above, who stated bluntly that 'I hate politics and politician[s]'. While other interviewees were not as forthright, the interview responses revealed a distinct political apathy from District Court judges, who instead perceived themselves as civil servants, performing an apolitical job for the benefit of all citizens, and to provide for their own families.

What explains this observed difference from Lev's writings? One possibility might be that, unlike the Guided Democracy and New Order eras, there are now many opportunities for political participation for young professionals in Indonesia, and hence those who voluntarily embark on a judicial career after completing their university education do so with a politically neutral civil service mentality.[96] Similarly, during Guided Democracy and the early New Order, Indonesian judges' political organisation and awareness was a historically contingent effort to

---

[94] Interview with District Court Judge #2, 17 May 2018; Interview with District Court Judge, 21 May 2018; Interview with Legal NGO Staff, 9 May 2018.

[95] Law 19/1964, art. 4(2); Law 14/1970, art. 6(2); Law 8/1981, elucidation; Law 48/2009, art. 8(1); Code of Ethics and Code of Conduct for Judges, 2006.

[96] See further Lev (1976: 162).

push back against an increasingly authoritarian political establishment (Bedner 2001: 21–2). As Pompe (2005: 411) has observed:

> [T]he political struggle of the judiciary in the 1950s contributed to a growing political awareness within the profession, as the judges changed from a politically atomized group of individuals to one that was much more cohesive. In addition, they moved from political innocence to a kind of maturity marked by broad agreement on the fundamental political goals to be achieved.

Another possibility is that Lev's position on politics implicitly influencing the courts remains vindicated today, albeit that political campaigns against certain crimes *unconsciously* influence judicial decisions on punishment. Nevertheless, the judges themselves do not recognise the implicit influence of national politics on their decision-making. Further empirical scholarship might explore the relationship between the prominence of certain crimes within the Indonesian political agenda and mass media coverage (see Tapsell, this volume), and the punishments accorded to those crimes at the trial level or on appeal.

Fourth, the interview responses on religious consciousness among judges also demonstrate divergence from Lev's writings. On the whole, the interviews suggested that District Court judges felt no need to distance their religious belief from their duties on the secular courts. Several examples were cited. Unlike with political parties, Indonesian judges are entitled to, and do, become members of Islamic non-governmental organisations such as *Muhammadiyah* or *Nahdlatul Ulama*.[97] There were instances of Muslim judges citing passages from the Qur'an or the Sunnah in their own judgements for illustrative purposes, and even an example of a Christian judge doing likewise. Interviewees also observed Muslim judges citing Christian or Buddhist texts to illustrate their reasoning.[98] Furthermore, although judges can only ever be responsive to prosecutorial trends, with the increasing prevalence of death-eligible cases (McRae 2012: 5–6: Pascoe 2019 : 160, 164–166) and blasphemy cases (mostly for blaspheming Islam) (Crouch 2012a, 2014) in post-Suharto Indonesia, District Court judges' religiosity arguably plays a growing role in criminal sentencing, even within Indonesia's secular criminal justice system. Within death penalty cases

---

[97] Interview with District Court Judge, 14 May 2018; Code of Ethics and Code of Conduct for Judges (2006).

[98] Interview with District Court Judge, 8 May 2018; Interview with District Court Judge #2, 17 May 2018; Interview with Legal NGO Staff #6, 21 May 2018.

and blasphemy cases, judges' overt religiosity might even have overtaken Lev's idea of the patrimonial village leader, to serve as the sentencing judges' foremost source of moral authority in pronouncing punishment. In cases such as these, no longer are District Court judges merely acting as community leaders or as bureaucratic functionaries, but instead they are religious arbiters of morality, thereby revisiting the age-old debate over Islam's potential role within Indonesia's criminal justice system (Hooker 2008: 265; Emont 2017). Indeed, if the proposed unlawful sexual intercourse (*zina*) and premarital cohabitation provisions are passed in the Revised Criminal Code (*Rancangan Kitab Undang-Undang Hukum Pidana* – RKUHP) during the next few years,[99] this trend will accelerate even further.

Fifth and further to the previous point, beyond cases where judges' moral authority to punish derives from religious belief, greater Jakarta District Court judges do appear to hold positions of patrimonial leadership in the communities in which they serve, by virtue of their status as legal arbiters. Judges tend to perceive themselves in this way, although for the public their moral leadership is also tainted by frequent allegations of corruption.[100] It remains a puzzle why judicial interviewees' responses in comparison with village-level *tokoh-tokoh masyarakat* were so negative. There are several plausible explanations. These include the *tokoh masyarakat*'s relatively informal role and separation from state institutions, judges' wider geographical sphere of responsibility beyond the village level, that judicial decision-making is not carried out unaided (as with a *tokoh masyarakat*) but in teams in three or five,[101] or perhaps due to the historically negative connotations of corruption, and political or military partiality associated with patrimonial village leaders (Kammen & Chandra 2010: 85; Antlov 2013: 82; Welker 2014: 78). Nevertheless, as described earlier, on a purely functional level, Lev's original equating of judges with *tokoh-tokoh masyarakat* appears to remain vindicated.

Sixth and finally, as in the Sukarno and early Suharto periods, judges still appear divided over whether their role involves tendering justice for local, provincial, or national needs and audiences. The continuity of this finding may be a result of Indonesia's unique geography, the age-old political debate over centralisation versus autonomy, the ethnic diversity

---

[99] See Institute for Criminal Justice Reform (2018) and Eddyono (2016).

[100] See note 73, above.

[101] Early in Lev's academic career, District Court trials were usually heard by a single judge only, potentially informing his characterisation of judges as patrimonial figures (Lev 2000d: 172 n20).

of the judges themselves, or their career trajectory, which involves frequent moves between different provinces before arriving at Jakarta's 'Class 1A' courts.[102] Lev also suggested in his work that judges in the Sukarno and early Suharto periods felt pressure to decide cases in a certain manner to please foreign audiences (Lev 1962: 210; Lev 2000d: 211). Indonesia was a far newer and less institutionally confident country back then. I found no evidence of that kind of thinking in the greater Jakarta District Courts today.

Recent innovations, such as the twenty-four-hour news cycle, instant communication across the archipelago and most importantly the rise of populist democratic politics, have elevated particular crimes (namely narcotics, corruption and terrorism) to the status of perceived national emergencies. These offences are now seen to require national coordination by police, prosecutors and the Supreme Court, and consistency of harsh punishment across provincial borders. At first glance, these developments, as reflected in the interview responses from various District Court Judges and observers, appear unique to the *reformasi* era. However, upon closer inspection, they accord closely with Lev's conception of politics affecting the operation of Indonesia's courts during the Sukarno and Suharto eras. In assessing political and judicial attitudes towards serious crimes, Indonesia-watchers will also note the echoes of the 'moral panic' over communist subversion (Wee 2012: 24–6), which was an important self-justifying feature of the Suharto military regime. In this sense, the more things change, the more they stay the same.

Conclusion

'Internal' legal culture, as a set of repeated practices, beliefs and behaviours on the part of legal professionals (Merry 2010: 43), is arguably more important in analysing civil law systems, where case law precedent is not as important in resolving legal disputes in the courts, as compared with common law systems. Legal culture is also important in transitional and developing societies with less of a tradition for formal 'legality' restricting judicial and prosecutorial behaviour in the criminal process. Indonesia falls into both categories, as a society where informal practices appear to govern judicial outcomes as much as the positive law does.

This case study has helped to reaffirm the importance of Daniel S. Lev's seminal work on legal culture in Indonesia, at least as it pertains to the

---

[102] See note 31, above.

District Courts of greater Jakarta in criminal cases. Only relatively minor updates to Lev's conception of Indonesian legal culture are required in light of contemporary judicial behaviour in the District Courts of greater Jakarta. Overall, this is surprising, given the seismic political and societal changes brought about by *reformasi* after 1998 (Arinanto 2018), and the academic literature that suggests more rapid changes to legal culture during periods of democratisation (Morn & Toro 1990; Bergoglio 2003; 54–5; Faivovich 2003: 130–1). While this may be good news for Lev's academic legacy, it is not so good for Indonesia's criminal justice system as a whole. With significant democratic progress in the twenty years since 1998, that Indonesia's judicial culture as an authoritarian state throughout the Guided Democracy and New Order periods still remains recognisable today is troubling for law reformers. It is an indication that legal culture, much like the broader societal culture on which it often depends (Nelken 1995: 438; Faivovich 2003: 111), changes only very slowly, if at all.

4

The Indonesian Prosecution Service at Work

The Justice System Postman

FACHRIZAL AFANDI

The Public Prosecutor is just the Postman[1]

It has commonly been assumed that the above statement accurately captures the role of the public prosecutor (*jaksa*)[2] in the Indonesian criminal justice system.[3] The Code of Criminal Procedure (KUHAP)[4] provides a minimal role for the public prosecutor in supervising police investigations. Theoretically, the public prosecutor has opportunities to supervise the use of coercive power and examine the facts during the investigation process. However, they rarely use such power. Once prosecutors proceed the trial with the case, they defend the facts as stated in the police file at all costs. During the trial, if they find false evidence produced by the police, they still prosecute the defendant and may ask the judge to give a minimum sentence that is similar to the length of their detention. The Indonesian Prosecution Service (hereafter the IPS) is a strict and

---

[1] See Kompas 2015. The Head of the IPS Legal Bureau, Jan Maringka, has complained about the position of the public prosecutor in the KUHAP. At the time of writing, Jan was appointed as the Junior Prosecutor General for Intelligence. He has promoted the importance of IPS position mentioned in the Constitution. He is also one of the initiators of the most significant Facebook group for Prosecutor (The Prosecutor Alliance [TPA]).

[2] The term 'jaksa' has a broader definition than the public prosecutor. The jaksa has many roles as the state attorney in civil and administrative cases and state intelligence. The KUHAP differentiates between the jaksa and the public prosecutor. The jaksa is an official who is granted the authority by the code of criminal procedure to be a public prosecutor and executor of a legally binding court order (KUHAP, art. 1(6)). The public prosecutor is defined as a jaksa who has authority to prosecute and carry out the court order (KUHAP, art. 1(7)). Historically, the term 'jaksa' was also used to refer to judicial officers who had tasks as the court advisor (Ravensbergen, 2018). In this chapter, I refer to the jaksa in English as the public prosecutor.

[3] I found the same reaction while conducting my PhD fieldwork in ten Public Prosecution Service offices in 2014–15. Some of the public prosecutors I met felt frustrated by their inability to screen cases from the police.

[4] Kitab Undang-undang Hukum Acara Pidana.

hierarchical bureaucracy, and its militaristic culture does not allow the public prosecutor to take initiative.

This chapter identifies and explains why the actual position of the public prosecutor is so weak in the current criminal justice system, while the prosecutors themselves believe that they are the *dominus litis* who control proceedings because he or she determines who to prosecute, like their Dutch prosecutor predecessor. The first part begins with a description of the role of the prosecutor from a historical perspective, with a particular focus on the position of the IPS in the broader legal system. In the early independence era, the IPS replaced the Dutch Prosecution Office (*Openbaar Ministrie*). In the late 1950s, efforts to reform the IPS ended when the political system changed with the rise of the military and authoritarian government. The government controlled the prosecutors as well as the judiciary to ensure that the outcome of criminal cases was favourable to the government. Since then, the prosecutor's role changed from an impartial criminal prosecutor to an effective tool to keep the authoritarian regime in power and silence or intimidate political opponents (Lev 1978; Lolo 2008). I then consider the bureaucracy of the public prosecution and its militaristic culture, which is shaped by previous authoritarian military regimes. I identify its militaristic cultural practices and prosecutors' understanding of their sense of mission and how it shapes how the law works (Merry 2010: 48; Wilson 1989: 95). Lastly, I discuss the work of public prosecutors in the criminal courts, as well as their relationship with police investigators and judges. I reflect on the problems that arise from the position of the public prosecutor as the postman in Indonesia's contemporary criminal justice system.

The Origins of the Indonesian Prosecution Service

The Reform Effort: From Native Prosecutor to the Officieren Van Justitie

The IPS originates from the colonial period when the Dutch organised the judicial system based on the race. The Dutch prosecutors (*officieren van justitie*) were organised in the European Prosecution Office (*Openbaar Ministrie*), structurally under the Attorney General of the Dutch East Indies High Court (*Procureur-generaal*) and organisationally part of the judiciary. The native prosecutor (*Jaksa*) was structurally subordinated to the resident and controlled by the governor general

(Tresna 1955: 14). In 1924, the colonial government opened the first legal training institution for Indonesians to produce public lawyers for the bureaucracy, including the public prosecution (Lev 2000d: 25). Then in 1940, the Dutch government unified the prosecution system in the Herziene Inlandsch Reglement (HIR). The Indonesian prosecutor was not structurally subordinated to the Resident any more but became part of the *Openbaar Ministrie* under the *Procureur-generaal* (Tresna 1955: 73).

After independence in 1945, the IPS employed and recruited many prosecutors who were trained in law school in the Netherlands (Lev 2000d: 82), while some had judicial experience. Former Prosecutor General Tirtawinata and Soeprapto were former colonial Judges. Many more were reputable Indonesian lawyers who started their career as a prosecutor, such as Prosecutor General Gatot Taroenamihardja, Prosecutor General Baharuddin Loppa, Omar Seno Adji, Adnan Buyung Nasution and Prijatna Abdurrasyid. They played a pivotal role in promoting the rule of law[5] and reformed the IPS to be more professional like their *Openbaar Ministrie* predecessor.

During the revolutionary era (1945–49), Japanese regulations were applied to criminal procedure.[6] Prosecutor General Tirtawinata sent a letter to the Minister of Information disagreeing with the view that prosecutors should apply Japanese regulations, because it did not guarantee human rights. Tirtawinata instructed the police and the public prosecutors to apply the HIR, which was considered to be superior to Japanese procedure in investigating and prosecuting criminal cases (PPS 1985: 83).

The transformation of prosecutors from government official (*executive ambtenaar*)[7] to the *magistraat* can be traced from Law 7/1947, Law 19/1948 and Emergency Law 1/1951. These laws deal with the structure and jurisdiction of the judiciary and the IPS.[8] These laws established the

---

[5] See art. 1(a) Persaja (The Prosecutor Association) Statute, which stated that the Prosecutor Association aimed to promote the rule of Law: *Indonesischtalige statuten van de Persatuan Djaksa-Djaksa*, 1955.

[6] Since the Republican government was at war with the Dutch military and its allies, there was little regard for the justice system.

[7] Jaksa was a native officer, who was supervised by the assistant resident to investigate and prosecute the criminal case. The colonial government used the native prosecutor/jaksa to maintain public order among the natives (Idema 1938, 67, 69). See Ravensbergen (2018) for more detail.

[8] Due to military conflict with the Dutch, this law never came into effect (Pompe 2005, 179).

Prosecutor General's Office and the Prosecutor General as part of the judiciary, like the previous *Openbaar Ministrie* and *Procureur-generaal*.

During the parliamentary period (1950–9), public prosecutors were responsible for supervising the police. In 1953, the police demanded the sole right to pretrial responsibilities. The police rejected the public prosecutor's supervision role and they refused to be called *hulpmagistraat* in the HIR, which is translated into Bahasa as *Pembantu Jaksa*. The word *pembantu* has two meanings in Bahasa: an assistant or a maid. Yet *pembantu* always has a negative connotation as maid. The police were concerned that their status as *pembantu* can be used by the public prosecutor to exploit and order the police to do anything they need (Rajab 2003: 197–8).

The public prosecutors defended their role in the pretrial process. They saw themselves as replacing the Dutch prosecutors (*officieren van justitie*) and *magistraat* in the Code of Criminal Procedure (*Herziene Inlandsch Reglement*, HIR) as mentioned in Emergency Law 1/1951 (Tresna 1955: 73). As the chairperson of the Public Prosecutor Association (PERSAJA),[9] Omar Seno Adji[10] believed that the prosecutor had to supervise the police investigation. PERSAJA argued that an independent police force that was not subject to any supervision would endanger civil rights (Lev 2000d: 91).

During the tenure of Prosecutor General Soeprapto (1950–9), in some cases the IPS used the *Reglement op de Strafvordering* (SV), which was much stricter and offered better protection for defendants.[11] Lolo and Lev refer to this period as the golden age of the prosecutor (Lev 2007b: 238; Lolo 2008: 70). Considering the poor legal knowledge of the pre-war prosecutors, Prosecutor General Soeprapto instructed high-ranking prosecutors who had a law background to assist low-level pre-war prosecutors to draft an indictment (Lev 2000d: 80).

Since the provisional 1950 Constitution guaranteed judicial independence and human rights[12] and prosecutors were part of the

---

[9] PERSAJA actively criticised the government and played an essential role in defending the position of the Public Prosecution Service.

[10] Omar Seno Adji was the Director of Criminal Investigation in the Supreme Prosecution Service Office. In 1955, he was appointed as the Chairman of PERSAJA. After resigning from the IPS following a conflict with Prosecutor General Gunawan, Seno Adji worked at the Supreme Court and later was appointed as the Chief Justice of the Supreme Court. When he was selected as the Minister of Justice, he introduced the concept of Examining Judge (Rechter Commissaries) in the draft of KUHAP.

[11] Article 6 Emergency Law 1/1951 did not clearly oblige the law enforcers to use the HIR as the criminal procedure.

[12] Of the 28 articles on human rights protection, several articles regulated the protection of human rights in the criminal justice process: the protection of unlawful arrests and

judiciary,[13] the prosecutor felt confident in their profession and was able to prosecute high-profile and politically sensitive cases without fear of political intervention. During the Soeprapto period, some ministers, and military and top government officials were prosecuted for serious crimes. Administratively the IPS was part of the Ministry of Justice, although this did not stop the public prosecutor from arresting and prosecuting the Minister of Justice Djody Gondokusumo on charges of corruption.[14] Soeprapto believed that the prosecution was a part of the judicial process and refused to grant President Soekarno's request to waive criminal cases involving his political friends (Yahya 2004: 197–206).

Public prosecutors believed that their positions were equal to judges and urged the government to raise their salary to the same level as judges.

> Whatever their backgrounds, prosecutors were, almost neurotically, con-
> stantly concerned to prove themselves authoritative officials of the inde-
> pendent state and to pursue symbols of high status. (Lev 2000d: 75)

Lev opines that prosecutors were struggling for a higher salary to increase their position and prestige after the revolution (Lev 2000d). However, his analysis does not take account of the fundamental reason behind this struggle. Lev did not analyse the role of the IPS leaders in this debate, who were dominated by prosecutors who had Dutch legal backgrounds like judges. Therefore, it was understandable that the prosecutor demanded the same salary as the judge.[15] Since PERSAJA believed that the HIR should be enforced as the guideline for criminal justice actors, they resisted the plans by the police to remove the supervisory role of prose-cutors during the investigation process. They perceived this would make

---

detentions (art. 12); equality before the law (art. 13); presumption of innocence (art. 14); the prohibition of criminal punishment such as the guilt's possession, deprivation or punishment, which resulted in losing the civil right (art. 15); a home search ban without a legal basis (art. 16); and protection of personal secrets (art. 17). This provisional Constitution also expressly prohibited the government from intervening in the judiciary (art. 103).

[13] The provisional 1950 Constitution established the Prosecutor General's position, similar to the President, as a high state official who is accountable to the Supreme Court when she or he commits crimes (art. 106).

[14] The public prosecutor prosecuted Mr Djody Gondokusumo for two years in prison for receiving Rp. 40.000 from Bong Kim Tjong in assisting him in the visa application. It was later revealed that the money was for the party which was chaired by Djody.

[15] Oemar Seno Adji contacted his friend judge and told him that the prosecutor could initiate a strike to urge the high salary. Later, Oemar Seno Adji's friend was appointed as the Chairperson of the Judges Association (IKAHI).

Indonesia a police state, with the potential that coercive powers such as arrest and seizure would be used for purposes other than legitimate searches for evidence.

Law 5/1950 stated that the prosecutor general was the chief of the military prosecution[16] and that the prosecutors were the military prosecutors who supervised military police investigations into criminal activity by the armed forces (art. 27). The prosecutor general had a double function in civilian and the military prosecutions, and could arrest and prosecute high military officers. For example, in 1952, the prosecutor general investigated and examined army commanders including Nasution for his role as the provocateur in the so-called '17 October affair' when the military faction suggested that the parliamentary government be dismissed. Despite the fact that this case did not proceed to the trial, the two-year investigation resulted in some high army officers being dismissed from their position (Yahya 2004: 179–96). The IPS also prioritised smuggling cases which often involve top military officers being arrested and prosecuted by the prosecutor (Abdurrasyid 2001: 155, 237, 254). These matters resulted in severe friction between the IPS and the army.

The government and military felt that Soeprapto's decision as prosecutor general to pursue these cases disturbed political stability. In 1957, the military started to exert control over the civilian administration with Law 74/1957 on Emergency Situation and tried to take over the IPS. This was not easy since Soeprapto was still in power. In 1958, the military proposed a government regulation stipulating that the IPS could only investigate military personnel if they had permission from their commander. Although Soeprapto was against this plan, the army succeeded in convincing the government to accept their proposal and enact the regulation (Yahya 2004: 57).

In 1959, President Soekarno issued a decree with support from the army, which effectively ended the parliamentary system (Sundhaussen 1986: 206–10). This decree, which re-enacted a strong presidential Constitution of 1945, became the turning point of the so-called Guided Democracy (Lev 2009). In the same year, the government succeeded in forcing Soeprapto to resign from his position in a much-publicised case. The tension between the IPS and the army increased. The Prosecutor General Gatot Taroenamihardja[17] arrested and detained several high-level military officials on charges of goods smuggling.[18] General Nasution

---

[16] Law 5/1950, art. 23.

[17] He was the first prosecutor general to be appointed as Soeprapto's successor.

[18] In some places in Sumatra, army commanders operated smuggling businesses to cover their expenditures (Kahin 1999).

claimed that Gatot's actions disrupted the public order and the army arrested Gatot.[19] Soekarno reconciled this conflict by dismissing Gatot as the prosecutor general and transferring the military officers who were accused of smuggling to other positions (Isnaeni 2017).

The army tried to contain the IPS. The army convinced President Soekarno to choose its preferred candidate, Gunawan,[20] as Gatot's successor for the prosecutor general's position. The President also positioned the prosecutor general under the coordination of the Ministry of Security, which was led by General Nasution. Besides the prosecutor, the army also gained control over the police and started to militarise its officers.[21] The responsibility for prosecuting the military was also transferred to the military, which greatly reduced the power of public prosecutors.[22] Gunawan's appointment marks the transformation of the public prosecutor from *magistraat* to the troops. He required public prosecutors to undergo military training and wear military uniforms.

However, the public prosecutors did not give up most of their power because they lost the contest against the police, as Lev believed (Lev 2000d: 97). The IPS did not lose their supervision power during the debate in parliament. Soeprapto was known as the close friend and mentor for Soekanto, the chief of police. The prosecutor could still work with the police in investigating some serious crimes. But when the military took control, the IPS and the police both lost their power and independence. After arresting Prosecutor General Gatot because he prosecuted the high army officials, the army ensured that a person loyal to them was appointed as prosecutor general, and this was the beginning of the militarisation of the prosecution.

The Weapon of the Government: Prosecutors as Troops

As the commander-in-chief of the IPS, Gunawan, with the support of the army headquarters, introduced a military-style hierarchy to the prosecution office. He reformed the public prosecution not as magistrates but

---

[19] Gatot was hit by a car and sustained serious injuries (Nasution 2004, 117).
[20] Gunawan was a junior Deputy Prosecutor General during Gatot period.
[21] The first chief of the police Soekanto who did not agree with the militarisation of the police was also replaced in 1959. Like Soeprapto, he was also known as the founder of the modern police after Indonesia's independence (Turan, Gunawan, Triharjoko, & Rochaedi, 2000).
[22] Even though the Law 5/1950 was not repealed, the Prosecutor General Ali Said delegated the military prosecutor mandate to the Army Commander in 1973 (PPS 1985, 237).

more like troops to strengthen the IPS as a tool of the regime. The militarisation process within the bureaucracy of the public prosecution enabled the military to appoint their generals as prosecutor general. In 1964, Soekarno appointed his close ally Brigadier General A. Soethardio as the Minister of the IPS.

President Soeharto followed this policy during the New Order authoritarian regime. Soeharto had selected his military loyalist to be the prosecutor general.[23] The prosecutor general and the commander of the armed forces (ABRI)[24] have the same status as a cabinet member. However, due to the strict military hierarchy the position of prosecutor generals, who were previously lieutenants or major generals, are now under the ABRI commander with four-star generals. Furthermore, the submissive attitude of the prosecutor general to the army was a bonus for President Soeharto, who already had control of the armed forces (Lolo 2008: 132). The public prosecutors silenced and intimidated political opponents of the regime. Even Prosecutor General Singgih admitted that Soeharto's first message to him before being appointed in 1990 was that he must use the Subversion Law to prosecute everyone who opposed the regime's policies[25] (Ritonga et al. 2003: 238).

After Soeharto stepped down in 1998, reformers sought legislation to guarantee the independence of the judiciary and to restrict the military from sharing power with the state. However, after succeeding to make laws on those issues and establishing the Corruption Eradication Commission (Komisi Pemberantasan Korupsi, KPK), reformers seemed unaware of the need to advocate for the IPS Law. The KPK is designed to be an independent institution and entitled to investigation and prosecution power (see Butt, this volume). However, in contrast, under the Law of the Public Prosecution 2004, the public prosecution is designed to be politically dependent on president and its powers remain the same. This has kept its bureaucratic and militaristic culture intact, the same as during the previous authoritarian regime.

After 1998, the amendment of the 1945 Constitution abrogated the president's control of the judiciary. The government transferred

---

[23] There were five military generals who became prosecutor general during Soeharto's rule. Four generals of the army: Lt. Gen. Sugih Arto, Lieutenant General Ali Said, Lt. Gen. Ismail Saleh and Major General Hari Suharto. Soekarton Marmosudjono is the admiral of the Navy.

[24] Angkatan Bersenjata Republik Indoenesia.

[25] Muchtar Pakpahan, Sri Bintang Pamungkas and many in opposition were prosecuted by the Subversion Law (Lolo 2008, 173–91).

administrative supervision of the courts to the Supreme Court.[26] The president must have approval from the parliament before appointing or dismissing the chief of police.[27] The government's ability to control law enforcement policies in regard to high-profile political cases was restricted once the KPK was established. The KPK can prosecute political elites without the president's permission, unlike the IPS and the police.[28] The government tried to maintain its control of the public prosecution as the only remaining supporter of the president in the justice system.[29] The government succeeded in hindering the parliament's draft of the Public Prosecution Law and replaced it with its own draft.[30] The power to appoint and dismiss the prosecutor general are the president's prerogative. The Constitutional Court in Decision 49/PUU-VIII/2010 confirms the position of the prosecutor general as a cabinet member.[31]

The public prosecution is managed hierarchically by the prosecutor general, so certain high-profile criminal cases may be dismissed if they contradict the president's political interests. A notable example occurred in 1998 when the Prosecutor General Soedjono C. Atmonegoro told President Habibie that the public prosecution would investigate the Soeharto corruption case. A day later Habibie dismissed him and appointed Army General Andi Ghalib as the prosecutor general (Moeljo Mangoenprawiro 1999: 37). Another example is when former State Secretary Yusril Ihza Mahendra witnessed Prosecutor General Hendarman Supandji coming to President Susilo Bambang Yudhoyono to receive directions about a public prosecution decision to investigate a corruption case.[32]

The IPS as the weapon of the government means that the prosecutor can serve as top-down and bottom-up monitoring and information-gathering mechanisms helping the government in the choice between repression and co-optation. IPS executives generate a sense of mission about this task, which is widely shared and endorsed by operators and managers[33] (Wilson 1989: 95).

---

[26] As mentioned in TAP MPR X/MPR/1998, Law 35/1999, Law 4/2004 on the judiciary.

[27] Law 2/2002 on the police.

[28] Law 30/2002 on the KPK.

[29] Interview with a former prosecutor general, 2 December 2015.

[30] See DPR 2002–4 (legislative minutes of IPS Law).

[31] This decision clarifies that the tenure of the prosecutor general depends on the president's term who appointed him.

[32] Constitutional Court Decision 49/PUU-VIII/2010, p. 21.

[33] Wilson's (1989) definition of executives, managers and operators helps me to differentiate among actors within the IPS.

The Bureaucracy of the Indonesia Prosecution Service
and Its Militaristic Culture

The public prosecution consists of one supreme public prosecution service office in Jakarta, whose jurisdiction covers the territory of the Republic of Indonesia, 31 high public prosecution service offices which cover the territory of the provinces, 393 district public prosecution service offices, which cover the districts, equivalent to a municipality or administrative city[34] and 86 sub-district public prosecution service offices.[35] The number of staff working in the IPS comprises 9,903 public prosecutors[36] and 12,875 administrative staff[37] (*Kejaksaan Agung* 2016: 38). The IPS arranges that prosecutors with high rank could not work in the district prosecution service offices, which are headed by prosecutors with lower ranks.[38] Since then, almost 11 per cent of public prosecutors, who have high ranks and long experiences, are concentrated in the supreme public prosecution service office.[39]

The IPS maintains a strict structure and ranking of officers. All levels are graded and given a strict numerical ranking. A prosecutor wears a uniform and badges in their daily work. To ensure the discipline and loyalty of prosecutors, the IPS holds morning and afternoon parades in military style. The IPS requires its officials to supervise their subordinates two levels below. Consequently, if the subordinate makes a mistake or acts inappropriately, the superior will also be punished.[40] In 1978, the Prosecutor General Major General Ali Said created a doctrine '*satya adhi wicaksana*' to strengthen the *esprit de corps* and loyalty to the government. This term is from Javanese Madjapahit Sanskrit language: *satya* means loyalty, *adhi* implies professionalism and *wicaksana* means being wise in using the power.[41] The doctrine is shared and endorsed by the IPS as legitimising its military culture. The prosecutor's candidacy training[42]

---

[34] President Regulation 38/2010 on IPS Organization classified the District Prosecution Office (DPO) into two types: A and B. It was classified based on the caseload and the complexity of the problems in that area.

[35] The Sub-district Prosecution Office (SDPO) is located in remote areas.

[36] 6,965 males and 2,949 females.

[37] 8,532 males and 4,523 females.

[38] Art. 8 Prosecutor General Regulation (Peraturan Jaksa Agung/Perja) PER-016/A/JA/07/2013.

[39] The prosecutor number in supreme public prosecution service office is nearly the same as the prosecutors' number in four provinces in Borneo.

[40] See Prosecutor General Decision (Keputusan Prosecutor Agung/Kepja) KEP-503/A/J.A/12/2000 on the supervision procedure in IPS.

[41] Prosecutor General Decision 074/J.A./7/1978 jo Prosecutor General Decision 052/J.A./8/1979; Prosecutor General Decision 030/J.A./1988.

[42] Pendidikan dan Pelatihan Pembentukan Jaksa.

is designed to strengthen this doctrine. The curriculum emphasises physical training such as marching and shaping prosecutors' obedience to their superiors. The prosecutor's morality is formed by inculcating the idea that loyalty to the organisation is of great importance (Wilson 1989: 92).

The militaristic culture has a significant impact on the IPS's view on the Dutch principle '*één en ondeelbaar*' (one and indivisible).[43] It originally refers to the public prosecutor's position during the trial and is concerned with minimising the charge disparity filed by the public prosecutor (Soepomo 1997: 136). During the authoritarian regime, the IPS reinterpreted this principle and used it as the basis for its militaristic culture within the IPS (Falaakh 2014: 428). Law 16/2004 stipulates that a prosecutor is responsible to the leader in her or his jurisdiction and hierarchically controlled by the prosecutor general.[44] In addition, the prosecutor general is above reproach. Because of this rigid chain of command, the prosecutor has no option but to hold the same view as the prosecutor general.

This culture plays an important role in influencing the public prosecutor's work within a limited budget. According to the 2011 Annual Report, the government set aside a budget to deal with just 10,100 cases, whereas the IPS received a total number of 99,770 general criminal cases from the police.[45] However, the IPS still processed 96,488 criminal cases. A number of them went through appeal and execution, and some even through review (IPS Annual Report 2011: 38). To use the limited budget strategically, the IPS reduced the budget allocation from 35 million rupiah to 3.5 million rupiah per case (Komisi Kejaksaan 2013: 10). It is taboo to ask their leader about the budget, so heads of the district office were reluctant to seek additional funds from the supreme public prosecution service office. They preferred to be strategic and seek funding by other means to cover their expenditures. These conditions enable the IPS to informally allow their staff to seek other sources for their expenditures. The head of the district office manages cases by using *subsidi silang* or cross-subsidy. This term means two things: first, using other funds to subsidise

---

[43] IPS Law, art. 3.

[44] See art. 8(2) and 18(1). As high-level officials under the prosecutor general, the head of the high public prosecution service office controls the operation of the offices under their jurisdiction.

[45] General criminal cases are all criminal cases excluding corruption cases, violation of human right cases, economic cases and other special criminal cases: Investigation report from police to IPS January until September 2011.

unexpected expenditures, and secondly, taking *Rezeki*[46] from big cases and allocating it to subsidise other cases (Bedner 2001: 234–5).

During the New Order regime, the IPS relied on a patronage system as a method to control and extract loyalty. Since there are no clear guidelines on the promotion and transfer process, prosecutors at the lower levels require their careers to advance under the auspices of their higher-ranking patrons. The leader of the public prosecution acts as a father (*bapak*) and relates to the subordinate like a child. The children then need to show their loyalty by giving *upeti*[47] (Butt 2012: 24; Lolo 2008: 123–4, 128, 419–20).

The IPS promotes the idea that its prosecutors are a part of the military and a tool of the government. Even though they built a statue of Soeprapto in front of Supreme public prosecution service office, the IPS attempted to restrain the prosecutors' memory of Soeprapto's legacy. They established the IPS's first anniversary on 22 July 1960. This is the date when the government established the IPS as a ministry and detached it from the judiciary. Further, to eliminate the prosecutor's critical attitude as practised by PERSAJA during the Soeprapto era, the IPS also rewrote the history of PERSAJA by deciding that its first anniversary was on 22 June 1993 (Badan Diklat Kejaksaan 2016).

The current political situation is more democratic than previous regimes and provides an opportunity for prosecutors to express their opinions. The prosecutors use the Indonesian Prosecutor's Association to advocate for the interests of the public prosecution. During the past few years, there has been an active Facebook group named The Prosecutor Alliance (TPA). Public prosecutors use this group to criticise the policy of the supreme public prosecution service office on human resource management (*Hukumonline* 2014i).

The military culture of the IPS is shaped by structural characteristics which are strongly influenced by the military doctrine in their career, belief, training and their connection to the political process (Merry 2010: 48). Furthermore, the IPS will be poorly adapted to perform tasks that are not defined as part of that culture (Wilson 1989: 95).

---

[46] *Rezeki* refers to gifts of a grateful party after or before a favourable prosecutor's decision.
[47] *Upeti* means gifts, which are provided by subordinates to their superior as a symbol of the willingness of the children to be under *Bapak* protection.

The Functions of the Public Prosecution Service

The IPS Law states that the public prosecution service is a government agency that has the power to prosecute (art. 2(1)). The IPS's role is not only as the prosecution service in criminal cases but also as the state intelligence in guarding the public order and acting as legal representative of the government. The IPS has two divisions that specialise in handling general and special criminal cases.[48] Although the Code of Criminal Procedure does not allow the public prosecutor authority to supervise police investigation, the IPS retains its authority to investigate special crimes such as corruption,[49] economic crime and human rights violations.[50] The IPS must have the president's permission to investigate corruption cases involving senior officials like mayors and legislative members. Despite this limitation, the IPS investigates more corruption cases than the police. For example, in 2016, the IPS investigated 307 corruption cases, while the police investigated 140 cases.[51]

The different powers within the divisions of the IPS are complicated when the special crime division handles a case in which a suspect has committed different offences[52] or a case whose offence is prosecuted by special and also general crimes.[53] Since the special crimes division cannot prosecute both general and special crimes in one case without cooperating with the police, the division usually only prosecutes special crimes and discards the general crimes from the case.[54]

The power of the IPS to guard the public order and operate in court is inherited from their old counterpart the Dutch Colonial Prosecution Service.[55] This goal has not been met because the IPS is considered a government apparatus. When Law 5/1986 was enacted, the authority of the public prosecution expanded to include cases in the administrative court (Jusuf 2014: 125). The administrative cases and other cases were

---

[48] IPS's categorisation of crimes is different from the police and the judiciary. For example, terrorism is categorised as special crimes by the police, but IPS classified it as the general offence.

[49] IPS special crimes division has its own *prosecutor* investigator.

[50] See Law 26/2000; Law 31/1999; Law 20/2001.

[51] See Kantor Berita Politik 2017. Since the KPK just have one office in Jakarta, it was not comparable with IPS or the police.

[52] *Concursus realis* (in Dutch: *meerdaadse samenloop*). See Indonesian Criminal Code, art. 65.

[53] *Concursus idealis* (in Dutch: *eendaadse samenloop*). See Indonesian Criminal Code, art. 63.

[54] Personal communication with a prosecutor in Special Crimes Division, 2015.

[55] Art. 55 RO.

merged into one division, which confused the function of the public prosecutor. The public prosecutor plays the role of government and state company representatives in civil and administrative cases. The public prosecutor has a poor reputation in handling administrative cases, and most ministries prefer to use their own in-house legal department in courts (Bedner 2001).

The prosecutor's function as an intelligence service was extended when the Soeharto regime used the IPS to purge the communist party affiliated with the government and civil society. The role of the IPS was also to search and ban books related to the ideology of communism. During the New Order, the position of junior prosecutor general for intelligence (JAMINTEL)[56] was appointed from among active army generals. In the post-Soeharto era, the prosecutor's function as the guardian of public order has failed.

Even though intelligence prosecutors are required to gather data to support blasphemy prosecutions and guarding the public order,[57] the prosecutor tends to adopt the fatwa from Indonesian Ulama Council (MUI) as the primary evidence (see Crouch 2017) rather than use the intelligence report from the intelligence prosecutor. Most of the intelligence prosecutors in the district prosecution service offices believe that their role as coordinators of the Board for the Monitoring of Mystical Beliefs (Bakorpakem)[58] is ineffective. The intelligence prosecutors have a heavy workload.[59] In addition, the IPS does not provide a specific budget for Bakorpakem. In some cases, other organisations like MUI hold regular meetings with Bakorpakem in its office. The MUI seems to dominate Bakorpakem meetings in deciding blasphemy cases.

Under the Jokowi government, the IPS was given additional duties to supervise plans on infrastructure development.[60] The role of the IPS is to guard the project and ensure that no prosecution is conducted during the

---

[56] Jaksa Agung Muda Intelijen.

[57] See Peraturan Jaksa Agung/PERJA PER – 019/A/JA/09/2015, art. 3.

[58] Badan Koordinasi Pengawas Aliran Kepercayaan Masyarakat. The role and function of Bakor Pakem is explained in Crouch 2012a: 6–10.

[59] The district intelligence prosecutor does the intelligence work and also prosecutes criminal cases.

[60] Jokowi instructed the police and IPS not to investigate and prosecute the infrastructure project built by the government. IPS then responded to this Jokowi instruction by issuing the Prosecutor General Regulation (Peraturan Jaksa Agung/PERJA) PER-04/A/JA/11/2016 on TP4 (team for guarding and securing the government and its development projects).

project (Kompas 2016e). Not surprisingly, the prosecutor seems to be confused with their multiple roles and does not perform well.

The Public Prosecutor at Work

The Master of the Pretrial Phase

In 1981, the IPS lost its supervision power over police investigations. The Prosecutor General Ali Said ceded this power to the police during the drafting process of the KUHAP[61] (Djamin et al. 2006: 399). The KUHAP introduced the Functional Differentiation (*Diferensiasi Fungsional*) principle, which means that investigation and prosecution are two different processes. The police are the sole investigators[62] and the public prosecutor cannot intervene in their investigation (Harahap 2007: 47–8). However, the KUHAP contains the 'mutual coordination' principle within the investigation process. The term mutual coordination means that the police and the public prosecutor are in the same position and must coordinate with each other (Harahap 2007: 49–51). This coordination encompasses four procedures.

First, the police investigator must send the notification letter to open the investigation[63] to the public prosecutor.[64] Although the police guidelines on investigation mention that the notification should be sent to the public prosecutor after the investigation starts, the police often carry the notification simultaneously with the dossier after they have finished the process. The IPS will command the public prosecutor to return the notification letter if the investigator does not send the investigation report within thirty days after the notification letter is received by public prosecutor.[65] Since

---

[61] The National Police Chief Awaloeddin Djamin initiated a meeting with Prosecutor General Ali Said and Minister of Justice Mudjono to discuss the KUHAP draft. Awaludin succeeded in convincing Ali Said to transfer IPS's investigation power to the police. Since the police were part of the military faction in DPR (House of Representatives), Ali Said left the KUHAP discussion to the police (Djamin, 1995, 218–23).

[62] PPNS (civil servant investigator) should coordinate with the police before handing their investigation dossier to the public prosecutor. Art. 107 KUHAP, art. 14 Law 2/2002 on the police.

[63] Surat Pemberitahuan Dimulainya Penyidikan.

[64] KUHAP art. 109(1). See also art. 25 of PERKAP 14/2012 (The Police Chairman Regulation), which states that the SPDP should be issued subsequently after the police start the investigation process.

[65] See PERJA 036/A/JA/09/2011 on the General Crimes Guidelines, art. 12(1) and (2). Meanwhile PERKAP 14/2012 states that the investigative process must be reported to the superior.

there are no legal consequences for the police investigator who does not carry the notification letter, from 2012 to 2014 almost 50 per cent of criminal investigations were not reported to the IPS (Zikry, Ardhan & Tiara 2016). This failure to report cases may be linked to the police efforts to mediate the cases as a source of illicit revenue. The police keep its investigation away from the public prosecutor since they try to reconcile and resolve the case out of the criminal justice system (Afandi 2013: 392; 2015: 29). Cases reported by Muradi (2014) also support the fact that the police conducts *parmin*[66] (criminal participation) to support the operational budget and their low salary (*Polri & KKN* 2004: 29).

Second, the police must get an extension permit from the public prosecutor to detain a suspect for more than forty days.[67] The public prosecutor cannot intervene in the investigation process based on the principle of Functional Differentiation, so almost every police request for an extension is authorised.[68] The Institute for Criminal Justice Reform reports that some officers use custody extension to intimidate suspects. They should give *parmin* if they want the police to hasten the investigation process and release them from custody (Eddyono et al. 2012: 225).

Third, the police must send a notification to the public prosecutor when they decide to drop a case (KUHAP art. 109(2)). In the event that the public prosecutor believes that the case should not be dismissed, the public prosecutor can examine the police decision in court (Art. 77(a) and 78). Nevertheless, at the time of writing, the public prosecutor has never used this authority to examine a police decision.

Fourth, regarding the pre-prosecution process, after completing its investigation the police must send the dossier to the public prosecutor. The public prosecutor must then examine the file within seven days. The public prosecutor will decide whether the investigation is complete or not. If the public prosecutor believes that the case does not have sufficient evidence, she or he will return the dossier to the police. The public prosecutor gives an annotation which must be used by the police to conduct the additional investigation within fourteen days (art. 14(b) and 138(2) KUHAP). In some cases, the investigator relies on the testimony of a criminal law lecturer as an expert witness to convince the

---

[66] Partisipasi Kriminal/Parmin, a term used for payment coming from criminal activities (Muradi 2014).

[67] KUHAP art. 24(2). The police can detain suspects for twenty days (KUHAP art. 20).

[68] No provisions about the extension of the police custody on PERJA 036/A/JA/09/2011 on the General Crimes Guidelines.

public prosecutor.[69] If the public prosecutor rejects the case, it means that the whole investigation fails and affects performance assessments.[70] To avoid this, the police keep criminal cases pending. In 2012, around 12,535 case files or 55 per cent of cases were kept pending after the public prosecutor rejected the dossier. In some cases, the district police chief lobbied the head of the district prosecution office to command the public prosecutor to accept the file. The police even threatened and forced the public prosecutor to receive the dossier (AJNN 2017; Berita Satu 2015). The Code of Criminal Procedure does not clarify whether the investigator conducts the additional investigation. The police believe that the KUHAP sets a limit on public prosecutor to accept the dossier fourteen days after the police complete the additional investigation. However, the IPS argues that they can return the dossier if the investigator is unable to fulfil the public prosecutor annotation in the dossier. The IPS stipulates that the police can declare its additional investigation optimal[71] or ask the public prosecutor to conduct additional inquiries into the case. The public prosecutor can decide to dismiss the case after the inquiries.[72]

Since prosecutorial discretion is monopolised by the prosecutor general, only criminal cases which have a high-profile political background are dismissed for public interest reasons. There are no guidelines and provisions about the definition of public interest. Even the police criticise and challenge the prosecutor general's decision when dismissing a case for this reason.[73] In 2015, various organisations affiliated with the police such as Association of Bachelor and Profession of Police Science,

---

[69] Art. 184 (1) of the KUHAP states that the expert witness is evidence. Choirul Huda, a famous legal expert in Indonesian courts, believes that since law enforcement cannot merely be based in the provisions in the law, the trial requires a legal expert to gain an understanding of the theoretical law, which is not written in the text (A'yun, 2014, 343).

[70] See PERKAP 14/2012 art. 94. Since the police have retained the military bureaucracy, the chief of police as the superior of investigator can also be evaluated because of the investigation process that was carried out by his subordinates.

[71] PERJA 036/A/JA/09/2011, art. 11(6), states that if the public prosecutor rejects the dossier more than three times because the investigator could not comply with public prosecutor supervision, the public prosecutor will recommend that the investigator stop the investigation. See also art. 76 PERKAP 14/2012.

[72] Although Constitutional Court Decision Number 130/PUU-XIII/2015 required the police investigator to send the SPDP to the prosecutor after no later than seven days, the Constitutional Court did not extend public prosecutor authority to conduct additional investigation.

[73] In response to the increased public outrage who believed that the criminal cases investigated by the police were retaliation for the KPK investigation of the corruption within the police, the prosecutor general issued Seponeering to formally drop the charges against

Indonesia Police Watch and Family of Police and Children urged the legislature to investigate the prosecutor general on suspicions that he had used prosecutorial discretion to drop the charges against KPK commissioners Abraham Samad and Bambang Widjojanto. The police filed a suit in the Constitutional Court on the authority of the prosecutor general's prosecutorial discretion with three lawsuits at once.[74]

The Postman in the Court

In 2008, the public prosecutor prosecuted a man known as Sugik for murdering Asrori in Jombang, East Java. This case was controversial because the public prosecutor insisted on prosecuting Sugik even though there was strong evidence that a police investigator tortured Sugik to confess. The police headquarters found that Asrori was killed by another person named Ryan and not Sugik. Despite this, the public prosecutor in Jombang district office persisted in prosecuting Sugik based on the dossier. The public prosecutor planned to summon the police investigator to defend its dossier. However, due to public pressure and strong evidence in favour of Sugik's innocence, the sub-district office ordered the public prosecutor to recommend the acquittal for the Sugik.[75] This case shows how public pressure can influence the decision of the prosecutor to release a defendant.

The KUHAP does not give power to the public prosecutor to present evidence that is not mentioned in the dossier. The IPS prefers to trust the investigators and summon the police as witnesses to back the dossier up in the trial.[76] Unlike the Sugik case, acquittal is rarely asked for by the public prosecutor in his or her closing statement. The IPS believes that the public prosecutor's decision to accept the investigation dossier must be based on firm evidence. If the judge acquits the defendant, the IPS will examine the prosecutor's performance. To avoid this situation, a public prosecutor may agree to help the defendant to ask for a minimum sentence from the judge.

KPK commissioners Chandra Muhammad Hamzah and Bibit Samad Rianto in 2011, and Abraham Samad and Bambang Widjojanto in 2015.

[74] Constitutional Court Decision Number 29/PUU-XIV/2016, Number 40/PUU-XIV/2016, and No 43/PUU-XIV/2016 reject those suits.

[75] For further details, see (Chazawi 2011, 143–74).

[76] Circular Letter of the Junior Prosecutor General for General Crimes: B-254/E/5/93, 31 Mei 1993.

The IPS believes that they manage the prosecution process according to strict procedures and in a faithful manner. Since the IPS has adopted a military culture, the superior supervises and controls the public prosecutor's charge and indictment. Even though the public prosecutor is the actor in a court hearing, they must have approval of their supervisor in order to recommend the offence the defendant is to be sentenced for and the severity of the sentence.[77] The public prosecutor must draft the indictment plans (Rentut)[78] and submit it to their superiors. If the draft is not approved, it must be revised based on the directive provided.[79]

The public prosecution acts on the assumption that the judge's decision should suit the public prosecutor recommendation.[80] If the judge's decision does not adopt the public prosecutor's indictment, the public prosecution requires the public prosecutor to appeal the decision.[81] The KUHAP does not give the public prosecutor the opportunity to appeal an acquittal. Since no provision restricts the public prosecution from filing a cassation to the Supreme Court, the public prosecution requires the public prosecutor to file a cassation for an acquittal decision.[82] To ensure that the Supreme Court decision matches the public prosecution's goals, the public prosecutor is required to file a review of the Supreme Court decision. The public prosecution insists on filing a review on a Supreme Court acquittal decision (Kompas 2016f), even though the KUHAP does not allow the public prosecutor to do so.[83] From 2008 to 2015 the public prosecutor was the applicant with the highest number of appeals in the

---

[77] See Inilah 2011. The Supreme Court complains of this Rentut procedure because sometimes the trial must be postponed because the public prosecutor needs to wait for direction from their superior in the sub-district office.

[78] Rencana Tuntutan. This Rentut procedure was initiated by the Prosecutor General Soeprapto to improve the indictment quality within the low-level prosecutors who had poor legal background. The *Rentut* was transformed during the Prosecutor General Gen. Ali Said's period. The concept was copied from the army operation model, which called the plan (Rencana) by the troops who got fully supervised by their leader. Personal communication Andi Hamzah, 2015.

[79] Before submitting the requisite charges, every public prosecutor should first ask how high the charges should be to the head of the district prosecution office for a case at the district level, the head of the high prosecution office for a provincial level case and the prosecutor general for a national level case.

[80] In 1962, Prosecutor General Gunawan urged the Supreme Court to accept his idea about the Consensual model (Pompe, 2005, 98).

[81] See the prosecutor general circular letter SE-013/A/JA/12/2011.

[82] In 2012, the constitutional court allowed the public prosecutor to file a cassation. See Constitutional Court decision 114/PUU-X/2012.

[83] Constitutional court decision no. 33/PUU-XIV/2016 prohibits the public prosecutor to file a Supreme Court decision review.

Supreme Court. This can lead to heavy caseloads and contribute to the Supreme Judges' performance (Arsil et al. 2016: 4).

This case illustrates the role of the public prosecutor as the postman who delivers the dossier to the court. In addition, since the IPS has lost its supervisory authority over police investigations, the prosecutor general position is like the postmaster general,[84] who is responsible for oversight of the delivery of criminal cases to the court throughout the nation. Under the previous authoritarian regime, the public prosecutor's mission was to ensure that cases that concerned the government were granted by the court. Currently, it seems that the public prosecutor's function is to deliver the case not only based on interests of the government but also other powerful actors such as political parties companies or the police. Since the police budget is higher than the IPS budget, some district offices handle more criminal cases than their budget anticipates.[85] In some cases, the police provide the budget for the public prosecutor.

Conclusion

As in other post-colonial countries, Indonesia has kept the former Dutch colonial legal system as a primary source of its national law after independence. A legacy of the Dutch civil legal tradition prevails in the existing judicial system and criminal justice system. However, the unfinished legal transplantation process at the end of the Dutch colonial administration, the Japanese military colonisation and different political ideologies from various regimes after independence contribute to the problems in adopting human right principles in criminal procedure.

Another possible explanation is the ambiguity of Dutch legal interpretation. During the 1950 provisional Constitution period, it is likely that the IPS's and the judiciary's views of the Dutch procedures were consistent to strengthen the rule of law.[86] When a more flexible 1945 Constitution was re-enacted in 1959, the government applied colonial law with an Indonesian-based interpretation. The development of this local legal interpretation began with the Minister of Justice Sahardjo as the primary person who shaped legal interpretation in the Guided Democracy era (1959–65).

---

[84] The name for chief executive officer of the postal service of a country like in Canada and US, responsible for oversight over the delivery of mail throughout the nation.

[85] In 2015 a District Prosecution Office (DPO) in Java prosecuted 406 criminal cases while they only have the budget for 350 cases.

[86] Albeit the government tried to intervene in the criminal proceeding, prosecutors and judges worked very well in cases involving high political actors.

Sahardjo introduced the concept of *Pengayoman*.[87] According to this concept, the rule of law must be based on community wisdom, which is represented by a leader's wisdom. Under the Guided Democracy, the idea that the president is the greatest leader and the wisest man of the community was promoted. Therefore, the president's discretion was the law itself (Sahardjo 1963). The Soeharto military regime (1965–99) expanded this *Pengayoman* concept not only for legal interpretation but also for the social and political understanding. Government officials in positions of leadership had the power to interpret the law based on their position as the representative of public wisdom. Thus, their discretion was considered as the policy and the wisdom, which was used to apply or ignore the rules legitimately. Moreover, the regime militarised the public prosecution and the police to legitimise their control over the criminal justice system to suit their political interests.

This situation has not changed even though the 1945 Constitution has been amended post 1998. Even though the Constitution now guarantees judicial independence, I conclude that the militaristic culture within the public prosecution continues and the position of the prosecutor general as a cabinet member prevents the public prosecutor from reforming. Instead of being a *dominus litis*, the public prosecutor works like a postman by prosecuting almost all criminal case dossiers received from the police. As a result, the Indonesian criminal justice system suffers from a heavy caseload[88] and overcrowding in prisons.[89]

---

[87] The *Pengayoman* is symbolised by the Banyan Tree and represents protection and succour (Lev 2000d: 119).

[88] See IPS Annual Report 2011 and LeIP research on the court case flow.

[89] World Prison Brief data (2017) shows that detainee and prisoner capacity in Indonesia is overcrowded by 174.9 per cent on average.

PART II

Specialised Courts Established under
the New Order

5

The Religious Courts

Does Lev's Analysis Still Hold?

STIJN CORNELIS VAN HUIS

In 1972, Daniel S. Lev was the first author to write a monograph about the Islamic courts in Indonesia.[1] Despite his longstanding and deep research of the Indonesian legal system, the Islamic courts are the only courts he has dedicated a monograph to. As a subchapter of his work *Islamic Courts in Indonesia. A Study in the Political Bases of Legal Institution* already indicates, Lev did not study the Islamic courts as a closed legal system but viewed them in the historical and political context of Indonesia to explain how and why the Islamic courts developed as they did procedurally and, to a lesser extent, substantively. He tried to explain why in Indonesia, unlike in other countries in the Islamic world, the Islamic courts not only survived the worldwide trend to unify and secularize the legal system, but even managed to grow. Lev convincingly argued that the strong position of traditional Islam in Indonesia, especially on the island of Java, resulted in a distinct political constellation, in which national governments always had to rely on the support of *Nahdlatul Ulama* (awakening of the ulama) – the political party representing traditionalist Muslim interests. The central position that Muslim traditionalists played in Indonesian politics led to a situation in which procedural reforms that were common in the Middle East – such as doing away with Islamic courts and placing Islamic family law under the civil courts – was unthinkable.

Lev's research on Islamic courts was conducted from the early 1960s till 1971. The year 1971 was an important year in Indonesian politics,

---

[1] The term 'religious courts' would be the direct translation of the Indonesian *pengadilan agama*. *Pengadilan agama* are the courts with jurisdiction over family law, inheritance and Islamic economic matters, such as Islamic banking, pertaining to Muslims. I follow Lev, who preferred to use the term 'Islamic courts' as he describes the development of the Islamic courts that had different names at different times and places, but always were Islamic in that the main point of reference was Islamic doctrine (*fiqh*).

because in that year the first elections since the rise to power of General Suharto after the crackdown of the communist coup in 1965 were held. In these elections, the Muslim parties suffered a severe defeat. President Suharto's political party *Golkar* (*Golongan Karya*; Functional Groups) won a majority of seats, 61 per cent, in parliament. The political constellation that had precluded profound procedural changes pertaining to the Islamic courts before no longer existed in parliament. However, as I will explain below, the *Nahdlatul Ulama* persevered in both society and politics. As a result, the Islamic courts managed to survive the first decades of Suharto's New Order and grew even further after 'the Islamic turn in Indonesia' (Liddle 1996). This chapter will explain how and why – contrary to Lev's predictions in 1971 – the Islamic courts survived the new constellation in Indonesian politics. Two questions are central in this chapter:

1. How did the religious legal system survive despite the weakened position of Islamic political parties in parliament?
2. To what extent has the civil legal system subjugated the Islamic courts after 1971?

In answering these questions, I reflect on Lev's analysis of the political dimensions of Indonesia's Islamic courts system. As a postscript in his last chapter, Lev tries to make sense of Indonesia's dual legal system, by which he means a system with distinct civil law and Islamic pillars. He looks into the question of what consequences the new political developments in 1971 might have for the future of the Islamic courts. According to Lev, the existence of a dual legal system may be interpreted in two ways. First, 'civil and religious legal systems reflect competing political principles and sources of legitimacy that cannot be tolerated for long'. In the end, because the systems are incompatible, civil institutions will expand their authority and subjugate Islamic administration and religious law to the overriding principles of state legitimacy and bureaucratic integrity. Lev argues that such development is likely in Indonesia 'in one form or another' (Lev 1972a: 264).

Lev adds this phrase because he believes that a second interpretation of the dual legal system in Indonesia is simultaneously valid: 'the competing principles of legitimacy [i.e. the constitution and Islam] are related in a political order that is itself legitimate. [. . .] Men may perceive their participation in a political system in terms of their conflict with other members of the political system, in something like a moiety structure' (Lev 1972a: 265). The religious and civil legal orders represent a religious–social–political cleavage which in turn 'relates to a complicated political order that men think of as Indonesia'. In other words, Lev believed in 1971 that the civil legal system in 'one form or another' would attempt to subjugate Islamic institutions to overriding principles of state legitimacy and bureaucratic integrity, but that the result of this process would be uncertain and dependent on the persistence and development of the religious–social–political cleavage, which is so distinctively Indonesian. Below I argue that such convergence between the civil and religious legal systems did take place after 1971, but that this was not the result of subjugation of religious law by the civil legal system but of an increased blending of the civil and the religious pillars within Indonesia's religious, social, political and legal domains.

The data used in this chapter builds on my earlier research on the Islamic courts in Cianjur and Bulukuma.[2] In my previous work, I have analysed and reworked this data with the abovementioned questions, analyses and insights of Daniel Lev concerning the Islamic courts in mind. I will argue that although during the New Order parliament became dominated by *Golkar*, through the Ministry of Religious Affairs the *Nahdlatul Ulama* maintained its strategic political position and its leverage on Islamic matters. Similarly, although the Indonesian state has increasingly regulated the Islamic courts system and brought it procedurally and substantively more in line with the civil legal system, it did so on the initiative of proponents of a more Islamic legal system in Indonesia within the government – the Ministry of Religious Affairs and an Islamist faction in the Supreme Court.

This chapter is divided into two parts: Part 1 analyses the interrelatedness of the Islamic courts and the civil legal system before 1971 – the last year discussed in Lev's study, and Part 2 discusses this interrelatedness for the period after 1971. I first turn to the colonial policies and regulations concerning the Islamic courts. The incorporation of the Islamic courts into the colonial legal system of the Netherlands Indies led to the birth of the dual legal system Lev speaks of. Subsequently, I discuss the political stalemate under Sukarno's Old Order after Independence and how this prevented the seemingly imminent abolition of the Islamic courts system from happening. I describe how after the rise of Suharto the elections of 1971 led to a totally new political situation in which one party held the absolute majority in parliament. Subsequently, in Part 2, I describe how and why, in 1973, despite the overwhelmingly

---

[2] See van Huis (2015), Chapters 2 and 4.

large support base in parliament, plans to drastically reform family law and the role of Islamic courts did not come about. In the 1980s, the Islamic turn in politics of the New Order signalled a total new political development. From now on there was sufficient political support to enhance the jurisdiction of the Islamic courts and to increase its standing. I show, following the analysis of Mark Cammack (2007), how this upgrading of the religious courts was achieved by modelling them on the civil courts. After the stepping down of Suharto in 1998, the emancipation of Islamic courts continued as they finally became a full-fledged part of the legal system under the roof of the Supreme Court. This full incorporation of Islamic courts into the legal system of Indonesia does not constitute a subjugation of the Islamic courts to the civil legal system but must be seen as a blending of the two. The result is a legal system in which core elements of the religious legal system can persist and thrive.

Part 1   The Religious Courts in Indonesia until 1971

The Colonial Origins of the Dual Legal System

When the first Dutch merchant ships arrived on the coast of Java in 1596, the Javanese Muslim sultanates of Demak (1475–1548), Cirebon (1479–1906), Banten (1527–1813) and the powerful sultanate of Mataram (1588–1681) had all integrated Islamic law into their judicial systems: the so-called *jaksa*[3] courts. The *jaksa* courts were sultanate courts at the regency level and held jurisdiction in all civil and criminal matters. As in the rest of the Muslim world (An Na'im 2002: 12), three systems of law in a broad sense operated in the sultanates: first, sultanic law consisting of decrees and regulations promulgated on the basis of the ruler's authority (*siyasa*); second, Islamic doctrines (*fiqh*), of the *syafi'ite maddhab*, and ultimately based on a divine authority; third, customary norms based in *adat* that ruled the daily lives of local communities. Within the *jaksa* courts an Islamic judge (*qadi*) passed judgments in Muslim family law and inheritance law. The position of *qadi* was filled by the *penghulu*, the local head of the Islamic bureaucracy (see Hisyam 2001; Bruinessen 1995; Lubis 1994: 58–9).

During the seventeenth and eighteenth centuries, Javanese territories under VOC rule increased considerably. In 1680 and 1752, respectively, the West Javanese sultanates of Cirebon and Banten became VOC

---

[3] *Jaksa* is Sanskrit for prosecutor.

protectorates. The legal system of the East Indies, designed for small Dutch East India Company (known as 'VOC') settlements like Batavia and other ports in the archipelago, became unsustainable and was, therefore, reorganized. On 30 November 1746, the VOC established the *landraad* in Semarang (Central Java), a general court for the indigenous population in which European judges were instructed to apply indigenous law. However, in practice, these courts focussed on criminal law and high-profile cases, whereas the *penghulus* continued their judicial work in family law and inheritance matters (Huis 2015: 22–6).

After the VOC went bankrupt and the short period of English rule (1811–16), the Dutch decided to regulate the jurisdiction of the *penghulus*. The Dutch, through the 1820 Regulations concerning the Duties, Titles and Rank of Regents on Java (the 1820 Regents Regulation),[4] now for the first time explicitly recognized the role of *penghulus* in settling marriage, divorce and inheritance in the areas under their rule. Article 13 of the 1820 Regents Regulation reads:

> The indigenous regency head (*regent*) supervises matters of the Muslim religion and guarantees that the priests, in accordance with the Javanese norms and customs, are free in practicing their profession, such as in marriage matters, division of property in divorce and inheritance matters (*boedelscheidingen*) and such.

After some inconsistency in *Landraad* judgments about whether this regulation had provided the *penghulu* with adjudication powers in matters mentioned in Article 13, the Supreme Court of the Netherlands Indies decided that they did not have such powers. The Governor General subsequently intervened and issued the Regulation concerning Judgments in Civil Actions Resulting from Disputes among the Javanese (S 1835/58)[5] to clarify the scope of Article 13:

> As ampliative and explication, in order to explain Article 13 of the regulation on the duties, titles and ranks of the district heads on the Island of Java [S 1820/ 22]; that in many instances disputes occur, among Javanese, about matters of marriage, [about] property after divorce and death and such, that must be decided according to Islamic law; that it is the priests who must give a judgment, yet that all civil actions, for settlement and payment, as a result of those decisions, will be brought

---

[4] *Het reglement op de verpligtingen, titels en rangen der regenten op het eiland Java* (S 1820/22).

[5] *Resolutie van den Gouverneur Generaal ad interim in Rade, van den 7den December 1835 no. 6. Uitspraak in civiele actiën, voortspruitende uit geschillen, tusschen Javanen onderling* (S 1835/58).

> before the general courts, in order to, while respecting those decisions and
> to ensure the executions thereof, do justice.

Thus, just when the civil legal system was in the process of subjugating
the judicial role of the *penghulu* on Java, the government of the
Netherlands Indies stepped in and formally recognized their adjudicating
powers. The Dutch created the dual system that Lev mentions by ruling
that enforcement orders of the *penghulus'* judgments could only be
issued by the civil courts (*Landraad*). The religious and civil legal systems
were procedurally linked to each other.

The incorporation of the Islamic courts system into the colonial legal
system would be formalized through the 1882 Priest Councils
Regulation.[6] The Priest Councils[7] Regulation laid down some founda-
tional aspects of the future Islamic courts. Article 1 stipulated that alongside every *landraad* on Java and Madura there should be an Islamic court.
Articles 2 and 3 stipulated that an Islamic court should consist of
a minimum of three and a maximum of eight *penghulus* and was presided
by the chief *penghulu*. The Governor General of the Netherlands Indies
appointed and dismissed the chief *penghulu*. Articles 4, 5 and 6 regulated
that to render a judgment valid, a panel of *penghulus* had to consist of at
least three members, including the chief *penghulu* as chair. The judgement, including the legal justification, had to be written down, signed by
all members of the panel of *penghulus* and kept in a registry.[8] The litigants
were to receive a copy of the judgement. Article 7, finally, stipulated that
when a priest council transgressed its jurisdiction, the judgements could
not be enforced through the *landraad*.

These procedural stipulations did not only constitute recognition of
the Islamic courts, but with the Priest Council Regulation, the colonial
government also sought to bring the *penghulus* under its bureaucratic
control – and this was probably the main rationale behind the regulation.
It pulled away the priest councils from the administrative control of the
Javanese regents and brought them under the direct administration of the
Department of Internal Affairs. Lev considered this separation of
the Islamic courts from indigenous governance of great importance as
it provided Islamic courts with more independence from the local

---

[6] *Reglement betreffende de priesterraden op Java en Madura (S 1882/152).*
[7] Because the Dutch colonizers saw a resemblance between the Islamic *penghulu* and
catholic priests, they called the Islamic courts that were preceded over by a *penghulu* as
'priest councils'.
[8] Raffles (1817) noted that the *penghulu* of the Islamic courts in the early nineteenth century
already wrote down their decisions and kept a registry.

Javanese government and a more supralocal orientation (Lev 1972a: 13). Thus, in 1882 the Dutch established the dual legal system that still exists today – a legal system that consists of a civil legal and a religious part.

From the early twentieth century onwards, the so-called *adat* law (*adatrecht*) school of the Dutch scholars Snouck Hurgronje, Van Vollenhoven and Ter Haar promoted the so-called reception theory (*receptietheorie*). Reception theory held that it was not Islamic law that ruled everyday life in Indonesia, but customary law (*adat* law). According to the *adat* law school, the role of Islamic law had to be limited to those Islamic norms that the local *adat* had incorporated or received in daily practices. The main argument was that in Indonesian legal culture, living norms (*adat*) rather than the prescribed norms of Islamic doctrine (*fiqh*) stood and ought to stand central.[9] In the opinion of the *adat* law proponents, the indigenous population should as much as possible be ruled by their own *adat* law norms and, therefore, the *landraad* should apply the local *adat* law (defined as *adat* norms with legal consequences) in their judgements. Van Vollenhoven was concerned about the 'encroachment' of both Islamic and European law on *adat* practices within society (1931: 70).

The influence of the *adat* law school was visible in the new proto-Constitution of the Netherlands Indies, the *Indische Staatsregeling* (S 1925/415; IS), which replaced the old 1854 RR (Nurlaelawati 2010: 48).[10] Article 134 (2) on the jurisdiction of the *penghulu* courts reads: 'civil lawsuits between Mohammedans fall under the jurisdiction of the religious judge, provided that this is in accordance with their *adat* law, and not contrary to stipulations in [colonial] legislation.' Hence, the 1925 IS made Islamic law subordinate to *adat* law, and the civil courts had to take local *adat* norms as the starting point in judgments concerning execution of *penghulu* courts' judgements.

From the perspective of legal practice, the IS did not form a significant legal change. From the early twentieth century onwards (and concurrently with the rise of the *adat* law school), the colonial civil court system had increasingly denied the Islamic court's judicial powers in disputes concerning maintenance, marital property and inheritance (Velde 1928; Huis 2015: 28–9). This silent transfer of jurisdiction in property and

---

[9] Although they saw *adat* law as a living law, the *adat* law scholars also tried to preserve local customary law, thus, whether intentionally or not, sustaining traditional hierarchies which facilitated colonial rule. For further reading, see Benda-Beckmann & Benda-Beckmann 2011; Burns 2004; Prins 1951.

[10] The *Indische Staatsregeling* came into force on 1 January 1926.

inheritance matters from Islamic courts to civil courts appeared not to be noticed by Muslim organizations. When existing legal practice was codified in the 1931 *Penghulu Courts* regulation, however, the Muslim organizations strongly objected.

These protests, after codification of legal practice, show how regarding sensitive issues involving symbols of religious authority, 'implicit legal change' is easier to achieve than 'explicit legal change' (Lev 1972a: 2). Despite protests of Muslim organizations, and after having postponed the implementation for six years, the government of the Netherlands Indies in 1937 adopted two Chapters of the 1931 *Penghulu* Courts Regulation.

In 1937, the Netherlands Indies also introduced an appellate Islamic court. This extension of the Islamic courts system appears to be at odds with the limitation of the *penghulu* courts' jurisdiction.[11] However, the colonial government had good reasons for this institutionalization of Islamic courts. Shapiro argues that the establishment of appellate courts generally is driven by concerns for political control (Shapiro 1981: 222). Indeed, the colonial government expected the Islamic high court to implement the reforms of 1931 and 1937, and to make sure the first instance *penghulu* courts would do the same. There is some proof that the Islamic high court indeed implemented the jurisdictional changes. For instance, as I have demonstrated elsewhere, it denied any judicial powers to Islamic courts in South Sulawesi on the grounds that the court had never been a customary institution there. This is an example of how the High Islamic Court applied the reception theory of the *adat* law school (Huis 2015, Chapter 6).

Lev argued that the legal culture pertaining to the Islamic courts in Indonesia of the 1960s differed significantly from those in other Islamic countries, because of its distinctive colonial legacy. Other than the French and the British did in their colonies, the Dutch did not interfere much in the dealings of the Islamic courts of the Netherlands Indies (Lev 1972a: 235). Lev was right if he meant that the Dutch did not interfere much regarding substantive legal practice *within* the Islamic courts, which remained based on the Shafi'i school of Islamic doctrine and *adat*. However, one should not underestimate the impact of procedural and relative jurisdictional legal changes that were introduced by the colonial

---

[11] The chapter concerning the Islamic high court (*Hof van Islamietische Zaken*) for Java and Madura in the 1931 *Penghulu* Courts Regulation came into force through *Staatsblad* 1937/610.

government and case law of the colonial civil court system of the Netherlands Indies. In my opinion, the cases described above are clear attempts by the colonial government and civil legal system to subjugate – or at least incorporate and control – traditional Islamic judicial practice.

Lev shows how the Islamic courts kept accommodating traditional Islamic legal culture by seeking conciliation and private settlements – and even continued to accept inheritance cases after 1937 – when formally they had lost jurisdiction. They did so, by acting as *ulama* issuing *fatwa* rather than judges issuing court judgments (Lev 1972a: 199–205). It is well possible that the transfer of jurisdiction from the Islamic courts to the civil court and their reliance on the civil courts to enforce judgments stimulated the already existing preference for private agreements and a dislike of judicial litigation in the legal culture of the Islamic courts.

The Development of Religious Courts from Independence until 1971

On 17 August 1945, Sukarno declared the independence of Indonesia. One of the most difficult political issues his government had to deal with was the place that Islam and Islamic law would take in an Independent Indonesian state. Initially, the 1945 Constitution contained the stipulation that the Sharia would apply to Muslims. However, because Sukarno and his advisers feared the reaction of the eastern, non-Muslim provinces to the Sharia stipulation, it was dropped from the Constitution. This, in turn, angered the Muslim militias that had fought against the Dutch and as a consequence the Muslim uprising of *Darul Islam* that was already raging in parts of West Java spread to Sulawesi, Sumatra and Kalimantan.

On 3 January 1946, the revolutionary government founded the Ministry of Religious Affairs, despite the fact that a large majority within the preparatory committee had voted against the establishment of such a ministry a year before. According to Lev, this was a clear attempt to appease those Muslim parties that were disappointed with the Constitution (Lev 1972a: 44). The Darul Islam rebellion, however, would rage on until it finally was defeated in the mid-1960s. The Ministry of Religious Affairs would develop into the guardian of traditionalist Islam in Indonesia, a harbour for members of the *Nahdlatul Ulama*. Only a few months after the ministry was established, Law 22/ 1946 on the registration of marriage, divorce and reconciliation (*pentjatatan nikah, talak dan rujuk*) was issued, largely based on colonial regulations, but now centralizing civil registration of Muslims under the Ministry's control (Huis & Wirastri 2012).[12]

A year later, the Minister of Religious Affairs issued Decree 6/1947, taking charge of three matters concerning the *penghulu* courts. First, it declared the ministry responsible for the appointment of *penghulus*, which under colonial rule had been the responsibility of the Governor General of the Netherlands Indies. Second, the decree transferred the administration of religious affairs, including the *penghulu* courts from the Minister of Home Affairs to the Ministry of Religious Affairs. Third, through the decree the Minister of Religious Affairs took over the administration of the Islamic high court, which previously had fallen under the Ministry of Justice. Through these actions the Ministry of Religious Affairs made clear its intention to unify the country's administration of Islamic family law matters under its authority. With the support of Muslim organizations, the ministry would turn into a countervailing power to the majority within the cabinet and parliament that wanted to unify Islamic family law under the civil courts. Proof of the latter intention is Act 19/1948, which would have abolished the Islamic court and created Islamic chambers within the general court. This Law was passed by parliament, but never came into force due to military setbacks during the independence struggle (Hanstein 2002: 59–60). Thus, the Islamic courts survived the revolutionary years merely by chance. In 1949, after the Dutch had recognized Indonesia's independence, the Indonesian government decided to continue the Islamic courts system. Emergency Law 1/1951 on the Jurisdiction and Procedures of the Civil Courts[13] abolished all indigenous *adat* courts, but not the Islamic courts.

The first general elections in Indonesia in 1955 resulted in a parliament in which the four main parties divided the seats almost equally: the Indonesian National Party (known as 'PNI'), the secular party of Sukarno, became the largest party with 24 per cent– of the votes, followed by the Muslim parties *Masyumi* (20.6 per cent) and Nahdlatul Ulama (18.5 per cent), the Communist Party (16.5 per cent) and a number of smaller parties. Because of the strong position of the Islamic parties in parliament, any proposals to abolish the Islamic courts were shelved. The results of the 1955 elections kept the increasingly polarized political parties in a stalemate and made the country, which suffered from an

---

[12] Because of administrative difficulties caused by the revolution, this law was initially only in force on Java and Madura. Law 32/1954 put the law into force throughout Indonesia.
[13] Emergency Law 1/1951 on Temporary Measures to Organize Unified Civil Courts in Form and Procedure.

economic crisis and local rebellions, even more difficult to govern. In 1957, President Sukarno decided to disband parliamentary democracy and to replace it with a 'Guided Democracy' with powers concentrated in the president's hands.

In 1957, Sukarno's government, which during the Guided Democracy was supported by the *Nahdaltul Ulama*, reaffirmed the continuation of Islamic courts on Java and Madura and regulated the expansion of the Islamic courts system to the other provinces through Government Regulation 45/1957.[14] Government Regulation 45/1957 stipulated the formation of an Islamic court in each district (*kabupaten*) where there was a general court and appellate Islamic courts in each province. This meant an enormous expansion of the Islamic courts in Indonesia. The lack of staff for the Islamic courts facilitated the appointment of female judges in Indonesia (Cammack et al. 2015: 6).

In 1959, Sukarno abolished the reformist Muslim political party *Masyumi*, because of the support part of its leadership had provided to the rebellions in the provinces. However, the hard stance towards the *Masyumi* in the last years of Sukarno's presidency did not signify suspicion towards traditional Islamic institutions. The 1957 Government Regulation on the Islamic Courts Outside Java and Madura was implemented and as a result their numbers continued to grow. Sukarno felt that he had better keep the support of the remaining Muslim organization – the *Nahdlatul Ulama*.

The year 1965 marks a defining moment in Indonesian politics. A coup by communist elements took place, which General Suharto successfully quelled in a military counteraction. As a result, President Sukarno's position was immensely weakened and in 1967 Sukarno stepped down. General Suharto became the new president of Indonesia. The *Nahdlatul Ulama*, which supported Suharto's crackdown of the communist party, had good hopes to be rewarded for its support. At first, this seemed to be the case. Law 14/1970 on Judicial Power made the Islamic courts into one of the four pillars of Indonesia's judicial system, alongside the general courts, the military courts and the administrative courts. It looked like the Islamic courts were safe in the New Order.

In 1971, however, Suharto's New Order organized the second general elections in Indonesia. The election turned out to be an enormous victory for the Golkar party – President Suharto's main political base in parliament, as it won 62.8 per cent of the votes. The *Nahdlatul Ulama* did well

---

[14] Government Regulation 45/1957 on the Islamic Courts Outside Java and Madura.

by winning 18.7 per cent of the votes, but the reformist Islamic political party *Parmusi*, the successor of the *Masyumi,* won a mere 5.4 per cent. Thus, in 1971, the year that Lev's analysis of the Islamic courts ends, the Islamic faction in parliament was significantly weakened. Lev thought that the likely trajectory of the Islamic courts system would be that it would be subjugated by the civil court system in one form or another. In the next part I will describe how, and the extent to which, such subjugation took place.

Part 2   The Religious Courts after 1971

The Political Events Leading up to the 1974 Marriage Law

In 1973, President Suharto's New Order regime introduced policies to increase its control over political parties and radically reorganize the political landscape of Indonesia. Only three political parties remained. The first one was Suharto's political machine, Golkar. The traditionalist and reformist Muslim parties – despite their doctrinal differences – were forced to merge into a single party, the United Development Party (*Partai Persatuan Pembangunan*, or PPP). The nationalist parties and the smaller Protestant and Catholic parties were joined together into the Indonesian Democratic Party (*Partai Demokrat Indonesia*, PDI).

In the context of this political transformation, a marriage bill was submitted to parliament. The 1973 Marriage Bill had been drafted by the Ministry of Justice and proposed far-reaching substantive legal reforms and a transfer jurisdiction on certain Islamic family law matters from the Islamic courts to the civil courts. The 1973 Bill would replace the religious basis of marriage with a civil one (Article 2) and would require men to seek permission from a general court for divorce (Article 40) and polygamy (Article 3) (e.g. Katz & Katz 1975 and 1978; Cammack et al. 1996; Butt 1999; Bowen 2003; O'Shaughnessy 2009). The Bill proposed a more secular basis for family law, meaning a further decline in the Islamic courts' jurisdiction. It was a clear attempt by the civil legal part of Indonesia's dual legal system to subjugate the Islamic branch of the legal system – an attempt that Lev had predicted would happen.

The new ruling party Golkar was overconfident as it could single-handedly pass the 1973 Bill. However, the Ministry of Religious Affairs, a stronghold of the traditionalist Muslim organization *Nahdlatul Ulama* and a strong supporter of the Islamic courts, did not agree. The ministry had not been involved in the drafting process and, as it appeared, Golkar had underestimated Islamic opposition to the 1973 Bill.

Protests mounted. The law was portrayed as an attack on the divine law of Allah, and led to emotional outcries in parliament (Hanstein 2002: 282–4).[15] On 27 September, two days before the start of the holy month of Ramadan, hundreds of young Muslims, many of them women, entered the parliament building, while a crowd of demonstrators took possession of the streets. By this time the government realized that opposition to the 1973 Bill had to be taken seriously. The Minister of Justice started negotiations with the Minister of Religious Affairs and the Muslim party PPP in order to work out a compromise. The New Order government decided to give in to most of the demands of the Muslim organizations and removed the most controversial articles of the 1973 Bill, while the Islamic courts retained their jurisdiction in divorce and polygamy matters (Nurlaelawati 2010: 69). Through this process, the Ministry of Religious Affairs, bypassed during the drafting process of the 1973 Bill, claimed its central position in Indonesia's Islamic affairs.

The events surrounding the 1973 Bill made the New Order realize that in the Indonesian context the clash between the civil legal and Islamic legal systems cannot be solved by simply subjugating one system by the other. Cammack et al. have called this 'the direct conflict between state positivism and Islam' (Cammack et al. 1996: 53). The political solution of the New Order was continued government support for the Ministry of Religious Affairs and the Islamic courts. As the Dutch had realized before, incorporation of Islamic courts into the national legal system fuses the State with the Divine to a considerable extent – while Divine law comes within reach of the state. In this way, a binary choice between the two loci of ultimate legal authority is avoided, and the state could exercise considerable control over ever-sensitive Muslim family law issues in an effective and legitimate way – as long as it does not tread on core Islamic issues. Evidently, the Marriage Law of 1974 also constituted a major legal change pertaining to the Islamic courts. For the first time in history, substantive secular family law rules for Muslims were established in national legislation, constituting a next step in the process of the

---

[15] For example, H. A. Balya Umar, a member of the PPP fraction in parliament, warned that the law would lead to 'alcoholism, drug addiction and extramarital intercourse.' He even predicted 'manslaughter, violence, rape, increased prostitution and hospitals full of sexually transmitted disease patients' if the law was implemented. See Hanstein (2002: 283).

rationalization of the Islamic courts administration of justice and a convergence with the civil law system.

The Islamic Turn in Politics and the Bureaucratization of the Religious Courts

Although the New Order did not shy away from resorting to violence to suppress Muslim resistance, from the mid-1970s onwards, it simultaneously applied a more peaceful strategy: the incorporation of Islamic institutions into the state (cf. Otto 2010). The case of the 1974 Marriage Law is the first example in which the New Order government created room for Islamic institutions within a civil law framework to operate in traditional Islamic ways. A year later, in 1975, the Indonesian *Ulama* Council (*Majelis Ulama Indonesia*, MUI) was established, which is often seen as the start of 'the Islamic turn in Indonesian politics' (Liddle 1996). By providing room for the MUI, the New Order sought both Islamic political support and Islamic legitimacy through supportive legal opinions (*fatwa*) of the MUI on sensitive issues such as, for instance, birth control (Bruinessen 1996; Hooker & Lindsey 2002; see also Feener 2010).

Similarly, a broadening of the jurisdiction of the Islamic courts was part of President Suharto's strategy to reach out to the Muslim organizations that disagreed with the obligation to adopt the New Order *Pancasila* ideology, rather than Islam, as the sole foundation of their organization (Nurlaelawati 2010: 81).[16] In the early 1980s, the Ministry of Religious Affairs and an Islamic faction within the Supreme Court managed to overcome the religious–social–political cleavage between them, and cooperation between the two institutions began. In 1982, Busthanul Arifin, Supreme Court judge and a strong proponent of Islamic legal institutions, became the first chair of the Islamic division of the Supreme Court. This was a major change, since previously there had been little support for the Islamic courts within the Supreme Court (Pompe 1996: 75; 387–9). Munawir Syadzali, Minister of Religious Affairs (1983–93), realized that the views of some members of the Supreme Court and the ministry had moved closer and approached the Supreme Court to develop a joint agenda for emancipation of the Islamic courts (Nurlaelawati 2010: 80–4).

---

[16] Nurlaelawati (2010: 81) describes how Busthanul Arifin had framed the Compilation of Islamic Law project in precisely this manner when he proposed the law-making project to President Suharto.

The rapprochement between the Ministry of Religious Affairs and the Supreme Court led to three programmes that were put into motion simultaneously: first, a standardization plan modelled to the civil courts to improve the management of Islamic courts; second, a law-making programme to draft a Bill on the Islamic Courts; and third, the drafting of a Compilation of Islamic Law that would be used as the main substantive legal source of Islamic law.

The standardization plan was issued in 1983 and 'set forth a bold agenda for improvement in the facilities and staffing of the courts' (Cammack 2007: 151). The pragmatic purpose of the plan was to manage the enormous increase in the caseload of the Islamic courts. In 1974, the Islamic courts processed only 23,758 cases, while in 1979, due to the legal stipulation in the 1974 Marriage Law that turned Muslim divorce (for both men and women) into a judicial proceeding, this number had increased to 257,337 cases (Cammack 2007: 150–1). The increased caseload required swift action, and in 1984 the plan was implemented in anticipation of its formalization in the Law on the Islamic Courts. In practice, the standardization plan unified the Islamic courts in several ways: their appearance; their equipment, including the books which were to be included in the courts' library; and importantly, the new judges, who now were to hold a secondary degree of Islamic academic training.

The second programme set in motion by the Ministry of Religious Affairs and the Supreme Court was the drafting of a Bill on the Islamic Courts. The main aim was to create a unified and more efficient Islamic court system, but at the same time the drafting team sought to increase the jurisdiction of the Islamic court and to amend and to annul colonial legislation which had favoured an *adat* law–based family and inheritance law.

The plea for a broadening of jurisdiction of Muslim family law was strategically framed within the framework of *Pancasila*. One year after the Tanjung Priok riots of 1984, which were crushed with excessive force by the special forces and left hundreds of Muslim anti-*Pancasila* protesters dead, Syadzali and Bustanul Arifin managed to convince President Suharto that support for a modernization and emancipation programme pertaining to the Islamic courts was a chance for the New Order to demonstrate to Muslim organizations that the New Order and its *Pancasila* ideology were not anti-Islam in character after all. Their strategy proved successful and in 1985 the drafting programmes of the Law on the Islamic Courts as well as the Compilation of Islamic Law took off. President Suharto even decided to support the project of the Compilation of Islamic Law personally, with his own private funds (Nurlaelawati 2010: 82).

The 1989 Law on the Islamic Courts adopted the recommendations of the above-mentioned standardization plan. Moreover, the 1989 Law on the Islamic Courts significantly increased the jurisdiction for the Islamic courts. The Islamic courts now held a shared competence with the civil courts in inheritance matters for Muslims and full competence in disputes concerning child custody, division of property and alimony which previously fell under the civil courts. The Islamic courts were also made competent to enforce their own judgments independently from the civil courts – a competence they never had under the legal system of the Netherlands Indies.

The issue of jurisdiction over inheritance and property disputes, however, provoked controversy. The drafting committee had initially proposed to provide the Islamic courts with exclusive powers over all matters of matrimonial property and inheritance. For the political party PDI, this was unacceptable. In terms of numbers, the PDI could not prevent the Bill being passed, but since it succeeded in gaining support from the influential Armed Forces Faction in parliament, the inheritance stipulations in the Bill became the subject of fierce negotiations (Cammack 2007: 157).

The PDI favoured the existing limited jurisdiction of the Islamic courts and opposed any transfer of jurisdiction from the civil to the Islamic courts. In the end, the members of the Armed Forces Faction succeeded in bringing about a compromise. The General Elucidation to the 1989 Islamic Judiciary Law includes the clause 'that prior to the [registration of the] case the parties can choose which body of law shall be used in the division of the estate.' In other words, parties in inheritance cases must agree first whether they want the lawsuit to fall under *adat* or Islamic law and based on this agreement the general court or the Islamic court handles the case.

The third project set in motion was the drafting of the Compilation of Islamic Law. The New Order government explained the project as a process of attaining *ijma*, or a consensus among the main Muslim scholars – one of the five traditional sources of Islamic law.[17] Sources for the Compilation were *syafi'ite fiqh* works,[18] case law, national legislation, foreign codes, and conferences and public debates. The *'ijma'*

---

[17] Islamic doctrine (*fiqh*) is developed by *ulama*, rather than judges who (according to the majority of Sunni *maddhab*, including the *syafi'i maddhab*) apply the sources of law in the following order: the Qur'an, the Sunna and Hadith, *qiyas* (analogy), *ijma* (consensus) and *ijtihad* (independent reasoning).

[18] For a thorough discussion of the *fiqh* books consulted, see Nurlaelawati (2010).

deliberation process was held with 166 *ulama* and Islamic court judges, other Muslim intellectuals and civil court judges.[19] The variety of sources consulted demonstrates that the Compilation's aim was to codify a substantive Muslim family law that was compliant with national legislation, and acceptable to Islamic court judges, Indonesian *ulama* and Indonesia's Muslim civil society. In 1988 the drafting process was finalised and the draft Compilation submitted to the president. In order to provide the document with Islamic legitimacy, the Indonesian government proclaimed that it was the result of a national consensus, or *ijma*, among Indonesian *ulama* and presented the Compilation of Islamic Law as constituting the 'living *fiqh* of Indonesia' – a unique Indonesian Islamic doctrine.[20]

The Compilation is a blend of civil and religious substantive law. The Compilation adopted all applicable rules from the 1974 Marriage Law, often in a form in which the text is reformulated or 'vernacularized' into more Islamic language, apparently with the intention of making them more acceptable to *ulama*.[21] Hence, like the 1974 Marriage Law, the Compilation stipulates judicial divorce on established divorce grounds, provides legal conditions for polygamy and recognizes the wife's equal right to marital property. In addition to this, the Compilation also regulates many issues on the basis of traditional *syafi'ite fiqh*, especially those matters not regulated by the 1974 Marriage Law and where the Marriage Law stipulates that religious law applies.

To preclude discord in parliament, which would destroy the carefully created image of a consensus among Indonesian Muslims, in 1991 the New Order government eventually chose to issue the Compilation of Islamic Law as part of a presidential instruction.[22] The fact that it was not issued as a law makes the legal status of the Compilation problematic.

---

[19] Technically speaking the 166 interviewed Muslim scholars were not all *ulama*; some were judges of religious courts, and three of them female judges. See Hanstein (2002: 385).

[20] The terminology used seems inspired by the Supreme Court ruling of 1960 – infamous from a conservative *ulama* point of view but well-known – in which it first used the term 'the living *adat* law throughout Indonesia' to justify a ruling contrary to *fiqh* that a widow has the right to inherit from her husband's estate (so *not* joint marital property). See Lev (2000g: 115).

[21] Sally Engle Merry (2006) has argued that human rights need to be 'vernacularized' or adapted to local understandings and conditions in order to become meaningful at local levels. In the same manner, Indonesian reforms often are linked to Islamic doctrine in order to make them acceptable to local power holders. For examples of the latter practices on the local level, see Van Doorn-Harder (2007).

[22] Presidential Decree Number 1 of the year 1991 on the Dissemination of the Compilation of Islamic Law.

However, in Decision 154/1991, the Minister of Religious Affairs is very clear on the application of the Compilation: all institutions falling under his powers, including the Islamic courts,[23] should to the largest extent possible rely on the Compilation as the main legal source. In practice, judges apply the Compilation as if it were a statutory law, even if they frequently make reference to additional *syafi'ite fiqh* sources as well (Lubis 1994: 321–2; Nurlaelawati 2010: 135–42).

The heated deliberation process of the Bill on the Islamic Courts and the decision of the New Order government not to allow deliberation of the Compilation of Islamic Law in parliament demonstrates that the religious–social–political cleavage in Indonesia that Lev signalled in 1971 had not been overcome – even following the Islamic turn of the New Order and the subsequent rapprochement between the Ministry of Religious Affairs and the Supreme Court. During the *reformasi,* however, the cleavage would become far less evident.

Developments after the Reformasi

In 1998, following the Asian financial crisis and subsequent mass demonstrations and riots, President Suharto stepped down. In the next few years Indonesia introduced far-reaching institutional changes. In this so-called *reformasi* period, Indonesia amended its Constitution four times, adopting a true division of powers, a decentralized government, democratic standards of government, human rights, and a Constitutional Court to guard the new reforms. At the same time, an attempt by the PPP and smaller Islamic parties to include references to the Sharia in the Constitution failed (Hosen 2005).

The Islamic court system was also affected by the *reformasi*. The third amendment of the Constitution adopted the Islamic court system as one of the pillars of Indonesia's court system in Article 24(2).[24] In other words, the position of the Islamic courts is constitutionally guaranteed. Moreover, Law 35/1999 as reaffirmed by Law 4/2004 on the Judiciary introduced a one-roof system, with the Supreme Court administering all court branches. By implication, the administration of the judiciary was

---

[23] This supervision of the Islamic courts by the Ministry of Religious Affairs lasted until 2004, when the administration and supervision of the Islamic court was brought under the Supreme Court.

[24] Article 24(2) of the Constitution: The judicial powers shall be carried out by a Supreme Court and by its subordinate judicatory bodies dealing with general, religious, military, state administrative judicial fields, and by a Constitutional Court.

transferred from the executive to the Supreme Court (Otto 2010: 457–8).[25] For the Islamic court this meant that in 2005, sixty years of financial and administrative supervision by the Ministry of Religious Affairs came to an end.

Wahyu Widiana, who from 2000 to 2012 acted as the director general of the Office of Islamic Courts of the Supreme Court (*Badan Peradilan Agama Mahkamah Agung, Badilag*), acknowledged that there were persons within *Badilag* and the Islamic courts who were sceptical regarding the transfer to the Supreme Court. However, the increase in funds and e-management programmes muted their criticism.[26] In terms of equipment and facilities, the transfer meant a significant improvement. Salaries of judges, clerks and other staff increased. The most visible change is the new Islamic court buildings along the main roads of district capitals. Only a few years before, most of the first-instance Islamic courts had been located in small buildings – often on the compound of the district office of the Ministry of Religious Affairs.

In 2005 a drafting team was composed to amend the 1989 Law on Islamic Courts. In February 2006, the draft was presented to parliament. On 22 March 2006, the president signed Law 3/2006 amending the 1989 Law on the Islamic Courts.[27] Most media attention centred on the Islamic courts' broadened jurisdiction, now including sharia economics (*ekonomi syariah*; Islamic banking, trading and such), and the special position of the Acehnese Islamic court (*Mahkamah Syariyah*) and its competence in Islamic criminal matters (*jinayat*).

Relatively unnoticed were the significant legal changes with regard to inheritance law.[28] As mentioned above, before the amendment litigants had the legal possibility to choose whether they wanted an inheritance case settled according to Islamic or *adat* law. This provision caused a lack

---

[25] With the notable exception of the Constitutional Court.

[26] Personal communication with Wahyu Widiana, director general of Badilag, 19 November 2009.

[27] In 2009, law 7/1989 would be amended for a second time. Law 50/2009 mainly concerns internal (by the Supreme Court) and external (by the Judicial Commission) checks on the Islamic court and includes a dishonourable discharge sanction for personnel demanding unofficial fees. Moreover, to increase the access to justice, law 50/2009 stipulates that every Islamic court has to create a legal aid office within its building which provides legal information to court clients free of charge.

[28] An exception was the website www.hukumonline.com, which provides information for legal practitioners in Indonesia. Hukumonline, Klausul *'Pilihan Hukum' Waris dalam UU Peradilan Agama Bakal Dihapus* [The 'choice of law' clause in inheritance in the law on the Islamic Judiciary will be erased], 22 February 2006.

of procedural clarity about how to proceed when there was no agreement between the parties about which body of law should apply. For defendants, it offered ample opportunities to delay and frustrate the adjudication process. Matters were complicated even further by the stipulation in Article 50 that ownership disputes were to be decided by the civil court first before a case could proceed to the Islamic courts. Law 3/2006 makes the procedures clearer by giving exclusive jurisdiction in those cases to the Islamic courts. It means, at least on paper,[29] that Islamic doctrine has become the standard in inheritance cases while *adat* has been reduced to an additional legal source that judges must consider in their judgments. The relatively smooth passing of the 2006 Amendment is remarkable, particularly in view of the strong opposition to very similar inheritance provisions from the PDI and the military faction in parliament in 1989.[30]

The Islamic courts' increased jurisdiction in the fields of sharia economics and Muslim inheritance is a continuation of the emancipation process that started in the 1980s. For those supporting a more Islamic character of Indonesian national law, this situation is applauded as a restoration of the rightful place that Islamic law held vis-à-vis *adat* prior to the 1931 *Penghulu* Courts Regulation (in force since 1937). In the words of Abdul Manan, the former head of the Islamic Courts Chamber in the Supreme Court:

> The Islamic community (*umat Islam*) had the opportunity to reclaim its jurisdiction that was brought to the fore by Van den Berg [architect behind the 1882 Priest Council Regulation] and his allies in the *receptie in complexu* theory: the laws that applies to Muslims are their religious law, specifically Islamic law, in the field of marriage, inheritance, *wakaf* and *sedekah*. (Manan 2008: 312)

In other words, 2006 marks the year that the Islamic courts have overcome the threat of subjugation by Indonesia's civil legal system in general, and the primacy civil courts attribute to *adat* in particular. As shown

---

[29] Keebeth von Benda-Beckmann (2009) has demonstrated that in the first years following the passing of the 2006 Amendment, most inheritance cases in the matrilineal Minangkabau area in Sumatra were still adjudicated by the civil courts on the basis of *adat*. The local population and civil courts clearly did not abide to the new stipulations of the 2006 Amendment that provided the religious courts with exclusive jurisdictional powers in inheritance matters pertaining to Muslims.

[30] A possible explanation for the smooth passing of the amendments of 2006 is that the government of President Yudhoyono heavily relied on the Islamic political parties for support, whereas the PDI-P, the successor of the PDI, which together with the armed forces had led opposition against an Islamic inheritance law for Muslims, rejected to join a broad cabinet.

above, this emancipation process involved a significant convergence of the Islamic court system with the civil law system.

What Does the Convergence of the Civil and Religious Legal Systems Signify?

Lev conducted his research about the Islamic courts with the purpose 'to understand, as precisely as we can, the political and social bases of institutional continuity and change in the legal systems of new states.' (Lev 1972a: ix). In this chapter I have attempted to reproduce Lev's study of Indonesia's Islamic courts and expand it from 1971 to the present. I started my analysis in the colonial period since Lev believed that the reason why Indonesian Islamic courts were not (yet) subjugated by the civil courts system is found in the lack of interference of the Dutch with Islamic justice. I argue that the opposite is true: continued interference by the colonial government in the jurisdictional conflict between civil courts and Islamic courts in the nineteenth century effectively meant a formal recognition of the adjudication powers of the Islamic courts. The 1882 Priest Councils Regulation is a benchmark as it resulted in a further incorporation of Javanese Islamic courts into the colonial legal system and unified Islamic courts that slowly evolved into symbols of a traditionalist Islamic identity. Dutch colonial and Indonesian policies that aimed at limiting the competence of the Islamic courts in comparison to the 1882 Priest Councils Regulation have been met with protests from Muslim circles even when those regulations simply codified legal practice. To those protestors such codification symbolized the subordination of Islamic law to *adat*.

In his book *'Islamic Courts in Indonesia'* Lev defines legal institutions and law 'as basically derivative from the primary institutions of political process. [...] What law is [...] depends upon what it is allowed to be by conditions of political power and authority, and these conditions in turn are determined by a wide variety of social, cultural, and economic forces.' Following Karl Renner (1949), Lev argues that because there are clear linkages between law, political process, and social, cultural and economic forces, law or at least the application of legal rules will accommodate changes in society: 'When the conditions change, the law must also change, sometimes explicitly but at the very least implicitly' (Lev 1972a: 2). As I have argued elsewhere (Huis 2015: 198, 199), in the case of Indonesian Muslim family law, it is often the other way around: the form of the core Islamic concepts cannot change, regardless of changed social circumstances. The scale of the protests surrounding the 1973 Marriage Bill clearly illustrates this. The reason for this is that doing away with core Islamic concepts jeopardizes the law's religious character. However, Lev is right that Islamic doctrine does change implicitly. When the legislator makes core Islamic norms conditional to external norms, or the judge applies the core norms with due consideration of changed social circumstances, or *adat*, the legal and social functions of Islamic norms change to a large extent. The 1991 Compilation of Islamic Law is an example of how external (secular and customary) norms were incorporated into the core of traditional Islamic doctrine. Of course, the package in which the Compilation of Islamic Law was offered – the increased jurisdiction of Islamic courts and thus an increased role of Islamic law in society – made it appealing for proponents of an increased role of Islam in Indonesia to state their agreement.

Clearly, the modernization of the Islamic courts was part of a strategy to appease Muslim organizations, or even generate support among them for Suharto's New Order government. The symbolism of a modern Islamic court applying an Islamic law compatible with modern times was surely appealing to most Muslim organizations. Of course, Muslim society in Indonesia is plural, and should not be equated with or reduced to supporters of a larger role of Islamic law and the Islamic court in society (Geertz 1976; Bruinessen 1996; Federspiel 1998). Nonetheless, Horowitz's observation about Malaysian Islamic courts applies to Indonesia too: 'While the urge to recapture Islamic authenticity has been strong, the secular system, within its sphere, remains the subject of considerable respect of the Islamic reformers' (Horowitz 1994: 244). This is reflected in the behaviour of the Indonesian *ulama* with regard to the reforms. Although some *ulama* initially voiced objections to the Indonesian state's increasing say in Islamic matters, in the end the *ulama* affiliated with the main Muslim organizations *Muhammadiyah* and *Nahdlatul Ulama* agreed to the reforms without much resistance (Nurlaelawati 2010: 82–4).

With Suharto's government in mind, Cammack argues that the New Order's agenda of emancipation of the Islamic courts was one of gaining control over the Islamic courts: 'when the plan to vest control over Muslim courts [through the Marriage Bill of 1973] proved politically unworkable, the strategy changed from an attempt to transfer the functions of the religious courts to the civil courts, to transforming the Islamic judiciary based on the model of the civil courts' (Cammack 2007: 154).

However, one must not overlook who within the New Order government initiated the programmes. The New Order cannot be viewed as a single entity. The main supporters of change came from within the Ministry of Religious Affairs and the Islamic faction within the Supreme Court. Throughout the New Order, the Ministry of Religious Affairs remained a stronghold for traditionalist Muslims. It had accepted the *Pancasila* ideology as the state's foundation, but '[i]n this Ministry and associated institutions, Islam is of high priority and its values are constantly lauded and put forward as worthy for the state and nation to follow' (Federspiel 1998: 97). By taking the lead in the standardization plan and the drafting processes of the Islamic Judiciary Bill and the Compilation of Islamic Law, the Ministry of Religion was in control of the agenda. The Ministry of Religious Affairs was part of the New Order government but had distinctive goals: the upgrading of the Islamic courts and, ultimately, the strong symbolic act of giving Islamic law its rightful place in Indonesian law – a place that was lost to *adat* in the last two decades of colonial rule. By comparison, this is a fundamentally different agenda from that of the 1973 Marriage Bill, which had been much more secular in character and was pushed by the Ministry of Justice.

After the *reformasi,* the emancipation of the Islamic courts continued, in a political constellation which is totally different from that of 1971. Islamism has become mainstream in Indonesian politics, secularism suspect. Today, it is unthinkable that the government would propose a draft law that would severely limit the powers of Islamic courts. Yet, the Islamic courts have been increasingly made fully part of the civil legal system – and are placed under the roof of the Supreme Court. The supervision of the Supreme Court should not be characterized as subjugation of Islamic courts system by the civil court system, as the Islamic legal system appears to be stronger than ever before, and the dual legal system, consisting of branches vested in the civil law and Islamic legal traditions, is very much alive.

Conclusion

The question of the extent to which regulation of the Islamic courts and Islamic law in Indonesia has resulted in the subjugation of the Islamic legal system by the civil legal system is, of course, difficult to answer. This is mainly because it implies placing a value on procedural legal changes regarding the Islamic courts and putting them into the categories 'Islamic' or 'civil'. It is clear that the 1973 Draft Marriage Law was an attempt by opponents of Islamic courts and traditional Islamic doctrine to significantly diminish the powers of Islamic courts. This attempt failed because of strong protests by Muslim organizations. Paradoxically, the more Islamic orientation of society from the 1980s onwards facilitated a larger convergence with the civil legal system. Part of the explanation for this convergence is the growth of the Islamic courts following the introduction of judicial divorce by the 1974 Marriage Law; it forced the Islamic legal system to operate in more efficient ways. The main explanation, however, is that Islamic politicians realized that modelling (or modernizing) the Islamic courts on the image of the civil courts would increase the standing of the courts in the eyes of society. In a context in which the balance in the political constellation regarding the 'religious–social–political cleavage' between proponents and opponents of Islamic courts has reversed, the question of which system conquers, and which system is being conquered becomes problematic. In present-day Indonesia, a dual legal system in which civil law and Islamic legal traditions coexist is no longer politically problematized. By extension, the convergence of the civil and Islamic legal systems no longer implies subjugation of the Islamic courts by the civil legal system. It may just as well be the other way around.

6

The Administrative Courts

The Quest for Consistency

ADRIAAN BEDNER AND HERLAMBANG PERDANA
WIRATRAMAN

This chapter looks at legal certainty in Indonesia's administrative courts. It provides a brief overview of the genesis and development of this branch of the Indonesian judiciary and then shifts its focus to how administrative court judges interpret and apply so-called 'general principles of proper administration' (hereafter 'General Principles'). These principles are one of the two grounds for which administrative courts can review administrative decrees, the other ground being the violation of a statute or regulation. The choice of these principles as a way of discussing legal certainty is deliberate: from the start of the administrative court system it was the intention of the legislator and the Supreme Court to develop these principles by means of judicial precedent. This is highly unusual in Indonesian legal practice, where legislative and executive lawmaking have always been dominant and little space is left for judge-made law. In other words, if ever there has been a field of law in Indonesia in which the judiciary is well-positioned to take the lead in developing consistent legal rules, it is in administrative law.

The administrative courts are of particular interest because of their history. In his account of the decline of the rule of law in Indonesia, Dan Lev paid much attention to judicial review. Effective judicial review, he argued, is the hallmark of an independent judiciary, and it was for good reasons that the judiciary sought to establish this power after the fall of Guided Democracy (Lev 1978). Although the judiciary and its supporters were unsuccessful in their attempt to gain such power, the New Order government felt compelled to provide symbolic compensation in the form of a watered-down version of judicial review: a new administrative court system. Even if these new courts could never achieve the kind of

political influence envisaged by the rule of law supporters, they still held
the promise of holding the government accountable. A consistent interpretation of General Principles would certainly help to promote such
accountability and could demonstrate that the government is not above
the law, which includes unwritten principles.

The chapter starts with a brief discussion of the problems with legal
certainty that are commonly encountered in the Indonesian legal system
(see also Assegaf, this volume). It then briefly outlines the position of the
administrative courts within Indonesia's judiciary, how it has developed
over the years and the reasons for this development. Next, we focus on
the interpretation and application of General Principles. We consider to
the extent to which these General Principles are actually applied, whether
the interpretation of General Principles has become more consistent over
the years, and how we can explain this. Our conclusion is that despite
positive developments in the conditions for consistent interpretation,
this objective has not been achieved yet, even if the situation in the
administrative courts is better than in the civil and criminal courts.

Problems with Legal Certainty in the Indonesian Legal System

Several studies of the Indonesian judiciary have drawn attention to the
lack of legal certainty.[1] The first and best known account is Sebastiaan
Pompe's book about the Supreme Court, which explains how this institution gradually lost control over the lower courts and thereby over legal
development. According to Pompe, legal certainty in Indonesia declined
over the years mostly because of political developments which put great
pressure on the judiciary (Pompe 2005: 468–9). One of the authors of this
chapter has discussed how, notwithstanding seemingly favourable conditions, the specialist administrative court has also fallen victim to the
problems discussed by Pompe (Bedner 2001, 2008). Similar arguments
have been made since about other courts and court branches.[2] Simon
Butt and Tim Lindsey noted that 'many, if not most, [judgements] are

---

[1] We are not even referring to 'real legal certainty' here, but legal certainty in a juridical
sense, meaning that 'there are clear, consistent, and accessible legal rules, issued or
acknowledged by or on behalf of the state' (Otto 2002: 5). This requires that judges provide
uniform interpretations of statutory rules, or that they create new ones which are then
followed by their colleagues in new cases.

[2] See, e.g., Tjandra (2016:249–50) about the industrial relations courts; Wiratraman (2014:
275–76) about civil and criminal cases against the press. The main exception are the
Islamic courts; see Nurlaelawati (2010) and Van Huis (2015: 251–4).

also unlikely to contain sufficient information to enable another court to follow them' (Butt & Lindsey 2018: 76). Simon Butt has identified how inconsistent the Supreme Court still is in its dealing with claims against regional regulations (Butt 2018). In summary, despite the judicial reforms implemented after 1998, a lack of legal certainty still is a hallmark of Indonesia's judicial system.

The reasons for this situation are diverse. It is clear that corruption plays an important role and it is tempting to reduce the problem to this phenomenon; the effects of corruption are visible at different levels and it is pervasive in all state branches. At the micro-level, legal certainty is undermined because judges may act based on monetary incentives instead of legal ones. This causes judges, lawyers and prosecutors to lose interest in legal reasoning and legal development, which ultimately leads to a shift in professional orientation and values (Bedner 2001: 240, 267–8). Corruption also undermines legal certainty in a subtle manner, by creating an incentive for judges to keep the law vague and thus widen the scope for decision-making (Bedner 2001: 238).

Yet, corruption cannot explain the full range of different judgements in similar cases. Some research refers to judges who prefer not to 'sell' a case to the highest bidder, but rather to the party with the strongest legal arguments (Bedner 2001: 239–40). Such corruption may yield judgements that are perfectly in line with the law. Neither can corruption explain the weak legal reasoning in judicial rulings where the substantive outcome does make sense.

A complementary explanation for lack of legal certainty is direct political pressure or even coercion, either by the government or other powerful actors. There is a long list of cases in which judges were forced to pass judgements that clearly go against positive law. The list of such cases under the New Order is long – *Kedung Ombo* and *Tempo* being the most notorious examples – but such pressure has continued after 1998. This has led to grave miscarriages of justice, such as the blasphemy cases (see generally Crouch 2014) including against Ahok in 2016 and Meiliana in 2018, or the long list of rulings against the press. While in the latter the Supreme Court overturned most of the lower courts' flawed judgements, in a few cases it has succumbed to the opinion of anti-liberal political forces (Wiratraman 2014).

Political pressure may also translate into lack of funding for the judiciary. While in a country like Singapore the judiciary is clearly subservient to the government in politically sensitive cases, it is well-funded and it provides a high degree of legal certainty in the day-to-day cases that it deals with in a routine manner (Silverstein 2008). By contrast, the Indonesian judiciary had a long history of underfunding before the significant improvements after the fall of Soeharto, and its effects are still visible. Such underfunding has not only demotivated judges, but also undermined material sources required for legal certainty, like publication of judgements and legal journals. Another effect of this has been the time pressure on judges it caused. In particular, the Supreme Court has been haunted by backlogs for decades (Pompe 2005: 281–303). Currently a Supreme Court justice may have to decide more than eight cases a day, with very limited staff support.[3]

Over the years this combination of factors has caused a deeper degree of legal uncertainty. It is produced by the structures of the Indonesian legal system and in turn reproduces them. The premise is that legal systems generate consistency through a set of interlocking mechanisms which may vary to some extent across jurisdictions, but whose main features are similar. Key is the law-making function of the judiciary in interpreting the existing body of legal rules. This function is supported by legal scholarship that criticises new developments in jurisprudence and helps to organise and understand the new rules within the broader legal system. Such legal scholarship is also required to educate new generations of law students, who can learn to master the main characteristics of legal reasoning more easily and gain the ability to apply such techniques by themselves. In Indonesia – as for that matter in many other countries – problems in the administration of justice, legal scholarship and legal education create friction, and together undermine legal consistency (Bedner 2016). Before we explore how these problems have worked out in the case of interpretation of General Principles by administrative courts, let us first look at these courts.

A Brief Overview of the Administrative Courts

In 1991, the administrative courts opened their gates to the first plaintiffs. Previously, citizens who felt that their interests had been violated by unlawful behaviour of the government could bring a claim on account of government tort to the civil courts. Now for the first time citizens could turn to an institution specialised in claims against government

---

[3] In 2017, the Supreme Court decided 16,474 cases (Mahkamah Agung 2017: 19). With about fifty judges available, this means an average of some 3,250 cases per judge per year. As judges sit on panels of at least three, the actual number of cases judges need to decide is three times higher.

officials. By all means this was a surprising development. Within twenty years, the authoritarian New Order government had managed to thoroughly emasculate the judiciary and it had demonstrated no inclination to allow the judiciary any control over the executive (Lev 1978; Pompe 2005). To many, the stifling political environment in which the new administrative courts were to operate looked like a guarantee for failure.

Yet, some observers saw glimpses of hope. They viewed the administrative courts as a sign of declining authoritarianism and an emerging *keterbukaan* (openness) – the Indonesian equivalent of the contemporaneous Russian *glasnost*. At the time, many hoped that the courts were a first step in a gradual transition to a more open, democratic political system. Not only was Suharto getting old, but the changing international political situation and the corresponding wave of democratisation were also supportive of such a development. Others pointed to the potential benefit the administrative courts could have for the central government, as controllers of lower levels of government. The Preamble to the Law on Administrative Courts (5/1986) explicitly referred to this function (Otto 1992).

If we look at the administrative court record during the New Order, we see that the more sceptical observers were right to have reservations about the court's potential. Even on paper the administrative court did not look too promising. Its jurisdiction was limited to written, individual, concrete and final government decisions; the amount of damages it could adjudicate was limited; its powers of enforcement looked ambiguous; and the grounds on which it could decide cases were not altogether clear – the Law on the Administrative Courts did not even mention the possibility of applying General Principles (Bedner 2001: 42).

In actual practice the limitations were even more conspicuous. Initially, the government introduced only six courts of first instance for all of Indonesia, and consequently most potential plaintiffs encountered insurmountable financial obstacles and time constraints when they wished to access the courts. Indeed, only a few people found their way to them and in more than twenty years their number has not grown much – relative to the number of courts. In its first year, the administrative court in Jakarta received 165 claims, a number that in 1997 had remained stable at 163 cases (PTUN Jakarta 2015a). For a court known to receive only a few cases such as the Yogyakarta court, we could not find a number earlier than 1998, when it received a single case (PTUUN Yogyakarta 2018). Other problems the courts had to confront included the tendency of government agencies to ignore administrative court decisions – in particular injunctions suspending these decisions. Parties often exercised undue influence on judges, mostly in the form of bribes, and if they made decisions the government did not like these judges had to face manipulation of their career paths (Bedner 2001: 205–8).

The increase in political freedom and judicial independence following the fall of Soeharto has not been accompanied by a sharp rise in the number of cases. Over the years their number has continued to grow slowly with the number of courts. In 2017, there were 31 administrative courts which received a total of 2,447 cases (Mahkamah Agung 2018: 21). This means that the average number of cases now stands at eighty-seven per court per year. However, cases are not evenly spread across Indonesia: in 2017, the administrative court in Yogyakarta registered 17 new cases, whereas the one in Jakarta received 191 (PTUN Yogyakarta 2018; PTUN Jakarta 2018).

On the other hand, the *symbolic* importance of the administrative courts should not be underestimated. A constant stream of newspaper reports drew attention to problematic government behaviour and the ill-will of the government to subject itself to judicial scrutiny, thus undermining the rulers' legitimacy (Bedner 2001: 261). No doubt the biggest publicity followed the judgements from the Jakarta administrative courts of first instance and appeal that annulled the ban on *Tempo*, Indonesia's most renowned weekly, in 1994. The *Tempo* case drew headlines for weeks and even provided the administrative courts with a brief moment of fame in the foreign press. Although the Supreme Court eventually succumbed to political pressure and reversed these judgements, they did establish the administrative courts' reputation as valiant defenders of the rule of law – even if ultimately impotent vis-à-vis political power (Bedner 2001: 179–82, 229–33).

After 1998, the political situation provided more leeway to promote an independent judiciary. For the administrative courts, this meant that outright government refusals to execute injunctions and judgements became rare and government pressure on judges greatly declined. However, problems *within* the organisation of the courts have continued. The paying of bribes, a practice that was widespread during the New Order (Bedner 2001: 234–7), is still common. In the absence of any new research on this issue it is not possible to make an informed estimation of the size and frequency of corrupt practices in the administrative courts, but at least one major case of bribery was exposed in recent years.[4] Its

---

[4] In 2015, a judge at the Medan Administrative Court was convicted and given two years in prison for receiving a bribe from the lawyer OC Kaligis (Tempo 2016).

seriousness gives us sufficient reason to assume that corruption has persisted and still is a serious problem.

Although we do not have the data that allow us to establish a causal link between the number of cases taken to the administrative courts and their actual performance – i.e. protection of citizens against unlawful behaviour of the government – it is likely that the perceived ineffectiveness of the administrative courts contributes to their limited popularity. Once again, there is a lack of research on the issue of whether the courts bring actual relief to citizens whose rights have been breached by unlawful behaviour of the government. The only research we know of that addressed this issue was conducted between the late 1990s and early 2000s by Irfan Fachruddin, who was at the time a judge in the Bandung Administrative Court and is now a Supreme Court Justice (Fachruddin 2004). Relying on the data in Fachruddin's work, one of the authors of this chapter calculated that the chances of actually winning a case and having its result implemented were very limited (Bedner 2008). This data supports the negative image explaining the reluctance of potential plaintiffs to take their cases to the administrative courts.

Another partial explanation of the limited growth in administrative court cases is the rise of other institutions that deal with claims or complaints against the government. These include the National Human Rights Commission (*Komnas HAM*), the Women's Rights Commission (*Komnas Perempuan*), the petitioning office of the President, etc. A particularly successful institution whose mandate effectively overlaps with the administrative courts is the Ombudsman of the Republic of Indonesia (ORI). Established in 2000, ORI has branch offices in all of Indonesia's provinces.[5] In 2017 the complaints brought to ORI outnumbered the claims brought to the administrative courts almost by a factor of four (2,447–9,446) (Ombudsman 2018). ORI's mandate is much broader than that of the administrative courts, so this higher number is in itself unsurprising. However, because ORI's 'jurisdiction' includes the decisions that can be addressed at the administrative court there is a huge potential for competition. Several features of ORI reinforce its relative advantage over the administrative court: it is easier to access (both on account of jurisdiction and because of its practical features), it is not bound by tight procedures, it takes less time of petitioners, and it is more flexible in providing redress (Bedner 2018). The single advantage of the administrative courts over ORI is that its judgements are backed up by

---

[5] Some regions have their own local Ombudsman; see Crouch 2007; 2008.

the threat of enforcement. However, because the enforcement record of the administrative court is so patchy, the perceived lack of 'teeth' of ORI loses much of its importance in deciding to bring a case to either one of these institutions.

Yet, the administrative courts have survived and continue to receive a stable number of cases. Recently, the new Law on Government Administration (LGA) (30/2014) has widened its jurisdiction which is no longer limited to decisions of an individual, concrete and final nature; it now includes decisions of a general nature as well as factual acts by the government (Art. 87). Another development is the consolidation of the grounds for review the administrative courts may apply. The absence of an explicit reference to General Principles in the Law on the Administrative Courts was rectified in 2004, when this law was amended to include them as a ground for review. In 2014 the LGA extended the number of General Principles, introducing a new, non-exhaustive list of them.

The next section will focus on these General Principles, to look more closely at the development of legal reasoning in the administrative courts. The question we intend to answer is whether the courts manage to produce a degree of consistency in legal interpretation. In order to do so, we first discuss the origins of this ground for review, before we look at its current application.

The Development of Legal Reasoning: General Principles of Proper Administration

The Law on Administrative Courts made no explicit reference to General Principles – surprisingly so, as parliament had agreed to include them in the new statute. However, in the end Minister of Justice Ismail Saleh decided that it was better not to make explicit reference in the law to any such principles and to leave it to the administrative court judges themselves to decide how they would develop this ground for review (Bedner 2001: 42). The legal basis for such elaboration was contested – either Article 53(2) of the Law on Administrative Courts or Article 27 of the General Law on the Judiciary (14/1970) – but no one disagreed that the General Principles were applicable (Bedner 2001: 97–8).

From the start, leading administrative court judges engaged in the task of elaboration. Having taken part in trainings from Dutch administrative law professors who emphasised the importance of General Principles, judges such as Indroharto, Olden Bidara, and Paulus Lotulung started applying and writing about these principles. As a basis they used the doctrine developed in the Dutch administrative judicial AROB (*Administratieve Rechtspraak Overheidsbeschikkingen*[6]) procedure, which had served as the general model for the Indonesian administrative court procedure. The most authoritative book was the one by Indroharto, who discussed the principles of carefulness, fair play, justification, legal certainty, trust and proportionality (Bedner 2001: 97–100). The first principle the Supreme Court applied in 1992 was the equality principle (Bedner 2001: 98). The acceptance of General Principles was underscored by the publication of this judgement and other ones in the administrative court review *Gema Peratun*, and in separate collections of court rulings (Bedner 2001: 97–100). In 1992 the Supreme Court moreover issued a circular letter (052/Td.TUN/II/1992), which put beyond doubt that General Principles constituted a lawful ground for review. It stipulated that

> If a judge holds that there is a general principle of proper administration as a basis for quashing a decision, there is no need for including this in the *diktum* of the judgement but it is sufficient to do so in the considerations (*pertimbangan*) while mentioning which principles of the General Principles have been violated.

Despite this promising start, problems in the application of General Principles soon became apparent. Of the principles discussed by Indroharto, the Supreme Court only applied those of carefulness and equality. Moreover, lower courts appeared reluctant to follow the precedent the Supreme Court had set in *Lindawati* (Bedner 2001: 98). Lower courts also provided some puzzling interpretations of principles. An example is the principle of trust, which according to the Bandung Administrative Court was violated when the government did not respond to the plaintiff's request for a housing permit – what this had to do with trust is a mystery (Bedner 2001: 99). More worrying still, some lower courts started to argue that if a defendant had made a decision according to the official procedure, this would mean that it could not have violated a General Principle. Such an interpretation rendered the General Principles effectively meaningless (Bedner 2001: 99–100).

The situation became worse after publication of judgements came to a standstill around 1998. In combination with the limited training candidate judges received, the situation led to confusion among administrative

---

[6] In English, this is the 'Judicial Procedure Regarding Government Decrees'.

judges – particularly but not exclusively at lower level courts – about how to apply the General Principles. The situation did not improve with the enactment of the 2004 amendment to the Law on the Administrative Courts (9/2004). This amendment went a step further by listing General Principles as a separate ground for review in Article 53. However, instead of codifying the principles that were being used in administrative court practice, the amendment referred to the General Principles of state administration listed in the Anti-corruption Law. These were of quite a different nature than the principles derived from Dutch practice the court had hitherto applied – and were not well-suited for use in the administrative court. They were designed for countering corruption, not for assessing lawfulness of government decisions. For example, it is hard to see how a principle as 'the general interest' can be used as a ground for review in an administrative court decision without the judges engaging in a full test that puts them in the position of the government.

A more positive change reinforcing the status of the General Principles was that the Supreme Court instructed the lower administrative courts to no longer *only* refer to the General Principles in the considerations of the judgement, but to include them as a ground for review in the *diktum* of the judgement, and moreover to specify which principle they applied. This put an obligation on judges to better explain how and why they thought this principle was applicable in the case at hand.

The most important change came with the enactment of the LGA in 2014. The original draft law did not provide for General Principles, but during the discussions in parliament about the Problem Inventory List (*Daftar Isi Masalah*), Deputy Minister of State Apparatus Empowerment and Bureaucratic Reform Eko Prasojo proposed the inclusion of General Principles. The political party representatives responded positively to Eko's list, which included the principles of legal certainty, expediency, impartiality, accuracy, prohibition of abuse of authority, openness and public interest. The spokesperson for the Golkar party then proposed another principle – 'the principle of good service' (*asas pelayanan yang baik*), which was indeed added. The entire list of cases resulting from these deliberations was laid down in Article 10(1). Moreover, the participants to the debate agreed that the proposed codification of principles should not preclude judges from creating new ones. This led to Article 10(2), in which we find the legal foundation for judges to develop General Principles on their own initiative. In so doing, they can rely on other laws and regulations, doctrinal writings by administrative law experts, and judicial rulings that have permanent legal force (see the Elucidation).

The LGA's codification of General Principles is a clear step forward in lawmaking in Indonesia. It unequivocally refers to a different model of legal development than is common: one relying – at least in part – on judicial precedents. The list of principles the law contains is itself the result of such a process, as it is based on jurisprudence (*yurisprudensi*) and doctrinal writings. This is quite unusual. As one of the authors of this article has argued elsewhere, there is a common disconnect between legal development by and within the judiciary and the legislature in particular, in the sense that judicial rulings are seldom taken into account as a source for lawmaking (Bedner 2016). Still, looking at all of the legislation that lists General Principles or similar principles, there is now a staggering variety of twenty-eight principles to be found in different pieces of legislation (Pratiwi et al. 2016: 47–8).

Another change favouring the use of precedent in administrative court practice is the Supreme Court's initiative to publish all of its judgements on its website. By making its judgements publicly available, the Court now has fulfilled an important precondition for legal development through judicial interpretation. Judges from the administrative courts can look for cases in which principles they think are relevant have been applied by the Supreme Court before.

The question then is whether these favourable changes have indeed promoted a more frequent and consistent use of General Principles. In research sponsored by the Dutch-Indonesian Judicial Sector Support Programme (LEIP 2018), two teams of researchers looked into this issue – the first focusing on the Supreme Court, the second looking at lower courts and government officials.[7] The first research team went through all of the 6,013 administrative court judgements published on the Supreme Court website. The first judgements date from 2002, the last ones from 2014. A total of 1,174 out of these 6,013 judgements referred to General Principles in one way or another, so more than one out of six judgements. This is an average, though, that does not show the sharp increase in references between 2002 and 2012 when this number went up from 2 to 296, to remain stable in 2013. If we look at the number of cases appealed for cassation (which fluctuates between 500 and 1,000 cases a year) the current average of cases referring to General Principles stands at one out of two cases, up from to one out of four cases.

---

[7] The researchers looked at a total of 1,174 cases from the period 2002–15 found at the Supreme Court website (Pratiwi et al. 2016: 24).

This increase can partly be attributed to the fact that plaintiffs now refer to General Principles more frequently than in the past. However, the way they use them does not show an increase in understanding of the separate principles. Most plaintiffs present a rather random list of General Principles, and only as a second ground: they *always* refer to a violation of the law first as a reason for quashing a decision. This suggests that plaintiffs read little beyond statutes while preparing a claim. Neither do most of them explain *why* the contested decision would violate the General Principles they list (Pratiwi et al. 2016: 9). This is particularly problematic because several judges of lower courts who were interviewed said that the application of General Principles depended on whether a claim mentioned them as a ground for review. Judges rarely supplement them as a ground (Wiratraman et al. 2017: 17fn.14). Moreover, according to one of the judges interviewed for the second report, at preliminary hearings judges advise the plaintiff to focus on the statutory violation and to only list General Principles as a secondary ground. In this manner, they suggest that a violation of General Principles does not offer sufficient basis for the review of an administrative decision (Wiratraman et al. 2017: 20). Another judge from a first-instance court even said in an interview that in matters of land law the statutes are so detailed that they leave no room for a violation of General Principles (Wiratraman et al. 2017: 46). This is similar to the views of the judges mentioned earlier, who argued that properly follow-ing a procedure suffices to prevent a violation of General Principles. At least one official interviewed in the framework of the Judicial Sector Support Program (JSSP) research corroborated this view, arguing that to realise General Principles is a part of following the procedure. If an official has the authority to take a decision and goes through the right procedural steps, this guarantees proper observance of the General Principles (Wiratraman et al. 2017: 86). There are also examples of cases where government officials issued new decisions following an annulment by the administrative court without taking into account the prescriptions of the court as contained in the judgement (Wiratraman et al. 2017: 87).

Neither have all officials taken notice of the changes implemented by the LGA. The most important one is that it changed the 'fictive negative' decision for a 'fictive positive' one. Under the Law on the Administrative Court, the failure to make a decision on request within four months led to the 'fiction' that the government had refused this request and that such a case could be taken to the administrative court – a so-called fictive negative decision. By contrast, the LGA determines that if the relevant statute does not stipulate otherwise the failure to respond within ten days leads to the assumption that the government has consented to the request – a fictive positive decision. This change has not been noticed by many officials, who continue to believe that the old regime still applies and who are unpleasantly surprised when requested to issue the decision they 'consented' to (Wiratraman et al. 2017: 89–91).

Judges at the lower courts themselves rarely clarify why and how a particular principle is applicable in a given case. Likewise, some courts of appeal overturned judgements built on the application of General Principles without explaining why they thought they were not applicable (Wiratraman et al. 2017: 55, 76). This promotes the mixing up of distinct principles, such as those of proportionality, equal treatment and carefulness (Pratiwi et al. 2016: 9–10, 41, 124). If judges provide an explanation, they use a variety of interpretational methods without providing sufficient information about their choices. The result is a variety in meanings ascribed to a variety of principles (Wiratraman et al. 2017: 23).

An interesting way to promote a well-considered application of a General Principle is when a case draws much attention in the media and becomes a focus of attention for activists and academics. An example is a highly controversial environmental license for mining in Rembang provided to the company PT Semen Indonesia. The case not only invited demonstrations and other forms of civil protest, but also initiatives by scholar-activists to examine the judgements in first instance and appeal in an open session. A number of them also sent an *amicus curiae* letter to the Supreme Court. The case was so politicised that the dean of the Law Faculty of Airlangga University in Surabaya refused to screen the documentary *Samin v. Semen*,[8] which argued against the license. In the end the Supreme Court agreed with the criticism and overturned the judgement of the appellate court (Wiratraman et al. 2017: 55–72). Because such cases get intense public attention (see Tapsell, this volume), the news about the interpretation spreads widely beyond the case at hand.

The principles the administrative courts most often apply are those of legal certainty, due care, the prohibition of misuse of power (*détournement de pouvoir*) and the principle of administrative orderliness. As we can see, this list only partly overlaps with the eight principles mentioned explicitly in Article 10(1) of the LGA. Judges seldom refer to the LGA but instead mention the Law on the Administrative Courts

---

[8] The Samin are a customary law community in Rembang.

Article 53 (as amended) (Pratiwi et al. 2016: 40; Wiratraman et al. 2017: 21). A large majority of the judges from first-instance courts and courts of appeal in interviews confirmed that they relied on the Law on the Administrative Court rather than the LGA (Wiratraman et al. 2017: 23). Moreover, some of them considered the General Principles in the LGA as rules that only apply to officials and cannot be used as a ground for review (Wiratraman et al. 2017: 25). The Supreme Court has consistently denied such a reading and has furthermore introduced newly invented principles, like the 'principle of personal responsibility' (463/K/TUN/2013) and the 'principle of protection of opinion or private life' (*asas perlindungan atas pandangan atau cara hidup pribadi*) (Wiratraman et al. 2017: 48). One problem with this trend is that the Court does not always clearly define these new principles (Pratiwi et al. 2016: 40).

The principle most often applied is legal certainty. However, many judges do not rely on a common understanding of this principle as requiring that a particular right the defendant gave to the plaintiff is honoured, or that laws cannot be applied retroactively. Rather, they use it as a way to reinforce a decision quashing an administrative act that has no legal basis, or if it contradicts the law in another way (Pratiwi et al. 2016: 55, 43). Interpreted in this manner the principle has no independent meaning. Other judges do use the principle as an independent ground for review, but they provide different interpretations of it. This is not surprising, given that the principle of legal certainty can be found in four different statutes, which provide three different definitions (Pratiwi et al. 2016: 54).[9]

One of the problems causing the lack of uniformity is that the current method of publication does not provide the 'added value' needed for the effective use of General Principles: cases are published in nine categories (civil, criminal, administrative, military, etc.) each subdivided into broad topics (e.g. tort, default, etc.), but their entry contains no information other than the case number. It does not say what the case is about, what statutory articles it refers to, etc. The only way to search the database is by entering particular terms that may be found in the document. This means

---

[9] The LGA carries the most elaborate definition: a principle in a state under the rule of law which prioritises the statutory basis, propriety, constancy and justice in every policy of the state authorities (Elucidation to Article 10). The Law on Regional Government (23/2014) refers to statutory basis and justice only (Elucidation to Article 58(a)), while the Law on State Institutions that are Clean and Free of Corruption, Collusion and Nepotism (28/1999) mentions statutory basis, justice and propriety.

that if one looks for cases concerning violation of a particular General Principle, one has to search all of the administrative court cases listed in the Supreme Court directory. So far, the Supreme Court or other legal authorities, for instance, law professors, have made no efforts to change this system. Therefore, in the short term we cannot expect a systematic development of General Principles.

While the Supreme Court itself carries responsibility for the lack of developing uniform interpretations of General Principles by not making its judgements available in a more accessible form or by providing clear guidance on which of its judgements should be considered 'leading cases', it is also true that judges of the lower courts themselves show little initiative to use the materials available. In interviews conducted with judges at first-instance courts, they indicated that they did not even know how to access the Supreme Court's judgements and never refer to precedents (Wiratraman et al., 2017: 24). In their training as judges, these skills are covered in just forty-five minutes and many administrative court judges never followed the relevant specialisation in law school, but only the general obligatory courses on administrative law (three study points) and administrative procedure (two study points). Specialisation is not a requirement for admission to become an administrative court judge (Wiratraman et al. 2017: 26–7).

Despite all of these problems, the research by Pratiwi et al. also found Supreme Court judgements that provided well-reasoned interpretations for each of the thirteen principles more frequently used by the administrative courts, which can potentially serve as precedents. The researchers suggest that the Supreme Court should use these judgements – which have been analysed and compiled in its report – as the basis for a guideline (*pedoman*). This seems an excellent idea.

Conclusion

Almost thirty years on, the administrative courts are a well-established presence in the Indonesian legal landscape. Despite competition from other, more flexible institutions such as the Ombudsman, they have continued to attract a consistent number of plaintiffs and there is no doubt that they have offered relief to citizens looking for a solution to a dispute with the government.

When it comes to the question of whether the administrative courts have managed to develop legal certainty in the application of General Principles, the answer is mixed. Pratiwi et al.'s careful analysis of

Supreme Court judgements indicates that the Supreme Court has produced and published judgements concerning all of the General Principles commonly used that offer clear guidelines for interpretation and can serve as landmark cases. On the other hand, the Supreme Court itself is not always consistent in its interpretations of General Principles and it has added to the confusion by introducing new principles without proper explanation.

At the level of the lower courts the picture is bleaker. Judges at these courts sometimes misjudge the meaning of General Principles as a separate ground for review and they seldom provide convincing reasons why they apply a particular General Principle. There are also indications that judges fully rely on the arguments of the plaintiff and that they do not apply General Principles of their own initiative. Courts of appeal furthermore feel no obligation to explain why they reject a General Principle applied by the court of first instance. Neither do judges at the lower courts show much inclination to look for precedents or doctrinal writings when they consider applying a particular principle.

The problems at the lower courts certainly have to do with the education and training judges receive, which gives little emphasis to the General Principles. It should also be noted that the Supreme Court has made available many relevant judgements, but that it has not spent much effort on presenting them in a 'user-friendly' way. The categories into which the Supreme Court uploads these judgements are quite broad and no other information is added to facilitate a search. This problem of communication extends to the group that should be reached in the first place: the officials who take decisions that affect the lives of citizens. Officials we interviewed about the General Principles indicated a lack of understanding of their meaning, showing a tendency to equate them with the proper following of a statutory procedure.

Despite all of these problems, there is progress. It is unlikely that problems of political pressure, corruption and other institutional issues will be fully resolved, but the conditions for a consistent interpretation of General Principles – and other legal tools – are more positive than they were before. It will take time, but we predict that the tide is turning in favour of legal certainty.

PART III

Specialised Courts as Judicial Reform Strategy

7

Indonesia's Anti-corruption Courts and the Persistence of Judicial Culture

SIMON BUTT

Indonesia has long been notorious for having very high levels of public sector corruption, which became particularly prevalent during Soeharto's time in power (1966–98). Transparency International's Corruption Perceptions Index (CPI), perhaps the most commonly cited corruption-related survey, has consistently rated Indonesia among the world's most corrupt countries.[1] However, in more recent years, the CPI has appeared to signal an improvement in Indonesia's corruption levels. For example, in 2007, Indonesia was the 143th most corrupt country of 180 countries reviewed by Transparency International, but by 2015 had improved to 88th of 168, and in 2017 had slipped slightly to 96th of 180. Whether these improvements in perception actually reflect corruption reduction is a matter of some debate.[2] But any perceived or actual improvements are likely due in large measure to the successes of two institutions established after Soeharto: the Anti-corruption Courts (ACCs) and the Anti-corruption Commission (*Komisi Pemberantasan Korupsi* or KPK).

The KPK was established in 2003 as an independent body with power to, *inter alia*, investigate and prosecute high-level corruption cases. In 2004, an ACC was established in Jakarta as the sole feeder court for all KPK investigations and prosecutions. I argue that the ACCs represent somewhat of a paradox in terms of Indonesian judicial culture. On the one hand, the 2004 ACC was established to circumvent what has arguably become the most prominent aspect of judicial culture in most other

---

[1] Transparency International, www.transparency.org/.

[2] There is some debate about whether corruption levels have dropped in Indonesia. Some argue that perceptions might have improved simply because more investigations and prosecutions are occurring, but that corruption levels remain very high, particularly in Indonesia's regions. The Index is based on the views of analysts, business persons and experts about the extent of public sector corruption. See www.transparency.org/research/cpi/overview.

Indonesian courts: having corruption levels so high that they affect or even determine judicial processes and outcomes.[3] The main design feature intended to reduce or avoid corruption in the ACC was the use of non-career judges (commonly called 'ad hoc' judges in Indonesia) to work alongside career judges in ACC cases. The main presumption here was that career judges are likely to be part of well-established corrupt networks through which bribes are extorted from defendants to ensure a light sentence or an acquittal (Satuan Tugas Pemberantasan Mafia Hukum 2010; ICW 2001; Fenwick 2008). Importantly, as initially conceived, there were to be three non-career judges and two career judges on each five-judge panel, so that non-career judges would outnumber career judges in all ACC cases. If a decision in a case was split along non-career and career judge lines, then the career judges would hold sway. Of course, having 'clean' ACCs is particularly important in the broader so-called 'fight' against corruption that has continued since Soeharto's fall. If corruption trials are themselves marred by corruption, successful prosecutions for corruption will be unlikely, providing near immunity for 'corruptors' and the judges who protect them.

Though various challenges to the initial institutional design of the ACCs have threatened their ability to resist this culture of corruption, the ACCs have retained these design aspects, at least in most cases. And, while some ACC judges, including some of its non-career judges, have been caught red-handed taking bribes themselves, the ACCs arguably have a reputation for integrity that is no worse than most other judges working in Indonesia's courts.

On the other hand, the ACCs frequently convict defendants – particularly in KPK-prosecuted cases, where the ACCs have issued guilty verdicts in 100% of cases.[4] This is widely regarded in Indonesia as a 'success', attributable to the ACCs having a majority of non-career judges on each panel. However, this conviction rate has led some commentators, both foreign and Indonesian, to question the objectivity and

---

[3] While corruption is said to be rampant in most Indonesian courts, it bears noting that complaints about corruption are rarely heard in relation to Indonesia's religious courts, discussed in Huis, this volume.

[4] Other civil law countries have similarly high conviction rates, with the conventional explanation for this being that various safeguards exist to prevent cases reaching trial in the absence of very strong evidence, including that prosecutors should themselves also consider and present evidence that supports the defendant's innocence. However, this rarely happens in Indonesia and, indeed, as mentioned below, once a suspected perpetrator is formally named a 'suspect', the KPK cannot drop the case, even if they discover exculpatory evidence.

impartiality of the ACCs, and even to ask whether the ACCs are even performing a 'judicial' function – that is, to rigorously examine the evidence put before them to determine whether it supports a finding of guilt. It is possible to speculate that these judges are in fact responding to public opinion, which, for reasons considered below, holds that a defendant brought before the courts is surely guilty. If the defendant is acquitted, then the general public are thought to presume that something improper must have occurred, such as the payment of a bribe to secure that acquittal. It is arguable that this apparent sensitivity to public opinion is also becoming increasingly part of Indonesia's judicial culture more broadly, which hardly bodes well for the rights of defendants and the rule of law. Nevertheless, in some cases it appears to have a mitigating effect on the judicial culture of corruption.

This chapter discusses the background to the establishment of the ACCs, the statutory powers they have been granted, their functions and workings, and their place within the broader judicial system. As this chapter demonstrates, the legal and institutional frameworks within which the ACC initially operated in 2003 have since undergone significant change – most notably, with the establishment of thirty-three new ACCs, so that all Indonesian provincial capitals now have one. This has brought real challenges to the way that the ACCs function that have significant potential to undermine their future efficacy. I conclude by discussing how these courts have been shaped by, and themselves shape, judicial culture in Indonesia.

It is impossible to discuss the ACC without also considering the role and performance of the KPK, which investigates and prosecutes many of the cases the ACCs decide. For this reason, I begin with a brief description of the background to the establishment of the KPK.

The Establishment of the KPK and the ACC

During Soeharto's authoritarian rule, corruption was very prevalent in government, and a significant portion of illicit funds made their way to Soeharto himself, his family and the members of his inner circle. Soeharto alone is estimated to have creamed somewhere between $USD 15–35 billion during his rule (Colmey and Liebhold 1999). Corruption was rampant in underfunded government institutions, including the courts (Butt and Lindsey 2011), which needed to seek external revenue streams in order to function. Corruption was also prevalent among underpaid government officials, many of whom participated in what has perhaps best been described as the 'Soeharto franchise' (McLeod 2000). Unofficial payments and kickbacks could be received with impunity, provided that a proportion was passed up through one's superiors (Goodpaster 2002). The courts were particularly bad, with prominent lawyers likening them to auction houses, where law and legal argument mattered little, if at all (Goodpaster 2002). Dan Lev was an important scholar who identified the dramatic increase in judicial corruption under Soeharto, and its various egregious consequences.

With Soeharto's fall came the dismantling of the pillars of his authoritarian system. Many commentators and politicians genuinely thought that Indonesia would disintegrate or Balkanise unless a meaningful and genuine programme of broader governance reform was achieved (Crouch 2010; Horowitz 2013). It was in this political context that important changes were made to Indonesia's anti-corruption legal and institutional framework; the idea for an independent anti-corruption commission with real power crystalised; and preparations for its establishment commenced.

It bears noting that Indonesia had certainly experienced no shortage of anti-corruption commissions and agencies – even during the Soeharto period (Assegaf 2002). But most were just public relations exercises to quell public anger after media reports of government corruption (Hamzah 1984), comprising task forces of existing police and prosecutors. The genuineness of the concern of many of these task forces to pursue corruption case was, quite rightly, called into question. Police and prosecutors had long been notorious for accepting bribes to drop cases, including corruption cases, and it became widely believed that many judges would issue a light sentence, or even acquit, in return for a bribe. Collectively, along with many lawyers, these officials form part of what Indonesians call the 'court mafia' (mafia peradilan).

Even when these task forces did seek to pursue allegations of corruption, including within Indonesia's courts, law enforcement institutions tended to close ranks around their embattled employees. This was widely seen by many as an attempt by senior law enforcers to protect the patronage networks of which they were part and from which they personally benefitted. A stark example was the pushback against the Joint Investigating Team for the Eradication of Corruption (*Tim Gabungan Pemberantasan Tindakan Korupsi*, or TGPTK), which was established in 2000 as a 'stop-gap' measure until the KPK could be formed. Its purpose was to help with difficult-to-prove corruption cases, but only by coordinating investigations and prosecutions that ordinary police and prosecutors conducted. It could not investigate or prosecute on its own initiative (Assegaf 2002).[5] When the Team began investigating allegations that Supreme Court judges had received bribes in return for favourable decisions, the judges responded by challenging, in the Central Jakarta District Court, the jurisdiction of the Team to investigate them. They were successful, albeit on highly dubious legal grounds, and the investigation into them was declared invalid. The judges also sought, before their brethren on the Supreme Court, a judicial review of the government regulation which established the Team. Again, they were successful despite questionable legal arguments. The Supreme Court invalidated the regulation, thereby disbanding the Team.[6]

And so, with what appeared to be the first genuine intentions to combat corruption for many decades, if not in Indonesian history, the KPK and the Jakarta ACC were born through passage of Law 30 of 2002 on the KPK. Both institutions were strong and independent in design. However, the Law did not require the KPK to handle *all* corruption cases; ordinary police and prosecutors continued handling them too. This was arguably a necessity; as a new institution, with limited resources, both human and budgetary, the KPK would likely have been overwhelmed if given responsibility for pursuing all corruption cases. It has handled, and continues to handle, a relatively small proportion of all corruption cases. In the period 2004 to 2011, for example, Indonesia's ordinary public prosecutors prosecuted almost 8,000 cases, while the KPK prosecuted around 230 (Butt 2012).

Perhaps the most significant feature of the KPK's introduction was the exclusion of ordinary police and prosecutors from handling serious corruption cases. As mentioned, their involvement had made effective pursuit of corruption cases difficult for many decades. The KPK Law itself explicitly recognises that the previous involvement of ordinary police, prosecutors and judges in handling corruption cases had contributed to the failure of previous anti-corruption efforts. The KPK has its own investigators and prosecutors and its primary task, at least concerning 'law enforcement', is

---

[5] Ultimately, however, the Joint Team was able to complete investigations leading to prosecutions in only around ten percent of the cases submitted to it: Assegaf, 2002, 135, leading the Head of the Team, former Supreme Court judge and respected reformist Adi Andojo Soetjipto to eventually resign in frustration: *The Jakarta Post* 2001.

[6] For a full discussion of this case, see Butt and Lindsey 2010.

investigating and prosecuting serious corruption cases, leaving run-of-the-mill cases to general police and prosecutors. More specifically, the KPK can initiate its own corruption investigations and prosecutions in cases that

1. allegedly involve law enforcers (that is, police, prosecutors or judges) and state officials, or people who have conspired or collaborated with law enforcers or state officials to engage in corruption;
2. draw the attention of, and disturb, the community; or
3. involve a loss to the state of at least Rp. 1 billion.[7]

More controversial has been the power of the KPK to take over existing corruption investigations and prosecutions if

- the KPK receives a report or complaint about police or prosecutors failing to pursue a case or protecting the real perpetrator;
- a corruption investigation or prosecution stalls for no good reason, is marred by corruption itself, or is interfered with by the executive, legislature or judiciary; or
- any circumstance arises that, according to police or prosecutors, makes a particular corruption case difficult to handle.[8]

These features of institutional design appear to have been effective, at least if successful prosecutions are used as a measure of success. Against the expectations of most, in the fifteen years since its establishment, the KPK has fearlessly and successfully prosecuted very high-profile figures. These include a relative[9] of former president Susilo Bambang Yudhoyono (SBY) and senior officials from SBY's political party, the Democrat Party, including its former treasurer Muhammad Nazaruddin (who received a four-year and ten-month sentence in 2012, extended to seven years by the Supreme Court in 2013); former party Deputy Secretary General Angelina Sondakh (sentenced to four and a half years in 2013, increased to twelve years by the Supreme Court later that year, then reduced to ten years on reconsideration (PK) appeal in 2015); former Sports Minister Andi Mallarangeng (who received a four-year jail sentence in 2014); and former party Chairperson Anas Urbaningrum (sentenced to eight years in 2014, and increased to fourteen years by the Supreme Court in 2015)

---

[7] Art. 11 of the KPK Law.

[8] Arts. 8–9 of the KPK Law.

[9] In 2009, Aulia Pohan, a former Bank Indonesia deputy governor, was convicted for his role in disbursing around $10 million from the Indonesian Banking Development Foundation for improper purposes: Crouch 2010: 72–3.

(Movanita 2015; Gabrillin 2016; *Hukumonline* 2013b). In 2013, serving Chairperson of the Constitutional Court, Akil Mochtar, was convicted and sentenced to life imprisonment for taking bribes to fix the outcome of cases (Rahmi 2014). Another Constitutional Court judge, Patrialis Akbar, was also successfully prosecuted and sentenced to eight years' imprisonment. Setyo Novanto, speaker of the national parliament, was convicted in 2018 for receiving money earmarked for an electronic identity card system (Cochrane 2018). Many other ministers and former ministers, other senior national party officials, legislators, governors, mayors and regents have also been tried and convicted (Rastika 2013; Kompas 2014).

The KPK has achieved these prosecutions despite very strong pushback from most of those it has pursued, or their associates. In both 2009 and 2014, for example, police arrested three of the KPK's five commissioners, effectively hobbling the KPK for several months and forcing it to drop some investigations (Butt 2012, 2015). These arrests were made based on obviously manipulated evidence or trumped-up charges, apparently at the behest of senior law enforcers who themselves were under investigation.

For example, in 2014, after newly elected President Joko Widodo announced his intention to appoint Commander General Budi Gunawan as police chief, the KPK revealed that it was investigating Gunawan for corruption and urged Widoyo not to appoint him. The police retaliated by charging all KPK Commissioners with various offences. These charges were not supported by convincing evidence, raising speculation that police had fabricated them, as they had in 2009 (Butt 2012). KPK Chairman Abraham Samad and well-respected human rights lawyer and anti-corruption activist, Bambang Widjojanto, were forced to resign. This is because Article 32(2) of the KPK Law allows KPK commissioners to be suspended if they are 'named as a suspect' in a criminal case. While this provision was apparently included in the KPK Law to protect the KPK's reputation if one of its commissioners was suspected of wrongdoing, it hands enormous power to police. Faced with a KPK investigation into one of their own, the police can and have simply charged a KPK commissioner with an offence. This will, at worst, stall the investigation and, at best, result in it being dropped altogether.

National parliamentarians, dozens of whom the KPK has also pursued, continually threaten to take away the KPK's powers, reduce its budget and even disband it. Most notable has been the threat to remove the

KPK's power to wiretap without a warrant from a judge (*Hukumonline* 2013i). The KPK commonly reports that wiretaps are crucial to the success of KPK investigations and that it routinely relies upon them for successful prosecutions. One fear is that if the KPK is forced to seek judicial pre-approval to wiretap, then corrupt judges might 'tip off' those under investigation about the wiretap in return for a bribe. If the suspect is forewarned, then the KPK is unlikely to obtain any admission or useful evidence from any ensuing recorded conversation.

Key figures in the national legislature have also attempted to discredit the KPK. A recent example of this is the response of the national parliament (DPR) to the KPK's investigation of the so-called 'e-KTP scandal'. According to the KPK, the case resulted in state losses of Rp. 2.3 trillion, making it the largest corruption scandal ever investigated by the institution (Firmanto 2017). The KPK alleges that all fifty-one legislators in DPR Commission II accepted kickbacks from project managers in 2010–12 in relation to the scheme, and, at time of writing, had indicted fourteen of them (Kompas 2017). The first person convicted was DPR speaker, Setya Novanto, who, as mentioned, was imprisoned for fifteen years for his involvement in the scandal.

In response, members of the national legislature sought to 'dig up dirt' on the KPK. In particular, they alleged that the KPK had misused its powers, manufactured key evidence and even mistreated witnesses and suspects. As part of this attempted smear campaign, key politicians launched a special inquiry into the KPK in April 2017, using its 'angket' power. The DPR has had this power for decades, which is defined, in Article 79(3) of Law 17 of 2014 on the MPR, DPR, DPD and DPRD (often called the MD3 Law), as the power to investigate

> the implementation of a statute and/or government policy, related to an issue that is important, strategic and has a wide impact on the life of the people and the nation, which is suspected to violate the law.

In the context of DPR–KPK relations, it seems clear that the DPR wished to compel the KPK to attend investigations to give the impression that it was stronger than and superior to the KPK and, ultimately, to find a justification to disband it. Realising this, the KPK initially refused to meet with any members of the special committee. It did so for various reasons. Legally, the KPK argued that the DPR had no power to compel it to attend. Politically, the KPK would undoubtedly have been reluctant to appear subservient to the DPR, whose members the KPK was investigating, and whose moral legitimacy was questionable, given that it is often rated as one of Indonesia's most corrupt institutions, if not the most corrupt, including by Transparency International (Indonesia Investments 2018).

Responding to the launch of the inquiry, in July 2017, the Forum for the Study of Law and the Constitution, along with a student and an academic, sought review of Article 79(3) before the Constitutional Court. These applicants asked for an order from the Court that Article 79(3) was unconstitutional unless interpreted to restrict the DPR to calling institutions that were part of the executive. They argued that the KPK, which by law is independent and free from government interference, was not subject to the DPR's hak angket power. However, the applicants were unsuccessful. The majority accepted that the KPK was part of the executive and that the KPK Law required that the KPK be independent in performing its functions. However, this did not mean that the KPK was immune from the *hak angket* process.

Three judges – I Dewa Gede Palguna, Suhartoyo and Saldi Isra – issued a joint dissent, and Maria Farida Indrati wrote her own dissent. The three-judge minority decided that KPK was not part of the executive. It could not, therefore, be compelled to attend investigation by the legislature. Indrati decided that the KPK was part of the executive but found that it was not subject to the angket process. For her, the KPK was not accountable to the head of the executive – the president – but rather only to the public, so it could not be called to account by the national legislature.

Even though the majority's views did not favour the KPK, it appeared to escape the controversy relatively unscathed. The special committee issued preliminary findings in September 2017, recommending that the KPK's operations be suspended. However, the committee eventually delivered a greatly watered-down list of recommendations on 14 February 2018. Ironically, one of the committee's findings was that the KPK had not done enough to improve Indonesia's corruption perception rating (KBR 2018).

The KPK's track record of successful prosecutions has traditionally been attributed to two main things. One is its high investigative and prosecutorial standards – at least relative to ordinary police and prosecutors. This, the KPK claims, is borne out of comprehensive training, stringent evidence handling and meticulous preparation, making conviction more likely. These high standards are necessary because the KPK

Law requires that the KPK must proceed to trial once it formally names an alleged perpetrator as a suspect. The second is that it has prosecuted all of its cases before specialised ACCs. It is to the establishment of these courts to which I now turn.

From Sole Jakarta ACC to Provincial ACCs

The 2002 KPK Law required the establishment of an anti-corruption (*Tindakan Pidana Korupsi* or Tipikor) court (ACC) to perform one function: hear corruption cases that the KPK prosecutes.[10] While formally independent, structurally the ACC was a chamber of the Central Jakarta District Court, although it was not housed in the Central Jakarta Court complex, but rather was located in separate premises. As mentioned, a panel of five judges presided over each case, with a majority of them being non-career judges.[11] They are legal experts, such as lawyers who are hired as corruption court judges for a limited period. The non-career judges were joined on each panel by two career judges – that is, judges who had worked in at least one of Indonesia's general courts and had been certified by the Supreme Court for work on the ACC.

The rationale for having this ratio appears to have been at least twofold. On the one hand, the career judiciary was, on the whole, considered largely corrupt. Indeed, Fenwick describes the establishment of the ACC as an

> [a]ttempt to circumvent entirely a judicial system known to be complicit in protecting corruptors, and – at the very least – capable of being unresponsive or incompetent in the administration of justice. (Fenwick 2008: 413)

It was presumed that having a majority of non-career judges, who were not part of the judicial corps, would improve the likelihood of corruption cases being decided on their merits, rather than being dictated by bribes, because they were 'less likely than career judges to be entwined in institutionalised corruption or to have divided loyalties' (Butt and Lindsey 2011: 208). Because career judges did not constitute a majority, the non-career judges would win the day if disagreement occurs along career and non-career lines. On the other hand, many non-career judges lacked the judicial experience to run trials and to write judgements. It

---

[10] Article 53 of the KPK Law. The ACC was initially regulated in Articles 53–62 of the KPK Law.

[11] Article 58(2) of the KPK Law.

was, therefore, felt necessary to have career judges on these panels, too. However, having them as a minority appeared to implicitly recognise that reformers considered integrity more important than judicial experience.

Rights of appeals lay to a high anti-corruption court and from there to the Supreme Court, which both maintained this ratio of non-career to career judges. Strict deadlines for case handling were imposed. First-instance courts were required to deliver their verdicts within ninety days of the trial commencing. Appeal courts had sixty days and the Supreme Court ninety days.[12] These timelines were intended to reduce the possibility of backlogs of undecided cases accumulating, for which the Supreme Court was notorious. This backlog problem was thought to be particularly acute in high-profile corruption cases, which often languished, often to the advantage of defendants who remained free pending appeal.

As mentioned, between 2004 and 2010, the Jakarta Court maintained a 100 per cent conviction rate in around 200 cases. Even so, some anti-corruption activists complained that the ACC did not impose sufficient penalties upon those it convicted, some of whom it found guilty of causing very large losses to the state. For example, the Court has imposed life imprisonment only once, and has never imposed the death penalty for corruption, despite its availability. There is merit in this criticism about leniency, particularly in light of the strong political and legal rhetoric – including in the KPK Law itself – emphasising corruption as an 'extraordinary crime' (*kejahatan luar biasa*) and the importance of taking strong action against it. The ACC's sentences are, however, conspicuously tougher than those traditionally issued for corruption by the general courts. For example, Indonesia Corruption Watch (ICW) estimated that the general court average sentence in corruption cases was just six months in the 2000s. But for the ACC, in 2008, the average was just over four years' imprisonment (ICW 2009b). This had dropped to just over two years' in 2016 and 2017 (ICW 2018).

Of course, not everyone sees this conviction rate, and the relatively higher sentences, as 'successes'. Defence lawyers and their clients commonly complain that the KPK simply cannot have got it right in all these cases and that the presumption of innocence is being compromised somewhere along the way. According to them, it is simply inconceivable that the KPK could 'get it right' in every single case. Surely at least

---

[12] Articles 58(1), 59(1) and 60(1) of the KPK Law.

sometimes has made mistakes or the defendant has adduced counter-evidence that led the judges to doubt whether the KPK had proven the defendant was guilty to the Indonesian standard: 'convincingly and legally'.[13] After all, many of the lawyers hired by defendants to represent them are among Indonesia's most highly regarded and successful. But this line has not got much traction yet in Indonesia, with many saying that corruption is such a big problem that some collateral damage can be justified.

One Indonesian legal expert, Professor Indriyanto of the University of Indonesia (who was a legal advisor for Abdullah Puteh, former Aceh governor, when he was tried before the ACC in the first case prosecuted by the KPK), has claimed that ACC judges are swayed by public pressure and the press to convict defendants, even in the face of unconvincing evidence of guilt (see Tapsell, this volume). In a similar vein, one lawyer who has appeared in several ACC trials claimed that, from his experience, the ACC was unfair and biased.[14] He stated that ACC court judges did not look for the 'truth', as required by Indonesian law, but rather were more interested in establishing 'guilt'. He claimed also that some of his clients had asked him to temper the vigour with which he represented them, fearing that putting up too much of a fight would cause them additional 'problems' during investigations and trials, and might result in an increased sentence.

As mentioned, this conviction rate is commonly explained as being a product of the KPK's professionalism.

> One ad hoc judge [indicated] that even though ad hoc judges and high public expectations to convict were important factors, the conviction rate was primarily due to the strong evidence presented by KPK prosecutors. As former Junior Attorney General for Special Crimes and KPK Commissioner for Enforcement (2003–7) Tumpak H. Panggabean put it, convictions were obtained because of "correct investigations, perfect cases files and sufficient evidence". Former KPK chairman Taufiqurrahman Ruki (2003–7) explained that the KPK was wary that losing a case would undermine public confidence in the KPK and thus put extra effort into collecting three to five pieces of evidence to present before the Court, instead of the legally required two, to ensure conviction. To these ends, the KPK invested heavily in training its investigators and prosecutors, encouraged cooperation between investigators and prosecutors of different professional backgrounds and allocated more resources to case-management than the Attorney General's Office (Butt and Schutte 2014: 607–8).

[13] Article 191 of the KUHAP.
[14] Interview with advocate, Jakarta, 15 July 2007.

Nevertheless, the newly appointed ACC non-career judges complained about receiving insufficient institutional and budgetary support, particularly in its early years.

> Tipikor Court judges had no access to secretarial and only minimal janitorial support and were initially required to pay for stationary from their own pockets. Worse, ad hoc judges were not paid for one year after their appointments. Tahyar describes how the presidential decree allocating ad hoc judges a monthly salary of Rp. 10 million (about US$ 1000) took one month to travel from the State Secretariat to the Supreme Court – a distance of around one kilometre (Butt and Schutte 2014: 607, citing Tahyar 2010).

In 2009, the national parliament issued Law 46 on the ACC, which required the Supreme Court to establish ACCs in the general courts located in each of Indonesia's thirty-four provincial capital cities.[15] The only exception is Jakarta, which has ACCs in each of its municipalities, again with jurisdiction over the same area as their corresponding district courts (Article 4). These new ACCs have now been established and have exclusive jurisdiction over corruption and money laundering cases that occur within the physical jurisdiction of their district court (Articles 3, 35). Like the Jakarta ACC, they were designed to have a majority of non-career judges serving on each panel.[16] However, ACC panels can now be either three- or five-judge. Critically, ordinary prosecutors must now use these courts, rather than the ordinary general courts, to prosecute in corruption cases. Both the KPK and ordinary prosecutors therefore appear there, though they continue to pursue their own cases, largely independent of each other.

The national parliament was moved to issue this statute by a decision of Indonesia's Constitutional Court, in which the 'two-track' system for resolving corruption cases was declared to violate the constitutional principle of legal equality (Article 28D(1) of the Constitution).[17] As mentioned, the KPK handled only the corruption cases it initiated or took over from the police or prosecutors, and its cases were decided by the ACC, which, as discussed below, could be expected to reliably convict. Cases handled by the general courts (which were brought by ordinary prosecutors, usually after police

---

[15] Article 3 of 2009 ACC Law.
[16] Article 4 of 2009 ACC Law.
[17] Constitutional Court Decision 012–016-019/PUU-IV/2006. The Constitutional Court is discussed generally in Roux, this volume; see also Butt, Crouch and Dixon 2016.

investigations) would result in conviction in only 50 per cent or so of cases. While the Constitutional Court did not mention these differing conviction rates in its decision, it did point to several differences in the KPK Law that made it easier for the KPK to investigate and prosecute corruption cases, compared with ordinary law enforcement institutions, such as to wiretap and record conversations, issue travel bans, block accounts, suspend transactions and seize evidence without prior judicial approval.[18]

Also not mentioned in the Court's decision, but perhaps implicit in its thinking, was that every person named as a suspect by the KPK had ultimately been convicted at trial. Relevant here is that the KPK lacks one power that ordinary police and prosecutors have – to issue Cessation of Investigation Orders (*Surat Keputusan Penghentian Penyidikan*, or SKPP). Article 40 of the KPK Law provides that once the KPK formally names a person as a suspect (*tersangka*), it cannot drop the case. This restriction was intended to prevent the KPK from ceasing investigations in questionable circumstances, as had police and prosecutors in many previous cases. They did so most notoriously in the case against Soeharto for corruption, when they used claims that the former president's health was failing, to justify dropping all charges against him. However, being named as a suspect became synonymous with guilt, because every person named as a suspect was ultimately convicted.

An optimist might applaud the expansion of the ACC network, particularly if the 'success' of the Jakarta ACC could be replicated across Indonesia. Indeed, NGOs had initially pushed for ACCs to be established in all provinces, though importantly, they also wanted them kept separate from the existing judiciary, attributing the failure of Indonesia's commercial courts to it forming part of the corrosive general courts (LeIP et al. 2002). Regional ACCs might result in convictions of subnational officials that might not have been possible in the general courts in those regions, or in the Jakarta ACC. This is because, as mentioned, non-career judges still formally 'prevail' in regional ACCs, just as they do in the Jakarta ACC. Even cases brought by ordinary prosecutors, then, are decided by non-career majority panels, reducing the potential for 'justice mafia' collaboration.

Some commentators have put forward more sinister explanations for the regional ACC model established in 2009. They have suspected that

---

[18] Articles 12 and 47 of the KPK Law.

parliamentarians established these new courts as part of a deliberate strategy to weaken Indonesia's anti-corruption framework, because they feared that the KPK and ACC were becoming too powerful. After all, many parliamentarians were either under KPK investigation themselves or be a political party whose members were under investigation. Having corruption trials in regional areas makes them more difficult to monitor, particularly by national-level NGOs and the KPK. Improper interference in proceedings thereby becomes more feasible. And allowing general prosecutors to prosecute in the ACCs, even the Jakarta ACC, might allow defendants to buy their way out of trouble – at least in cases the KPK does not pursue. Potentially, then, the work of the KPK could be undermined despite its popularity, without directly attacking it.

There are various weaknesses in this explanation. One is that if the national parliament had wanted to hobble the KPK's efforts indirectly by targeting the ACC, it could have done so much more effectively by choosing a different strategy. The Constitutional Court decision that prompted the 2009 ACC Law gave the national legislature a three-year deadline to enact a new statute on the ACC that did not establish a two-track system. If that deadline was not reached, then the statutory basis for the ACCs that existed at that time would automatically have become invalid, meaning that the ACC would no longer have a legal basis under which it could perform its functions. If this deadline had been missed, then the Jakarta ACC would probably have needed to close down, leaving the ordinary courts to regain exclusive jurisdiction over all corruption and money laundering cases. In this context, it would have been much easier for the national parliament to have simply done nothing, and then to have blamed the Constitutional Court for the ACC's demise. It is unclear precisely why the national parliament did not take this course, but one can surmise that it would have drawn significant public and press criticism, given that, at that time, the KPK and ACC were among the most publicly popular institutions in Indonesia, and the government appears to have become accustomed to complying with decisions of the Constitutional Court as a matter of course (Butt 2015).

Assessing the Regional ACCs

Regardless of the true motivations for regionalisation, in 2011, in one of the first cases brought by an ordinary prosecutor before the Jakarta ACC, the court issued its first acquittal, apparently due to errors that prosecutors made in presenting their case (Butt 2011a). Several further acquittals followed soon thereafter. Although ACC case disposition statistics are difficult to obtain, in the first year these regional ACCs heard 466 cases and acquitted in 71 of them. Although acquittals do not necessarily reflect judicial decrepitude, in Indonesia this news made headlines and was perceived as an indication of impropriety, as discussed in more detail below.

Since regionalisation, the ACCs have been under almost continuous threat of reduced efficacy for reasons both external and internal to them. Internally, ACC judges have become embroiled in corruption scandals themselves, with several of them caught red-handed by the KPK when receiving bribes, and others being criticised for acquitting defendants. The Surabaya ACC, for example, has made headlines for acquitting more defendants than any other. Nineteen of these acquittals were issued in the first four months of the court's existence.[19] The Samarinda ACC also received criticism for acquitting fourteen regional parliamentarians from the Kutai Kartanegara DPRD in four days. The Semarang ACC, too, has been targeted for acquitting, with one of its judges, Lilik Nuraini, even being punished by being transferred to another court on the recommendation of the Judicial Commission. Nuraini had chaired panels that had acquitted in at least six cases (Kompas 2012b; Parwito 2012). (As argued below, however, acquittals alone are a poor indication of judicial performance and less emphasis should be placed on them.)

Worse, in August 2012, the KPK arrested Semarang ACC non-career judge Kartini Juliana Magdalena Marpaung for allegedly receiving a bribe. According to media reports, she was caught red-handed receiving around Rp. 150 million (US$15,806) from Heru Kusbandono, a ACC judge from Pontianak, West Kalimantan, who was acting as a 'case broker' for a matter the Semarang ACC was deciding and delivered the money to Kartini. The media named Sri Dartuti as the person who gave Heru the bribe to pay to Kartini. Sri Dartuti is the younger sister of the former speaker of the Grobogan Regional House of Representatives, Muhammad Yaeni. The KPK revealed to the press that it suspected that the payoff was intended to ensure the acquittal of Yaeni in a corruption case concerning the misuse of funds for maintenance of the Grobogan parliament's official cars in 2006–8, a case involving around Rp. 1.9 billion (Tempo 2012). Other judges on the panel hearing the case

---

[19] According to some media reports, the Surabaya court has only twice handed down prison sentences exceeding five years (Surya Online 2012). Most sentences have been only one or two years (Ambarita 2012).

were also reported to have received bribes. In fact, *Tempo magazine* reported that one judge, Pragsono, in a meeting with the Supreme Court Chief Justice about the case, acknowledged being the first judge to meet with Heru in an effort to 'fix' the Yaeni case. Pragsono even admitted to protesting that the bribe was only Rp. 100 million and pushing Heru to increase it to 150 million (Tempo 2012). According to *The Jakarta Post*, Kartini had also acquitted four corruption defendants in other cases (*The Jakarta Post* 2012). As a result of these allegations of judicial impropriety, the KPK itself has asked the Semarang ACC to hand over particular cases to the Jakarta ACC for trial.

Critics of the regional ACCs appear to presume that these acquittals are, at least for the most part, indications of judicial impropriety and, to add weight to this claim, they point to the Semarang ACC judge bribery investigation. They also refer to research conducted by ICW which found that eighty-four career judges in fourteen ACCs had 'problematic' integrity, quality and administrative skills (*Hukumonline* 2012d). This assessment was based on the failure of most of these judges to comply with mandatory asset reporting requirements and on some of them having been reported to the Judicial Commission and Supreme Court for breach of the Judicial Ethics Code, including by continuing to work as lawyers and meeting with lawyers outside of court. In short, critics appear to assume that the acquittals in corruption cases are inevitably the result of a bribe paid by the defendant to one or more judges presiding over his or her case.

Some legal commentators, including former Constitutional Court Chief Justice Mahfud, criticised the ACCs, implying that they were making the problem worse, and called for them to be disbanded. And the then KPK Chairperson Abraham Samad said, 'I appreciate our many [anti-corruption court] judges who are good, but I cannot close my eyes to the many of our career judges who are bad' (Antara 2012). Another fear initially raised was that there was a shortage of non-career judges and that this would mean that ad hoc judges might no longer make up a majority on ACC panels. Of course, this would be a major backward step given that excluding career judges from important corruption cases was the main rationale for establishing the ACC in the first place.

While the corruption scandals involving ACC judges have significantly undermined the credibility of the ACCs and many of the decisions they issue, the precise extent of corruption within the ACCs is unclear, as it is for other Indonesian courts. It is quite possible that there has been some over-hysteria about this; it is by no means clear that the integrity of ACCs is any worse than other Indonesian courts. The KPK has ensnared judges working in other courts, too. And most of these non-career judges were caught within a couple of years of the regional ACCs being established. Generally speaking, fewer corruption court judges have been arrested in more recent years.

Externally, the ACCs have been affected by recruitment problems, which have resulted in a shortage of non-career judges to serve on ACCs, leading some commentators to express fears that career judges might be forced to constitute the majority on ACC panels. Indeed, the ACC Law seems to permit a majority of career judges to sit on ACC trials. The chairperson of the district court housing the ACC is also the chairperson of that ACC (Article 9(2)). For each case, he or she determines whether the ACC panel will have three or five judges and the ratio of non-career to career judges on that panel. There must be either one or two non-career judges on three-judge panels and two or three on five-judge panels.

Some commentators have also expressed concerns about a lack of good-quality non-career judges. Of course, the ACCs can do little about this, given that non-career judge recruitment is primarily the responsibility of the Supreme Court. The Supreme Court has encountered significant difficulties in recruiting sufficiently qualified non-career judges to sit on regional ACCs ever since regionalisation (*Hukumonline* 2016a). There are several apparent reasons for this, including that the pool of qualified applicants appears to be small, especially in Indonesia's outer provinces, and that the budget allocation for recruitment has been too low (Detik News 2011b). NGOs such as ICW have argued that many of those recruited have highly dubious backgrounds, including because of their party affiliations, insufficient legal experience and questionable legal qualifications, and in some years have even complained that no credible candidates have been appointed (ICW 2015).

As for panel representation, the fears about non-career judges being outnumbered by career judges on most corruption court panels do not appear to have transpired. As part of my recent research, 1,050 corruption cases hosted on the Supreme Court's website were examined. Only around 5 per cent did not have non-career judges as a majority. A handful of cases had panels comprising only non-career judges. The acquittal rate of the ACCs has been about 10 per cent. As for concerns about the quality of decision-making, it is very difficult to determine whether ACC decisions are any better or worse than those produced by general courts – no comparative analyses have been produced.

There is almost no data upon which to assess the performance of these new ACC courts, much less any established measures to assess that performance in the Indonesian context. However, there are clearly much better indicators of judicial performance than conviction rates and sentences. Relying on conviction rates presumes that defendants are guilty if brought to trial, and that if they are acquitted then judicial impropriety was the cause. This presumption is, however, deeply flawed, for two main reasons. First, prosecutors may have put forward a weak case. Under Indonesian law, as elsewhere, defendants are presumed innocent until proven guilty. Though judges have scope to independently call witnesses, the prosecution is primarily responsible for proving the defendant's guilt 'convincingly and legally' (*secara sah dan menyakin-kan*) – Indonesia's equivalent to 'beyond reasonable doubt'. If the prosecution fails to do so, then the defendant must be acquitted. The Supreme Court has made comments to a similar effect in defence of its acquittals in corruption cases:

> It needs to be understood that not all cases brought before the Courts have enough evidence. In these cases, no one can force a judge to convict the defendant for any reason.[20]

Second, evidence of guilt adduced at trial might not withstand in-court examination. A primary objective of trials in Indonesia, as elsewhere, is to scrutinise relevant physical evidence and witness testimony pointing towards guilt or innocence. At trial, the defence might successfully challenge the evidence upon which the prosecution's case is based. For example, the credibility of a key prosecution witness might deteriorate under cross-examination.

Furthermore, corruption is, generally speaking, more difficult to pursue than many other types of crimes – it is a 'secret crime, [usually] carried out by powerful and often sophisticated perpetrators intent on silencing potential witnesses ... ' (Wagner and Jacobs 2008: 183, 18; Pearson 2001: 39). Evidence is, therefore, often difficult to obtain. Low conviction rates in corruption cases are commonplace in most countries – even developed states (ADB 2006). It may be, then, that a 10 per cent acquittal rate is low, especially given that general prosecutors now bring the vast majority of cases before these courts. Much research remains to be done, but all in all, the performance of the ACCs might not be as bad as initially expected.

---

[20] Hukumonline, 'MA Tantang ICW Uji Data Vonis Kasus Korupsi'.

Conclusion: The ACCs and the Pervasiveness
of Judicial Culture

Indonesia's ACCs find themselves in a difficult position, almost a decade after their expansion. On the one hand, it seems clear that the public expects them to continue convicting, as does the KPK, which is perhaps the most publicly popular government institution in Indonesia today, given the progress it is making, at least in high-profile cases. However, this public pressure appears to significantly influence the ACCs' decision-making – that is, to push them to convict. This pressure is reinforced by the media criticism the ACCs face when they acquit defendants in corruption cases. However, to the extent that the ACCs succumb to pressure to convict as a matter of course, even when the circumstances of the case (such as weak evidence or a flawed indictment) point towards an acquittal, they cannot be said to be performing a 'judicial' function. That is, they are not objectively applying the law to the facts presented before them. Yet, without public support, the very existence of the ACCs is by no means certain: politicians would likely seek to abolish them or discredit them, because many politicians quite rightly anticipate that they might appear as defendants in them. The same thing that allows them to continue in existence also raises questions about their contribution to the rule of law.

Comparisons between the performance of ordinary law enforcers (that is, police and prosecutors) and the KPK on the one hand, and the general courts and the ACCs on the other, raise an important question: is it possible to insulate a single judicial institution from negative aspects of judicial culture prevalent in other courts? More specifically, has the ACC experiment – to keep important corruption cases from the general courts – worked? Unfortunately, there is presently insufficient data to definitively answer this question, much less any agreed-upon criteria upon which to judge success. If the higher conviction rate, and generally higher sentences (at least compared with the general courts), indicate a higher level of professionalism, then this might indicate that the experiment has been successful. But the continuing potential for career judge majorities on ACC panels and corruption scandals involving ACC judges themselves has led some commentators to speculate that the corrupt practices of career judges have in fact already infected some ACC non-career judges, taking Indonesia's anti-corruption drive 'back to square one', where corruption cases are, in essence, decided by judges willing to acquit for a bribe.

While it appears that the vast majority of trials take place with a majority of non-career judges on the panels, there is, of course, no guarantee that these judges are immune from the general judicial culture of corruption, thought to be prevalent among their career brethren. That several non-career judges have been convicted of accepting bribes confirms this, though it is important to note that this is not exceptional within Indonesia's judiciary.

It also bears noting that, from an institutional perspective, the establishment of the KPK and ACCs has never taken *all* aspects of corruption cases to the courts, even in cases the KPK initiated or took over from ordinary police. The initially intended insulation has not, therefore, been complete. This is because suspects have always been able to challenge the validity of their arrest or detention using the so-called pretrial hearing (*praperadilan*) process outlined in Articles 77–83 of the Code of Criminal Procedure. This has been loosely compared to the principle of *habeas corpus* in common law countries but is much narrower and more restricted. Importantly, a single judge hears the challenge in the general courts.[21] Because pretrial hearings are decided by a single judge and determinations cannot be appealed, standards of decision-making are generally low, with outcomes notorious for lack of uniformity and predictability (Fitzpatrick 2008: 506). However, there is no right of appeal from a pretrial determination to a high court or the Supreme Court. If the *praperadilan* judge finds the arrest or detention to be unlawful, then the accused is released (Article 82(3)(a)).[22]

Before 2015, the *praperadilan* process was not particularly contentious. If a defendant won at the pretrial stage, police or prosecutors could continue to pursue that suspect by recommencing their investigations or prosecutions. If, for example, a suspect was released after being illegally arrested without a warrant, police could simply obtain a warrant and re-arrest that suspect. However, this changed in early 2015 when police chief candidate Budi Gunawan, who faced KPK prosecution for corruption, challenged the legality of his being named a suspect by the KPK in *praperadilan* proceedings. This was controversial, because 'being named a suspect' is not a ground upon which *praperadilan* proceedings can be brought under the Code of

---

[21] A decision must be reached within ten days of the application being made (Articles 78 and 82(1)).

[22] A suspect or accused person can receive compensation for unlawful detention (Article 95). See also Articles 77(b) and 81. If an issue relating to arrest or detention is not raised in a pretrial hearing, courts usually refuse to allow it to be raised at trial.

Criminal Procedure. This decision was widely condemned as an illegitimate expansion of judicial power and as indicating judicial impropriety, though this was never proved. A few months later, the Constitutional Court expanded the matters that can be challenged in pretrial motions, to allow applicants to challenge the legality of being formally named a suspect by law enforcement officials.[23] While instinctively this appears to be a sound decision, it has been subsequently used by alleged corruptors to challenge their being named a suspect, successfully in some cases (*The Jakarta Post*, 12 May 2015).

This has had critical implications for the handling of corruption cases in Indonesia. In particular, it allows suspects to defend themselves before the general courts in the face of KPK investigation. Issues that may have been considered at trial by an ACC can now be judged by a single career judge. These include whether there was sufficient evidence upon which to proceed against the subject. Under Indonesian criminal law, a suspect cannot be arrested, or a defendant convicted, unless two pieces of legal evidence are produced (Butt 2008). Though the precise processes are yet to be confirmed, it appears that a general criminal court can now assess the strength of the evidence police claim to have against criminal suspects – including KPK commissioners – as a basis for charging them. Presumably, the court can order that charges be dropped if based on insufficient evidence.

Another issue that has been considered in *praperadilan* hearings is whether the KPK had jurisdiction to pursue the particular case. So, for example, in one *praperadilan* case, a judge decided that the KPK's investigations into the suspect were invalid because they were not conducted by seconded police but rather the KPK's internal staff (Assegaf 2015). Similar jurisdictional issues were successfully raised in the Budi Gunawan case itself. As Assegaf explains:

> the court invalidated the KPK investigation on the grounds that Budi's alleged offence was not within the jurisdiction of the KPK. The KPK had accused Budi of accepting bribes paid by other police officers to secure higher and more prestigious postings. The court ruled that this type of corruption allegation could only be investigated by police or prosecutors. The KPK was then forced to hand the investigation over to the Attorney General's Office, which, in turn, handed it over to the police. They, unsurprisingly, dropped the case against one of their most senior and powerful officers. (Assegaf 2015)

---

[23] Constitutional Court Decision No. 21/PUU-XII/2014.

Assegaf argues:

> The legal questions raised in this case are serious, and go to the core of the KPK's operations. Such questions require extensive discussion, with an opportunity for review by a higher court through an appeals process. A single court session that cannot be appealed is not enough. (Assegaf 2015)

In other words, very important matters of jurisdiction and evidence are now able to be decided by a single general court judge, who, apart from being a career judge and hence perceived to be more susceptible to bribery, is arguably easier to bribe than a panel of three judges. Despite the best efforts of reformers in the immediate post-Soeharto period, corruption – perhaps the centrepiece of judicial culture in Indonesia – remains a significant threat to judicial impartiality, the anti-corruption movement and, ultimately, the rule of law in Indonesia. In this regard, Dan S. Lev's scepticism of quick-fix reforms of the judiciary remains relevant today.

8

The Commercial Courts

A Story of Unfinished Reforms

GUSTAAF REERINK, KEVIN OMAR SIDHARTA, ARIA
SUYUDI AND SOPHIE HEWITT

The Commercial Courts are specialized courts that were established in April 1998 as part of the legal reform program initiated by the International Monetary Fund (IMF). The reforms were conditional upon an IMF loan to bail the country out of a major financial crisis. The aim was to do away with the old culture of unprofessionalism and corruption pervasive in the courts by creating new courts with new judges applying a new system for bankruptcy administration. The Commercial Courts were also envisaged to act as "a wedge into the judiciary": by acting as model courts, it was hoped the Commercial Courts would influence the rest of the court system.[1]

Early assessments of the court were highly critical (Lindsey 1998: 119–21). In 2004, a project evaluation commissioned by the IMF concluded that the results of the reforms were "mixed" (IMF 2005: iv). These evaluations arguably came too early, only five years after the start of the reform program, or in the case of Lindsey even just a few months, to draw any final conclusions on the establishment or operation of the court.[2] Twenty years later, there have been further reforms to the Commercial Courts and broader reforms to the judicial system, not as part of conditional funding from international financial institutions, but as voluntary actions with policy formulation and decision-making by the government.

---

[1] Quote from Professor Mardjono Reksodiputro; interview with resident advisor to IMF Technical Assistance Team, August 21, 2018.

[2] This was also acknowledged by the IMF's evaluation team (IMF Report 2005: xii). The institution's programmatic approach inherently required an evaluation at a relatively short period after the program's implementation.

In light of these reforms, this chapter offers a fresh consideration of the performance of the Commercial Courts, with a focus on bankruptcy cases.[3] It first discusses bankruptcy reforms and the introduction of the Commercial Courts and the practical experiences with the courts between 1998 and 2004. The chapter then addresses further reforms after 2004 and evaluates more recent experiences with the Commercial Courts. Finally, it analyzes factors that explain the Commercial Courts' performance in bankruptcy cases, especially by the Commercial Court at the Central Jakarta District Court. This evaluation leads to the conclusion that the reforms initiated by the establishment of the Commercial Courts were substantial and aimed at contributing to an effective bankruptcy regime and encouraging investor confidence, although they remain largely unfinished.

Bankruptcy Reforms and Introduction of the Commercial Courts

In the mid-1990s, proposals for reforms to the bankruptcy law, administration, and courts emerged (see Bedner and Wiratraman, this volume). Calls for judicial reforms were translated into action after August 1997, when the Asian monetary crisis reached Indonesia. The Rupiah plunged from IDR 2,500 to IDR 17,000 per US$1, resulting in an estimated 65–75 percent of all loans in Indonesia becoming nonperforming loans (Halliday & Carruthers 2009: 253). This forced the government to invite the IMF to help stabilize its currency. As a condition to further IMF funding, the government agreed to reform the country's bankruptcy law. The objective was to create speedy, efficient, and transparent restructuring and bankruptcy proceedings. It was agreed to make amendments to the existing, Dutch-based system, and introduce Commercial Courts. These immediate reforms were conducted under the supervision of the IMF, while the World Bank focused on medium-term policy, later taking over from the IMF, and introducing an out-of-court restructuring mechanism, known as the Jakarta Initiative (Halliday & Carruthers 2009: 175–80).

On April 22, 1998, just a few months after an agreement had been reached with the IMF about the need for bankruptcy reform, the

---

[3] The Commercial Courts also have jurisdiction in the field of intellectual property and the liquidation of banks by the Indonesia Deposit Insurance Corporation (*Lembaga Penjamin Simpanan*). For an evaluation of the Commercial Courts' performance in intellectual property cases, please refer to Linnan 2010.

government passed Government Regulation in lieu of Law No. 1/1998.[4] The Parliament finally ratified it to become Law No. 4/1998 and President Habibie signed it on September 9, 1998,[5] followed by implementing legislation. Law No. 4/1998 provided for the introduction of specialized Commercial Courts, which would have exclusive jurisdiction in bankruptcy matters (Art. 280(1)). The Commercial Courts could handle other cases in the field of commerce subject to issuance of a Government Regulation (Art. 280(2)). Indeed, the intention was to realize broader judiciary reforms, and bankruptcy reforms would only be the start. As one advisor noted, the establishment of the commercial courts on the basis of an "emergency" government regulation was like entering the house of the judiciary through the window instead of the front door.[6]

The first Commercial Court, consisting of seventeen judges, was established within the District Court of Central Jakarta and opened its doors in August 1998 (Churchill 2000: 177). A year later, Commercial Courts were established in four other major centers of trade – Makassar, Medan, Surabaya, and Semarang. Until that time, the Commercial Court within the District Court of Central Jakarta had jurisdiction over all Indonesian territory.

Law No. 4/1998 contained several articles that pointed to a new approach in court procedures relating to bankruptcy. It would now be possible to appoint by Presidential Decree and at the proposal of the Chief Justice of the Supreme Court certain legal experts to become ad hoc judges (Art. 283(3)).[7] Furthermore, judges could give dissenting opinions.[8] Procedures for the administration of cases would now have

---

[4] Government Regulation in lieu of Law No. 1/1998 on the Amendment of the Bankruptcy Law.

[5] Law No. 4 of 1998 concerning ratification of Government Regulation in lieu of Law No. 1 of 1998.

[6] Quote from Professor Mardjono Reksodiputro as conveyed to one of the authors.

[7] Each panel of three judges would have only one ad hoc judge, which means that career judges would always form the majority. Only one ad hoc judge actually served in bankruptcy cases (IMF 2004:11).

[8] The possibility for ad hoc judges to issue dissenting opinions found its basis in Article 9 Regulation of the Supreme Court No. 2/2000. Note that the concept of dissenting opinions was not foreign to the Indonesian judiciary. Prior to 2000, it was already common for judges to give dissenting opinions, but these were never published. They were filed internally and could be used for evaluation of performance and promotion (interview with resident advisor to IMF Technical Assistance Team, August 21, 2018). Judges made little use of the possibility to issue dissenting opinions. According to the IMF, out of 300 bankruptcy issues that were issued between 1998 and 2004, there were only five dissenting opinions, which consisted of four by Commercial Court judges and one by a Supreme Court judge. Notably, all four dissenting opinions were upheld in cassation (IMF 2004:12).

time limits.[9] Finally, underlying legal reasoning of decisions would be made explicit, and decisions would be published (Elucidation Art. 284 (1)c). These measures were meant to protect the Commercial Courts from the pervasive problem of corruption that existed within the judiciary (IMF 2005: vii).

The reform program did not only involve amendments to bankruptcy law and the establishment of Commercial Courts, but also training programs for candidate judges, receivers, and administrators, registrars, and bailiffs. In August 1998, participants who successfully completed the course established the new Indonesian Association of Receivers and Administrators (*Asosiasi Kurator dan Pengurus Indonesia* or AKPI). Membership of the AKPI would be a requisite for appointment as a receiver or administrator. The training efforts were supported by the publication of a textbook on the new bankruptcy law, compilations of decisions of the Commercial Courts and Supreme Court, and the launching of a debt settlement journal and a website with relevant resources, including legislation and full text court decisions (Churchill 2000: 179/181).

Operation of the Commercial Courts: The First Five Years

The first five years of operation produced mixed results. Procedurally, the decisions of the Commercial Courts met the new requirements set by Law No. 4/1998. According to Schröeder-van Waes and Sidharta, 99 percent of the decisions were issued within the prescribed thirty days' period. Furthermore, legal reasoning was made explicit in the decisions, and all the decisions were published (2004: 194–5). Observers were less positive about the substance of the Commercial Court's decisions in bankruptcy cases. The Commercial Court in Jakarta issued its first decisions in late September 1998 and concerns began to emerge as early as December (Churchill 2000: 179–80). Early cases that raised concern were the Dharmala case (1998) and the Ometraco case (1998), in which local debtors were, at least initially, successful in preventing being bankrupted by foreign creditors.[10] In the Dharmala case, the petitioning ING Bank applied for bankruptcy of customer PT Dharmala Agrifood Tbk, which had defaulted on a credit agreement by failing to repay the loan by

---

[9] Article 4(3–6), 6(2) and (4), 8(2), 9(2–4), 10(1–3) and (5) Law No. 4/1998.
[10] Commercial Court of Central Jakarta Decision 16/Pailit/1998/PN. Niaga/Jkt, PT ING Indonesia Bank et al. v. PT Dharmala Agrifood Tbk.

the due date. The Commercial Court rejected the request, arguing that the agreement itself had not yet expired. In the Ometraco case (1998), the Commercial Court dismissed a bankruptcy petition against a parent company because the creditors had already filed a bankruptcy petition against its subsidiary, which together with the parent company, the court argued, were one and the same economic entity (Tahyar 2012: 211–13).[11]

In other cases, such as the Davomas case (2000)[12] (Goodpaster 2000) and the POFI case (2001),[13] local debtors allegedly used fictitious creditors to prevent being bankrupted and to force the real creditors to accept the restructuring terms being offered in the composition plan (which usually were not commercially favorable) (Hukumonline 2000a, 2001, 2004). Two other cases that raised international attention were the Manulife case (2002) and the Prudential case (2004), which were actually commercial disputes turned into bankruptcy cases by local parties that wanted to put pressure on their foreign counterpart (Tahyar 2012: 211–13).[14] The decisions of the Commercial Court in both the Manulife case and Prudential case were later overturned by the Supreme Court.[15]

Based on these early experiences, major creditors such as the IFC soon stopped filing bankruptcy requests to the Commercial Courts (Halliday & Carruthers 2009: 186). There was a general perception, particularly among foreign observers, that the Commercial Courts tended to decide against the interests of foreign creditors, benefitting local debtors. This perception was not entirely true: between 1998 and 2002, slightly more than half of the 315 cases were decided in favor of creditors (Suyudi 2004: 3). Statistical analysis also found that both at the level of the Commercial Courts and the Supreme Court, there was no correlation between the nationality of creditors (i.e. foreign or Indonesian) and the outcome of

---

[11] Commercial Court of Central Jakarta Decision 05/Pailit/1998/PN.Niaga.Jkt.Pst, American Express Bank Ltd et al. v. PT Omertreco Corp. Tbk.

[12] Commercial Court of Central Jakarta Decision 02/PKPU/2000: PT. Davomas Abadi Tbk (voluntary suspension of payments).

[13] Commercial Court of Central Jakarta Decision 16/PKPU/2000/PN.JKT.PST jo. 65/Pailit/2000/PN.JKT.PST International Finance Corporation vs. PT. Panca Overseas Finance Tbk.

[14] Commercial Court of Central Jakarta Decision 10/Pailit/2002/PN.Niaga/Jkt.Pst, Paul Sukran (receiver of PT Dharmala Sakti Sejahtera Tbk. (in bankruptcy)) v. PT AJ Manulife Indonesia; Commercial Court of Central Jakarta Decision 13/Pailit/2004/PN. Niaga.Jkt.Pst, Tuan Lee Boon Siong vs. PT. Prudential Life Assurance.

[15] Commercial Court of Central Jakarta Decision 10/Pailit/2002/PN.Niaga/Jkt.Pst jo. Supreme Court Decision 021 K/N/2002; Commercial Court of Central Jakarta Decision 13/Pailit/2004/PN.Niaga.Jkt.Pst, jo. Supreme Court Decision 8 K/N/2004.

bankruptcy cases (Suyudi 2004: 10–11). However, there was a negative correlation between the value of debt (i.e. more than USD 1 million) and courts' rejection to award a request for bankruptcy (Suyudi 2004: 14). A similar negative correlation could be identified between the involvement of a lawyer in cases and courts' rejection to award a request for bankruptcy, raising questions regarding integrity (Suyudi 2004: 21). Suyudi concluded that decision-making by the Commercial Courts was relatively consistent, with more than 70 percent of the cases having a predictable outcome (Suyudi 2004: 14). Around two-thirds of the decisions could be legally justified (IMF 2005: 15). Schröeder-van Waes & Sidharta concluded that 73 percent of all Commercial Court decisions and 64 percent of all Supreme Court decisions ranged from A ("in accordance with the law") to C ("justifiable"), while 27 percent of the Commercial Court decisions and 36 percent of the Supreme Court decisions were against the law (D and E). They also saw indications that judges were generally willing to apply the law and were consistent in their reasoning when addressing various questions of law (Schröeder-van Waes & Sidharta 2004: 195–8).

In the first two years, there were interpretation issues as both the judges and the litigants were unfamiliar with Law No. 4/1998, resulting in incorrect applications of the law (Suyudi 2004: 15–7). The Supreme Court, which handled bankruptcy cases in cassation, appeared to do better. In fact, all decisions by Commercial Courts identified as problematic that were appealed, were overruled by the Supreme Court (Suyudi 2004: 20). This is a remarkable finding, as the Supreme Court has no specialized chamber to handle bankruptcy cases.

On the appointment of receivers, Law No. 4/1998 provided that debtors or creditors submitting a request for bankruptcy had the right to nominate a receiver for court appointment (Art. 13(2)). However, the Commercial Courts would often reject creditors' nominees and instead appoint other receivers without clear reason. This increased suspicion that judges, receivers and debtors, and their lawyers worked together to achieve a debtor-friendly outcome, in return for kickbacks for the judges (Halliday & Carruthers 2009: 194–5).

Larger firms pulled out of receivership practice because it was not profitable. The Ministry of Justice issued a decree providing that receivers' fees would be calculated as a percentage of the estate.[16] However, in deviation from the decree, the courts calculated receivers' fees on the

---

[16] Decree of the Minister of Justice No. M.09-HT.05.10.Tahun 1998.

basis of hourly rates. Most receivers and administrators were working for small litigation firms and were familiar with the "wheeling and dealing" in the courts. It soon became commonplace for judges to ask for contributions before they would appoint receivers, to be paid at the end of their appointment through deduction of receivers' fees (*uang terima kasih*) (Halliday & Carruthers 2009: 195–6).

There were rumors that corruption within the Commercial Courts was pervasive. It was easy for lawyers to influence judges, due to their low salaries (Halliday & Carruthers 2009: 200). The fact that many of these lawyers represented local debtors against foreign creditors and local jobs were at stake when ruling against these local debtors perhaps made it easier for judges to accept money (Halliday & Carruthers 2009: 202–3).

The alleged corruption in the Commercial Courts raised questions on the professionalism of judges, but perhaps even more so of bankruptcy lawyers. They were criticized for their alleged lack of integrity, but also for their organizational structure and lack of knowledge and skills. It was sometimes questionable who the bankruptcy lawyers involved in the case represented, the debtors, creditors, or the receiver, or all. Lawyers typically worked for multiple law firms, making it impossible to trace them or to perform a necessary conflict of interest test (Schröeder-van Waes & Sidharta 2004: 194). Their knowledge of bankruptcy law and lawyering skills was also limited, and considered inferior to judges (Schröeder-van Waes & Sidharta 2004: 193).

AKPI and the Indonesian bar associations, which before 2003 consisted of as many as eight different organizations, did little to improve the professional standards of their members, e.g., by organizing training sessions and imposing sanctions. In 2002, AKPI received three complaints for breach of professional ethics by two of its members, but no sanctions were imposed (Hukumonline 2002c). The complaint against one member was revoked, while the other member who was subject to the two other unrevoked complaints resigned from AKPI and together with forty-five other AKPI members, established a rival receiver's organization, in the name of the Indonesian Bond of Receivers and Administrators (*Ikatan Kurator dan Pengurus Indonesia* (IKAPI)) (Halliday & Carruthers 2009: 196; Hukumonline 2002a). These two rival receiver organizations were soon caught up in court battle, claiming public and government recognition, triggering a tort lawsuit filed by IKAPI against AKPI for allegedly organizing an unlawful board election process (Hukumonline 2002b). The Central Jakarta District Court dismissed the case due to the absence of a legal connection between AKPI and IKAPI (Hukumonline 2003).

The weak professional standards, including professional ethics, of receivers and lawyers posed a particular concern in the stage after the Commercial Courts had decided to award a bankruptcy request or a suspension of payments request, as receivers and lawyers played an important role, while the Commercial Courts' supervision role is limited. In practice the Commercial Courts' supervisory role was limited as most receivers failed to submit periodic reports to the supervisory judge (USAID 2007: 21).

The low and declining number of bankruptcy cases indicated a loss of faith in the Commercial Courts. By 2003, the Commercial Courts had handled 353 bankruptcy cases, with an upward trend in the first two years. After 1999, there was a steep downward trend from 100 cases to 38 cases in 2003.[17] Of these bankruptcy cases, a total of forty-six were converted into suspension of payments cases. These figures were nowhere near the actual number of companies that were in dire straits financially. Restructuring may have been conducted out of court or through the Jakarta Initiative, which continued until June 2003 (Suyudi 2004: 1–2).

By 2004, there was consensus that establishment of the Commercial Courts had not met its objectives. The IMF evaluation concluded that the Commercial Courts failed to contribute to an effective bankruptcy regime and proved incapable of encouraging investor confidence (IMF 2005: iv). This is because the commercial courts were never separated from the larger judicial system. Wider systematic problems prevented the Commercial Courts from functioning effectively and credibly (IMF 2005: xii). These disappointing results gave rise to the discontinuation of the project. The evaluation team recommended that future funding follow Indonesian priorities and focus on wider judiciary system improvements more generally (IMF 2005: iv).

Reforms Introduced by Law No. 37/2004

Pressure grew on the government to address misinterpretations and abuses of the law. In 2001, the IMF included a provision in its Letter of

---

[17] The Commercial Courts handled 31 cases in 1998 (August–December), 100 cases in 1999, 84 cases in 2000, 61 cases in 2001, 39 cases in 2002, and 38 cases in 2003 (Schröeder-van Waes & Sidharta 2004: 202).

Intent requiring amendments to the bankruptcy law by 2002. No action was taken until the Manulife case (2002) and the Prudential case (2004), which created a real threat to Indonesia's life insurance business. In 2004, Parliament passed revisions to address defects in the implementation of Law No. 4/1998. On October 18, 2004, Law No. 37 of 2004 on Bankruptcy and Suspension of Payments (Law 37/2004) replaced the 1906 Bankruptcy Ordinance as amended by Law No. 4/1998. Law 37/2004 introduced a complete new set of rules, entirely in the Indonesian language. This was a step towards creating effective bankruptcy procedures.

To highlight a few important changes, Law 37/2004 provides a new set of definitions for terms such as "debt", "creditor", and "debtor". A request for suspension of payments can now be submitted by not just a debtor, but also a creditor or, in the case of the entities enjoying protections, by a certain government institution (Arts. 222–3). Finally, the law creates further protections for secured creditors in approving permanent suspensions of payments (Art. 229(1b)) and composition plans (Art. 281(1b)) by requiring approval, in addition to the existing requirement of unsecured creditors' approval in the Law No. 4/1998, from more than half of the total amount of secured creditors representing at least two-thirds of the secured creditors' total claims. The secured creditors rejecting the composition plan shall be compensated by the lowest value between the secured amount and the actual claim directly secured by *in rem* rights (Art. 281 (2)).

In addition to the introduction of a new law, further reforms took place within the Commercial Courts. In 2004, the Supreme Court of Indonesia adopted the Blueprints and Action Plan for the Commercial Court and the Anticorruption Courts. From late 2006 to early 2010, USAID initiated the Indonesian Anticorruption and Commercial Court Enhancement (IN-ACCE) Project. The project aimed to support the implementation of the Blueprints and Action Plan for the Commercial Court and the Anticorruption Courts (USAID 2010: 2). The IN-ACCE project focused on improving IT facilities and training of court staff. It encouraged the courts to consider more rigorous ethical standards for judges, court staff, and lawyers; greater support for judicial reform; public service and responsiveness; transparency; accountability; increased capacities for critical thinking and problem-solving; research and analysis; and cross-training opportunities among judges, court staff, NGOs, and the legal community. After the completion of the IN-ACCE Project, the project activities became part of the broader Changes for Justice (C4 J) Project

(2010–15). The C4 J Project was implemented on the basis of the IN-ACCE Project findings that any effort to improve the Commercial or Anticorruption Courts must include institutional reforms of the district courts generally (which expanded the project to include development of a case management system for all types of civil and criminal cases) (USAID 2015: 5). Towards the end of the C4 J project, the Supreme Court lost interest in improving the Commercial Courts' performance. In 2013, at the request of the Supreme Court, funding for the Commercial Court Judges Certification (CCJC) program was redirected to a new certification program for judges hearing juvenile cases. Furthermore, the Supreme Court dropped its plans to host another CCJC program in 2014, instead focusing on training to judges handling larger volumes of cases and cases raising more serious social concerns (USAID 2015: 58).

Contemporary Performance of the Commercial Courts (2012–2017)

There has been a significant surge in the number of bankruptcy petitions from 2015 to 2017, based on data from the Commercial Courts of Central Jakarta and Surabaya, compared to the period just after the establishment of the Commercial Courts (Table 8.1, below).

The surge in suspension of payments petitions is particularly remarkable (Table 8.2, below). This development can at least in part be explained by the fact that a request for suspension of payments can now not only be submitted by a debtor, but also by a creditor.

Despite the surge in bankruptcy and suspension of payments cases, it is unlikely that this reflects the actual number of companies with payment issues. Indonesia's economy is performing well, but even in less established economies the number of bankruptcy cases is far higher. Many parties who are confronted with companies with payment issues will look for another strategy, such as imposing criminal charges, or if unsuccessful, giving up their claim.

Aside from the number of cases, it is important to consider the quality of decisions, although this is harder to evaluate. It appears that the quality of the courts' decisions in certain notable cases remains questionable. Following the introduction of Law 37/2004, certain unprecedented practices can be identified, giving rise to questions of independence and impartiality of the Commercial Courts (Hukumonline 2014b).

An important example is the Telkomsel Case (2012) (Hukumonline 2013e). PT Telekomunikasi Seluler (Telkomsel) is the largest Indonesian

Table 8.1 *Number of bankruptcy petitions in the commercial courts in the Central Jakarta and Surabaya district courts (2015–17)*

Bankruptcy	Commercial court central Jakarta			Commercial court Surabaya		
Year	2015	2016	2017	2015	2016	2017
Incoming	55	67	73	24	31	23
Decided	36	54	66	24	31	23
Withdrawn	11	12	8	3	8	4
Unable to meet requirement	-					

Data collected from the Commercial Courts in the Central Jakarta and Surabaya District Courts.

Table 8.2 *Suspension of payment petitions in the commercial courts in the Central Jakarta and Surabaya district courts (2015–17)*

Suspension of payment	Commercial court central Jakarta			Commercial court Surabaya		
Year	2015	2016	2017	2015	2016	2017
Incoming	106	145	168	14	23	37
Decided	100	119	138	14	23	37
Withdrawn	3	22	8	2	8	3
Unable to meet requirements	-	1	3			

Data collected from the Commercial Courts in the Central Jakarta and Surabaya District Courts.

telecommunication carrier and a subsidiary of a State-Owned Enterprise, PT Telkomunikasi Indonesia Tbk. In 2012, one of Telkomsel's vendors filed a bankruptcy petition against Telkomsel based on a claim of around IDR 5 billion (International Financial Law Review 2013). The Central Jakarta Commercial Court declared Telkomsel bankrupt on September 14, 2012. Telkomsel filed for cassation against the decision to the Supreme Court. The cassation process did not cease the commencement of the bankruptcy proceeding of Telkomsel. On

November 21, 2012, the Supreme Court approved Telkomsel's cassation petition and overturned the Central Jakarta Commercial Court decision revoking the bankruptcy declaration and stopping the bankruptcy process (Hukumonline 2013d). Furthermore, in April 2013, the Supreme Court sanctioned the Central Jakarta Commercial Court judges involved in the Telkomsel case, transferring them to regional courts (Hukumonline 2013c), due to unprofessional conduct (Hukumonline 2013d).

Following the revocation of the bankruptcy declaration, the Telkomsel receiver requested the Central Jakarta Commercial Court to approve the receiver's fee, calculated on the basis of Decree of the Minister of Justice No. M.09-HT.05.10.Tahun 1998 (the 1998 Regulation).[18] The Central Jakarta Commercial Court decided to approve the receiver's fee in the amount of IDR 293.6 billion on January 31, 2013, but Telkomsel refused to make any payments (Hukumonline 2013a). A few weeks earlier, on January 11, 2013, the Minister of Law and Human Rights, who had been warned by one of the presidential agencies supervising the Telkomsel case, rushed to issue Regulation No. 1 of 2013 (the 2013 Regulation), replacing the 1998 Regulation.[19] The 2013 Regulation provides that in case a bankruptcy declaration is revoked following cassation or case review the bankruptcy petitioner alone shall be liable to pay the receiver's fee, rather than the debtor as stipulated under the 1998 Regulation. Telkomsel subsequently filed a case review to the Supreme Court against the decision of the Commercial Court regarding the Telkomsel receiver's fee, arguing that instead of the 1998 Regulation, the 2013 Regulation should be applied in determining the Telkomsel receiver's fee, given the Telkomsel bankruptcy process was not yet completed by the time the 2013 Regulation was issued. On August 16, 2013, the Supreme Court revoked the order of the Commercial Court (Hukumonline 2013h),[20] although in a previous case, the Supreme Court had declared that no legal remedy can be filed against a court order on the receiver's fee.[21] In September 2013, the Telkomsel receiver filed another case review petition against this decision (Hukumonline 2013i), but to no avail.

---

[18] Decree of the Minister of Justice No. M.09-HT.05.10.Tahun 1998 on the Guidance of the Receiver/Administrator Service Remuneration.

[19] Regulation of the Minister of Law and Human Rights No. 1 of 2013 re Guidelines for the Honorarium of Receivers and Administrators.

[20] Decision Supreme Court No. 48 PK/Pdt.Sus-Pailit/2013.

[21] Article 91 Law No. 37/2004 and its elucidation; Hukumonline 2011c.

In June 2013, the Telkomsel receiver (Hukumonline 2013f) and nine receiver professionals filed two separate judicial review petitions to the Supreme Court against the 2013 Regulation (Hukumonline 2013g). The Supreme Court approved one of the judicial review petitions and invalidated the 2013 Regulation as it contradicted Article 17(3) of Law 37/2004 (Hukumonline 2014a). On October 9, 2014, following the judicial review decision, the Minister of Law and Human Rights issued Regulation No. 23 of 2014 (the 2014 Regulation) amending the 2013 Regulation to be in line with Law 37/2004. On January 22, 2014, the Telkomsel receiver filed a tort lawsuit against Telkomsel, Telkomsel's lawyers and the Minister for Law and Human Rights. On May 5, 2014, the South Jakarta District Court dismissed the lawsuit and declared that it is not authorized to examine the case, for the reason that lawyers were protected under the advocate immunity doctrine (Hukumonline 2014f).

Other unprecedented practices relate to suspension of payment filings by creditors, an option introduced by Law 37/2004 that led to a significant increase of the number of suspension of payments filings. This option has been used by many local banks—either state, local, or foreign owned—to force their debtors to restructure under the suspension of payments process. If debtors cannot provide a favorable composition plan acceptable to all creditors during the suspension of payments process, they will be declared bankrupt and dissolved. However, this same new feature has also been (ab)used by the publicly listed companies, through suspension of payments petition filing by friendly creditors, to force creditors to restructure their claims through the suspension of payments process. This new feature has overcome the obstacle encountered by the publicly listed companies desiring to file voluntary suspension of payments petition as they would be required to obtain prior approval from their shareholders (including their public shareholders), which in practice may be very cumbersome, costly and time consuming.

One noteworthy case in which a creditor filed for suspension of payment is the Bakrieland case (2013).[22] In this case, the trustee of notes issued by BLD Investments Pte. Ltd. and guaranteed by PT Bakrieland Debelopment Tbk (Bakrieland) filed a suspension of payments petition against Bakrieland on grounds that, *inter alia*, Bakrieland had failed to comply with its obligation to repay the outstanding amount of the notes when noteholders exercised their put

---

[22] Commercial Court of Central Jakarta Decision 53/Pdt.Sus-PKPU/2013/PN Niaga. Jkt.Pst.

option under the terms of the notes. The Central Jakarta Commercial Court dismissed the suspension of payments petition, *inter alia*, for the reason that as the trust deed relating to the notes was governed by English law, all disputes arising out of or in connection with the trust deed had to be settled by English courts and therefore the Central Jakarta Commercial Court did not have jurisdiction. The Supreme Court in cassation confirmed the Commercial Court's decision.[23]

In all cases under Law No. 4/1998 allegedly involving fictitious creditors, most if not all of the fictitious creditors held unsecured claims.[24] Due to the new obligation under Law 37/2004 to involve secured creditors, in addition to unsecured creditors, in voting to approve the composition plan in the suspension of payments process, the creation of fictitious creditors holding unsecured claims alone may no longer be sufficient to achieve the expected goal, especially in the suspension of payments process. A creditor will be deemed as a secured creditor if it holds *in rem* security which, with the exception of the pledge on shares, requires valid registration of such *in rem* security with the relevant public registry maintained by the government bodies, e.g., the national land office for a land mortgage, *fiducia* registration office for *fiducia* security, directorate general of sea communications for a hypothec over a vessel. Therefore, any effort to create fictitious creditors holding a secured claim would involve backdating the security registration, which is clearly much more difficult and cumbersome, if not impossible.

Given these constraints, rather than using fictitious creditors, a more sophisticated technique has allegedly been developed. It is suspected to involve the use of an "intercompany creditor" to control the suspension of payments process and sideline real third-party creditors, as can be seen in Bakrie Telecom case (2014) and Trikomsel case (2015).

In the Bakrie Telecom case (2014),[25] Bakrie Telecom Pte. Ltd issued notes which were guaranteed by PT Bakrie Telecom Tbk (BTEL). The proceeds from the offering of the notes were disbursed to BTEL pursuant to a certain intercompany loan agreement. The Central Jakarta Commercial Court granted the suspension of payments petition against BTEL filed by one of BTEL's creditors. During the BTEL suspension of payments process, BTEL's administrator rejected the claims submitted by

---

[23] Decision Supreme Court No. 555 K/Pdt.Sus-Pailit/2013.

[24] This practice was noted by parliament during the deliberation of Law No. 37/2004. See: DPR 2004d, p. 8.

[25] Commercial Court of Central Jakarta Decision 59/Pdt.Sus-PKPU/2014/PN. NiagaJkt.Pst.

the trustee and the noteholders on the ground that such claims were not stated in BTEL's records and reports, therefore not satisfying Article 271 of Law 37/2004. BTEL's supervisory judge further determined that the trustee and the noteholders were not able to participate in the voting of BTEL's composition plan in the BTEL suspension of payments process. By contrast, Bakrie Telecom Pte Ltd, which is a subsidiary of BTEL, was accepted as BTEL's creditor holding the claims with the notes total amount and voted in favor of the composition plan that BTEL offered, which content was not commercially favorable to the trustee and the noteholders (Danubrata 2015; Detik 2015). The Central Jakarta Commercial Court ratified BTEL's approved composition plan. The Supreme Court confirmed the decision in response to a case review petition filed by the Minister of Communications and Information Technology.[26]

In the Trikomsel case (2015),[27] almost the same structure was used as in the Bakrie Telecom case: Trikomsel Pte. Ltd. had issued notes, which were guaranteed by PT Trikomsel Oke Tbk (Trikomsel), its parent company. The Central Jakarta Commercial Court granted the suspension of payments petition against Trikomsel filed by one of Trikomsel's creditors. During the Trikomsel suspension of payments process, the Trikomsel administrator decided to accept a huge secured claim submitted by a Trikomsel affiliate (Boey 2016). At the same time, the administrator rejected the claims submitted by the trustees on the ground that no documents had been submitted in the claim submission process that explicitly confirmed the authority of the trustees in representing the noteholders in the Trikomsel suspension of payments process. Nevertheless, Trikomsel administrator accepted the claims being submitted by the individual noteholders and a controversial affiliate of Trikomsel, which despite objections from other creditors was allowed by the Supervisory Judge to participate and vote in the Trikomsel suspension of payments process. Trikomsel's affiliate later pulled out from the Trikomsel suspension of payments process for unclear reasons and cancelled its participation in the voting process. Trikomsel's composition plan was ultimately approved by its creditors in the voting and was legalized by the Central Jakarta Commercial Court.

---

[26] Decision Supreme Court No. 83 PK/Pdt.Sus-Pailit/2015.
[27] Commercial Court of Central Jakarta Decision 98/Pdt.Sus-PKPU/2015/PN.Niaga. Jkt.Pst.

The Bakrieland case, Bakrie Telecom case and Trikomsel cases have again raised major concerns among foreign investors, especially those involved in transactions involving the issuance of international bonds/notes/securities by Indonesian debtors. These cases are now commonly flagged as some sort of an "enforcement risk" in the risk factor section of offering memoranda of subsequent transactions of foreign securities issuance by or involving Indonesian company using a similar structure.[28]

A final suspension of payments case that illustrates the questionable quality of decisions in bankruptcy cases is the AKT case (2016). This case goes beyond the Commercial Courts' jurisdiction and the outcome remains pending. PT Asmin Koalindo Tuhup (AKT), the holder of coal contract of work (CCoW), filed and was granted a voluntary suspension of payments petition by the Central Jakarta Commercial Court. During the AKT suspension of payments process, AKT administrators and the Supervisory Judge denied the admission of a claim under a corporate payment guarantee submitted by an international bank, securing the obligation of PT Borneo Lumbung Energi & Metal Tbk, AKT's parent company, on the ground that AKT, the issuer of the guarantee, was not in possession of an approval from the Minister of Energy and Mineral Resources for the amendment of its investment and financing sources registration. The AKT administrators held that the enforcement of the AKT corporate guarantee constituted such an amendment. As a consequence, the claim under that guarantee was not included in the creditors' voting process over the composition plan proposed by AKT. However, the AKT composition plan did not deny the validity or the enforceability of the AKT corporate guarantee as a contractual obligation. It expressly stated that the loan facility provided by the international bank to PT Borneo Lumbung Energy & Metal Tbk (AKT's parent company), which was secured by a security package that included the AKT corporate guarantee, as well as the AKT corporate guarantee itself (which constitute the finance documents underlying the claims of the international bank on AKT), continued to be valid.

---

[28] See, for instance, Offering Memorandum of USD 550 million 4.95 percent Senior Notes due 2026 dated September 7, 2016, issued by Listrindo Capital BV, unconditionally and irrevocably guaranteed by PT Cikarang Listrindo Tbk, available online at: http://infopub.sgx.com/FileOpen/Final%20Offering%20Memorandum%20dated%20September%207,%202016.ashx?App=Prospectus&FileID=29833; Offering Memorandum of USD 300 million 7.125 percent Senior Notes due 2022 issued by PT ABM Investama Tbk dated July 25, 2017, available online at http://infopub.sgx.com/FileOpen/Excalibur%20OM%20-%20Part%20I.ashx?App=Prospectus&FileID=32423.

During the AKT suspension of payments process, AKT administrators denied the admission of another claim of a coal trader based on an advanced prepayment made pursuant to an offtake agreement with AKT and secured by the fiduciary security over AKT's coal inventory, on the ground that such contract was within the scope of Article 250 of Law 37/2004 (forward transaction), which therefore was deemed terminated by operation of law. The coal trader was invited to instead submit a compensation claim due to such termination, which it did not file. With respect to the "security" status of this claim, the AKT administrators reasoned that (i) according to the CCoW, AKT was not able to use the mine (including the coal) as collateral without the prior approval of the Indonesian government, which approval had not been obtained; and (ii) AKT would only own the coal (and therefore be entitled to encumber the coal with security rights) after paying royalties to the State, which AKT had failed to do. The AKT composition plan was subsequently approved by the AKT's creditors and ratified by the Central Jakarta Commercial Court. The bank and the coal trader filed a cassation against the Central Jakarta Commercial Court decision. The coal trader withdrew its cassation filing in the middle of the cassation process, but the Supreme Court in cassation confirmed the decision following the bank's cassation filing.

It should be noted that just as in the period between 1998 and 2004, most decisions of the Commercial Courts in bankruptcy cases between 2004 and 2018 generally appear to be uncontroversial. Nonetheless, the above cases, which reflect the Commercial Courts' most questionable decisions and practices in recent years, do give reason for concern.

Ongoing Issues with the Legal Framework, the Lack of Expertise, and Legal Culture

While the number of cases handled by the Commercial Courts has increased, the quality of the decisions in certain notable cases remains still questionable. This can be explained by three main issues: inadequacies with the procedural and substantive law relating to bankruptcy, the limited expertise within the courts, and the continuation of a pervasive culture of unprofessionalism and corruption. This culture is fed by the broader environment in which the Commercial Courts operate.

The legislation is still insufficient to resolve bankruptcy cases. The flaws go beyond the scope of this chapter, but it is important to note that most of the issues have already been identified as part of the Blueprints, the IN-ACCE project, and the C4 J Project. The government is also aware that the legislative framework for bankruptcy needs improvement, but support from the executive and legislative branch has been limited. There is a lack of leadership within the government in pushing the reforms. There may also have been misperceptions on judicial independence among government circles, resulting in reluctance to introduce court related reforms.

The Jokowi administration has shown some willingness to strengthen the performance of the Commercial Courts in order to improve the country's Ease of Doing Business ranking.[29] In 2016, the World Bank made detailed recommendations for bankruptcy reform. The recommendations resulted in a Circular Letter on efficiency and transparency.[30] Around the same time, the Minister of Law and Human Rights issued Regulation No. 11 of 2016 (the 2016 Regulation), which decreased the administrator's fee in the suspension of payments process and introduced the maximum hourly rate of IDR 4 million (Rayanti 2016).[31] In 2017, the Minister of Law and Human Rights once again decreased the receiver/administrator's fee.[32] These measures are quick fixes pending the introduction of more fundamental reforms. In December 2017, the National Law Development Agency (BPHN) issued an academic paper identifying seventeen reforms to Law 37/2004. However, the academic paper is criticized not only by the World Bank, but also by legal practitioners, for failing to address the real issues.[33] Notably, most of the World Bank recommendations were not included in the academic paper.

Aside from procedural and substantive issues with the law, the expertise within the Commercial Courts is limited. Before 2004, judges were reluctant to follow a certification training to be placed in a Commercial Court. In fact, there is now an oversupply of judges with a certificate: 355

---

[29] The government's efforts to improve the country's Ease of Doing Business ranking have been successful, at least as far as its resolving insolvency ranking is concerned: Indonesia's ranking improved from 71 in 2014 to 36 in 2019. The ranking is based on a survey reflecting the calculation of the time and costs needed to resolve insolvency as well as the recovery rate, but this does not necessarily say something about the performance of the Commercial Courts.

[30] Circular Letter of the Supreme Court No. 2/2016 on the Improvement of Efficiency and Transparency for Handling Bankruptcy and Suspension of Payments at Court.

[31] Regulation of the Minister of Law and Human Rights No. 11 of 2016 on Guidelines for the Honorarium of Receivers and Administrators.

[32] Regulation of the Minister of Law and Human Rights No. 2 of 2017 on the Revision of Regulation of the Minister of Law and Human Rights No 11/2016.

[33] See presentation of the World Bank Group titled Insolvency in Indonesia, Opportunities for Reform, August 24, 2018; interview with a representative of a receiver/administrator association, October 3, 2018.

District Court judges and 197 Court of Appeal judges.[34] Training sessions are not organized on a needs basis. Judges who have more than ten years' working experience are invited to attend the training, without any clear prospect that they will be placed in a Commercial Court. As a result, even those judges who have a Commercial Court certificate may not have up-to-date knowledge of bankruptcy law when being placed in a Commercial Court.

Once judges are placed in a Commercial Court, their exposure to bankruptcy law is limited, because the Commercial Courts receive a low number of bankruptcy cases. This means that practically, many Commercial Court judges handle a variety of other cases, including cases that are not within the jurisdiction of the Commercial Court but the broader jurisdiction of the District Court of which the Commercial Court forms part, such as criminal cases, juvenile cases, etc. Even in the Central Jakarta Commercial Court, the largest Commercial Court in the country, a judge in the Commercial Court would only serve 1/3 of the time handling bankruptcy cases.[35]

A further cause of the limited expertise is the rotation system, which requires judges to serve in a court for three years, after which they are transferred to another (often noncommercial) court. Given these circumstances, few judges can specialize in the field of bankruptcy law. For instance, in Central Jakarta, out of thirteen of a total thirty-two judges in the District Court that serve as Commercial Court judges, only three judges have prior experience serving in another Commercial Court, and only one judge is academically specialized in bankruptcy law.[36]

In 2011, after a supervisory judge in the Commercial Court was caught red-handed accepting a bribe, it was decided that not only judges but also registrars would be rotated. It appears that registrars also handle other cases within the jurisdiction of the District Court and have no prior training when they are assigned to handle bankruptcy matters. This contributes to the poor documentation in bankruptcy and suspension of payments cases.[37]

Judges' command of English is usually limited. Formally speaking this should not be an issue, as all foreign language documents submitted to an Indonesian court should be translated by a sworn translation. However,

---

[34] Information from the Directorate Development of Technical Staff, Directorate General Court Jurisdiction, Supreme Court.

[35] Interview with Judge of Commercial Court of Central Jakarta, September 27, 2018.

[36] Ibid.

[37] Interview with a representative of a receiver/administrator association, October 3, 2018.

in practice this may create confusion, particularly in large bankruptcy cases that have a cross-border dimension.

While in 2004 the quality of judges was better than of receivers, administrators, and lawyers, this situation is nowadays reversed. During the twenty years of bankruptcy practice, a small group of receivers, administrators, and lawyers, particularly based in Jakarta, has developed strong expertise in the field of bankruptcy. As a result, judges now commonly rely on these lawyers' knowhow.

This is not to say that bankruptcy lawyers have sufficient expertise. Particularly outside Jakarta, where few bankruptcy cases are handled, the knowledge of receivers, administrators, and lawyers of bankruptcy law may be limited. The existence of different receiver/administrator associations makes it difficult to create a common standard of knowledge. After the enactment of Law 37/2004, a third receiver/administrator association was established, Indonesian Assembly of Receivers and Administrators (*Himpunan Kurator Pengurus Indonesia* (HKPI)).[38] In 2014, the Minister of Law and Human Rights rendered a decree creating a Joint Committee, consisting of a representatives of the Supreme Court, the Ministry of Law and Human Rights, and the receiver/administrator associations, which has the purpose of providing recommendations to the receiver/administrator associations for the preparation of a training curriculum and carry out the training and examination for receivers/administrators.[39] In 2016, the Minister of Law and Human Rights issued another decree concerning the Joint Committee with similar content to the 2014 decree, but now also referring to HKPI.[40] However, in the end the receiver/administrator associations have their own responsibility to develop a training curriculum and carry out the training and examination for receivers/administrators. In practice the three receiver/administrator associations apply different training standards. Lower training standards make it easier to attract new members.[41]

Finally, there remain issues of unprofessionalism and corruption. Since 1998, only one judge has been arrested and convicted for bribery.

---

[38] It appears that there was a conflict between the current Chairman of HKPI, who was an IKAPI member, and the Chairman of IKAPI. Before the IKAPI Chairman sacked him, he resigned and established HKPI. These events are like those that led to the establishment of IKAPI.

[39] Decree of the Minister of Law and Human Rights No. M.HH-01.AH.06.06 Tahun 2014 on the Joint Committee.

[40] Decree of the Minister of Law and Human Rights No. M.HH-01.AH.06.06 Tahun 2016 on the Joint Committee.

[41] Interview with a representative of a receiver/administrator association, October 3, 2018.

On June 1, 2011, Syarifuddin Umar, a supervisory judge in the Commercial Court of Central Jakarta, was caught and arrested by the Corruption Eradication Commission (KPK) for accepting a bribe of Rp. 250 million from the court-appointed receiver, Puguh Wirawan, in connection with the bankruptcy proceedings of PT SkyCamping Indonesia. When raiding the judge's house, the KPK found a significant amount of other currency, including US$ 116,000 and SGD 245,000. The bribe was sourced from the sale of land. The receiver approached Syarifuddin to approve the receiver's report concerning the sale of a land plot in the name of PT Tannata Cempala Saputra (which based on the supervisory judge's previous order was classified as a bankruptcy asset), performed by means of a nonbankruptcy asset sale, without obtaining a new supervisory judge's order revising the previous one (Hukumonline 2011b; Jpnn.com 2011).[42] On February 28, 2012, Syarifuddin was found guilty by the Corruption Court at the Central Jakarta District Court for corruption, sentenced to four years' imprisonment and fined Rp. 150 million (Kompas 2012d). Syarifuddin's appeal to the High Court,[43] cassation to the Supreme Court[44] and case review to the Supreme Court[45] were all rejected. The SkyCamping receiver was convicted by the Corruption Court at Central Jakarta District Court for corruption and received a sentence of 3.5 years imprisonment and a fine of Rp. 150 million (Tempo 2011). In a court hearing, Puguh Wirawan testified that the money given to Syarifudin constituted his token of appreciation after completing a complex case (i.e. Skycamping bankruptcy), which he also shared with other parties (e.g. laborers of the bankrupt company, advisors) so that he could obtain subsequent cases from the money recipients (Hukumonline 2011d; Kompas 2011). Puguh Wirawan was appointed as Skycamping receiver to replace the previous receivers after being proposed by representatives of the laborers of the bankrupt company. Rumor has that Syarifudin became target of a KPK sting operation after, in his previous role as Corruption Court judge, he had acquitted the accused in more than thirty cases (Berita Satu 2011a, 2011b). If it is true, then the KPK did not really target Syarifudin as a Commercial Court judge.

In 2012, there was another criminal case relating to bankruptcy, when two receivers were caught for embezzlement of part of the proceeds of the sale of a hotel that formed part of the bankruptcy estate of PT Sarana

---

[42] KPK's indictment as quoted in Supreme Court Decision No. 167 PK/PID.SUS/2015.
[43] Decision Court of Appeal Jakarta No. 23/PID/TPK/2012/PT.DKI.
[44] Decision Supreme Court No. 1824 K/Pid.Sus/2012.
[45] Decision Supreme Court No. 167 PK/PID.SUS/2015.

Perdana Indoglobal (SPI). In addition, they incurred expenses that were not supposed to be claimed or could not be justified. The total amount of embezzled funds amounted to Rp. 10.85 billion, while the 2,184 creditors were only to receive Rp. 8.19 billion as compensation for outstanding debt (Detik 2011b; Gatra 2012a). The receivers were both convicted for embezzlement and sentenced to three years imprisonment.[46]

Although to the best of our knowledge, only one judge in the Commercial Court and three receivers have been convicted since the enactment of Law 37/2004 (Hukumonline 2014c, 2014e, 2016b, 2016c; Kontan 2018),[47] there are strong indications that the above cases are only the tip of the iceberg. A representative of a receiver/administrator association, commenting on the corruption case, indicated that it is still common for supervisory judges to ask for a financial contribution. This is normally done at the end of the bankruptcy process, when the receiver/administrator's fees need to be approved by the Commercial Court. Receivers/administrators commonly feel pressured to pay, regardless of the risk of being prosecuted for corruption. The representative also admitted that certain practitioners pay supervisory judges to obtain the orders they want.[48] There are strong rumors that certain bankruptcy lawyers use a network of law firms. They act at the same time as receiver/administrator of the company in bankruptcy or suspension of payment and lawyer of certain real or fake creditors and the debtor. This allows them to control the process, also through their contacts in the Commercial Courts, obviously at the expense of real creditors, not rarely foreign banks facing significant financial exposure.

The government has been addressing the problem of legal mafia (*mafia hukum*): in 2009, President Susilo Bambang Yudhoyono established the Legal Mafia Eradication Task Force (Kompas 2010; Viva 2010).[49] However, concrete results are still awaited. The KPK is increasingly active in investigating, arresting, and prosecuting judges and lawyers (see Butt,

---

[46] District Court Central Jakarta Decision 2081/Pid.B/2011/PN.JKT.PST.

[47] We note that numerous police reports have been filed against receivers and administrators, but these did not result in a conviction and indeed may not always relate to actual criminal conduct. It may be a strategy to replace receiver or administrator or at least frustrate the bankruptcy/suspension of payment process. In any event, it is common in Indonesia to criminalize commercial disputes.

[48] Interview with a representative of a receiver/administrator association, October 3, 2018.

[49] Presidential Decree No. 37 of 2009 on the Legal Mafia Eradication Task Force; "Legal Mafia" is informally defined by the Task Force as any actions committed by a person or group that are well planned for certain interests that affect the law enforcer and public official which deviate from the prevailing laws and regulations.

this volume). Although unrelated to a bankruptcy case, the founder of IKAPI, the infamous lawyer, receiver, and administrator Lucas, was recently arrested by the KPK for obstruction of justice. He faces a maximum sentence of twelve years' imprisonment (Kontan 2018).

The receiver/administrator associations do little to improve ethical standards and ban these practices. The largest receiver/administrator association, AKPI, does have a complaint mechanism. However, the complaining party has to pay an administrative fee of Rp. 5 million before a complaint is processed. This fee is supposed to filter out frivolous complaints but may be a financial barrier for those with a serious complaint.

One question that remains is whether the above corruption cases are just instances or illustrations of a systematic problem. If it is indeed a systemic problem, it will likely take decades before the Commercial Courts perform as envisaged when they were established in 1998. Furthermore, whether they are true or not, negative perceptions regarding the Commercial Courts now serve as a self-fulfilling prophecy. Lawyers with high ethical standards and/or sound knowledge of bankruptcy law are reluctant to get involved as a receiver or administrator in bankruptcy or suspension of payments cases, keeping the performance of the Commercial Courts weak and transforming the Commercial Courts into a potential playground for "fixers".

Conclusion

A fresh consideration of the performance of the Commercial Courts in this chapter suggests that while some of the old problems identified in the first years after the establishment of the Commercial Courts have been solved and most decisions of the Commercial Courts in bankruptcy cases between 2004 and 2018 generally appear to be uncontroversial, the quality of the decisions in certain notable cases remains still questionable. This can be explained by three main issues: inadequacies with the procedural and substantive law relating to bankruptcy; the limited expertise within the Commercial Courts; and the continuation of a pervasive culture of unprofessionalism and corruption. This culture is fed by the broader environment in which the Commercial Courts operate.

This sobering conclusion, twenty years later, does not mean that the establishment of the Commercial Courts has been useless. Many of the approaches introduced as part of the establishment of the Commercial Courts are now applied in other courts, thus indeed acting as "a wedge into the judiciary." Ad hoc judges are used in the Human Rights Courts, Anticorruption Courts, and Industrial Relations Courts. Dissenting opinions have become common outside the Commercial Court. Time bound procedures are used in the Human Rights Courts and the Anticorruption Courts. Publication of decisions is now the standard.

This also does not mean that the Commercial Courts should be written off as a failure. It is still possible to improve the performance of the Commercial Courts in the coming years, but this will require more than the quick fixes that have improved Indonesia's Ease of Doing Business – Resolving Insolvency ranking in recent years. If there is sufficient political commitment, it should be possible to overcome the inadequacies with the procedural and substantive law relating to bankruptcy by introducing further revisions or replacements to Law 37/2004. The expertise within the Commercial Courts can be improved by organizing the trainings better, only inviting judges who are to be appointed as Commercial Court judge to participate and reorganizing the rotation system. It appears there is now willingness within the courts to implement the specialized courts strategy fully, even by separating the Commercial Courts from the District Courts or at least by introducing a chamber system, where judges strictly focus on Commercial Court cases or even only on bankruptcy cases.

Creating a conducive legal culture will be the biggest challenge. As Lev noted when evaluating the result of the IMF Project, "There are basically two approaches to deep reform. One is dramatic, quick, and effective, essentially Napoleonic, and consists quite literally in getting rid of old institutions, replacing them with new ones, and inventing new rules. This sort of approach depends on a rare opportunity, however, one in which an existing elite has disappeared or has surrendered its authority or fled, as in the French revolution of 1789 or, say, the Meji Restoration in late 19th century Japan. Otherwise, the process of change is slow, gradual, difficult, expensive, and in constant need of rethinking, readjustment, adaptation" (2005). The Asian Monetary Crisis created some room for reform, but it did not realize the opportunity for a dramatic, quick, and effective approach. This means that a slow approach, as part of a wider program of reform, is the only option.

9

The Small Claims Court

An Innovation in Judicial Reform

BINZIAD KADAFI[*]

In my capacity as a judicial reform program manager in Indonesia, I have consulted with various justice sector stakeholders to assist the planning and the mobilization of resources to execute judicial reform policies. Promoting small claims-related policies marked by the enactment of Supreme Court Regulation No. 2 of 2015 concerning Procedures for the Settlement of Small Claims has been among the easiest law reform projects, with no significant constraints. The explanation lies not merely in the widespread support for the procedures, but also in the substance of the policy, which has the backing of many stakeholders. The most significant source of support came from the Supreme Court (*Mahkamah Agung*) itself. The Supreme Court has long sought to limit the number of cases it receives. There are frequent complaints about the high number of cases, and the backlog of unresolved cases. The justices, clerks, and even the employees of the Supreme Court have been affected by the situation. Indeed, the aspirations to limit cases resulted in new legislation. In 2004, the law on the Supreme Court was amended to exclude certain types of cases from the possibility of cassation. Pretrial judgments in criminal cases are one category that was precluded from cassation. Criminal cases sentenced with a maximum imprisonment of one year or a fine were also prohibited from making a request for cassation. The amendment also excluded from cassation claims against a decree from a local authority.

[*] Currently works as a lawyer at Assegaf Hamzah & Partners (AHP) and a lecturer at Indonesia Jentera School of Law. Previously worked as adviser to the Australia Indonesia Partnership for Justice (AIPJ) and the Indonesia Netherlands National Legal Reform Program (NLRP), two prominent technical assistance programs for the reform of Indonesian law and justice. The author would like to thank Peter de Meij for his comments and suggestions to this chapter.

However, the amended law was limited to criminal and administrative cases. Not one provision regulated the limitation of civil cases. It was understandable that, as the idea of having a small claims mechanism gained traction and emerged as an opportunity to limit legal remedies in civil cases, the Supreme Court did not have to think twice to support the small claims system. Moreover, in 2010, the Supreme Court had already agreed that the judiciary should have summary proceedings with a single judge to examine civil actions lodged by individuals with a specified amount for claims or a small amount of damages (Mahkamah Agung 2010: 31–2).[1] According to the Blueprint for the Reform of the Supreme Court, a panel of judges should only be convened to examine more complicated cases (Mahkamah Agung 2010: 31–2).

The Blueprint noted that summary proceedings should be implemented in the district court (general court of first instance), and although this would not be a special court, the proceedings should take place in a specially designated chamber under special procedural rules and a simplified case administration process. The summary proceedings, as envisioned by the Blueprint, could also be held through circuit courts in locations where there are many everyday cases of minor offences and misdemeanors.

A second form of support for the introduction of a small claims mechanism came from the government. In its National Medium-Term Development Plan (*Rencana Pembangunan Jangka Menengah Nasional/ RPJMN*), the Government of Indonesia declared its commitment to support improvements in the investment climate by pushing for the effective resolution of civil cases (BAPPENAS 2014: 120). An agenda was set out to achieve sustainable economic growth and to regulate matters regarding the economy, ensure sufficient legal protection and enforcement, and certainty for business investors and industries (BAPPENAS 2014: 120). The government outlined a number of strategies in the plan to achieve this. The major step to be undertaken is to revise legislation in civil matters in general and in contract law in particular. Among the concrete goals was to increase the use of mediation, including the introduction of summary proceedings for dispute settlements (small claims court) (BAPPENAS RI 2014: 120).

---

[1] An early idea about small claims court can be found in the Supreme Court's 2003 Judicial Reform Blue Print, where particular mechanisms for small cases are discussed in the context of limiting cases eligible for appeal to the Supreme Court.

It was not a coincidence that the existence of a small claims settlement mechanism became one of the indicators in the assessment of enforcement of contracts. The assessment constitutes an integral part of the Ease of Doing Business (hereafter "Doing Business") survey conducted annually by the World Bank. It was hoped that the existence of a small claims mechanism would increase Indonesia's score on enforcement of contracts in the Doing Business survey. The government, of course, had a strong interest in improving Indonesia's ranking in the survey, which has significant value politically (in terms of obtaining quantitative indicators for achievement) and economically (in terms of adding attraction to investment).

The third area of support came from civil society, which has long demanded the expansion of access to justice, including and especially for cases of low economic value. Those who work in justice sector reform have suggested that cases with small economic value should be treated differently from regular cases, namely by having such cases resolved through summary proceedings with limitations on legal remedies (LeIP 2010: 45–7). The forum should be physically (and psychologically) attractive, so that the public will feel comfortable and confident (LeIP 2010: 45–7).

The small claims mechanism had several unique features that ensured it had the support of these three actors in the field of legal and judicial reform. Besides its potential to fulfill the three goals described above (case limitation, improving the business climate, and access to justice), the exceptional nature of the small claims mechanism lies in the fact that it was born amid an impasse in the Indonesian civil justice system, which the author will describe as follows.

Background to the Small Claims Court

For years, the number of civil lawsuits in courts throughout Indonesia has been low and the number tends to remain static. The data on the number of civil lawsuits over the last five years, taken from the latest Supreme Court annual reports, is as follows (Table 9.1):

The number of civil lawsuits is worthy of scrutiny because it is one indicator of how the courts are perceived as a formal dispute resolution mechanism by the community. In a civil lawsuit, citizens voluntarily come to court to settle their disputes. A civil lawsuit is different from the civil petition in which people go to court to meet the civil administration, as required by laws and regulations. Civil lawsuits must also be

Table 9.1 *Number of civil claims*

Year	No. of District court judges	No. of claims
2013	3,171	17,258
2014	3,034	26,431
2015	3,199	28,374
2016	3,852	30,741
2017	3,040	30,504

Extracted from Annual Report of the Mahkamah Agung RI 2013–17.

distinguished from criminal cases in which people come to court after being forcefully brought or summoned by law enforcement agencies.

Over the years, the ratio of the number of civil lawsuits to the total Indonesian population (per-2017: 261,890,872) (Subdirektorat Statistik Demografi 2013: 59) has never been more than 0.01 percent. This means that the civil justice system only serves 0.01 percent of Indonesians. When compared with the number of micro, small, and medium enterprises (SMEs), which in 2015 amounted to about 60,700,000 (BAPPENAS 2016: 4), the ratio has never been more than 0.04 percent. This means that the civil justice system in Indonesia serves only 0.04 percent of the people that are most likely to face business disputes. If the ratio is taken against the number of the available judges, then between 2013 and 2017, every judge of the District Court handled an average of about eight civil cases each year. When compared to the same data from several other countries, one gets a sense of how small that number really is. Based on the data available, in 2008 alone, in Japan, there were 2.3 million civil cases in the courts at all levels (Ramseyer 2010: 8). Likewise, in the United Kingdom, during 2007, there were 2.01 million lawsuits filed into all county courts (Ramseyer 2010: 8).

One conclusion is that, when facing civil disputes, citizens, including the SMEs, tend to give up rather than go to court. People may consider the dispute as God's ordeal or a matter of bad luck (Kadafi 2016). In 2001, a survey of Citizen's Perception on the Indonesian Justice Sector was conducted among 1,700 respondents. The survey was organized by The Asia Foundation in collaboration with AC Nielsen. The survey indicated that out of 63 percent of respondents having experienced justiciable legal disputes of some kind, 32 percent of them did nothing to solve the dispute (AC Nielsen 2001: 6). The reasons cited by those who took no action whatsoever included lack of knowledge of what to do (ranging from 24 percent of urban respondents to 47 percent of rural respondents) and the belief that the problem was not sufficiently significant to be taken up by the police or the court (AC Nielsen 2001: 6). Another reason was that too much time would be required to reach a solution, with an additional consideration being that action of any kind would damage relations with the other party or cause problems for the families involved (AC Nielsen 2001: 6). Concerns that the costs would be too high were among the reasons as well, with insufficient evidence to support a claim also creating another disincentive to do something to solve their case (AC Nielsen 2001: 6).

The lack of civil lawsuits in Indonesian courts is not new. Similar findings were obtained by J. J. Burns who researched civil courts in North Sumatra in the 1970s. According to Burns, the frequency of court use by economic actors was very low (Burns 1980: 365). Civil courts were not ordinarily used by business people to collect debts or to develop and reinforce acceptable business standards (Burns 1980: 365). Through the study, Burns doubted whether the civil courts influenced economic behavior, even if only indirectly by threatening to sanction unacceptable behavior (Burns 1980: 365).

Daniel Lev studied legal culture in Indonesian courts. According to Lev, the judicial system does not have a positive image among the majority of the people (1972b: 280). According to him, the legal profession is considered an urban phenomenon, serving only a specific part of society (1972b: 280). Although courts are widespread, Lev observed that these institutions were not a common or entirely legitimate means of settling disputes (1972b: 280). Lev even maintained that cultural emphases in conflict resolution tend to turn people away from the courts (1972b: 280). He believed that in Java and other aristocratic societies, most issues of conflict were left to the village or family, and the usual mode of a settlement was to compromise (1972b: 249). Social values stress personal solutions to guard communal solidarity and avoid disputes (Lev 1972b: 281). There was almost no support for the idea that conflict may be functional (Lev 1972b: 281). The court in this kind of society is seen as an external factor (Lev 1972b: 284). Going out of the village to resolve disputes would introduce external interests and unfamiliar concerns (Lev 1972b: 284). A government court is considered to be unaware of the relationships at stake in a local dispute, which may bring alien standards to matters of custom (Lev 1972b: 284). Under Suharto's New Order, Lev underlined that legal processes, and especially courts, became more and more irrelevant to the private economy (1972b: 259).

The Criminalization of Civil Disputes

In addition to compromise or deciding not to pursue the dispute further, other explanations can be put forward to clarify the reluctance to go to court. The low number of civil suits has occurred at the same time as there has been an increase in the criminalization of civil disputes. A growing number of civil suits have been followed or replaced by police reports, either in the name of litigation or negotiation. In most cases, the reports are served by the police, so they often run simultaneously to the civil process.

In 2016, for example, the cassation of general criminal cases, which entered the Supreme Court, consisted of fraud (19.27 percent), embezzlement (12.27 percent), and forgery (8.8 percent) (Table 9.2). Overall, these three types of criminal offences constitute about 40 percent of the volume of cassation cases for general crimes. These three types of offences are criminal acts originating from or very strongly intertwined with civil disputes. According to Article 1328 of the Indonesian Civil Code, fraud is one of the reasons for invalidating a contract where it has to be proven and not merely alleged. There is a strong incentive for someone who wishes to invalidate an agreement with others to pursue criminal charges of fraud.

It is the same with embezzlement as provided in Article 372 of the Indonesian Criminal Code. The wording of the Criminal Code by itself is sufficiently precise to indicate that the source of the alleged embezzlement is a civil transaction. Embezzlement by law is defined as intentionally and unlawfully possessing goods, which belong to another person, either wholly or partially. Although it is said to be unlawful, the possession of goods in embezzlement is set out clearly enough not to be because of a crime. Similarly, in 2017, the cassation of general criminal cases that went to the Supreme Court consisted of fraud (18.4 percent), embezzlement (11.1 percent), and forgery (10.4 percent) (Table 9.2). It can even be said that fraud and embezzlement have been the general crimes at the top of the list of cassations submitted to the Supreme Court.

By looking at the typology of ordinary criminal cases that go to the district courts, the number of cases of fraud and embezzlement is not insignificant. In 2017, the number of embezzlement cases reached 5,891,

Table 9.2 *Types of criminal cases entering the Supreme Court*

Type of case	2013 (%)	2014 (%)	2015 (%)	2016 (%)	2017 (%)
Fraud	13.94	13.63	19.89	19.27	18.4
Embezzlement	13.82	13.27	10.63	12.27	11.1
Forgery (letter)	10.76	9.94	10.17	8.8	10.4
Defamation	1.8	2.2	2.57	2	
Total	40.32	39.04	43.26	42.34	39.9
Other crimes	59.68	60.96	56.74	57.66	60.1

Extracted from Annual Report of the Mahkamah Agung 2013–17.

while there were 4,527 fraud cases (Mahkamah Agung 2018: 49). Of all criminal cases, 44,172 cases are related to narcotics. However, the volume of criminal cases that concern civil disputes cannot be ignored. Criminalizing civil matters occurs frequently and this deters people from going to court for civil cases. Furthermore, approaching civil disputes from a criminal law perspective is an old existing phenomenon. According to Lev, the police are particularly prone to lending a hand in common disputes, not always just for biased reasons, but often because they actually conceive dispute settlement to be a proper part of their responsibilities (1972b: 290).

Moreover, when it is both necessary and possible, there is a tendency among litigants to voluntarily and intentionally turn away from civil actions in favor of criminal prosecutions (Lev 1965a: 99). The civil process may take a very long time, which consequently allows the debtor to maintain control over the debt owed while inflation erodes the value of the money. Accordingly, claimants try to persuade the police to take the debtor into custody, usually on charges of fraud (Lev 1965a: 99).

This situation has led some advocates to note that the law seems to be moving back towards a "primitive" condition in which civil and criminal actions are indistinguishable (Lev 1965a: 99). The inefficiency of the civil process has directed business people to disguise civil problems as criminal complaints in settling commercial disputes (Burns 1980: 366). The expectation is that, when faced with possible imprisonment, the debtor will pay if she or he can (Lev 1965a: 100). Since the civil justice system cannot be expected to facilitate the settlement of disputes, the criminal justice system is also used. The civil courts have nothing to offer, not even as an instrument of control in commercial conflicts (Lev 1965a: 100).

The Negative Public Perception of the Courts

Apart from these cultural explanations, the most significant cause of the impasse of the civil justice system is the growing negative perception of the courts in society, especially among the business community. This perception erodes trust in the courts. This is in line with Lev who once stated that the avoidance of government courts by commercial interests is mainly due to considerations of trust (besides efficiency and utility) (1972b: 287). As specified by Lev, civil trials are perceived to be painfully time consuming (1972b: 287). This observation is also consistent with Burns's study, which shows that the average completed cases that entered the Medan court in 1971 took 222 days from filing to decision, and the average for such cases entering in 1972 was 208 days (1980: 359).

Lev also asserted that decisions in commercial cases offer little legal guidance, partly because judges have neither time nor inclination to write carefully reasoned conclusions (1972b: 287). Business actors generally complain that the courts are too inconsistent and unpredictable to use in settling disputes (Burns 1980: 355). Inconsistencies, in turn, lead to a perception of lack of integrity in the court process. According to Lev, the integrity of judges in rendering fair and just decisions is often seen as a source of unpredictability for litigants. Lev pointed out that "the living law of actual practice" is a significant source of law in Indonesia (1965a: 103). He suggested that there are two slightly related systems of law: a formal one and a real one, where the latter operates through an intricate network of personal and family relationships, bribes, payoffs, and many ad hoc deals (1965a: 103).

The findings of Burns's study further verify Lev's statement. Burns said that each element in the judicial system must be mobilized separately to achieve the desired outcome (1980: 354). Many channels have to be used to settle matters and each of them cost money (Lev 1972b: 288). Finally, Lev indicated that judicial decisions do not always carry their guarantee of execution (1972b: 287).

All these negative perceptions result in courts being accused of not being able to meet the demands of the private economy (Lev 1972b: 287). Business people find courts inadequate and fundamentally unsympa-thetic to their problems and needs (Lev 1972b: 287). Factors including

procedural inadequacies, slowness, and uncertainty of execution of decisions help to explain why private enterprises have tended to stay away
from the courts (Lev 1965a: 99). Some of these perceptions are also
mapped in a nonprobabilistic survey of seventy-five respondents conducted by the Indonesian Center for Law & Policy Studies (PSHK) and
Institute for the Independence of the Judiciary (LeIP) on issues regarding
completion of civil cases in five district courts (Central Jakarta, Cibinong,
Mataram, Selong, and Makassar). The study was organized for the preparation of the Supreme Court regulation on small claims. The report on
the study suggests that 60 percent of respondents felt that civil court
procedures are "complicated", 33 percent observed that the procedures
are "very complicated", and only 7 percent stated that the procedures are
"simple enough" (Kelompok Kerja Mahkamah Agung RI 2015: 15–16).
The respondents recommended that several critical factors need to be
addressed in the civil court procedures, including the cost of the case
(66 percent), the time frame for case finalization (14 percent), and the
effectiveness of the ruling (5 percent) (Kelompok Kerja Mahkamah
Agung RI 2015: 15–16).

Regarding timelines, based on analysis of the case registers in five district
courts, the study revealed that the average period to finalize a civil case at the
level of the first-instance courts is 154 days. This duration can be broken
down into categories of cases, namely tort (165.5 days) and breach of
contract (145 days). Breach of contract includes debts (118 days), sales and
purchases (149 days), and other types of contract cases (170 days)
(Kelompok Kerja Mahkamah Agung 2015: 16–17).

The negative perceptions of the courts are also substantiated by
a series of Doing Business reports. According to the World Bank, in
2017, the time needed to finalize a civil dispute in Jakarta (with a sample
taken from the Central Jakarta District Court) is 390 days. The time
frame can be broken down into lodging claims (60 days), hearings, and
decision-making (150 days), and enforcing court decision (180 days)
(World Bank 2017: 116). It is important to note that this has decreased
from the previous years, when it took 460 days in 2015 and 2016
(Table 9.3).

As for the costs of settling civil cases, in 2017, the costs on average are
74 percent of the value of the claim. The most prominent component is
the lawyer's fee (50 percent) (World Bank 2017: 116). Previously (2015
and 2016), the estimate of the costs for settling civil disputes was 118 percent of the claim value (Table 9.3). This means that the fee to process
a case is even higher than the value of the claims in the case.

Table 9.3 *Time and cost of civil cases settlement in Jakarta*

Enforcement of contracts EoDB	2015	2016	2017
Time (days)	**460**	**460**	**390**
Filing and service	60	60	60
Trial and judgment	220	220	150
Enforcement of judgment	180	180	180
Cost (% of claim value)	**118**	**118**	**74**
Attorney fees	90	90	50
Court fees	3,1	3,1	13
Enforcement fees	25	25	11

Extracted from Doing Business Report of the World Bank 2016–18

Legal Framework

Before explaining how the small claims mechanism responds to this context, it is necessary to first clarify the regulatory framework of the mechanism, and why the Supreme Court Regulation (*Peraturan Mahkamah Agung*/Perma) has become the chosen regulation. It has been a long time since the government first planned to produce a Code of Civil Procedure to replace the *Herziening Indonesisch Reglement* (HIR), a civil procedural law of Dutch heritage.

Between 2012 and 2013, the government, through the Directorate General of Legislation of the Ministry of Law and Human Rights, communicated its intention to establish a small claims mechanism. In the draft Code of Civil Procedure a number of provisions addressed the examination of cases in a speedy manner (arts. 79–86). However, neither the draft of the Code of Civil Procedure nor the special law on small claims was included as priorities of the 2015–19 national legislation program (Kelompok Kerja Mahkamah Agung RI 2015: 32). In fact, it would be better for the small claims mechanism to be implemented by law rather than a regulation of the Supreme Court. However, with strong consideration of the various problems that surround the legislation process, and growing aspirations related to the ease of doing business, the Supreme Court regulation has been used to address the legal vacuum. The choice is not without reason. Law No. 12/2011 concerning the Establishment of Laws and Regulations mentions that the rules of the Supreme Court have binding legal force to the extent that it is ordered by higher legislation or established by authority (Law No. 12 of 2011 re. Legislation Art. 8 (2) & (2)).

The Supreme Court has the power to issue orders by higher legislation and to regulate the small claims mechanism. The law provides that the Supreme Court may further regulate the matters necessary for the smooth conduct of the judiciary if there are matters that have not been adequately regulated in the Supreme Court Law (Law No. 14 of 1985 re. Supreme Court Art. 79). In addition, the authority of the Supreme Court also comes through Law No. 48 Year 2009 on Judicial Power, which provides that the judiciary be organized in a simple, fast, and low-cost manner (Law No. 48 of 2009 re. Basic Provision of Judicial Power Art. 2 (4)). The same law authorizes the courts to assist justice seekers to over-come all obstacles and hindrances to achieve a simple, speedy, and low-cost trial (Law No. 48 of 2009 Art. 4 (2)).

The Supreme Court's authority to regulate procedural law has become an accepted norm within the Indonesian legal system. For example, the Supreme Court issued a Circular Letter No. 3 of 1963 related to the status of the Civil Code as law in order to abolish some provisions of the Code (Kelompok Kerja Mahkamah Agung RI 2015: 32–3). Likewise, the issu-ance of another regulation was the first framework for a legal basis for the mechanism of revision *(peninjauan kembali)* in Indonesia.[2]

Features of the Small Claims Mechanism

The Supreme Court decided to establish a small claims mechanism to address existing challenges. The combination of challenges leading to a lengthy and complicated dispute resolution process was to be addressed by a number of features of the envisioned small claims mechanism.

Simple Substance

The simplicity of the substance of a case is determined by the value of the law suit, which is at most IDR 200,000,000. Any breach of contract or tort with such value can be settled by the small claims mechanism. At the

---

[2] Supreme Court Regulation No. 1 Year 1969 and Supreme Court Regulation No. 1 Year 1980 on Revision. Although in its history, Supreme Court Regulation no. 1 of 1969 on Revision was frozen by the Supreme Court because of its enactment that provoked the protests of many parties, especially the parliament, on the allegation that the substance should have been regulated in the law and thus the Supreme Court has taken over the legislative role of the parliament.

initial deliberation of the Regulation, the maximum value of small claims was determined to be IDR 100 million. The value was determined as two times the gross domestic product per capita of Indonesia, which in 2015 was around IDR 45–50 million. However, the leadership meeting of the Supreme Court that was organized to deliberate and approve the regulation eventually agreed that the value would be increased to IDR 200 million.

As with most small claims models, there was initially an effort to restrict incoming cases to those concerning breach of contract. Breach of contract (*wanprestasi*) occurring from the nonfulfillment of a contract of either written or unwritten agreement (Mahkamah Agung RI et al. 2015: 10). The expectation was that the existence of the agreement in a dispute would facilitate the process of proof of nonfulfillment. However, some judges argued that torts cases should also be incorporated into the small claims mechanism. A torts case arises from the damage suffered by one party due to the actions of the other party with no prior agreement (Mahkamah Agung RI et al. 2015: 10). A small claims mechanism was formed to solve the legal problems faced by the community. Judges, especially career judges who began in the lower courts, feel that one of the most significant legal issues faced by the community at the grassroots level is tort, while the breach of contract is considered an urban dispute.

The limitation that a small claim does not cover land right disputes also represents the feature of simplicity of the substance. Land disputes often entail complex issues, with high cultural sensitivity (Kelompok Kerja Mahkamah Agung RI 2015: 35). The limited number of parties involved in a case also reflects substantive simplicity. The regulation stipulates that a small claim must be direct; there can be only one plaintiff and one defendant, unless they have the same legal interests, for example, when husband and wife are both seated as defendants in a dispute related to a credit agreement.

Simple Process

The regulation ensures the process remains simple by requiring that cases be heard by a single judge. A single judge minimizes the complexity of scheduling of the hearing and decision-making processes. The use of a single judge with simple trial procedures has also become common practice. For example, the Code of Criminal Procedure recognizes a fast examination process handled by a single judge for minor crimes and traffic violations (Kelompok Kerja Mahkamah Agung RI 2015: 41; Law No. 8 of 1981 re. Criminal Procedural Code Art. 205 (3)). So is the use of a single judge in pretrial procedure (Law No. 8 of 1981 Art. 78 (2)).

The simplicity of the process is further represented by a provision which removes some of the agenda items of the trial that are deemed unnecessary. The regulation provides that in the process of examining a small claim, neither provisional demands can be filed, nor *eksepsi* (objections), *rekon-vensi* (counterclaims), *replik* (replies), *duplik* (rejoinders), or *kesimpulan* (summations). A provisional demand is a demand for temporary action on behalf of one party before a final decision is made. The *rekonvensi* is a claim filed by a defendant as a counterattack against the lawsuit that the plaintiff filed against him or her. To sue the plaintiff, the defendant does not have to file a new lawsuit, but directly advances it along with the answer to the plaintiff's lawsuit. *Eksepsi* generally means objections addressed to matters concerning the terms or formalities of the lawsuit that might result in the lawsuit being declared inadmissible. The primary purpose of the filing of an objection is to end the examination process without further examining the merits of the case. Reply and rejoinder processes can be implemented at once during the process of proving the claim. This is possible due to the active role of the judge, who can clarify the claims of the plaintiff to the defendant. The removal of these reply and rejoinder actions is possible because the normative provisions of the proceedings are not strictly regulated in the HIR (Kelompok Kerja Mahkamah Agung RI 2015: 40–1).

A summation is an additional effort made by each party (both the plaintiff and the defendant) to submit a final opinion on the results of the examination in the verification process. The summation is usually just a repetition of what has been said in the process of giving and explaining evidences. Judges are not dependent on the summation, because after the stage of proof, the judges deliberate to formulate a verdict. These limits can help simplify court processes.

Finally, the simplicity of the process is also represented by a simple appeal or objection mechanism that is adequately submitted to the same district court for review and decision by the panel of judges. The decision at the objection level is a final verdict, which is not available for formal appeal, cassation, or revision.

Accelerated Settlement and Reduced Costs

The settlement of a small claim is limited to a maximum of twenty-five days from the date of the first hearing at the single judge level. The verdict on the appeal or objection must be determined by the panel of judges no later than seven days after the date of their appointment. A video graphic produced by the Supreme Court on small claims stated that in general the entire process from registration to verdict in the objection would last for 58–60 working days.

The most important factor of costs in a small claim is a provision that requires the plaintiff and the defendant to appear directly in each hearing, as well as a provision allowing the parties not to be accompanied by a legal counsel. The need for legal counsel becomes increasingly irrelevant because in settling a small claim, the judge is required to take an active role. The active role of the judge includes providing explanations to the parties concerning the small claim procedure, pursuing a peaceful settlement of the case, guiding the parties in the proof, and explaining the legal remedies that can be taken by the parties.

The Doing Business Report 2018 finds that attorney fees constitute 50 percent of the total cost of the case, which in total can reach 74 percent of the value of the claim (Table 9.3). In the 2017 and 2016 reports, the figure was much higher, where the attorney's fee could reach 90 percent of the total cost of the case, which totaled as 118 percent of the value of the claim (Table 9.3). It is understandable that the provisions that discourage the parties to use attorneys significantly contribute to the efforts to reduce the cost of the process in a small claim.

Implementation

The Supreme Court has monitored the implementation of the small claim mechanism. *First,* the Legal and Public Relations Bureau of the Supreme Court issued a report on one year of implementation of the regulation on the small claims mechanism, between August 2015 and August 2016 (Sahbani 2016). According to the data of the Supreme Court, at that time there were 404 simple lawsuits registered in 124 District Courts throughout Indonesia (Sahbani 2016). It was reported that the five District Courts with the highest number of handling small claim cases were Cianjur, West Java, with twenty cases followed by Jember, East Java, as runner-up with sixteen cases and Batam, Riau Islands, with fourteen cases, in third rank. The fourth and fifth ranks were, respectively, for Bandung, West Java, with thirteen cases, and Tangerang, Banten, with twelve cases (Sahbani 2016).

In 2016, the duration of the settlement process of small claims varied depending on the weight of the case. For example, 67 percent of cases

Table 9.4 *Number of incoming small claims*

Year	Number of small claims	Notes
2015	21	Initial setup period
2016	754	Increased 3,590% from 2015
2017	3,966	Increased 525% from 2016

Extracted from Annual Report of the Mahkamah Agung
2015–17.

were decided in less than twenty-five days, and 30 percent of them were even decided in less than ten days. However, there were still about 33 percent of cases settled in more than twenty-five days, the maximum limit for simple settlement of claims, at the level of a single judge (Sahbani 2016).

In 2017, a second monitoring report released by the Supreme Court highlighted the implementation of the small claims regulation throughout 2016. Among small claims cases handled by the courts throughout 2016, 81.2 percent were lawsuits concerning breach of contract and 18.8 percent were tort claims (Mahkamah Agung 2017: 98–9). In 2016 the number of small claims increased approximately 36-fold from 2015 (the beginning of the functioning of the small claims mechanism), when only twenty-one cases were received. By 2017 the number of small claims had increased by about five times from 2016 (Table 9.4).

Consistent with its design, the average civil case dealt with by the small claims mechanism was straightforward and required only the court's decision as an objective third party on who has the legal rights and obligations. However, that does not mean the judge has no room at all to refer to the provisions of legislation or jurisprudence to approach the pertinent legal facts more argumentatively.

An example of this is a small claim handled by the District Court of Palangkaraya, where the main issue was a debt agreement worth IDR 30,000,000, with an interest rate of 10 percent per month, for two months.[3] The debt agreement involved collateral in the form of a Certificate of Ownership on a plot of 162 m^2 land owned by the defendant. From the evidence and witness testimony in the hearing, the judge determined that based on Article 1765 of the Indonesian Civil

---

[3] District Court of Palangkaraya, Decision No. 4/Pdt.G.S/2016/PN.Plk.

Code the defendant had indeed defaulted. The judge considered provisions in the legislation and jurisprudence, namely:

(1) That contracting interest on borrowed money is allowed (Article 1765 of Civil Code);
(2) The definition of interest by law, according to *Staatsblad* 1848 No. 22 is six percent per year;
(3) If the rate of interest is not specifically contracted, pursuant to Supreme Court Decision No. 8 K/Sip/1974 then the amount of the interest is six percent per year;
(4) Reimbursement of costs, losses and interest due to the late implementation of the engagement is in the form of payment of money, based on Article 1250 paragraph 1 of Civil Code consisting only of interest determined by law;
(5) The contracted interest may exceed the interest according to the law;
(6) The amount of interest that is contracted in the agreement, according to Article 1767 of Civil Code, shall be stipulated in writing.

The judge considered that the interest of 10 percent per month agreed by both parties had been stipulated in writing determined by the testimony of the witnesses in the hearing. There was no evidence of coercion in this case. However, the judge explicitly rejected the amount of interest the plaintiff calculated in his lawsuit, amounting to IDR 30,000,000 (10 percent multiplied by ten months), which according to the Judge of the District Court of Palangkaraya was excessive and not previously agreed upon.

In a separate decision of a panel of judges of the District Court of Blora, it was argued that the objection of the petitioner (originally the defendant) and the objection of the defendant (initially the plaintiff) had been considered by the single judge examining the case.[4] According to the panel of judges, nothing new had been said, and the objection was only a repetition. The judges agreed with the single judge's conclusion.[5]

In another case, a judge considered a plaintiff's lawsuit for the auction of collateral in the form of a plot of land with proof of ownership if the defendant did not fully repay the remaining loan. The judge was of the opinion that the request could not be filed through a small claims mechanism because an auction with an Intermediary of State Wealth Service Offices is a complicated process.[6] In order to avoid nonexecutable

---

[4] District Court of Blora, Decision No. 4/Pdt.G.S/2016/PN.Bla.
[5] District Court of Gorontalo, Decision No. 4/Pdt.G.S/2016/PN.Bla.
[6] District Court of Gorontalo, Decision No. 9/Pdt.G.S/2017/PN.Gto.

judgments, the judge was of the opinion that the plaintiff's claim in the case did not fall in the category of small claims, and the judge should issue a determination to declare that the lawsuit was not a small claim.[7]

Evaluation

The Supreme Court's aspiration to limit cases through the regulation of small claims has not yet been achieved. The increasing number of small claims handled by various courts over time has not been consistent with the significant reduction in the number of civil cases in the Supreme Court. In 2015, for example, the year in which the regulation on small claims mechanism was issued, 3,615 general civil appeals were submitted to the Supreme Court (see Table 9.5). In 2016, when the regulation was effectively implemented, the number of civil cassations that went to the Supreme Court increased slightly (3,817). Even in 2017, when the small claims handled by the Court reached 3,966 cases, civil cassation that went into the Supreme Court was only slightly reduced, to 3,536.

The aspiration to limit cases through the establishment of the small claims mechanism was not defined carefully, which should have been done by looking at the compatibility between the character of a civil cassation case and a small claim case. It now seems civil cases that are limited through the small claims mechanism are disconnected from the civil cases that have been entering the Supreme Court for cassation.

Aspirations related to increased ease of doing business at least can be seen from the score and ranking of Indonesia in the Doing Business reports following the enactment and the implementation of the regulation. In 2015, during the early implementation of the small claims mechanism, Indonesia's Doing Business rating remained at No. 109 with enforcement of contracts ranking at 170 (Table 9.6). In 2017, two years after the implementation of the small claims mechanism, where the number of cases continued to rise, the Doing Business rating was 72, and Indonesia's enforcement of contracts rank was 145 (Table 9.6).

The desire to open a wider channel for community legal issues to be resolved by the Court has been achieved. The number of incoming small claims throughout 2017 alone was more than 10 percent of the total incoming ordinary civil lawsuits that enter each year. This figure is

---

[7] District Court of Gorontalo, Decision No. 9/Pdt.G.S/2017/PN Gto.

Table 9.5 *Incoming cassation to the Supreme Court*

Year	No. of cases
2015	3,615
2016	3,817
2017	3,536

Extracted from Annual Report of the Mahkamah Agung RI 2015–17.

Table 9.6 *Indonesia's rank in the ease of doing business and enforcement of contracts*

Year	Ease of doing business	Enforcement of contracts
2015	109	170
2016	91	166
2017	72	145

Extracted from Doing Business Report of the World Bank 2016–18

indeed promising, though not sufficient because of the various problems that still surround the small claims mechanism, particularly those related to the execution of decisions.

Until now, the most dynamic user of the service of the small claims mechanism is the banking community, including various Rural Banks that distribute small amounts of credit. Banks dominate the news about the use of small claims mechanisms. Even, in some areas, cooperation between banking institutions and the court in providing training for credit staff is evident (PN Kota Cirebon 2018). But that does not mean that most people have not benefited from the small claims mechanism, like the housewife whom the author accompanied in filing small claims against her defaulting business partner (Kadafi 2017). The view that small claims provides a promising solution for breaking the deadlock that overshadows the legal problems of society might begin to be found in many communities.

Conclusion

If adequately developed and disseminated, the small claims mechanism could be a useful medium for ending old practices and encouraging new legal practices. The small claims mechanism has the potential to make the civil justice system relevant to economic life. It may become part of community expectations, particularly among small and medium business actors. With support gained from various stakeholders, as well as acceptance from justice seekers, the small claims mechanism has the potential to become an entry point for the improvement of the civil justice system as a whole (Kadafi 2016). With a significant increase in the number of cases handled over time, evidence suggests that the public will welcome systematic and structured efforts to simplify the civil justice process (Kadafi 2016).

This is an opportunity to shape the interests and logic of the judicial system, which according to Lev so far often stands alone, rather than in line with public interests and logic. Traditionally, the judicial system responded to the court's institutional concern and established rules (Lev 1972b: 284). One of the ways would be by making regulatory breakthroughs concerning the justice system, which address the public's negative perceptions of the court.

The legal framework constrained such efforts. The new Supreme Court regulation is adequate although it is not strong enough on its own to institutionalize this new judicial mechanism. There is a sense of temporariness among court actors considering that the small claims mechanism is based on regulation rather than a law. Attempts to develop it into a solid structure have been half-hearted, resulting in concerns that one day the system may easily be changed due to its weak legal framework.

The Supreme Court has managed to take bold steps to make breakthroughs in the regulation of court procedures. Many burdensome civil procedures are no longer used in these cases. It is therefore worth considering the incorporation of the small claims mechanism in the provisions of a law. There are other examples of a Supreme Court regulation later being regulated by law. Sometimes the parliament does not have the legislative capacity or will to produce a quality law in a relatively fast time. Consequently, the Supreme Court must use its technical knowledge to issue a regulation first. The legislative process will follow by adopting regulations that prove themselves in practice.

The small claims mechanism is a breakthrough in Indonesia. It has established a new and simplified means of hearing and resolving small claims in the courts. In so doing, the regulation of the small claims mechanism has enhanced Indonesian civil procedural law.

10

The Fisheries Court

Government-Led Judicial Development?

INDRIASWATI DYAH SAPTANINGRUM[*]

> *...the court I inaugurated has failed me. I am very disappointed and I ask the government to close down the (Fisheries) Court in Ambon. We do not need it anymore!*
>
> Minister of Maritime Affairs and Fisheries Susi Pudjiastuti (Kompas 2015)

In May 2015, Ambon Fisheries Court issued a controversial decision by returning the vessels caught for illegal fishing to their owners, instead of destroying the boat and fining the captains 100 million rupiahs (6,000 USD) for committing illegal fishing instead of a jail term.[1] According to the current law on fisheries, a crime of illegal fishing carries a penalty of up to six years' imprisonment and six billion rupiahs' fines.[2] The court's decision provoked outrage from Minister Susi Pudjiastuti (also known as 'Ibu Susi' or 'Bu Susi'), the Ministry of Maritime Affairs and Fisheries ('the Ministry')[3] and the wider fisheries communities, as they expected the ships to be scuttled. Bu Susi expressed her frustration publicly to the media. A month before, the same court also issued a controversial decision to MV Hai Fa, a Panama fishing fleet of 5 gross tonnage that was said to be the biggest fleet caught by the Illegal Fishing Taskforce of the

---

[*] All graphs and tables in this chapter are compiled by the author from data contained in the Supreme Court Annual Reports 2013–17 and the General Court annual review 2013–2017.

[1] Overall there are five vessels (Sino 15, 26, 27, 35 and 36) of PT Sino Indonesia Shunlida Fishing (PT Sino) that were brought before the Ambon Fisheries Court. According to the decision of the Fisheries Court at the first level, all vessels were returned to their owners; for example, the decision on Sino 15 issued by the Fisheries Court of Ambon No. 04/Pid. Sus.PRK/2015/PN.Ambon. However, the High Court of Ambon revoked the decision about the vessel and ordered the vessel to be confiscated and scuttled (Decision No. 33/Pid.sus-Prk/2015/PT.Ambon).

[2] Art. 93(3), Law no. 45/2009 on the Amendment of Law no. 31/2004 on fisheries.

[3] The name of the Ministry has changed over time, for example, under the Susilo Bambang Yudhoyono, the Ministry was titled 'Department'. It was first established in 1999 under the name of 'Ministry of Maritime Exploration', but since 2001, the name changed to the Ministry of Maritime and Fisheries (which is the name used in this chapter).

Ministry. The court found the captain guilty of illegal fishing, but fined him just 200 million rupiahs (12,000 USD) and returned the vessel to the owner.[4] The decision was released only six months after the Ministry launched the Fisheries Court in December 2014. It was hoped that the court would act as a deterrent and display the government's strong stance against illegal fishing to other neighbouring countries, backing the government's ship-sinking policy by judicial authority.

Responding to Ibu Susi's disappointment, the prosecutor's office of the Fisheries High Court of Tual (Maluku) reminded the Ministry to respect the trial to ensure the court is free from pressure and intervention. Although appealing to the value of judicial independence, the response did not seem to win public support. The ship-sinking campaign led by Ibu Susi has already gained popularity among the public. Ibu Susi has built a reputation as a tough leader and has a unique background. She is one of the most popular ministers in Jokowi's cabinet and has cultivated her popularity on social media. She is the only minister in Jokowi's cabinet who does not have a degree beyond high school. Prior to holding this ministerial position, she was a leading business woman in the fisheries industries. Her ministerial campaign to scuttle foreign vessels has caused tension with the Vice President Jusuf Kala and Luhut Panjaitan, a Coordinating Minister on Maritime Affairs. Despite this opposition from within government, her campaign of sinking foreign vessels continues and is live-streamed in media-savvy ceremonies. This sends a strong message to neighbouring countries on the government's firm commitment to eradicate illegal fishing, which according to Ibu Susi is necessary to uphold Indonesia's sovereignty over the sea.

The notion of upholding national sovereignty over the sea was first introduced in the Joko Widodo's inauguration speech before the People's Consultative Assembly (MPR) in October 2014, through which he promised to reclaim Indonesia's strength as a maritime archipelagic country in the past. Furthermore, he reiterated his vision in the East Asian Summit in Myanmar a month after, when he launched his 'Global Maritime Fulcrum' (GMF), a maritime axis doctrine aiming Indonesia as a force between Indian Ocean and Pacific Ocean. In 2016, he issued a presidential regulation on Indonesia Maritime Policy to accelerate the implementation of GMF doctrine, bringing maritime affairs and the

---

[4] See Fisheries Court of Ambon, Decision No. 01/Pid.Sus/PRK/2015/PN.Amb. The decision was strengthened by the High Court of Ambon in their Decision no. 15/PID.SUS-PRK /2015/PT.AMB.

Ministry of Maritime and Fisheries at the centre of Indonesia's development policy. Against this backdrop, the Fisheries Court, as part of the
ship-sinking policy, regained momentum – in Ibu Susi's words – to be the
stage where justice is revealed.

The Fisheries Court was introduced for the first time in 2007.[5]
However, it was only in 2014 when Ibu Susi launched a campaign against
illegal fishing that the Fisheries Court began to receive more attention
from the media (on media and the courts, see Tapsell this volume). This
friction between two institutions displayed by the press is worth noting
for it reflects a development in the function of the judiciary that is unique
to Indonesia. The Fisheries Court discussed in this chapter warrants
attention, as it portrays the limits of the claim of judicial independence
gained by the Supreme Court post 1998. In particular, it shows the extent
to which the courts exercise their power independent from external
political interference, and how its independence is contested and
negotiated.

This chapter draws on the legislative records containing discussion of
the draft Fisheries Law in 2004 and 2009, as the legal foundation for the
Fisheries Court. This archival information is combined with secondary
data on the institutional development of the Fisheries Court and the work
of the Fisheries Court. The chapter is structured in three parts: the first
part will discuss the Fisheries Court as one type of special court in the
Indonesian legal system. The second part will discuss the development of
the Fisheries Court in detail and look closely into the early development
of the court, which to a large extent reflects the contestation of different
political interests shaping its organisational structure, and the extent to
which it has affected the Supreme Court. The third part will discuss major
problems that hinder the Fisheries Court from effectively functioning
and lessons that can be learned from this initiative.

Specialised Courts in Indonesia Legal System

Specialised courts are not alien to the judicial institution and have been
recognised since the early development of judicial institution in
Indonesia. Under the Dutch, there were three forms of specialised courts,
namely, the Religious Courts, the Adat Courts and 'Swapraja' Court,

---

[5] See, Government Regulation in lieu of Law no. 2/2006 on the postponement of the
function of Fisheries Court as contained in article 71(5) of Law no. 31/2004 on
fisheries.

which were established specifically for indigenous peoples. The establishment of these courts reflected the practice of racial divisions of the
population as part of the colonial strategy in controlling the colony
(Lev 1965b). These courts shared similar features and served specific
political or development agendas of the Dutch colonisers. The need for
a special court came from the recognition of the need for cases to be tried
by courts with special expertise and competence. In the postcolonial era,
Adat Court and 'Swapraja' Court continued to be established in different
regions although very small in numbers and had only been fully eliminated by the issuance of Emergency Law no. 1/1951, which mandated the
unification of the court (Zoelva 2013: 172).

Under Guided Democracy, two specialised courts were established:
a specialised court for economic crimes (1955) and a special court within
the Supreme Court to prosecute the abuse of power by high-ranking public
officials such as the President and ministers (Zoelva 2013: 171–2). In 1963,
another special court was established under the military court based on the
Presidential Regulation no 16/1963. This extraordinary military court had
jurisdiction over crimes that were a serious threat to national security or other
special cases to prosecute crimes related to national security. When the New
Order came to power in 1966, this regime established an extraordinary
military court to prosecute military personnel who were allegedly involved
with the Communist Party. The second special court established during this
period was the land reform court in 1964 as part of Sukarno's land reform
project. The project aimed at addressing disputes over the redistribution of
lands and other cases related to land reform. The court introduced the idea of
a mixed composition of career and non-career judges on its panel. Each panel
of judges was comprised of three non-career judges representing peasant
organisations, one high level official from the Agrarian Department, and one
career judge (art. 19 of the Law no 21/1964 on the Landreform court). In
1970, this court was abolished due to the lack of expertise and commitment of
non-career judges, and conflict over jurisdiction between this court and the
District Court, for example, on the case of fiduciary dispute.[6] The Supreme
Court was in favour of maintaining the traditional jurisdiction of the District
Courts and issued a circular letter to the effect that the land reform court
jurisdiction should only cover cases related to the implementation of land
reform. Any cases brought before the land reform court were required to have
a letter from the land reform committee where the dispute took place.[7] The

---

[6] See Law No. 7/1970 on the Judiciary.
[7] See Supreme Court letter no. 6/KM/a 6/KM/845/M/A/III/67.

Supreme Court's attitude in supporting the District Court in its conflict against this special court has remained consistent up to the present, as demonstrated in its response to the Fisheries Court, as I will show.

It was only after the reformation era in 1998 that special courts regained popularity among legal reformers and legal reform agendas. This partly reflects the awareness that the judiciary was plagued with substantive problems, which made it less promising for achieving a quick win judicial reform programme. The Supreme Court has suffered from substantive decline of its institutional independence under the New Order and has been plagued with corruption (Pompe 2005). This situation has increased the distrust of the judiciary. The idea of specialised courts was seen as more promising as it helped to create a relatively autonomous space for reform to take place. Since 1998, different legal reform projects introduced often required judicial reform components. The pressure for quick reform with clear results and the need to modernise particular areas of law targeted by the reform is seen as more viable compared to reforming the general courts. This situation was clearly demonstrated by early legal reform initiatives such as the establishment of the commercial court in 2002 (Gustaaf et al. this volume), established as part of the IMF's conditionality for the post-crisis monetary fund provided to the government.

Since then, the special court strategy has continued to be applied in different reform projects. It may reflect a realistic approach to reform, because reforming the judicial system, which has long been plagued with corruption, is difficult. Establishing a new institution that has no such historical burden may give greater opportunity for the reform to yield success (Lev 2007c). During the period of 2000–14, seven specialised courts were established in different fields. Similar to the commercial court, the establishment of the human rights court in 2000 has a strong international dimension element (Setiawan, this volume). It was established partly to prevent the attempt to bring atrocities in East Timor pre- and post-referendum 1999 to the international accountability mechanism under the United Nations (Cohen 2003). Most special courts initiatives come from both the house of the representatives (DPR) and the executive when they prepare for draft laws or drafts of amended laws.

The academic draft of the law does not usually adequately discuss the extent to which the establishment would affect the management of judicial institution held by the Supreme Court. For example, the special court implies additional cost for the Supreme Court to ensure the court room allocation, trainings and certification for judges, and appointing more court clerks. The requirement to have ad hoc judges also adds financial burden to the Court. Apart from the selection process, the Supreme Court has to provide monthly salaries for ad hoc judges, which varies from 17.5 million rupiahs for the first-instance level to about 40 millions at the cassation level.[8] In 2017, in total, there are 383 ad hoc judges managed by the Supreme Court, of which 302 judges serve at the first-instance court, 71 judges assigned at the appeal level and 10 judges at the cassation level (Mahkamah Agung 2017: 146).[9]

There are sometimes delays with the establishment of the special courts or factors that hinder the court from fully functioning. The Supreme Court is always briefly consulted by the government in preparing the draft Law, but its views may not be considered. The Supreme Court often shows a lack of support for either the idea of a special court or the appointment of ad hoc judges on the bench. The Supreme Court does not take part and is not invited to attend hearings by the DPR during the deliberation of the draft Law. However, the Association of Indonesian Judges (IKAHI) is invited to attend public hearings in the DPR and generally voices the interests and concerns of the court and of judges. Yet, the final decision for establishing a special court lies with the legislature. This helps to explain why special courts have continued to be established regardless of the Supreme Court's lack of support. For example, the Law No. 18/2013 on the Prevention and Eradication of Forest Destruction follows the Fisheries Court model, in which the law provides a special criminal procedure to address crimes related to forestry destruction. The law does not establish a special court as a separate entity that differs from the general District Court, but provides for special trial procedures, which includes a requirement for the District Court to prioritise and to expedite the trial for crimes related to forestry over other general crimes. The composition of the judges includes two ad hoc court judges.[10] Five years after the stipulation of the law, this court has not yet been established, and the case of illegal lodging continued to be tried at the District Court.

Sometimes the Supreme Court does show a more supportive response. For example, it deals with cases under the Law on Environmental

---

[8] See Presidential Regulation No. 20/2011 on support and other entitlements for the ad hoc judges of the Industrial Relations Court; Presidential Regulation No. 87/2010 for ad hoc judges of the Fisheries Court, and Regulation No. 86/2010 for ad hoc judges of the Anti-corruption Court.

[9] The total number of ad hoc judges amounted to 10 per cent of the total number of judges serving at the first and second instances, or 3,895 judges (Mahkamah Agung 2017).

[10] See Law No. 18/2013 on the Prevention and Eradication of Forest Destruction.

Protection and Management No. 32/2009. Similar to the Fisheries Law, the law introduces a new type of environmental crimes and special criminal procedures to prosecute crimes. These procedures substantially differ from the general criminal procedure provided in the Law no. 8/1981 concerning Criminal Procedure (KUHAP), including the use of strict liability principles, the use of scientific evidence, and the minimum and maximum criminal sanction for environmental crimes offences. However, it does not require a special court to be established to hold those perpetrating environmental crimes accountable nor does it introduce the need for ad hoc judges.

In response, the Supreme Court issued some circular letters to bring environmental court into existence (on the role of circular letters, see Assegaf, this volume). In 2011, the Supreme Court issued a circular letter to establish a certification programme for judges who will serve on the court. It issued another circular letter providing guidelines for judges handling environmental crimes. Gradually, some District Courts produced landmark decisions in this field, such as in the case of forest fires issued by the Palalawan District Court in Riau (2012)[11] and Meulaboh Court (2014)[12]. The response of the Supreme Court might influence the efficacy of special court strategy in judicial reform, as some specialised courts demonstrate a positive influence to enhance the performance of the judiciary (Bedner 2008).[13] The Human Rights Court, for example, has not received any cases since 2004 (see Setiawan, this volume), and since

---

[11] The case provides an example in which a corporation is held accountable for crimes. The corporation's executive management were held criminally accountable and served imprisonment for the corporation's criminal offences against the Environmental Law. The District Court initially charged the executive director and the project manager who represented the corporation to pay 100 million rupiah (10,000 USD) fines, but acquitted them from imprisonment; see Palalawan District Court, Decision no. 08/Pid.B/2012/PN. Plw. The prosecutors appealed the decision, and the High Court revised the decision, and added a one-year imprisonment sentence with 6-month probation period (Decision no. 235/Pid.Sus/2012/PTR). Prosecutors furthered filed cassation to the Supreme Court, which revised the High Court decision by omitting the probation period and charged the defendants to serve one-year imprisonments aside from the sanction to pay fines (Decision no. 1266K/Pid.sus/2014).

[12] The case was filed under the civil lawsuit procedure (District Court of Melauboh, Decision no. 12/Pdt.G/2012/PN.BO). The appealed court revised the decision and freed the company from the obligation to replant the destroyed peatland as contained in the District Court decision; see High Court of Banda Aceh Decision no. 50/PDT/2014/PT. BNA. The decision was strengthened by the Supreme Court in Decision No. 651 K/PDT/2015.

[13] Bedner's research (2008) on the Administrative Courts suggests there are ways in which specialized courts can promote judicial performance and the professionalism of judges.

2012 the Directorate of Human Rights Violations of the Attorney General's office was closed due to a lack of cases (Wiwoho 2017).

To date, the special court strategy, which often is perceived as providing space to address special problems pertinent to a particular field such as forestry, fisheries or taxes, and to provide special legal procedures for accountability of crimes related to these fields continues to be popular among different actors proposing a new law or amending the law. It continues to appear in a number of new laws and amended laws discussed by DPR. For example, the draft of the Agrarian Law, discussed in Commission II of the DPR since 2013, introduces an Agrarian Court, a special court to address land disputes. In 2014, in the public hearing with the DPR, the Supreme Court rejected this plan (Hukumonline 2016d). In 2015 the Supreme Court conducted an evaluation which supported its earlier recommendation to the DPR that establishment of a special court specific for land disputes is both unnecessary and less effective. In 2017, IKAHI, which was consulted by the DPR on the plan to establish special court for land disputes, echoed the position of the Supreme Court to reject the plan. It highlighted and recommended the DPR to integrate the plan into the existing judicial organisation and structure under the Supreme Court (Hukumonline 2015c). In addition, in the recent deliberation of the amendment to Law No. 35/2009 on Narcotics, the National Bureau of Narcotics (BNN) expressed its interest to establish a special court for drugs-related crimes in the DPR hearing. Referring to the Anti-corruption Court, the BNN suggested it should have greater power in prosecuting drugs-related crimes (Kusuma 2016).

The Fisheries Court: An Overview

The Fisheries Court was first introduced in Law No. 31/2004 on Fisheries, which amended the Law on Fisheries No. 8/1985. The attempt to establish a Fisheries Court was first discussed as part of the demand to amend Law No. 9/1985 on Fisheries. The demand for a new law on fisheries also reflected the emerging role of fisheries and marine exploration in the national development agenda post 1998, after so many years of neglect under the land-centred development policies of the New Order. Under the New Order, fisheries were only managed by a small department under the Ministry of Agriculture, therefore the first law on fisheries focused on fresh water fish farming and small-scale coastal fishing catchment areas. The institutional landscape changed under Abdul Rahman Wahid, when he established the Ministry of Marine Exploration in 1999

(Presidential Decree No. 355/M/1999) and appointed a renowned environmentalist Sarwono Kusumaatmadja as the first Minister for Marine Exploration. In this period, the economic scale of marine products, including high-sea fishing, has rapidly increased. The total export of fisheries produced in 1999 was about USD 1.5 million and was gradually expected to reach USD 1.6 million in 2000.[14] High-sea fishing produce was recorded at 4.9 million tons in 2000 and increased to 5.6 million tons in 2003 (Kata Data 2016).[15]

During the period 2000–4, the strategic policies of the Ministry of Marine Exploration concentrated on supporting the small fisheries communities, mainly to improve the freshwater production capacities and poverty alleviation programmes for coastal areas. The existing law was seen to be adequate and there was no strategic plan to reform the law on fisheries. The Law on Fisheries no. 8/1985 did not address large-scale commercial fishing activities, including ocean fishing catchment, and although it regulated fisheries-related crimes, the scope of the crimes is limited and narrowly defined. For example, fisheries crimes are briefly defined into two broad categories, namely offences related to the use of tools and materials that endanger marine resources and the environment (art. 6), and activities which pollute the environment (art. 7).

During the period of 2000–3, one of the driving factors for reform came from the House of the Representatives, which organised consultations with different stakeholders to discuss the problem of illegal fishing in high seas by foreign fleets. Foreign fleets often are more technologically advanced and benefit from corrupt practices in licensing by the local administration. This issue has been broadly discussed in public as well as in several consultation meetings between the government and the DPR during 2002–3.

In general, Law No. 31/2004 aims to address issues in the emerging fisheries industry, particularly large-scale commercial fishing in the ocean. The amendment expands the scope of offences covered by the fisheries crimes, which under Law No. 8/1985 was briefly defined into two categories. The first is misdemeanours which includes offences related to fraud licensing or commercial fishing without adequate license (art. 26, 27), and offences which include the use of chemical or other

---

[14] Keputusan Menteri Kelautan dan Perikanan No.: Kep. 18/Men/2002 tentang Rencana Strategis Pembangunan, Kelautan dan Perikanan tahun 2001–4.

[15] See Kata Data, 2016, Produksi Ikan Tangkap di Indonesia 2000–2004, accessible at: https://databoks.katadata.co.id/datapublish/2016/08/08/produksi-ikan-tangkap-indonesia-2000–14.

commercial fishing facilities that potentially endanger the marine resources or polluted the environment (art. 24, 25). The law did not specifically regulate large-scale commercial fishing activities in the ocean but mainly focused on fostering the development of small-scale fishing activities in coastal areas, and fresh water fish farming. It excludes fishery-related offences committed in the Exclusive Economic Zone from its jurisdiction.

The Fisheries Law maintains the two classifications of crimes contained in the previous fishery law, but substantially expands the scope of fisheries-related crimes to include governance of the large-scale commercial fishing activities including commercial fishing activities in the Economic Exclusive Zone. It also introduced at least thirteen fisheries-related crimes, including crimes related to fish importation (art. 88), commercial processing and distribution (art. 89–92). It also extended criminal liability of fisheries crimes to include individual criminal responsibility of fleets' operators, owners, captain (art. 93, 97–8), and legal personae such as companies and foreign companies (art. 101) in which the criminal sanction weighs to one-third of the sanction to individual offenders.

To support the enforcement of fisheries crimes, the law established a special court with special criminal procedures to prosecute these crimes. According to the Fisheries Law, five fisheries courts shall be established within two years after the enactment of the law, and further courts can continue to be established gradually if required.[16] The second amendment of the Law strengthened the Fisheries Court's speciality by inserting words to the effect that the Fisheries Court is a special court established within the District Court.[17] Up to the present, there are ten fisheries courts established (see Figure 10.1).

The Fisheries Law requires the composition of the Fisheries Court to include two ad hoc judges together with one career judge. The ad hoc judges are expected to have expertise in the field of fisheries either from academic trainings or professional experience. According to the recruitment procedure of ad hoc judges of the Fisheries Court, the candidate is expected to have at least five years' professional experience in the field of

---

[16] See Law No. 31/2004 on fisheries, art. 71(6).

[17] According to the amended 1945 Constitution, the Supreme Court comprises four special courts, namely the general court, the administrative court, the military court and religious court. Law No. 5/2004 further emphasized this category by stipulating that any other special court could only be established based on Law and has to be under one of the four categories (art. 15(1)).

Figure 10.1   Fisheries Courts timeline (2008–2014)

fisheries.[18] The recruitment process for ad hoc judges began in 2006 and twenty-eight ad hoc judges were appointed.[19] Following the establishment of two Fisheries Courts in 2009, the Supreme Court recruited nineteen additional ad hoc court judges. In 2012, another twenty new ad hoc judges were appointed. The number of ad hoc judges to career judges has changed over time (see Figure 10.2).

Based on the assumption that the elements of the crimes are unique to fisheries and substantially different from crimes recognized in the Penal Code, the law also requires the trial to follow special criminal procedures that significantly differ from the general criminal procedures contained in the Code of Criminal Procedure (Kitab Undang-Undang Hukum Acara Pidana/KUHAP).[20] These special procedures enhance the powers of prosecutors to produce evidence for fisheries crimes. According to the government representatives during the deliberation session of the law, the KUHAP provides only the generic rules in prosecution; therefore, it will be insufficient for any special court investigation (DPR 2018; DPR 2004a). In short, fisheries are a specific subject that requires specific rules (*lex specialis*); therefore, it requires a special legal procedure, and the generic rules in the KUHAP are insufficient to determine crimes committed in the sea (DPR 2004b). Within this special procedure framework, the law gives prosecutorial power to three government bodies, namely the Ministry of Marine and Fisheries (the Civil Servant investigator, known as PPNS), the

---

[18] See Government Regulation No. 24/2006 on the procedures for recruitment and dismissal of ad hoc judges for the fisheries court, art. 3(g)–(h).

[19] The list of the ad hoc court judges can be found in Keppres No. 22/P/2005.

[20] See General Elucidation of Law No. 31/2004.

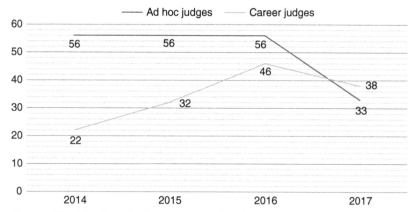

Figure 10.2 Number of Fisheries Court judges from 2014 to 2017

national police and the Navy. The wording of this clause indirectly strengthens the position of the Navy to carry out criminal investigation outside the Exclusive Economic Zone. Initially, the Navy had exclusive authority as the only criminal investigator for crimes committed within the Exclusive Economic Zone. The second amendment of the law in 2009 strengthened the position of Civil Servant investigators by extending their authority to cover Exclusive Economic Zones, and by giving them priority as the key investigator for crimes committed in the harbour areas.[21]

Although most aspects of the trial are still based on KUHAP, the Fisheries Law emphasises the need to have a speedy trial in prosecuting fisheries crimes. As detailed further in chapter XIV of the Fisheries law,[22] once the case dossier is submitted to the prosecutor's office, the case has to be submitted to the court within twenty-five days and the trial shall be completed in thirty days. In absentia trial is permitted to support this speedy process (art. 79). Overall, the criminal prosecution at the first-instance court shall be completed within fifty-five days. The trial at the appeal level shall be completed in another thirty days, and if the case goes to the Supreme Court, the final decision needs to be issued within thirty days (see Figure 10.3).

---

[21] See Law No. 45/2009 on the Amendment of Law No. 31/2004 on fisheries, art. 73 (2) and (3).

[22] See Law No. 31/2004 on fisheries, art. 72–83.

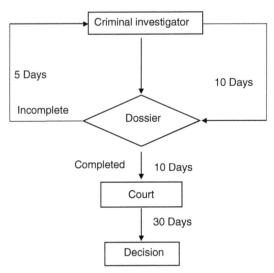

Figure 10.3   Fisheries trial procedure

Major Challenges of the Court

The Fisheries Court is established based on the notion that crimes unique to fisheries entail specific procedures of proof and evidence and require specific expertise which substantially differs from that acquired by judges who serve the general courts. However, after more than ten years of its establishment, and despite the number of ad hoc judges appointed to serve on the ten fisheries courts, the performance of the court does not seem to have improved. On the contrary, some decisions issued by the Fisheries Courts have spurred public debates and controversies such as in decisions to release foreign vessels that were caught for illegal fishing in Indonesian waters, such as Panama vessel MV Hai Va, five Tiongkok vessels owned by Sino Group and the MV Sellin, a vessel with a Guinea Equatorial flag. The weak performance of the Fisheries Court and high-profile dismissals of important cases have led to a call for review of the court.

Overall, there are two major challenges hindering the Fisheries Court from fully functioning. The problems stem from two levels: first, the text of the law, particularly the wording of some articles that are legally problematic such as the problem of scope and definition of the jurisdiction of the Fisheries Court; second, problems arisen from the lack of institutional support, as reflected in the rivalries among government agencies holding criminal investigation authority, which further led to the problem of coordination, and the lack of support from the Supreme Court.

The Problem of Jurisdiction

From the outset, as recorded in the deliberations of the bill in the DPR, the Ministry of Marine and Fisheries wanted the Fisheries Court to have autonomy, which is reflected in the special procedure in prosecuting the crimes, and jurisdiction unique to the court. Although at the beginning the Fisheries Courts would only be established in a few places where fisheries crimes are reported in high numbers, the intention was to establish the courts across the country. However, the issue of jurisdiction was problematic as the court was assumed to have a different jurisdiction from the general court, although during the deliberation process the committee did not define it in detail. Moreover, in the absence of prior consultation with the Supreme Court, the scope of the Fisheries Court's jurisdiction and other technical issues in preparing the establishment of the court failed to be properly discussed (DPR 2004a: 1190–4).[23] Although during the deliberation some DPR members raised the question about the budget required for the day-to-day operation of the court, which includes salaries and recruitment of the court clerks and judges, and maintenance of the court facilities, these important practical questions were left unanswered until the final draft was adopted. The choices of locations and the number of courts to be established for the first time were made – based on the government's preference – simply by identifying where a high number of fisheries crimes are reported.

Recognising the lack of support from the Supreme Court to establish the Fisheries Court, representatives of the Ministry insisted on having a provision to secure the existence of the court, by detailing the minimum number of courts that must be established. Consequently, a provision defining the jurisdiction of the Fisheries Court had to be included. In order to address this issue, the final draft adopted a definition of the jurisdiction of the Fisheries Court that is consistent with the District Court's jurisdiction (art. 71(4)). This formulation has created difficulties for prosecutors and the Fisheries Court to fully function as many offences

---

[23] During the session, a representative from the National Police reminded the committee that the law may not be enforceable without the presence of the Supreme Court, the key institution in the establishment of the court in the discussion. Therefore, the chair of the Committee ordered the government to consult the Supreme Court about the plan. But the consultation did not seem to take place until the DPR stipulated the Law in 2004.

take place outside the general court jurisdiction or the crime scene located closer to the other court, which further reduces the cost of the trial. Therefore, fisheries crimes continue to be tried at the general district court instead of the Fisheries Court. When DPR initiated the second amendment of the law in 2009, the Ministry of Maritime and Fisheries Affairs took the opportunity to omit this problematic article.

The problem in the definition of the court's jurisdiction coupled with ambitious provisions to create speedy criminal procedures in which the prosecution is expected to be completed in ninety days (art. 73–5 Law no. 45/2009) have made prosecutions in the Fisheries Court more difficult. A very short detention period of ten days has restrained prosecutors from preparing a good quality of dossier to be submitted to the court, particularly if the defendant is a foreign citizen who needs a translator. Some prosecutors interviewed in the study carried out by Attorney General office on the effectiveness of the court in 2017 also confirmed this problem (Sunartri 2017).

In addition, prosecuting fisheries crimes is often more expensive compared to general crimes. A study carried out by the Attorney General office in 2017 on the effectiveness of the court revealed that some elements of pre-criminal investigation make prosecution of the crime costly. Among them are the costs to carry out crime scene investigation on the sea, the on-site examination in the trial, as most of the evidence cannot be brought to the court room, and pretrial detention for defendants who in many cases are foreign citizens (Sunarti et al. 2017). To avoid the problem, many prosecutions of fisheries crimes are carried out without pretrial detention, and the trial is conducted *in absentia*. In addition, as many defendants cannot speak the Indonesian language (as they are foreigners), prosecution of the crimes requires additional costs for translation at each level from criminal investigation to the trial. In some cases, translators are provided by the government of the defendants.

According to the law, the jurisdiction of the Fisheries Court is limited to fisheries crimes contained in the Fisheries Law (art. 74(1)). The formulation is problematic as in many cases fisheries-related crimes involve other crimes as well such as slavery, people smuggling and trafficking in persons, which are not necessarily crimes under the fisheries law, but are crimes according to other laws. To date, the clause on jurisdiction has restrained prosecutors from choosing the different courts' jurisdiction which may bring the best result. Once the case is submitted to the fisheries court, in many cases it will be unlikely to be submitted to other courts, notwithstanding the opportunity to successfully prosecute them in general court is higher. As a result, many other offences such as violation of labour law and corruption in fisheries crimes failed to be held accountable while the prosecution under the Fisheries Court often yields no success.[24] Therefore, a few high-profile cases like the Benjina case were not tried in the fisheries court. Benjina case was a high-profile case reported internationally by Associated Press (AP) which revealed the practice of slavery in the fishing companies of PT Pusaka Benjina Resources (PBR) in 2015. Although the case could have included fisheries crimes, the prosecutors filed the case in the District Court for trafficking in persons. The court charged eight of the companies' personnel, five of whom are foreign citizens, for three years' imprisonment and pay restitution to the victims of 884 million rupiahs (USD 88,000).

More and more fisheries-related crimes are brought to the District Courts (see generally Pascoe, this volume; see Figure 10.4). The crimes include illegally selling fish product without a proper license,[25] fishing outside legally designated fishing areas[26] or without permit from port officer,[27] and illegally recruiting and employing ship crews without proper documents. This situation has raised the issue of the effectiveness of the Fisheries Court. In a hearing with the DPR in 2015, the IKAHI reported that some Fisheries Courts did not receive any cases for two years. IKAHI raised additional problems, such as the failure of the Supreme Court to pay the salary of ad hoc judges appointed for the courts (DPR 2015).

The formulation of criminal procedures specific to the fisheries crimes is also criticized for failing to comply with relevant international standards, such as the imprisonment of foreign crews if they fail to pay the fines. Under the UN Convention on the Law of the Sea (UNCLOS), of which the government has been a party since 1985, imprisonment cannot be applied

---

[24] Interview with M. Yunus and Harrimuddin of the 115 Taskforce against Illegal Fishing, 26/1/2018.

[25] See, for example, a 2017 case against Ibnu Walid in Banyuwangi District Court, who was charged for two months and fifteen days jail and fined Rp. 2 million, which upon the failure to pay would be replaced by two months' confinement, Putusan P. N. Banyuwangi No. 202/Pid.Sus-PRK/2018/PN Byw.

[26] For example, in 2018 the Ternate District Court fined Robert Boyke Sumampouw Rp. 7 million, which will be replaced by four months' imprisonment if he fails to pay; see District Court of Ternate Decision No. 134/Pid.Sus/2018/PN Tte.

[27] For example, in the case of Government vs Hamjah Bin Hamid, tried at Tarakan District Court, the court charged the Chief of Captain of the TB Alexander III ship for sailing without an official permit issued by the Chief of the Port, and sentenced him for five months' imprisonment and fines of 10 million rupiahs; see District Court of Tarakan Decision No. 90/Pid.B/2018/PN Tar.

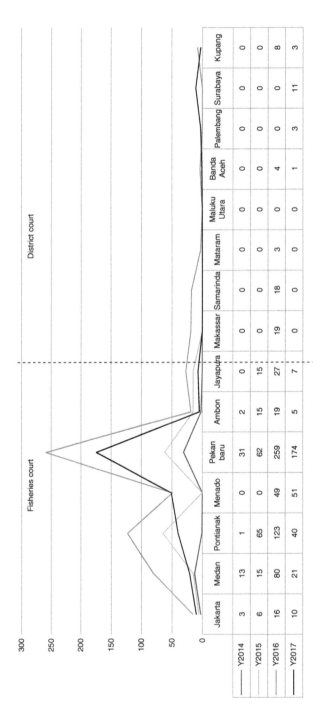

	Jakarta	Medan	Pontianak	Menado	Pekan baru	Ambon	Jayapura	Makassar	Samarinda	Mataram	Maluku Utara	Banda Aceh	Palembang	Surabaya	Kupang
Y2014	3	13	1	0	31	2	0	0	0	0	0	0	0	0	0
Y2015	6	15	65	0	62	15	15	0	0	0	0	0	0	0	0
Y2016	16	80	123	49	259	19	27	19	18	3	0	4	0	0	8
Y2017	10	21	40	51	174	5	7	0	0	0	0	1	3	11	3

Figure 10.4 Number of fisheries crimes cases tried at the Fisheries Court and the District Court

for crimes committed in EEZ areas unless there is specific agreement on that matter between two countries (art. 73(3)). However, the second amendment of the Fisheries Law allows the use of imprisonment to any offender's committed crimes in the EEZ areas (Law No. 45/2009, art. 102). Judges' views vary, as reflected in their decisions. Some judges apply imprisonment, while some others limit the sanction to fines in accordance with UNCLOS (Lubis 2016). In response to this criticism, in 2015, the Supreme Court issued a circular letter to prohibit judges from applying imprisonment in the crimes committed in EEZ areas.[28] Yet, judges' practices continue to vary.

A Lack of Institutional Support from the Judiciary

Generally, the Supreme Court is reluctant to support the establishment of any special court, especially when the new court also implies the appointment of ad hoc judges. The Ministry of Maritime and Fisheries Affairs was well aware of the Supreme Court's position in regard to the special court; however, it supported the government's desire to have a special court. When the law was discussed in the DPR, the Ministry of Justice and Human Rights echoed the Supreme Court's position, asserting that the most important consideration was to have a speedy trial on fisheries crimes rather than the option for a special court as it might limit the forum to prosecute fisheries crimes at the District Court.[29] The view also received support from representatives of the National Police, who argued that the establishment of the court should be initiated by the Supreme Court as part of respect for judicial independence (DPR 2004b). However, the proposal put forward by the Ministry of Maritime and Fisheries Affairs to have a special court won support from most factions in the DPR and was adopted in the final draft of the law.

The proceedings of the Working Committee during the deliberation also reflect the lack of consultation with the Supreme Court in this regard. The absence of discussion on the technical details such as the impact on court management by the Supreme Court, the budget, physical infrastructure and human resources also reflects the absence of consultation

---

[28] Supreme Court Circular Letter No. 3/2015.

[29] The Supreme Court was previously under this Ministry. A few months before the closed session with the DPR to discuss the draft law took place; the Ministry of Justice and Human Rights officially handed over the management of the Fisheries Court to the Supreme Court through which the court enjoyed its institutional independence. This helped to understand how the Ministry shared the same views with the Supreme Court (DPR 2004b).

with the Supreme Court. These factors partly contributed to the delay in implementing the law, in particular to establish the courts within two years after the enactment of the Fisheries Law. In responding to this situation, the Ministry of Maritime and Fisheries Affairs had to allocate its own internal resources to implement the law. This includes providing a venue for the court and funds to recruit ad hoc judges. The Ministry also allocated funds and sought international cooperation to provide trainings for fisheries judges and prosecutors. According to the Supreme Court Annual Report 2014, the Ministry's contribution in the form of buildings, transportations and other facilities for seven fisheries courts is worth around Rp. 6.6 billion (USD 6,600,000) (Supreme Court 2014: 218).

In 2005, based on the agreement between the Ministry of Maritime and Fisheries Affairs and the Vice Chairperson of the Chief Justice for the judicial sector, a working group to prepare for the establishment of the Fisheries Court was appointed. However, until the end of the two-year transition period mandated by the law (2006), no Fisheries Court was established. Therefore, the Supreme Court appealed for a regulation in lieu of the law to the president to postpone the implementation of the Fisheries Law, particularly regarding the obligation to establish fisheries courts in five places, namely North Jakarta, Medan, Pontianak, Bitung and Tual. The delay also reflected a lack of institutional support from the Supreme Court, in terms of both human resources and the infrastructures necessary for the Fisheries Courts to function.

The Regulation in Lieu of the Law extended the time limit for the first establishment of the court by the end of 2007. However, it was only in 2008 that the Fisheries Court began to function, so its performance was first evaluated in the Supreme Court annual report in 2009. The number of cases heard in five courts was among the lowest in the criminal chamber of the Supreme Court, recorded at seventy-six cases, or 0.002 per cent of the total cases received by the general courts. In 2009, the slow progress of the implementation of the law has led the DPR to table a proposed amendment of the Fisheries Law in the national legislation programme (Prolegnas). The plan also was supported by KIARA, a coalition of NGOs that advocates the rights of fisher folk along the coastal areas, and small-scale commercial fishing, which asserted the criminal procedures contained in the Law hindered the court from hearing more cases. As a result, only a few cases were charged under the fisheries crimes, but many cases were tried as common crimes under the Penal Code (KUHP). In a focus group discussion held by the Secretariat

General of DPR in 2015, KIARA highlighted that the existing law failed to prosecute the key actors, such as the company owners, but mainly could only hold accountable low-level staffs of the company (Khopiatuziadah 2017).

The DPR led the initiative for the second amendment of the Law and, within less than one month, had finished the deliberation and submitted the final amended draft for adoption to the Plenary Assembly.[30] In regards to the Fisheries Court, one salient change put forward by the DPR was the word 'specialised court' (*pengadilan khusus*) to emphasise the existence of the court as a specialised court (art. 71(2)). This also implied that all fisheries cases could only be brought before the Fisheries Court, and therefore, eliminated the jurisdiction of the District Court to hear cases on fisheries crimes. The Ministry did not agree with this change and instead suggested retaining the existing text of the law (DPR 2009). The government argued that the current art. 71(2) as contained in the Law No. 31/2004 should be retained. Instead, the special character of the court could be developed through technical coordination with the Supreme Court, for example, by a jointly developed certification system for judges before they served the Fisheries Court. This view reflected a substantial change of the Ministry's position in regards to the establishment and management of the special fisheries court. Having observed the weak performance of the court and the major problems in ensuring the court to properly function, including in addressing the problem of coordination among government institutions with criminal investigation authorities on one side and the continuous reluctance of the Supreme Court in supporting the court, the Ministry was forced to take a more realistic strategy in maintaining the existence of the fisheries court.

As far as the Fisheries Court was concerned, the Supreme Court consistently displays lack of interest and support. The establishment suffered from significant delays, as the Supreme Court failed to allocate both financial and human resources necessary to set up the court, which according to the Supreme Court required at the minimum 3.5 trillion rupiahs (USD 350 million). After more than two years of delay from the designated plan as contained in Law no. 31/2004, the Ministry covered almost all the cost to establish the court, such as preparing for the recruitment of ad hoc judges, training for law enforcement officers

---

[30] DPR 2009. The amended draft was submitted on 9 September 2009, and on 30 September, the final draft was submitted for adoption to the DPR plenary assembly.

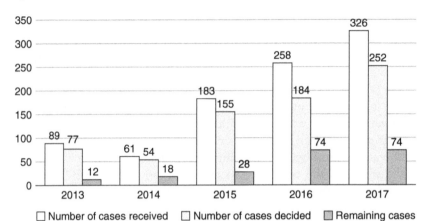

Figure 10.5   Number of cases at the Fisheries Court (2013–2017)

and buildings for the court. As reflected in the deliberation of the Law in 2002, the DPR and the Ministry intended to establish the Fisheries Court across the country similar to the District Courts in numbers (DPR 2002). However, four years after the law was enacted, it became clear that such interest would never be realised, and the number of the courts was unlikely to increase.

In addition, considering the limited resources of the Supreme Court and the Directorate General Protection and Control of Marine Resources (P2SKP), the Ministry argued that the new text proposed by the DPR limits the opportunity for fisheries crimes to be prosecuted at the District Court. This further affects the performance of the ministry in increasing the number of prosecutions of fisheries crimes. The shift in the position of the government towards the specialised court presumably was influenced by a series of consultations with the Supreme Court in preparing the implementation of the court. As previously mentioned, both institutions set up a working group to prepare for the establishment of the Fisheries Court, through which the two institutions could better communicate. Yet, DPR insisted that the change be adopted at the final draft. However, as shown in the chart above, the amendment made to the law in 2009 failed to improve the performance of the Fisheries Court. Although the number of cases has gradually increased, in total the number of cases remains lower than the other special courts, such as the corruption court (see Figure 10.5). The lower number of cases brought to the Fisheries Court was partly due to the issue of jurisdiction, which I discuss earlier.

In December 2017, the Supreme Court criticised the performance of the Fisheries Court, and called for the Ministry of Maritime and Fisheries Affairs to review the Fisheries Courts as they continued to be problematic (Kumparan 2017a).

The lack of support for the Fisheries Court is clearly reflected from the low number of judges and clerk to the court. In the last five years, their numbers are among the lowest compared to the other specialised courts established and managed by the Supreme Court. No data were recorded on the number of clerks to the court specific to Fisheries Court until 2016, when the number of clerks to the court for Fisheries Court first appeared in the annual report of the Directorate General of General Court of the Supreme Court. There is no data on the number of clerks to the court specific to Fisheries Court until 2016, when the number of clerks to the Fisheries Court first appeared in the annual report of the Directorate General of General Court of the Supreme Court. There were nine clerks to the court across the District Court and Appellate Courts in that year (Badilum 2016). Similarly, the total number of career judges and ad hoc judges for the Fisheries Court are low compared to other special courts. Until 2013, there were 243 career judges who obtain certification as fisheries judges.

The Ministry seems to be aware of the lack of interest and support from the Supreme Court to the Fisheries Court. As the court could not fully support its campaign against illegal fishing in creating strong deterrent effect to the offenders, since 2015 it has shifted the focus of creating deterrent effects against illegal fishing away from the court, but intensified the attempt to confiscate and sink foreign vessels allegedly committing illegal fishing in Indonesia's water territory. However, the attempt to burn down foreign vessels is often restrained by the requirement to obtain a district court order as the vessels are considered to be evidence before the court. In March 2015, the Supreme Court supported this attempt by issuing a circular letter to ease the requirement as contained in the Fisheries Law (art. 76A). The circular letter provides that in order to have a deterrent effect against illegal fishing, the criminal investigator does not require a district court order to sink or to burn down a confiscated foreign vessel caught for illegal fishing. Through this circular letter, require a Supreme Court halts the enforcement of the Law, which provides that criminal investigator require a court order to burn down or to sink a confiscated foreign vessel caught for illegal fishing in Indonesia water territory. Therefore, the Ministry can sink any foreign vessel allegedly committing illegal fishing in Indonesia territory even before the trial is concluded. The impact of this circular letter to the number of scuttled foreign vessels is noticeable. In 2014, there were only eight foreign vessels scuttled by the Ministry. The number increased significantly to 112 vessels in 2015, 113 vessels in 2016, and in 2017 the Ministry sank in total 317 vessels (Kumparan 2017b).

Institutional Rivalry on Criminal Investigation Power

One of the problems hindering the work of the Fisheries Court lies in the continuous rivalry among four institutions holding criminal investigation powers in fisheries-related crimes. They are the National Police, particularly its Air and Water Police Unit (PolAirUd), the Navy, for crimes committed in the Exclusive Economic Zone territory, and the Directorate General of the monitoring of maritime and fisheries resources (PSDKP) of the Ministry of Maritime and Fisheries (on the public prosecution, see Afandi this volume). The three institutions obtained their power from different laws. Prior to the stipulation of the fisheries law, these institutions expect for PSDKP individually exercised their authority and therefore overlapped with each other, except in the area of Economic Exclusive Zone where the Navy enjoys monopoly of criminal investigation power.

Before the enactment of the Fisheries law, criminal investigation power lay in two institutions, namely the Navy, and the National Police, which also has a specialised unit for securing water territories. The National Police is the main criminal investigator body according to the Law on Criminal Procedure (KUHAP). Within the National Police, authority lies with the water Police unit. The Police water unit was established in 1950 and its mandate includes conducting criminal investigation in Indonesian waters.[31] It is also equipped with the necessary facilities to carry out water patrol and to maintain security in Indonesian waters. The directorate also has representation at the local level, which is coordinated under the provincial police.

The adoption of the Economic Exclusive Zone has given the Navy exclusive criminal investigative powers for crimes committed in Indonesian waters within the limit of 200 nautical miles of the outer strip bordering the Indonesian territorial sea. The power is granted to the Navy as part of the national defence role in maintaining the sovereignty

---

[31] See Peraturan Kapolri No. 21 tahun 2010 tentang Susunan Organisasi dan Tata kerja Satuan Organisasi di Tingkat Maber Polri.

of the country in the sea and was strengthened by the 1985 Fisheries Law. The initial amended Draft Law on Fisheries in 2002 eliminated this role and shifted the authority to the Ministry of Maritime and Fisheries Affairs office which functioned as Civil Servants with Criminal Investigator power (PPNS). As the principal institution implementing the Fisheries Law, the Ministry wanted to increase its power in the field of maritime affairs and fisheries to include not only controlling the fishing industry through licensing but also law enforcement through criminal procedures. The Ministry was well aware that in order to secure the authority and scope given to PPNS it had to be detailed in the law.

The Navy represented by the TNI/Polri faction in its written response called for the Committee to revise the draft law to retain its investigative authority (TNI Polri 2002). Two other factions, FKB (Kebangkitan Bangsa Faction) and FPP (Persatuan Pembangunan Faction) in the DPR supported the call to retain its criminal investigation power and confront the government's interest represented by the Ministry. These two factions argued that the law, while accommodating the interests of the Ministry also needed to sustain the existing powers held by both the Navy and the National Police. Therefore, the law needs to ensure that the three institutions have equal position in exercising their investigation powers, as reflected in the final draft adopted by the plenary assembly. For the Navy, the consensus adopted in the final draft not only secured its prosecutorial power in the EEZ but also extended its jurisdiction outside the EEZ areas.

The equal position of three different institutions in conducting criminal investigation has raised the issue of coordination and the division of labour in criminal investigation. The Ministry wanted the law to regulate in detail roles and responsibility of each institution to secure its position as criminal investigator. But this interest did not get support from most DPR factions, including the Police and the Army, whose position as criminal investigator had already been secured and been regulated in detail in other laws namely KUHAP for the National Police and Law on Exclusive Economic Zone for the Navy (DPR 2004a). Having failed to secure consensus from the Committee members, the government through the Ministry of Law and Human rights raised the issue of coordination which might arise from unclear division of labour among the three institutions. The Committee members accommodated the concern on the need for coordination, but refused to add more clauses to detail roles and responsibility of each institution in criminal investigation. In order to address this potential problem, the Committee added an article on a coordination forum to be organised by the Ministry of Maritime and Fisheries Affairs to be established when it deemed necessary, including at the local level (DPR 2004b).

In the implementation of the law, the Navy and the police have better facilities and expertise in carrying out water patrol operations and criminal investigation in water territories, while the PPNS might be the weakest in regard to facilities and expertise among the three. One year after the amended Fisheries Law was enforced, the Ministry of Maritime and Fisheries Affairs had produced 374 civil servant investigators (Pusat Data, Statistik dan Informasi 2009: 102). The number steadily increased and reached 495 investigators in 2015 (Pusat Data, Statistik dan Informasi 2015: 175). Despite the increase in number of investigators, the capacity in prosecuting fisheries crimes continues to be weak. In 2015 alone, the total number of fisheries crimes prosecuted stood at 184 cases. In addition, the Ministry also increased its investigator power by extending the power of PPNS to cover crimes committed in the EEZ together with the Navy. With the absence of Navy representation in the DPR, the proposal was smoothly accepted without substantial objection.[32] Further, it also increased the authority of the civil servant investigator by prioritising them for investigation of crimes committed in port areas (art. 73(3)), preventing the police from conducting criminal investigations in these areas.

The issue of coordination among the three institutions, which is partly due to institutional egos, has hindered the Fisheries Court from fully functioning and was among the key issues listed in the proposal for the second amendment of the law in September 2009. The issue of coordination due to institutional rivalries persisted after the second amendment was adopted until 2015 when Susi Pudjiastuti became Minister and established Task Force 115 on illegal fishing.[33] The establishment of the task force gave her authority to control and lead criminal prosecutions against illegal fishing, including to glean intelligence from the Navy directly, which prior to the establishment of the task force could not be accessed (Salim 2015). The task force also addresses the issue of coordination and has played pivotal roles in mediating competing interests among the three institutions.

---

[32] Since 2004, the TNI/Polri faction was eliminated from the DPR as part of the democratic reform process.
[33] Presidential Regulation No. 115/2015 on the task force on illegal fishing.

Conclusion

A closer look into the establishment of the Fisheries Court helps to advance understanding of judicial development in Indonesia post 1998. One of the most interesting findings of this research lies on the contested interests – in the absence of the judiciary – that lie behind the establishment of the Fisheries Court. The deliberation process of the two legislative amendments in 2004 and 2009 of the Fisheries Law reveals important insights about how different state agencies negotiate their interests in the establishment of the Fisheries Court. The executive, represented by the Ministry of Maritime and Fisheries Affairs, intended to establish the Fisheries Court as a symbolic representation of its authority. Yet the executive has had to negotiate and contest its interests with the Navy and the Police. The presence of these two institutions, which are the political representation of the army, is possible only because the process took place shortly before the wave of democratic reform in 2004 eliminated these institutions from the legislative body. The contestation of the aforesaid interests continued through the second amendment to the Fisheries Law that took place in 2009. These two institutions had been powerful institutionally in the field of maritime and fisheries criminal prosecutions and did not seem to be affected practically by any changes put forward in the law.

From a different angle, this political process also reflects the limits and vulnerability of the judiciary in its struggle for institutional independence from the other branches of government. When the deliberation of the law took place from 2002 to 2004, the Supreme Court was occupied with the implementation of its first blueprint of institutional reform which was intensified under the leadership of Bagir Manan, who took over as chairperson in 2001. Under his leadership, the Supreme Court exercised its institutional independence through the implementation of one roof system, through which the Supreme Court has full control of the court organisation and management (see Assegaf, this volume). In February 2004, the first blueprint of judicial reform was launched, which outlined the strategic direction of reform within the judiciary. To a large extent, the paper also is a symbol of political statement of the Supreme Court against any political interference from the other branches of government, particularly the executive. Yet as shown earlier in this chapter, lawmaking opened the opportunity for other government institutions to perpetuate influence to shape the course of judicial development.

The dynamics in the implementation of the law, as elaborated above, reflects the Supreme Court's response to negotiate this externally driven initiative. Its reluctance in implementing the law as previously discussed suggests a silent yet clear display of irritation against external influence into judicial institutions, as the complete dismissal of the newly established court seems to be less likely. To date, despite strong criticism of the efficacy of special courts established post 1998, there was no decision to abolish any special court. These findings raise intriguing questions regarding the continuity of the evolution of judicial institutions in post-revolutionary Indonesia as previously considered in the work of Daniel S. Lev, who sketched the landscape of two major battles between the Supreme Court, the police and the prosecutors, which shaped the judicial organisation in Indonesia (Lev 1965b). The findings of my research suggest a different picture that extends the battle to include other government institutions. Further, looking into the legal process of the establishment of the court clearly demonstrates that special court strategy does not always represent the aspiration of reform, but is rather symbolic of political authority.

11

The Constitutional Court

A Levian Take on Its Place in the *Reformasi*

THEUNIS ROUX[*]

Dan Lev was famously wary of the term 'culture'. Like several other scholars of his generation (Friedman 1997; Cotterrell 1997; Nelken 2004), he warned of the dangers of using it as a catch-all phrase to explain complex social processes in ways that dispensed with the hard work of causal analysis. In Lev's view, 'culture' and its cognate, 'legal culture', were the go-to concepts of researchers who had not done enough research. Conversely, the more you knew about a society, the less you needed 'culture' to explain what was going on (Lev 1978: 38, Lev 2005a: 346–9).

My work over the last ten years has probably committed many of the sins that Lev warned about. In seeking to explain, first, the South African Constitutional Court's approach to its mandate after 1995 (Roux 2013), and then, the general process through which 'judicial review regimes' evolve (Roux 2018), I have stressed the importance of legal culture as an explanatory variable. While one of the reasons for this is that I have only lately come to Lev's work – and was thus deprived of the benefits of his cautionary remarks – I also want to defend the use of legal culture in certain kinds of carefully designed research. Many of the problems with the term, as Lev himself recognised (Lev 1993: 335n21), may be avoided if legal culture is understood more narrowly to refer to legal–cultural ideologies, complexes of legitimating ideas about law and legal institutions and their place in society.

In addition to coming late to Lev's work, the other reason for my greater willingness to deploy legal culture as an explanatory variable has to do with my scholarly background. As a legal academic, I escaped the

[*] I would like to thank Melissa Crouch for inviting me to write for this volume and, more importantly, for introducing me to Dan Lev's work. Thanks also to Melissa Crouch, Martin Krygier and Abdurrachman Satrio for comments on an earlier draft of this chapter.

admonitions against using this term that political scientists have drummed into them, seemingly from birth. My ignorance on this score may yet prove to be my undoing but, in the meantime, it has allowed me to blunder in where others have feared to tread, perhaps with some beneficial results. Like most academic lawyers, the driving force behind my research has been a desire to solve practical problems – in my case, the challenge of getting a constitutional system off the ground in countries that lack a developed tradition of the rule of law and judicial independence, or whose political tradition in these respects has at some point been compromised. The more I have researched this issue, the more I have become convinced of the need to understand the dynamic interaction of one dimension of every society's legal culture – conceptions of the law/politics relation – and the institution of judicial review (Roux 2018).

In continuing to pursue this line of research, I take some comfort in the knowledge that Lev, although mostly devoted to examining the specific nature of the Indonesian case, was not averse to comparative generalisation (see, for example, Lev 1972b: 246). He would thus have approved (or at least not totally disapproved) of scholarship that attempts to extract out of the mass of particularistic detail about developments in a range of societies certain core concepts and causal mechanisms. While his own method was inside-out and then back in, in the sense that he would first arrive at his core concepts inductively, briefly test them against other examples and then proceed to deploy them in close ethnographic analysis, he would have seen the sense, I think, of a more traditional comparative approach. There is a place, at least, for research that endeavours to strike a balance between, on the one hand, the exhaustive ethnographic study of one society, and, on the other, deductive, empirically aloof scholarship (I am thinking here particularly of rational choice) that takes a relatively crude model of human behaviour and relentlessly applies it to explain everything, everywhere.

This chapter deploys such a midway approach to explain aspects of Indonesia's constitutional development after 2002. It begins by interrogating Lev's account of law's authority and then modifies it by suggesting (1) a broader view of the factors that motivate proponents of the rule of law and (2) a different understanding of how law works its legitimating effects. One of the central tensions running through Lev's work, I argue, is that he wants, as a political scientist, to say that law's authority is always a function of politics – of sectional interests that promote the rule of law ideal under certain conditions. As an advocate of the law-state (*negara hukum*) in Indonesia, however, he was acutely aware that societies prosper where there is public confidence in law as an *autonomous* source of authority – as a social subsystem that has somehow managed to float free of the particular interests it serves to become a general public good. This tension runs through a lot of his work and undercuts what is otherwise a powerful account of the struggle for *negara hukum* in Indonesia after 1945. After noting this tension, I proceed briefly to set out my own conceptual framework, one that sees claims to legal and political authority as being capable, under certain conditions, of supporting each other in a stable ideational complex. The third section then applies this framework to examine the development of conceptions of legal and political authority during Indonesia's *reformasi*. The central, though not the only, legal–cultural actor, in this story, I argue, has been the Constitutional Court. It is thus possible to learn a great deal by looking at how successive chief justices have sought to assert and justify the Court's role in national politics. My conclusions on this score, despite differences of conceptualisation, demonstrate how vitally important Lev's work on the pre-*reformasi* period still is to an understanding of the fate of the Indonesian law-state.

Modifying Lev's take on Law's Authority

Lev's work, by his own admission, was not guided by 'a compelling theoretical perspective' (Lev 2000c: 6). He never produced, in one place, a complete and general statement of his abiding concern – the conditions under which 'new states' (i.e. states emerging from a history of colonial domination) might establish functioning constitutional systems. Instead, what we have is a series of short, conceptually dense introductions and conclusions to his major articles. Rather than setting out Lev's theoretical commitments in positive terms, these passages mostly take the form of powerful critiques of the fallacies underlying the traditional Eurocentric view of the path that new states should (normatively) or inevitably will (descriptively) follow. Nevertheless, by piecing these passages together, it is possible to reconstruct a reasonably coherent account of Lev's implied theoretical framework.

One of Lev's core theoretical commitments was that law, both as it figures in a society's legal–cultural imagination and as it operates as an instrument of government, is a function of political interests. Law's authority, on this approach, is derivative of politics – it is only ever as extensive as the degree of political support for autonomous law, which in turn is a function of the balance of political power. In distinguishing the concept of a 'legal system' from that of 'legal culture', for example, Lev wrote:

> A legal system's primary source of authority is the political system, whose legitimacy (or lack of it) extends to the substantive rules which legal systems apply and whose organization, traditions, and style determine, indeed, how far specifically legal processes are (or can be) used for social management and the pursuit of common goals. (Lev 1972b: 247)

Other representative formulations include 'law does not stand alone, but rests on a political base' (Lev 2005b: 6), and the statement that law and legal institutions 'represent a configuration of power relationships, masking it with a cover of legitimate authority' (Lev 1985: 57). The direction of influence in these passages is all one way – from politics to law. A political system – whether authoritarian or democratic – has whatever legitimacy it has, and the authority of the legal system is derivative on that legitimate political authority. Any notion that autonomous law might reciprocally legitimate political authority is either suppressed or derided as an illusion.

In another formulation, Lev does appear to recognise that in certain circumstances autonomous law may legitimate political authority – indeed, that the heart of the appeal of constitutionalism is the promise it holds out of constraining the exercise of political power and, in the process, legitimating it. In his essay on 'Social Movements, Constitutionalism and Human Rights', Lev thus wrote: 'Constitutionalism ... means little more (nor less) than the limited state, one in which official political power is surrounded by knowable laws whose acceptance transforms power into *legally* specified legitimate authority.' (Lev 1993: in 2000 reprint 322 – emphasis in the original; also discussed in Crouch 2018). Here, the project of subordinating political power to legal constraints emerges as a project through which a legally unconstrained form of political authority (patrimonial authority, for example) may be transformed into rational–legal authority in Weberian terms. Even on this account, however, law's authority is a function of politics: constitutionalism and its promise of autonomous law are depicted as an ideology that certain political groupings propound under particular historical conditions in furtherance of their interests.

In other work, Lev was quite explicit about whose political interests he thought constitutionalism served: the middle class, including intellectuals, students and notably also the legal profession. In his essay on

'Judicial Authority and the Struggle for an Indonesian Rechtsstaat', for example, Lev endorsed Marx's view that demands for the rule of law were principally driven by the middle class, with variations in outcome associated with how closely connected the middle class was to political elites (Lev 1978: 39–41). In writing about the legal aid movement in Indonesia and the advocates' profession, Lev likewise stressed the self-interested motivations that lay behind seemingly general appeals to the value of constitutional government (Lev 1976, 1978, 2000c: 309–10). The reason that professional advocates were so insistent on the need for *negara hukum*, Lev argued, was that they lacked real access to political power, first under Soekarno's Guided Democracy, and then under Soeharto's New Order regime (Lev 2000c: 309). It was largely for strategic reasons that their demands were sometimes couched in ways that appealed to less-privileged social groups (Lev 2000c: 335–6).

Seeing constitutionalism as the product of a successful middle-class movement to promote its interests in this way, Lev was sceptical about the potential of this form of government to transform society:

> [C]onstitutionalism is not an obvious solution to many of the most serious, compelling problems that humanity has to deal with ... It does not eliminate economic poverty, or social discrimination, or political abuse, or the incompetence, greed, or stupidity of political leadership ... for all these miseries, the only sensible solutions remain relevant knowledge, clearly articulated ideology, and effectively organised power in whatever kind of political structure exists. (Lev 2000c: 324)[1]

'[G]roups without power', Lev concluded, 'fare little better in constitutional than non-constitutional regimes' (Lev 2000c: 336). In other formulations, he went even further. Not only was constitutionalism no help. It was in certain circumstances a hindrance. 'It is also unnecessary to argue', Lev said, 'that "law" is the best thing that can happen to everybody. For some it may be disastrous' (Lev 1978: 39). These conclusions flow logically from Lev's theoretical premise. Since law's authority in a constitutionalist regime is only as extensive as the balance of political power permits it to be, the poor have little to gain from constitutionalism.

---

[1] Note that there is an obvious contradiction in this quoted passage. On Lev's own view, constitutionalism is a 'clearly articulated ideology' about 'effectively organised power' that draws on 'relevant knowledge' about the conditions for human freedom. This passage thus at once denies that constitutionalism is a solution for pressing social problems while at the same time defining the required solution in a way that makes constitutionalism seem like the ideal choice. This contradiction betrays the tension in Lev's views on this issue that I analyse below.

As soon as law's authority begins to intrude into politics in ways that give the poor more power, it is retracted. Or rather, this would never even happen in the first place because political power holders would not permit it.

There is clearly much to admire in this uncompromising, decidedly unromantic account of constitutionalism. The idea that it is just one ideological conception of appropriate state/society relations which competes with other powerful conceptions is a necessary corrective to liberal wishful thinking on this score. Had he been alive today, Lev would have been less surprised than most of us, I think, about all the illiberal backsliding that is going on.[2] His emphasis on the political interests that drive the demand for constitutionalism in new states, and ultimately support it after its establishment, was also ahead of its time. Long before comparative lawyers began to question the simplistic model of constitutional transplants, Lev was counselling caution (Lev 2000c: 323). Finally, Lev's insistence that liberal constitutionalism masks unequal power relations and may be a barrier to social transformation must also be taken seriously. It is the proponents of liberal constitutionalism's failure to do that which arguably lies behind this form of government's current vulnerability to populist retrenchment.

All of this is true. Nevertheless, Lev's hard-nosed scepticism about the benefits of constitutionalism is something of an overreaction to the (admittedly simplistic) views he was refuting. It is one thing, after all, to recognise that 'law ... rests on a political base' (Lev 2005b: 6), another to conclude that constitutionalism has no value apart from the immediate political interests it promotes. At times, at least, Lev appears to be substituting a kind of vulgar American political science view of law as everywhere subordinate to politics for a vulgar Marxist view of law as a superstructural reflection of a particular mode of production. This is regrettable because the question whether constitutionalist government may deliver benefits beyond satisfying the political interests that immediately support it is ultimately an empirical one. To deny this possibility by theoretical fiat is to take up a position in advance of the facts, something to which Lev was usually opposed (Lev 2005a).

Another problem for Lev is that the great sociological treatments of the conditions for the emergence of autonomous law on which he relies

---

[2] Twenty years before this became a hot topic, for example, Lev wrote that '[i]f we take seriously the study of constitutionalist evolution ... we must take equally seriously the study of constitutional decay' (Lev 1993: 322 n 2).

(Weber 1968; Unger 1976) suggest that this process is not just a question of the middle class convincing a political elite to accede to its demands. Rather, autonomous law emerges when political power holders (of whatever sort and whatever their connections to the middle class) see some virtue in it – typically its legitimating value. More than this, as E. P. Thompson taught us, the ideology of autonomous law (for which we may substitute constitutionalism in this context) only works its legitimating effects if it actually does blunt the naked exercise of political power in certain respects (Thompson 1975: 266). Thus, the intriguing thing about the constitutionalist ideal, which Lev portrays as just one 'myth' competing for ideological dominance with other 'myths' (Lev 1993: in 2000 reprint 321), is that its promises may under certain conditions come true. And when they do, the benefits of law's autonomy potentially (subject to empirical confirmation) extend beyond the political groups that demanded it.

Lev's apparent insensitivity to this point is in tension with the celebration in much of his work of the tenacity of what he called the Indonesian 'law movement' (Lev 1976, 1978, 1988, 1993). Of course, it is possible to reconcile Lev's lifelong commitment to the advocates of legal reform and judicial independence in Indonesia (see Pompe 2012: 201) with his views of constitutionalism as a self-interested middle-class project. Perhaps his closeness to the people involved caused him to see their all-too-human failings. But if all that the members of the Indonesian law movement were doing was promoting their class interests, Lev hardly would have admired them as much. It was precisely because people like Adnan Buyung Nasution and Yap Thiam Hien[3] risked their livelihoods (and sometimes their lives) for an ideal that was larger than themselves, that he devoted so much attention to them. He was inspired by the nobility of their cause, and when, towards the end of his life, they emerged victorious, he celebrated with them something larger than the triumph of an illusion.

Admittedly, the adoption of a liberal constitution (or in Indonesia's case, the amendment of an illiberal one) is only ever a temporary victory. In post-authoritarian settings, particularly, the formal constitutional promise of law's autonomy that the adoption of a liberal constitution represents is just the beginning of the (never assured) process of instantiating this ideal in practice. Perhaps that is all that Lev meant to convey

---

[3] See Lev 2011 for his full account of Yap Thiam Hien's contribution; and Crouch 2012c for a review.

by his scepticism. But he would have been more faithful to his methodological commitments if he had explicitly held open the possibility that constitutionalism may under certain conditions turn back the tide of naked power politics, or at least contain it.

If we do countenance that possibility, then we must also accept that constitutionalism comes in different forms depending on how deeply the ideal of law's autonomy is entrenched in the society we are looking at and on what form of political authority it is combined with. Just as we posit various forms of political regime between authoritarianism and democracy, so might there exist various politico-legal orders, i.e. legitimating ideologies about the relationship between legal and political authority and the appropriate degree of law's autonomy from politics.

As I have argued elsewhere (Roux 2018), there are four main conceptual possibilities in this respect, each of which may be embodied to a greater or lesser degree by actually existing politico-legal orders. On the authoritarian side, the first possibility, illustrated by Indonesia itself under Soeharto's New Order regime (and moving towards this ideal type even under Guided Democracy), is that of law's complete subordination to authoritarian political ends. In this type of politico-legal order, legitimate political authority is the product of an official, state-sanctioned ideology that explains why the political power holder, despite the lack of an authentic democratic mandate, has the right to govern. The list of legitimating rationales here includes appeals to a revolutionary anti-colonial tradition, national security, economic prosperity and the need for interethnic harmony. Little reliance is placed on the legitimating power of autonomous law in this kind of politico-legal order. Rather, law is enlisted in service to the national interest that the power holder claims to be promoting. In such an order – call it 'authoritarian instrumentalism' – law's authority is indeed entirely derivative on politics. This possibility represents Lev's default case in this sense.

But there is another authoritarian possibility as well, and that is a situation where *partial* reliance is placed on autonomous law's legitimating power. Under this scenario, legalism – the ideology of law's autonomy from politics – serves authoritarian ends by carving up social life into areas where law rules (in the sense of being genuinely free of political influence) and areas where it does not. In Singapore, for example, judges are given considerable independence to rule on commercial and family law matters (Rajah 2012). It is only when they start to enforce political rights of government opponents that their wings are clipped (Thio 2012). In this style of politico-legal order ('authoritarian legalism'), a formal commitment to electoral democracy is maintained, but the real basis for power holders' claim to legitimate political authority is not the authenticity of their democratic mandate (as policed by independent courts enforcing liberal political rights), but their claimed privileged role in promoting some ultimately democracy-trumping conception of the national interest.

On the democratic side of the divide, there are also two main possibilities. The first corresponds to the conventional view that sees all variants of liberal constitutionalism as one or another kind of democratic legalism – as politico-legal orders, that is, where the ideal of law's autonomy from politics has triumphed, and where law's authority extends to all aspects of social life, including the political process (which is what distinguishes this kind of order from authoritarian legalism). In combination with a democratic conception of political authority, the ideology of legalism drives a powerful complex of legitimating ideas in which the courts' impartial enforcement of political rights certifies claims to political authority based on the authenticity of a democratic mandate. The political branches' respect for judicial independence in turn fortifies law's claim to authority as a separate social system with its own extra-political values and impartial reasoning techniques. On this view, the differences between, say, the German conception of the appropriate relationship between law and politics and the American conception are simply a matter of degree. Both societies in the end place their faith in autonomous law's capacity to authenticate democratic mandates.

But it is clear from developments over the last century in the US that there is in fact a real difference in kind between the American politico-legal order and more straightforwardly democratic legalist ones. Americans, almost everyone agrees, lost their faith in law's autonomy in a gradual process that began with the controversy over the *Lochner* line of cases, was aided and abetted by legal realism, was given further impetus by the instrumentalisation of law under Roosevelt's New Deal, was finally revealed in the Warren Court's treatment of the US Constitution as a vehicle for progressive social reform, and which now sees both sides of the political divide in the US competing to enforce their partisan conception of the American constitutional project. Law's authority in this politico-legal order has long since ceased to be legitimated by any plausible claim to autonomy from politics. Instead, it lies in the Constitution's usefulness as a vehicle for the out-of-electoral-cycle entrenchment of partisan political values – a politico-legal order to which both liberals and conservatives are equally addicted (when they possess the power of federal judicial appointment) and by which they are both equally enraged (when they do not).

This fairly unusual, instrumentalised conception of law in a democratic state (India is the only other example that I have been able to think of) (Roux 2018: 146–92) has certain advantages. For many, this style of politico-legal order (call it 'democratic instrumentalism') presents a more candid, because more realistic, portrayal of law's irreducibly political character, particularly in constitutional adjudication. It exactly punctures the liberal myth of constitutional judges' ability somehow to escape the influence of politics. In a democratic state, moreover, political power by definition rotates. Thus, the most unappealing quality of *authoritarian* instrumentalism, where citizens are forced, with the exception of the occasional strategic readjustment, to accept a single, state-sanctioned view of the instrumental purposes law is expected to serve, is missing under democratic instrumentalism. Instead, there are at least two democratically competing views of those purposes, which allows some periodic refreshment of political goals under the threat of electoral replacement.

But there is also a dark side to democratic instrumentalism. For one, the political system may be locked up by two dominant parties to the exclusion of more marginal voices. Worse than this, after many years of such bipartisan conflict, constitutional politics, as the American case illustrates, may become so polarised that any notion of the public interest, or of supra-political constitutional values to which both sides of politics subscribe, is lost. There are in reality two partisan constitutions, bitterly fought over in an apparent zero-sum game. In another scenario, one represented by the Indian case, constitutional judges, relying on politicised readings of the Constitution that the dysfunctionality of the democratic system has permitted to emerge, perpetuate democratic pathologies by acting as a kind of legitimacy crutch on which the political system comes to depend (Roux 2018: 187–92). Thus, democratic instrumentalism, for all its appeal as a more candid portrayal of the real nature of judicial review, has certain drawbacks. It is also, as will become apparent in the next section, a legitimating ideology that is particularly difficult to promote in new states, where autonomous law is usually not seen as a decadent liberal illusion, but as the very essence of what the transition to constitutional democracy is all about.

In summary, there are four theoretically conceivable politico-legal orders – relatively stable combinations of legal and political authority. Only two of these are dependent on a legitimating ideology of autonomous law (democratic and authoritarian legalism). In the other two, law is instrumentalised, either to a single authoritarian conception of the national interest or to two or more democratically competing ones. It is an open empirical question which of these four politico-legal orders a society's dominant conception of the law/politics relationship will resemble, and, in cases of transition from authoritarianism to democracy, which of the two democratic variants (if at all) will emerge. Using this typology as a heuristic, the next section considers the evolution of conceptions of the law/politics relationship in Indonesia under the *reformasi*. Particular attention is paid to the ideas that underpinned the adoption of judicial review during the constitutional reform process and to the legitimating ideologies that the Indonesian Constitutional Court has subsequently tried to promote. While the Court is obviously not solely responsible for the outcome of this complex social process, it is an influential legal–cultural actor that has the capacity to shape public perceptions of its legitimate claim to authority and thus of law's authority more generally. After describing what has happened, the lawyer in me concludes by suggesting practical steps that the Court might take to cement the transition to *negara hukum* that the 1999–2002 constitutional reforms ushered in.

Evolving Conceptions of Law's Authority under the *Reformasi*

Constitution-making processes are obviously moments of political bargaining about how governmental power is in future to be allocated and controlled. But they are also legal–cultural moments – moments, that is, when a society (or more often, in Southeast Asia, a political elite) reflects on its constitutional tradition and decides what to reject, what to keep and what to attempt to change. Discussions over particular institutions bring out different aspects of a society's tradition. In the case of judicial review, which by definition elevates law to a position of coequal status with politics (Roux 2018: 1), the discussion necessarily focuses on understandings of law's legitimate claim to authority and its relationship to political authority. In contemplating whether to give judges the power to strike down democratically adopted statutes, constitution makers need to reflect on the role that law has played in the past in controlling the arbitrary exercise of power, and whether they think that the counter-majoritarian effects of judicial review are offset by the need for a neutral, third-party enforcer of constitutional ground rules. They then need to calibrate the powers that they give to judges to what they decide is the legitimate scope of law's authority.

The 1999–2002 constitutional reform process in Indonesia did not conform to this idealised picture. Like most constitution-making processes, it was messy and conflicted (Horowitz 2013). The decision to adopt judicial review, in particular, was by all accounts quite haphazard because of the way the *Majelis Permusyawaratan Rakyat* (MPR) first decided on the need for a constitutional court to oversee the impeachment process and then on what other powers to confer on it (Butt 2015; Siregar 2016; Hendrianto 2018). There was a sense, then, in which not all members of the MPR realised exactly what they were creating. While there had been a longstanding demand for judicial review, as Lev's work inter alia reveals (Lev 1978: 56–63), this institution had always been rejected in past constitutional reform processes as a step too far. In the 1999–2002 constitutional reforms, too, no major political party initially backed judicial review (Hendrianto 2013: 46–8). The idea of creating a constitutional court achieved prominence only after President Abdurrahman Wahid's impeachment on 14 July 2001. Fearing a repeat performance, Megawati Soekarnoputri's Indonesian Democratic Party of Struggle (*Partai Demokrasi Indonesia – Perjuangan* – PDI-P) convinced the other parties of the need for a constitutional court to oversee the impeachment process (Hendrianto 2018: 44). Article 7B providing for this process was adopted in October 2001. It was only after this, in November 2001, that the MPR reached agreement on the Constitutional Court's other powers (Hendrianto 2018: 48–9).

In total, just three weeks passed from the decision to create the Constitutional Court in mid-October 2001 to the adoption of Article 24C on 9 November 2001 setting out the Court's powers (Hendrianto 2018: 49). While the debates in the MPR were intense, Article 24C cannot therefore be said to represent the culmination of a long and considered, cross-party political commitment to judicial review. Civil society groups, for their part, had been excluded from the constitution-making process. Their input on the nature of the institution that was being created was accordingly also limited. Finally, the text of Article 24C reveals some hesitancy about what was being done. On the one hand, Article 24C gives the Constitutional Court the power to review statutes for conformance with the Constitution, including a new list of fundamental rights. On the other, it does not confer on the Court the power to review subordinate regulations, the real framework of administration. The justices' terms of office, at five years once renewable, are also quite short, suggesting that the MPR was a little wary of creating a separate centre of power.

This somewhat haphazard process meant that the 1999–2002 constitutional reform process did not really function as a crucible in which Indonesia's compromised tradition of thinking about the legitimate basis for law's authority could be melted down and remade. While the adoption of judicial review and the creation of the Constitutional Court clearly did signal the triumph of the demand for *negara hukum*, the constitutional reform process did not clarify in exactly what form this demand had been granted. Rather, it was left to the first members of the Constitutional Court, and particularly the first Chief Justice, Jimly Asshiddiqie, to decide how to assert the Court's authority and justify its powers.

In this respect, Indonesia appears to have had both the good fortune and the bad fortune to have appointed an exceptionally talented person to undertake this work. Asshiddiqie possessed, as he still does, a formidable intellect and depth of learning about the nature of judicial review and the requirements of his role as chief justice (Siregar 2016; Hendrianto 2018). He was thus able, as explained in more detail below, to map a clear and generally sensible course for the Court. That was Indonesia's good fortune. Its bad fortune, however, was that Jimly had few people around him with the same depth of understanding of what was required. He was accordingly somewhat isolated and the one strategic mistake he made had a great influence on the Court's trajectory.

The very sensible steps that Jimly took included the following. First, he insisted that the Constitutional Court should be accommodated in a fashion worthy of the role it had been asked to perform. The Court's imposing Graeco-Roman building, with its nine pillars and central location in Jakarta, has done much to ensure that its decisions are taken seriously (Hendrianto 2018: 79). In addition to this, the Court under Asshiddiqie's chief justiceship worked hard to develop consistent standards, both for the way judicial conferences were held and for what was expected of judges when writing their opinions. One of the things Asshiddiqie did, for example, was to establish a new practice of reasoned opinion writing that departed from the declaratory style associated with Indonesia's civil law tradition (Butt 2015: 65; Siregar 2016: 123). He also encouraged the writing of dissents, thus presenting the decision-making process as one in which judges strive to give their own good-faith account of the law (Butt 2015: 67). At the same time, the first Bench's remedial orders were generally non-intrusive – a species of weak-from review (Hendrianto 2018: 5). By suspending orders for invalidity, using pro- spective overruling and granting conditionally constitutional orders, the Court under Asshiddiqie's leadership preserved a sense of the political branches' primary responsibility for policy. Together with the other steps taken, this helped to promote a democratic-legalist understanding of law as an autonomous system of logically ordered norms that have the capacity to constrain both politically partisan and ideologically motivated judicial decision-making.

Despite this considerable achievement, Asshiddiqie made one crucial error in justifying the Court's authority. That was to explain publicly, when its first decisions caused some controversy, that its role was limited to that of a 'negative legislator'.[4] In introducing this phrase into Indonesian public discourse, Asshiddiqie was playing his usually very helpful educative role. The Indonesian Constitutional Court, as a specialised constitutional court, had been built on the so-called 'Kelsenian model'. To this extent, Asshiddiqie's stance was technically correct. Kelsen, the Austrian legal theorist, had coined the term 'nega- tive legislator' in explaining why, despite the political function that constitutional courts inevitably perform, they are nevertheless distinct from the regular legislature (Kelsen 1928). No doubt Asshiddiqie was convinced at the time, given the phrase's pedigree and the uncertainties surrounding the adoption of Article 24C, that this way of depicting the Court's powers was a viable route to legitimating its authority. But there is nothing in Article 24C that obviously limits it powers in this way. Moreover, since Kelsen wrote, there has been a tremendous growth in international understanding of the role that constitutional courts may legitimately perform as positive legislators ((Brewer-Carías 2013). While Asshiddiqie could not have assumed that this developed under- standing would necessarily be embraced in Indonesia, he was a little too hasty in associating the Court's legitimacy with its ability to stick to a negative legislator conception of its mandate. As explained in a moment, the Court's perceived violation of this self-imposed limita- tion has been at the heart of the most serious political attacks on it.

Despite this oversight, by the time he came up for re-election as Chief Justice in 2008, Asshiddiqie's overall record was that of someone who had

---

[4] This paragraph relies on a discussion with Pan Mohammad Faiz, a Senior Researcher at the Constitutional Court who has written on this topic in Bahasa Indonesian. The normative assessment is my own and should not be attributed to him.

done much to legitimate the Court's authority around the idea of democratic legalism. The particular version of this politico-legal order that he
and his Court had helped to construct was one in which the Court's claim
to authority rested on its reputation for impartially enforcing the ground
rules for sound democratic governance. Had Asshiddiqie continued in
the role of Chief Justice, it is likely that this legitimating ideology would
have become even further entrenched. But Asshiddiqie was not re-
elected. For reasons that are hard to establish with certainty, he was
defeated in an intra-curial vote for the chief justiceship by Mohammad
Mahfud ('Mahfud MD'), a then newly appointed judge who had undertaken at his nomination hearing to return the Court to its negative-
legislator mandate (Roux and Siregar 2016: 10).

Much has been written about the Court's change of direction under
its second chief justice (Butt 2015; Siregar 2016; Hendrianto 2018). For
present purposes, the key point is that Mahfud MD's accession to the
chief justiceship undermined the democratic-legalist understanding of
the Court's authority that Asshiddiqie had propounded. This was the
consequence not so much of a deliberate change in strategy as the fact
that Mahfud MD had a very different conception of his duty as a judge.
Taking shape during his doctoral research at Gadjah Mada University,
Mahfud MD's personal judicial philosophy was influenced by two theorisations of law in particular: Nonet and Selznick's idea of 'responsive
law' (Nonet and Selznick 2009) and Satjipto Rahardjo's so-called 'progressive legal approach' (*hukum progresif*) (Siregar 2016: 115; Hendrianto
2018: 161). Both of these theorisations conceive of law's authority as
residing, not in its autonomy from politics, but in its capacity to promote
a certain kind of politics: participatory, engaged and social justice-
seeking.

On his elevation to the Bench, Mahfud MD began to operationalise
this conception of law's authority in the form of a 'substantive justice'
approach to decision-making (Butt 2015: 80; Siregar 2016: 115;
Hendrianto 2018: 167). Under his chief justiceship, the Court's opinions
became more reliant on broad concepts like justice and fairness as
opposed to direct references to the constitutional text (Butt 2015: 63).
Ideologically, too, the Mahfud Court began to articulate a more explicit
pro-poor agenda (Hendrianto 2018: 163). As Butt puts it, the Court
under Mahfud became 'arguably more concerned with resolving
immediate political issues and building popularity than with applying
or creating legal principles that could be readily applied in future cases'
(Butt 2015: 64). Its remedial orders at the same time became more

intrusive (Butt 2015: 124). If Asshiddiqie's leadership style had been one of 'prudential-minimalism', Mahfud MD was a chief justice in a more traditionally 'heroic' mould (Hendrianto 2018: 4). In the conceptual vocabulary used here, the Court under Mahfud MD's chief justiceship began to stake out its claim to authority on noticeably more instrumentalist grounds. What mattered was the consequences of the Court's decisions, and whether they were perceived to be just or not.

As should now be clear, this second way of conceiving of law's authority is perfectly valid in the abstract. Other constitutional courts have consolidated their authority in this way and this has proved in certain circumstances to be a basis for stable constitutional governance. There is a question in Indonesia's case, however, about whether the timing of the Court's adoption of such an overtly instrumentalist conception of its authority was right – both because this conception came as such a sudden corrective on the Asshiddiqie Court's approach and because Indonesia's constitutional democracy was still in its infancy.

It is interesting in this respect that Mahfud's views were so strongly influenced by Nonet and Selznick's work. In their book, *Toward Responsive Law*, these authors distinguish three kinds of legal order – repressive, autonomous and responsive – and express a normative preference for the latter (Nonet and Selznick 2009). They are careful to say, however, that there is no necessary developmental progression between these modes and that there are considerable risks associated with a transition to responsive law. In particular, because the responsive conception (which is similar to what this article has been calling an instrumentalist conception) is founded on law's openness to political influence, there is a risk that a deliberate attempt to drive a transition towards it will politicise the judicial process, making it harder for the Court to establish its authority.

Nonet and Selznick's advice is borne out by comparative experience. As we have seen, there are two countries in which a transition to democratic instrumentalism has successfully occurred – the US and India. In both these cases, however, judicial review was firmly established by the time the transition took place. Each country had also enjoyed a long tradition of judicial independence. In the US, the transition to democratic instrumentalism came on the back of profound economic changes and the sustained ideational work done by the legal realist movement. In India, the transition was aided by the damage done to legalism by the Court's performance during the 1975–7 Emergency and the charismatic leadership provided by the post-Emergency justices, Bhagwati and

Krishna Iyer (Roux 2018). Another crucial factor in India's case was that these two justices had the backing of Prime Minister Indira Gandhi, whose pro-poor political program they were in effect implementing (Austin 1999: 485–97). In both the US and India, therefore, the risks that Nonet and Selznick talked about were reduced.

The situation was quite different in Indonesia. As noted, Mahfud MD had been appointed on the back of a promise to adopt a more restrained approach. He consequently lacked the political support that Bhagwati and Krishna Iyer had enjoyed when implementing their pro-poor vision of the Indian Supreme Court's role. Without that kind of political support, there was a risk that Mahfud MD's well-intentioned efforts to turn the Court into a forum for promoting substantive justice would be misconstrued as the pursuit of a purely private agenda.

These processes are complex and the lines of causation are far from clear. But the Mahfud Court's move to a more politicised conception of law, coupled with the greater intrusiveness of its remedial orders when compared to the Asshiddiqie Court, certainly did not help to fortify the Court's position. By abruptly changing the basis for the Court's claim to authority, Mahfud's substantive justice approach arguably exposed the Court to charges of judicial overreach. In 2011,[5] and again in 2013,[6] the *Dewan Perwakilan Rakyat* (DPR) amended the Court's governing statute in an attempt, on the one hand, to return it to its negative-legislator mandate and, on the other, to improve judicial accountability mechanisms.

Over and above their immediate policy rationales, the 2011 and 2013 amendments must be understood as moves to redraw the boundary between law and politics. As the Presidency and the DPR saw things, the Court had expanded the scope of its authority beyond what had originally been intended. This was not a question of a return to authoritarian instrumentalism. Rather, what was being attempted was a readjustment along the lines of what had occurred in the US in 1937 when the Supreme Court, under the threat of Franklin Roosevelt's court-packing plan, relinquished its authority to review the substantive reasonableness of economic legislation (McCloskey 2005: 101). Understood in these terms, the 2011 and 2013 amendments constituted an important opportunity for the Constitutional Court to try to build a shared understanding of its legitimate role in national politics. This opportunity, however, was not taken up. Instead, the Court struck down the bulk of

---

[5] Law 8 of 2011 (discussed in Butt and Lindsey 2012: 144–6).
[6] In presidential emergency interim order (PERPPU) 1 of 2013, confirmed by Law 4 of 2014.

the 2011 amendments[7] and all of the 2013 amendments,[8] holding that
they were an attack on its independence.

While drawing on a rich tradition of defiant legal–professional (if not
always judicial) defence of judicial independence under Soeharto (Lev
1978), the Court's forceful rejection of many elements of the 2011
reforms, especially those introducing new judicial accountability measures, was arguably misjudged. The 2011 amendments were partly
a response to a realisation on the part of the DPR that Mahfud MD,
despite the undertaking made at his nomination, was in fact ramping up
the Court's positive-legislator role, particularly by increasing the rate of
so-called 'conditionally constitutional' orders (i.e. reading down) and
even turning them into conditionally *unconstitutional* orders (Butt
2015; Siregar 2016). Since the countervailing, negative-legislator depiction of the Court's mandate was the product of Asshiddiqie's early,
textually unrequired attempt to defend its authority, there was arguably
good reason for the Court not to accept this aspect of the amendments.
At the time, the 2011 amendments were introduced, however, there were
also growing concerns about the personal moral integrity of one of the
justices (Hendrianto 2013: 170). Some of the amendments were therefore
directed at improving judicial accountability measures. In rejecting these
amendments, too, the Court's defiance was arguably less justified. Rather
than adjusting its understanding of its independence to the changing
quality of Indonesia's democracy (Fiss 1992: 55; Holmes 2004: 9), the
Court adopted a somewhat dogmatic conception, one more suited to the
Soeharto era. At the very least, its emphatic rejection of improved judicial
accountability measures was not appropriate to a situation where there
were genuine reasons for the political branches to introduce such
reforms.

Something similar happened in 2013, when there was even more
reason for the Court to accede to the introduction of effective judicial
accountability measures. On this occasion, the amendments followed
a huge scandal in which Mahfud MD's successor as chief justice, Akil
Mochtar, had been found guilty of corruption and eventually imprisoned
(Hendrianto 2018: 196–8). Undaunted, the Court struck down the entire
legislative reform package, once more finding an interference with its
constitutionally guaranteed independence.[9] While the Court's decision

---

[7] Constitutional Court Decision 48/PUU-IX/2011 and Constitutional Court Decision 49/
PUU-IX/2011.
[8] Constitutional Court Decision 1–2/PUU-XII/2014.
[9] Constitutional Court Decision No. 1–2/PUU-XII/2014.

again appeared forceful, it was the wrong kind of forcefulness. A Court's legitimate claim to authority in a new state, on either a legalist or an instrumentalist conception, comes not from a dogmatic defence of its independence, but from its ability to present a defensible account of its role in national politics. It is not clear how the Court's decisions on the 2013 amendments did that.

While the Court has recovered from the damage done to its public support by the Mochtar scandal (Dressel and Inoue 2018), its somewhat inflexible response to the 2011 and 2013 amendments raises questions about its future role in Indonesia's democracy. To be sure, the Court is still an influential actor – demonstrated, for example, by its decisions on the losing candidate, Prabowo Subianto's challenge to the 2015 presidential election result[10] and on the so-called 'MD3 law',[11] which threatened rights to freedom of speech and association. But the Court has on other occasions avoided taking decisions on democracy-threatening measures. In the first of these, the Court suspended its order of invalidity on the constitutionality of staggered legislative and presidential elections until after the 2014 elections.[12] In the second, it first rejected a challenge to a 20 per cent presidential election threshold requirement,[13] and then delayed deciding a renewed challenge until after the 2019 elections (Satrio 2018).

These decisions suggest that the Court is more reticent than it used to be about directly confronting the political branches. Part of the reason for this, this chapter has argued, is its equivocation between a legalist and instrumentalist conception of its authority. Until the Court settles on one or the other of these conceptions (preferably the former, given the problems with democratic instrumentalism in the transitional context), its public support will continue to depend on fluctuating perceptions of the moral and intellectual qualities of the justices and the relative performance of other institutions. While this has proved sufficient so far, Indonesia's constitutional democracy is facing serious threats from two quarters: those who wish to create a theocratic state and those who wish to revive its authoritarian traditions (Aspinall 2018; Mietzner 2018). In the circumstances, the Court needs to re-dedicate itself to the work that Asshiddiqie began. That means

[10] Constitutional Court Decision 1/PHPU.Pres-XII/2014.
[11] Constitutional Court Decision 16/PUU-XVI/2018.
[12] Constitutional Court Decision 14/PUU-XI/2013.
[13] Constitutional Court Decision 53/PUU-XV/2017.

paying close attention to the technical quality of its decisions, presenting an account of its authority as stemming from the impartiality of its reasoning processes rather than from the justices' extraconstitutional views of social justice, and engaging in continued efforts to educate the public about the importance of its role in Indonesia's democracy.

PART IV

Courts and Rights

12

The Juvenile Courts and Children's Rights

Good Intentions, Flawed Execution

PUTRI K. AMANDA, SHAILA TIEKEN, SHARYN GRAHAM
DAVIES AND SANTI KUSUMANINGRUM[*]

This chapter draws on Daniel S. Lev's (2000d) concept of legal culture as a tool to understand Indonesia's juvenile justice system. Despite limitations that arise when using the concept of legal culture, it provides significant value in revealing how the Indonesian juvenile justice system works, in understanding relations among authorities, and revealing how social and technological developments bring legal change (Kurkchiyan, 2010, cited in Nelken, 2016). This chapter will also exercise Lev's approach in identifying key actors and evaluating how the reform of a legal system produces behavioral change. Contextualizing these concepts in Indonesia's juvenile justice system will make a significant contribution to knowledge as there has yet to be an examination of this change. Significantly, this chapter provides support for one of Lev's most influential ideas: law reform without a corresponding supportive change in legal culture will render the former deficient.

Indonesia has seen growth in the size and role of its judicial systems. The area of juvenile justice is no exception. The most recent changes to the area of juvenile justice occurred in 2012 when a new law was adopted (Law No. 11/2012 on the Juvenile Court). This law brought hopes of a positive change in the area of juvenile justice since it increased the minimum age of criminal responsibility from eight to twelve, introduced diversion mechanisms to keep children from being prosecuted, put incarceration of children as a last resort, guaranteed children's rights to legal representation and special protection within the justice system, and pushed for rehabilitation and reintegration of victims and offenders.

[*] The authors would like to acknowledge the assistance of Feri Sahputra and Cendy Adam, who are both research and advocacy assistants at PUSKAPA.

Despite such major legislative reform, there have been challenges in implementing these advances effectively.

Part of the reason reform has been challenging is that Indonesia has a population of over 260 million people, spread across thousands of islands, speaking more than 300 languages. Adding to this complexity is that six world religions must be accommodated, although most Indonesians are Muslim, at around 88 percent of the population. In addition, Indonesia's public institutions are rife with corruption meaning that even if good policies are implemented their execution is left wanting. Until 2012, Indonesia had a particularly draconian system for treating juvenile defenders, including eight being the age of culpability. The 2012 Juvenile Criminal Justice System Law, which we discuss in this chapter, is thus a significant step forward for Indonesia, although implementation remains inadequate.

In exploring the dynamics of Indonesia's juvenile justice system, this chapter is organized into four substantive sections. After an abstract and this brief introduction, we first provide background to the evolution of Indonesia's Juvenile Justice Law before then discussing the 2012 Juvenile Criminal Justice System Law. The third section evaluates the state of Indonesia's Juvenile Justice System as of 2018. Fourth, we assess the challenges and opportunities present in Indonesia's juvenile justice system by employing Lev's legal culture analysis.

Evolution of Indonesia's Juvenile Justice Law

In 1990, Indonesia ratified the International Convention on the Rights of Child. Seven years later, Indonesia enacted its Law on the Juvenile Court (Law 3/1997). Law 3/1997 regulates juvenile courts in Indonesia and augments several provisions in Indonesia's Criminal Code (KUHP) and Criminal Procedural Code (KUHAP) in relation to juveniles. Under Law 3/1997, law enforcement officials should not wear an official uniform during any aspect of the process in order to create a more friendly atmosphere. The Law stimulates that detention must be a last resort and children should be separated from adults to prevent further harm against juvenile offenders. Court hearings should be led by just one judge and closed to the public. Legal counsel, counselors, and parents/guardians must attend the hearing process in order to support the child and ensure their rights are protected. In terms of punishment, the law states that the death penalty cannot be imposed on children. The law banning the death penalty for juveniles is significant because a range of offences in Indonesia, particularly drug-related offences, attract the death penalty and Indonesia has been active in carrying out the death penalty for those on death row in recent years (Pascoe 2017). The Law also accommodates options for the court to return the child to their parents or social welfare centers in order to receive education and training. Law 3/1997 also established the role of probation officers (P. K. Bapas) to provide written assessments of juvenile offenders' individual data, family situation, education background, social situation, and special needs. This assessment was required to be taken into consideration by police officers, prosecutors, and judges before making any decisions. The Law's provisions differentiate treatment of children from adults in the justice system to "protect children," give children a "second chance by providing training and education" in order to create "independent and responsible human beings," and to enable children to be "productive members of the society."

After its enactment, concerns were raised about the difficulty of implementing Law 3/1997 because of the high number of juvenile offenders and their appalling treatment within the justice system. A study conducted in six provinces of Indonesia found that almost every child who came in contact with the law was detained during the judicial process (Dermawan et al. 2007). Data from the Ministry of Justice and Human Rights shows that the number of children detained increased from over 1,000 children across Indonesia in 2004 to more than 1,900 in 2012 (DGC 2004–12). This was almost a 100 percent increase in less than ten years and worryingly this number excludes an unidentified number of children detained in police facilities. UNICEF and the Department of Criminology at the University of Indonesia also identified that in 2007 law enforcement officers placed 735 child detainees in adult detention centers and 456 in adult prisons (Dermawan et al. 2007). There were therefore significant problems not only in the increase in the number of children coming in contact with the law, but in the detainment of juvenile offenders in adult prisons.

After the enactment of Law 3/1997, many children remained exposed to ill-treatment during the judicial process. Indeed, there were, and continue to be, insufficient mechanisms to control and evaluate law enforcement officers' performance and behavior when dealing with juvenile cases (Kusumaningrum 2012). UNICEF and the Department of Criminology at the University of Indonesia found the use of intimidation and violence by police officers toward juvenile offenders, including pinning children's legs down with a table, punching and kicking them, and pointing a gun at children to force confessions (Dermawan et al. 2007). Reports of physical abuse and forced confessions of children are particularly concerning.

Further, it remained common for judges to impose a sentence of imprisonment on children, rather than treating imprisonment as a measure of last resort. In 2007, judges approved just 114 of 1,294 recommendations by probation officers to return the child to their parents. Further, in 2007, judges only approved 422 of 2,328 recommendations by probation officers for the judge to impose imprisonment with probation (Dermawan et al. 2007). While serving their prison term, children were often denied access to necessary and appropriate services and rehabilitation programs (Dermawan et al. 2007). The prisons also faced overpopulation problems. In 2004, Indonesian prisons held 29 percent more inmates than they were designed to accommodate. This rate of overpopulation continued to increase, with jail overcrowding at 43 percent in 2005 and 55 percent in 2006 (Widayati 2014). By 2012, the year the new Juvenile Justice Law was established, this figure had reached 153 percent overcrowding (Republika 2012). While we cannot find any reliable statistics, this figure is likely to be higher today.

Law enforcement officials faced limitations in terms of their capacity to handle criminal cases as numbers increased while government resources declined. In 1999–2000, for example, the judiciary was only able to adjudicate a third of cases involving children suspected of committing a crime. In 2011, the Office of the Attorney General had to handle more than 96,488 cases, while the budget only covered 10,100 cases (MaPPI FHUI 2015). The lack of financial resources prevented children receiving proper treatment or access to education or basic services while they were in the justice system (Dermawan et al. 2007; Ismawati 2013; Irwanto 2013). Further, Law No. 3/1997 contained no requirement for authorities to divert children from the judicial process. The absence of such a provision, in addition to the other negative impacts stated above, was the reason that Indonesia was forced to change its juvenile justice law.

The 2012 Juvenile Justice Law

Due to mounting domestic and international pressure, in 2012 the Indonesian parliament repealed Law 3/1997 and enacted Law No. 11/2012 on the Juvenile Criminal Justice System (Law 11/2012). Pressure was coming from several organizations (Mulyadi 2005; Davies & Robson 2016). For instance, United Nations, through its various bodies and treaty recommendations, began demanding early on that Indonesia implement a justice system sympathetic to children (UNICEF 2004). In achieving this end, UNICEF worked closely with international partners, including external experts from New Zealand, the Philippines, and France (UNICEF 2004). UNICEF also worked with domestic partners including law professors, NGOs and NGO lawyers, anthropologists, sociologists, journalists, judges, and probation officers (UNICEF 2004). It also worked with the Supreme Court, the Attorney General's Office, national police, the Ministry of Justice and Human Rights, academic institutions and other levels of the judiciary, law enforcers, and social workers (UNICEF 2004). Partnership with civil society was also a key in developing a child-friendly justice system (UNICEF 2004). This work continued through until 2012 when the new law was finally ratified.

The new law introduced significant changes to juvenile court mechanisms. The first key change was increasing the minimum age of criminal responsibility from eight years old to twelve years old. This change was justified on the basis that by twelve years of age, children have completed their basic education and supposedly have the mental capability to face judicial proceedings (Policy Brief 2018). The law also defined "children" based on only their age—"people aged below eighteen years old" —without looking at their marital status. Previously, Law 3/1997 placed children involved in young marriage in a vulnerable and disadvantaged position because once married a child was considered an adult.

The second key change related to use of restorative justice as a tool to prevent children from being processed through the judicial system. Policymakers defined restorative justice in Law 11/2012 as a process where every party involved in the crime should be involved in finding solutions to repair, reconcile, and reassure without revenge. Restorative justice was thus aimed at solving conflict at the community level by bringing the offender and victim together to work toward a just outcome. This was a novel concept and innovation in the context of Indonesia. Under Law 11/2012, the offender, victim, the parents/guardian of the offender, and related parties can hold a conference where alternative solutions to prison are discussed. The use of the principle of restorative justice changed the focus of criminal proceedings from a traditional approach to one adopting alternative measures to judicial proceedings (Foussard & Melotti 2016). Foussard and Melotti indicate that there are three key objectives in this approach: that the victims of crime should be compensated; that the perpetrators need to be rehabilitated and reintegrated into society; and that a process of relationship building should take place among the victim, offender, and the community. This process of relationship building, which must protect both the victim's and offender's interest, is understood to be a diversion mechanism.

According to Law 11/2012, law enforcement officers must prioritize diversion mechanisms for children involved in criminal cases. This was a significant break from past practice. At every step of the process, police officers, prosecutors, and judges are required to facilitate diversion. Law 11/2012 provided several options related to diversion, including resolution with or without compensation; returning the offender back to parental/guardian care; obligatory participation in education or training for no longer than three months; or an obligation to do community service.

The third key change relates to the process of criminal proceedings and the actors involved. Law 11/2012 states that victims are no longer merely witnesses. Rather, victims can help determine what action should be taken in respect to diversion. Further, parole officers' roles are no longer limited to developing assessment reports, but they can also support the police, the prosecutor and judge in facilitating the diversion process. Law 11/2012 requires law enforcement officials to appoint legal counsel for children at every stage of the judicial process. Another important difference between the new and old law is the standard competency of law enforcement officers. Law enforcement officers are now required to enroll in integrated training regarding juvenile justice, as a means of enhancing the skills and expertise of officers involved.

The fourth key change relates to protecting child witnesses and victims. Law 11/2012 requires the police to develop an assessment report on child victims and witnesses, and to cooperate with social workers to provide rehabilitation and reintegration services. Law enforcement officers are also required to consider the social worker's recommendation and they may refer the victim or witness to a child welfare institution based on the social worker's report. In an emergency, the law also allows law enforcement officers to refer child victims or child witnesses to hospital or child welfare institutions even if the social worker's report is not available.

The fifth key change relates to pretrial detention. Law 11/2012 makes it harder for law enforcers to place juvenile offenders in detention centers. However, law enforcers can detain juveniles aged fourteen years or over who commit a crime punishable by more than seven years of imprisonment. Juvenile detention must be used only as a last resort and only after considering the child's best interest. A child can be placed in special detention centers (Lembaga Penempatan Anak Sementara/LPAS) or in an institution provided for by the Ministry of Social Affairs (MoSA) (Lembaga Penyelenggaraan Kesejahteraan Sosial/LPKS). Law 11/2012

Table 12.1 *Comparison of Maximum Detention Period*

Judicial process	Law 3/1997	Law 11/2012
Investigation	30 days	15 days
While prosecution is taking place (after police investigation but before trial)	25 days	10 days
District court trial	45 days	25 days
Appeal trial (Provincial court)	45 days	25 days
Appeal trial (Supreme court)	55 days	35 days
Additional detention period that can be sought	Maximum 30 days on each stage	–

also reduces the maximum detention period children can serve from the previous law, as can be seen in Table 12.1.

The sixth key change in Law 11/2012 from the preceding law is the ability of law enforcers to provide an alternative to detention for children. Law 11/2012 also gives judges a wider array of options to enable rehabilitation for children through various measures other than imprisonment. Article 71 of Law 11/2012 stipulates several alternative sentences, including warnings, probation (e.g. rehabilitation outside prison facilities, public service, and supervision), rehabilitation inside prison facilities, and training (see Table 12.2). These alternatives to detention were not available under the old system.

Addressing the Concept of Legal Culture in the Juvenile Justice System

Lev's work affirms the importance of including cultural factors in understanding the justice system (2000d: 161–200). Our attempt to understand legal culture around juvenile justice in Indonesia is constrained due to very limited data and documentation on the topic. Referring to Merry's (2010) proposed dimensions of legal culture, this section will focus on analyzing legal practice dimensions. This section will also extend the concept of legal culture as it does have limitations.

The concept of legal culture has been used in a variety of ways, thus leading to some confusion (Nelken 2014: 225). Cotterrell (2006) also adds that the term legal culture is too vague and not useful in constructing

Table 12.2 *Comparison of penalties under Law 3/1997 and Law 11/2012*

Punishment category	Law 3/1997	Law 11/2012
Basic punishment	a. Imprisonment b. Fine c. Confinement d. Supervision	a. Judge warning b. Conditional sentence c. Job training d. Rehabilitation outside the institution e. Imprisonment
Additional punishment	a. Confiscation of certain items b. Payment of compensation	a. Confiscation of certain items b. Fulfillment of customary obligations
Measurement	a. Return to parents b. Put in state care in order to receive education c. Deliver to a state department	a. Return to parents b. Return to a guardian c. Rehabilitation in a mental health hospital d. Treatment in a Social Welfare Institution e. Enroll in formal education and/or training conducted by the government or private entity f. Revocation of driver's license g. Recovering damage caused by criminal act

explanations. It is also often difficult to see the causal relationship between culture and behavior. Questions that could show how beliefs and actions work are extraordinarily complex: Does the legal system not work well because people distrust the court, or do people distrust the courts because the legal system does not work well? How much do people's attitudes, beliefs, and assumptions determine their social environment, and how much does the social environment determine their attitudes? To complete the narrative of the dynamics of the implementation of Law 11/2012, this part will describe the structural and institutional context, identify the key actors involved, and examine the dynamic interplay between relevant actors (cf. Domingo & Denney 2013).

Shifting the Paradigm under Law 11/2012

Law 11/2012 acknowledges the importance of family and kinship within the community and includes this in a formal, written, and accountable process of criminal justice, just as Lev recommends (2000d, p.163). Indonesia's Law 11/2012 enhances the legal system with a new spirit and concept of restorative justice, influenced by programs of social, economic, and legal change. As previous sections have mentioned, Law 11/2012 has brought substantial change from the institutional-based treatment of child offenders to alternatives of detention within a family or community setting (Schubert et al. 2015). For example, one important point to note is the shifting definition of children in juvenile justice laws. The term used to define children in contact with the law was "delinquents" in Law 3/1997, a term often considered to be demeaning and stigmatizing. In the new law, the term was replaced with 'children in contact with the law'. The use of this definition is neutral and nonstigmatizing. The term was included because of Indonesia's ratification and adoption of the United Nations' Convention on the Rights of the Child (UNCRC) in respect to Law 23/2002. This is the first law in Indonesia to use this term and it is an important shift in terminology.

Law 11/2012 also shifted the law enforcement paradigm in handling juvenile cases and reframed the understanding of children as developing and dependent individuals (Syukur & Bagshaw 2015: 4). This paradigm shift strengthened the view of law enforcers that children's deviant behavior was a result of a poorly functioning society and other external factors (Hockey & James 1993). Law 11/2012 also specified the social understanding of children as a future asset and as dependent beings whose misbehavior is often the result of outside factors beyond the control of the child. The emphasis on these factors offers a new perspective on children's responsibility for their action and the consequences.

There is no doubt that Law 11/2012 has brought improvements in the protection of children in the justice system. The changing laws in Indonesia's juvenile justice system are one indication of changes in legal culture in redefining juvenile offenders, in defining the way law enforcers should treat children, and in handling juvenile cases. Beginning with the enactment of the KUHP, to Law 3/1997, and then to Law 11/2012, there have been major changes in the roles of various authorities including police officers, prosecutors, judges, and probation officers. The new law even places social workers and the community as key actors in supporting rehabilitation and reintegration for juvenile offenders, child victims, and witnesses. This is the first time that such important actors have been recognized as playing a key support role in the judicial process. However, these legislative reforms have not automatically been implemented. In practice, juvenile justice is continuously shaped by practices within the legal system as interpreted by police, prosecutors, judges, legal professionals, and social workers (Lev 2000d, p. 175). In other words, just as Lev notes, without a corresponding change in social attitudes, progressive laws will not necessarily ensure children receive justice.

The Characteristics of Juvenile Offenders

Law 11/2012 offers noninstitutional alternatives for children in contact with the law. Moreover, Indonesia is moving toward a rights-based and family-based care approach for such children (Schubert et al. 2015). Law 11/2012 challenges the previous notion that children as young as twelve and thirteen years of age should, even before they were convicted of a crime, be placed in detention (PUSKAPA 2014; Angga, Napitupulu, & Hernowo 2016). Law 11/2012 clearly stipulates the use of diversion as an alternative mechanism. However, the use of detention and imprisonment is still the favored method in practice and continues to be used by those with power in the criminal justice system (Anggara, Napitupulu, & Hernowo 2016). In 2014, the Convention of the Rights of the Child Concluding Observation observed that large numbers of children are still sentenced for petty crimes, and they are often detained in poor conditions (Van Welzenis 2016).

What is particularly worrying about young children being detained is that they are being placed in detention primarily because they are poor, uneducated, and lack family and community support (PUSKAPA 2014). International research has found the latter factor leads children to undertake criminal behavior (Hirschi 2017). Moreover, detaining drug users is not only detrimental to the individual but also ineffective for deterrence (Mitchell et al. 2017). These factors are not reflected in the way the law enforcement system responds to children in Indonesia. Crimes like theft and drug abuse still result in the detention of children (PUSKAPA 2014; Anggara, Napitupulu, & Hernowo 2016).

The problematic nature of detention is also apparent in its duration and conditions. Although there has been a reduction in the maximum period children can be held pretrial, presentence detention is still usually exercised to its maximum period. A study from PUSKAPA in 2014 even found law enforcers still using the previous law (Law 3/1997) as a basis to identify children's maximum detention period. Even though Law 11/2012 allowed maximum sentencing for children during investigation for fifteen days, at least 28 percent of children who were police detainees were detained for over thirty days, fifteen days longer than Law 11/2012 permitted. The study also found that 21 percent of court detainees exceeded 230 days of detention, 160 days longer than Law 11/2012 permitted. According to Indonesia Criminal Justice Reform, most children held longer than 230 days were accused of a crime against life, a sexual crime, drugs, or violent crime (Anggara, Napitupulu, & Hernowo 2016).

Studies also show that there are issues with the conditions under which children are incarcerated. For example, in 2015, of 3,228 children incarcerated, 2,408 of them were housed in adult facilities and were only separated from adults by cell walls (Amanda 2014; Purwati and Alam 2015). In 2018, there does appear to be some improvement with 51 percent of children placed in thirty-one juvenile facilities, while the rest (49 percent) are spread across 224 adult facilities (DGC 2018).

One of the problems of housing children in conflict with the law is the demand for correctional facilities. In 2000, there were just thirteen children's correctional facilities across the entire country. In 2018, there were thirty-one facilities, which is a significant increase in the number of facilities but still not a sufficient number (Meuwese 2003). The available centers are still not equipped with programs or activities suitable for children, and there is usually nowhere within the facilities for trainers to be able to offer rehabilitation services (Davies & Robson 2016; PUSKAPA 2018). Children in detention also experience physical violence and harassment, and families are often unable to visit children due to living in remote locales and not having sufficient economic resources to fund the visit (Amanda 2014; Amaliyah et al. 2015).

Law 11/2012 provides a wide array of alternatives to detention, although there are still various challenges to its implementation. While alternatives are available to those who can prove that they classify as a child, it is often difficult for children to prove their age as documentation, such as a birth certificate, is a privilege not all children have—see, for example, the report *Detention of Indonesian Minors in Australia* (2012) which found that Indonesian children were being inaccurately defined as adults and imprisoned in adult prisons. From the poorest families in Indonesia, only 42 percent of children aged 1–17 have birth certificates (PUSKAPA 2014). There are thus approximately 15 million children currently in Indonesia without a birth certificate (based on statistics provided by SUSENAS 2013). If children are unable to prove they are below the age of eighteen, they may be at risk of being tried and sentenced as an adult.

Dynamics among Police, Prosecutors, and Judges

Lev (1972b) noted that in Indonesia there is frequently conflict between prosecutors, judges, and police over control in all aspects of criminal proceedings and that this has been ongoing since the early formation of the Indonesian state. This conflict persists today, and one example that reflects this conflict in the juvenile justice system is the different practices of diversion. At every stage of examinations, Law 11/2012 allows police, prosecutors, and judges to execute diversionary efforts. There remains confusion among officers, though, in applying diversion mechanisms as there have been no sufficient guidelines developed to implement the process.

One constraint in applying diversion is that the Supreme Court's Regulation (PERMA 4/2014) allows diversion but police and prosecutors may impose different procedures since they define the requirement for diversion differently to the law as written, especially regarding maximum sentences. For instance, Article 3 on PERMA 4/2014 opens the possibility to apply diversion for children who have been prosecuted for more than one criminal offence, if one of the offences is under the maximum sentencing of seven years' imprisonment. This article is based on the idea that law enforcers tend to combine charges laid against juveniles. However, combining charges is inconsistent with Law 11/2012, which states that diversion only be applied to criminal offences under the maximum sentencing of seven years' imprisonment. Further, the key aims of mediation—restorative justice and rehabilitation—are often not understood by court workers and are thus not effective (Syukur & Bagshaw 2015). Adding to the complication of diversion practices is the fact that there is no reliable data to show the exact number of diversions granted. In December 2017, the Supreme Court online database noted 173 diversion arrangements for juveniles, but detailed information was either missing or inaccessible.

The Relationship between Law Enforcement Officers and Nonlegal Stakeholders

In a broader context, law enforcement bodies cannot work alone to build a comprehensive system to mitigate against the risks children face. As Lev (2000d) notes, all changes can only be implemented with the combined efforts of policy makers, judicial services, and the wider community. As of 2018, the MoSA has been given the capacity to provide alternatives to detention through its facilities in the Social Service Center (LPKS). Alternatives to child incarceration rely on social workers' and probation officers' reports to assist law enforcers navigate the system in the best interests of the child. While it is possible to obtain these reports, the quality of recommendations contained in these reports is often questionable (Amaliyah at al. 2015; Anggara, Napitupulu, & Hernowo 2016). This points to a need to strengthen the expertise of social workers and probation officers in this specialized area of juvenile justice.

During any stage of examination, law enforcement agencies can take noncustodial measures by returning children to their parents or placing them in LPKS. LPKS facilities take a social work approach and assist children from arrest to release. They also extend the support offered to include monitoring after the child has returned to their family and community. The MoSA has established 66 LPKS facilities nationwide (CNN Indonesia, August 15, 2016). However, there is limited availability of these social rehabilitation mechanisms and facilities, which do not necessarily guarantee a positive outcome for the child. In 2015, only 4 percent of juvenile offenders were placed in LPKS facilities, while more than 50 percent of all children in contact with the law were imprisoned in adult facilities (Ministry of Women's Empowerment and Child Protection 2017: 66).

The stark difference between the law and the reality may be caused by various problems faced by both LPKS and law enforcement agencies in implementing social rehabilitation. Legal institutions are not built to be particularly democratic, but to serve the functions of control and the establishment of order (Lev 2007c). Social institutions that are represented by LPKS are intended to fulfill a range of different functions. LPKS has three main aims: to guide the social rehabilitation process for children in contact with the law, to protect such children, and to increase the quality and reach of LPKS services (Ministry of Social Regulation No. 15/ 2014). The differences between the law trying to maintain control and social services trying to reintegrate children are also found in the different structure between the law enforcement sector and other sectors. Both the institutions of the police and prosecutors are centralized under the president's cabinet, while judges report to the Supreme Court. In contrast, social, health, and education sectors are decentralized under a local governor's office (Van Welzenis 2016). This means that centralized state authorities must cooperate with decentralized authorities.

In addition to the conflicting approach between law enforcers and social workers, the lack of regulation also hampers the effective implementation of services to rehabilitate children in conflict with the law. Guidelines on the duration of a child's placement in a facility, as an alternative to detention, have not been issued yet. There is no certainty about the length of time a child should be in the facility during the investigation process, and at the same time, LPKS cannot return children to their parents. This situation of uncertainty is exacerbated by poor coordination between law enforcement agencies and LPKS. It is also common to find cases where children escape from LPKS. There is also no regulation governing the prevention and response mechanism if the child escapes from LPKS. While there are no statistics, anecdotal evidence suggests that escapes are common, especially as children are often not locked behind bars. Further, the responsibility for monitoring and returning children to their family or the facility remains unclear.

Adding to the complicated relations among stakeholders, juvenile justice has become a part of the child protection remit, which is coordinated by the Indonesian Ministry of Women's Empowerment and Child Protection (MoWECP). Law 11/2012 gives MoWECP the roles of overseeing coordination, monitoring, and evaluation. Their role includes an overview of the budget related to integrated training among law enforcement officers. Very little has been accomplished as of 2018. The failure to produce implementing regulations regarding Law 11/2012, now six years after its establishment, along with the minimum amount of training given to staff, warrants that MoWECP as the coordinating agency be highly scrutinized (PUSKAPA 2018). The Ministry of Development Planning (Bappenas), as the central planning agency, has held coordination meetings to update the situation; however, MoWECP rarely attends these multistakeholder meetings. This suggests that MoWECP was given jurisdiction over this area despite not having the motivation or willingness to undertake the task.

Clarity of Laws and Policies

The practice of diversion often faces challenges because of weak regulations, and because of the lack of knowledge about diversion procedures among law enforcers (Krisnawati 2012). Law 11/2012 states that law enforcement officials should facilitate diversion if the juvenile is a first offender and the maximum punishment for the juvenile criminal act is seven years of imprisonment or less. Under this provision, the child that is tried for grand theft, burglary, or consensual sexual intercourse with a minor—the latter is the most common juvenile 'crime' (PUSKAPA 2014; Anggara, Napitupulu, & Hernowo 2016)—cannot be diverted because it is punishable by more than seven years' imprisonment.

The technical regulation on diversion issued under Government Regulation No. 65 of 2015 on Guidelines for the Implementation of Diversion and Handling of Children under twelve years of age does not clarify which cases can be diverted. Diversion is also vague because Law 11/2012 and Government Regulation 65/2015 state that diversion can only be implemented if both parties (victim and defendant) agree. This provision potentially overrides the child's best interest because sometimes the victim or his/her family wants the offender to receive severe punishment or demands an amount of money that the offender cannot afford (Jumadi 2013; Herdiyanto, Achmad, & Aldhiyati 2013).

The provision that both sides must agree on an outcome is also incompatible with the development of criminal law in Indonesia. Rather than trying to facilitate an agreement, the Indonesian government often responds to requests to improve the justice system by issuing more punitive regulations. For example, narcotic use has prompted the government to enact Law 35/2009 on narcotics that means that a child drug user can be given a maximum sentence of four years imprisonment and the drug supplier twelve years' imprisonment. Drug use or drug supply for adults can result in the death penalty if someone is convicted of that crime. In eleven cases monitored by the Institute of Criminal Justice Reform (ICJR), all children accused of drug use were unable to access diversion because they were also accused of supplying drugs (Anggara, Napitupulu, & Hernowo 2016).

Regarding the issue of violence against children, the Indonesian public often vocally demands that the best response is to implement tougher punishments to deter such violence. For instance, severe penalties have been imposed as punishment for those convicted of carrying out sexual violence against children (Amanda 2014). As the current juvenile justice system relies on adult criminal laws, the higher punishment imposed on adults also applies to children convicted of similar crimes. This increased penalty bars children from accessing alternatives to detention and it challenges Indonesia's move toward establishing restorative justice approaches in its juvenile justice system.

In 2018, the latest pressing issue concerns debates and discussion on the revision of Indonesia's penal code (RKUHP). Child protection organizations have highlighted a number of articles within the proposed revision that could potentially bring more children into the criminal justice system, thus increasing their risk of being imprisoned. The current draft being discussed in parliament consists of hundreds of criminal offences and harsher criminal sanctions, which will automatically lower the chance of juvenile offenders accessing diversion practices (PUSKAPA 2018).

RKUHP also opens the possibility of the criminalization of offences under customary law (*adat*) (PUSKAPA 2018). With the diverse range of customary laws across Indonesia, this article will increase political–legal authority vested in administrators at the local government level (Lev 1996). This situation will increase diverse standards regarding what is considered criminal behavior, opening the door to misinterpretation and ill practices toward children (PUSKAPA 2018). This already happens in the province of Aceh where the local government criminalizes citizens (including children) for "khalwat" (a term used when an unmarried woman and man meet in a secluded place). In practice, the enforcement of Aceh's local law puts children accused of such a crime into detention and through unnecessary interrogation. The result of a woman and man being found guilty of khalwat is that they might be forced to marry. They might be forced to marry because, according to Acehnese religious and moral beliefs, it is unacceptable for an unmarried couple to be alone together, even if they are just talking. The "sin" of being together is considered void if the couple then marries (HRW 2010). This regulation has the result of increasing rates of the forced marriage of minors.

Legal Representation and Assistance

Indonesia has a sufficient regulatory framework to ensure legal representation for children. Article 23 of Law 11/2012 and Law No. 16/2011 on legal aid requires law enforces to appoint legal counsel for children, especially to those who are poor and threatened with imprisonment of five years or more. The Indonesian legal aid system was built to address structural oppression toward the poor. As a result, people in poverty should receive legal aid, as required by Law No. 16/2011. However, while this framework is a compulsory part of the justice system, very few children are legally represented after arrest. In fact, only 34 percent of all children facing imprisonment have a lawyer to defend them (PUSKAPA 2014). Further, if the case goes to trial, children often have no legal representation. In 2012, only 51 percent of cases observed involved a child with legal representation (Hutabarat, Isnur, & Tobing

2012). This number appears to have declined, and in 2016, only 11 percent of cases observed involved a child with legal representation; the rest of the cases had no lawyer involved (Anggara, Napitupulu, & Hernowo 2016).

In responding to this lack of legal representation, the Supreme Court routinely provides budgets for legal aid. In 2015, the general courts provided legal assistance for 11,551 people (Indonesian Supreme Court 2017). In 2016, the Ministry of Law and Human Rights provided a total budget of 45 billion rupiah (or US$ 3.2 million) to support 405 accredited legal aid organizations. However, this budget can only provide legal aid for 9,000–10,000, cases and the money was distributed unevenly to legal aid organizations (BPHN 2018). According to Law 16/2011, local government can also provide legal aid. However, research in Jakarta, Riau, West Borneo, and Gorontalo found that only the West Borneo Provincial Government provided a legal aid budget (Fajriando 2016). Meanwhile, neither the National Police Department nor the General Prosecutor's Office has ever had a special policy to provide legal aid for suspects.

Budget Politics in Providing Training for Specialized Personnel

Training of specialized personnel is deemed important to develop an effective juvenile justice system. Its importance is emphasized in the Indonesian government's 2018 Workplan, which prioritized integrated training programs for people involved in law.[1] Article 92 of Law 11/2012 obligates the government to conduct integrated education and training for law enforcers and other related stakeholders. Presidential Regulation 175/2014 states that trainees should include police, attorneys, judges, advocates, and social workers. The purpose is not only for educating law enforcers and other related stakeholders but also for improving the general perceptions of law enforcement parties. Until 2017, training was undertaken by several institutions including the Ministry of Women's Empowerment and Child Protection, the Ministry of Law and Human Rights, the national police, the Supreme Court, and the Attorney Office (PUSKAPA 2018). Even the Supreme Court and the police have committed to the training by allocating an annual budget of 10 billion rupiah to integrated training services. But this budget is not supported by the readiness of judges for training. Since judges are reviewed based on cases handled, not on certifications earned, they are reluctant to attend training

---

[1] Presidential Regulation No. 79 of 2017 on the government's 2018 Workplan.

due to the time required (three weeks full-time). Low attendance rates also occur in other agencies, especially among advocates. Other issues that arise are that the training only covers laws and regulations, not the psychosocial needs of children, whereas those working in the criminal justice system also need adequate knowledge of psychology and sociology.

In 2015, the MoSA budgeted for the education and training of its 1,000 employees. However, research by MoSA found that there were many social workers who did not become certified, although many of them had already gained qualifications as a counselor for children. The certification requirement is aimed at ensuring the quality of service provided by social workers. But this provision limits the number of social workers available to provide services to children. As a result, children find it difficult to obtain assistance because the number of social workers who have certification is low and they are not available in all districts. Furthermore, the issue of lack of budget also arises in relation to the development of programs aimed to implement restorative justice principles. In addition, there is no budget invested in data collection, monitoring, or evaluation of the system, so it is difficult to know how well the system is performing (Foussard & Melotti 2016).

Institutional Dynamics toward Integrated Data and Information Systems

The extent to which the principle of restorative justice is being implemented in Indonesia's juvenile courts remains unclear. Limited knowledge of the court's process is due to insufficient administrative data and dispersed institutional registers, both for child offenders, victims, and witnesses. This makes it difficult to track down cases, particularly those where diversion was granted (PUSKAPA 2014). Moreover, the lack of monitoring and evaluation mechanisms concerning implementation contributes to the unavailability of data on the juvenile justice system and on children in contact with the law.

The collection of data for administrative purposes is regulated by Government Regulation No. 9 of 2017. On its implementation, there was very little information management to allow for national, or even provincial, law enforcement offices to understand the scale of cases involving children. Correctional institution data is made available online, and the Supreme Court does have an electronic database, but the data does not categorize cases involving children nor allow tracking by the age of defendants. Other databases are not easily retrievable, and even when they are available, such as police data on children, it is spread across different units based on the category of criminal case rather than on age (PUSKAPA 2014). It is also difficult to get useful data because there is little coordination among legal sectors and little exchange of data or information (Syukur & Bagshaw 2015).

The lack of data reveals the government's inability to conduct monitoring or evaluation of the new law, although this is not necessarily unusual in Indonesia. There is no evidence to show the extent of implemented restorative practices or evidence to allow for an assessment of its effectiveness. While further changes are needed to assist children in conflict with the law, Indonesia does at least have legislative measures to assist in preventing reoffending and further harm.

Conclusion

Lev's work helps us to understand the development, implementation, and improvement of Indonesia's juvenile justice system. Understanding legal culture in relation to juvenile courts is not, as Lev reveals, a mere set of processes, but involves reciprocity between the legal system and society in the reproduction of the meaning of law. As the meaning of law itself is constantly changing, the interrelationship between systems and culture cannot be explained without having a proper understanding of the social setting and, regarding the juvenile court, society's perception of juvenile justice.

Utilizing Lev's legal culture concept, understandings of the culture in Indonesia's justice system can be increased. Such understanding can also be increased when Lev's concept is accompanied by other components such as social and political norms and values. In a practical manner, it is extremely difficult to measure the factors that affect the legal system. This is a challenge to our understanding of the interventions needed. What our chapter suggests is that Lev's work is important but that we also need to incorporate other approaches to understand how the legal system works in Indonesia.

This chapter has explained the role of Indonesia's juvenile court in providing justice to children. While this role fits into a broader judicial system and legal culture in theory, in practice Indonesia continues to fall short. Law 11/2012 has theoretically improved the way officials deal with children in contact with the law, providing them with options of restorative justice, diversion, and alternative resolution approaches. The law should thus be used to push the criminal justice community to improve their data management systems and data sharing. But as with any law, it is embedded in a sociopolitical system and to date there has been little improvement of the justice system vis-à-vis children.

As Lev emphasized in *Between State and Society* (2008), legislative reform unaccompanied by institutional reform is unlikely to result in any positive change. For all its failings in practice, Law 11/2012 confirms the importance of considering the legal rights of children, and it constitutes recognition of children's rights and well-being in the legal system. The establishment of Law 11/2012 is useful for reformers to continue to push for political and legal change. Importantly, the law should also be supported with evidence-based strategies to be implemented effectively. Regulation needs better enforcement. Governance, monitoring, accountability, and the interaction of all stakeholders must be improved. Indonesia's children deserve justice.

13

The Human Rights Courts

Embedding Impunity

KEN SETIAWAN

[. . .] for the most fundamental sorts of change,
law is probably always of limited value

(Lev 1972b: 317–318)

Since the fall of President Suharto in May 1998, one of the most contentious issues in Indonesia has been the question of what to do with the
country's immense legacy of human rights violations, particularly those
that occurred under authoritarian rule (1966–1998).[1] Organisations and
individuals favourable to the promotion of human rights have argued
that accountability for these violations will break the cycle of military
impunity, in turn a crucial aspect of strengthening democracy and the
rule of law in the country (Linton 2006: 202). In the early *reformasi* years,
there has been significant activity in the realm of human rights, including
law-making and the creation of new institutions with a human rights
mandate. One of the most important developments has been the establishment of Human Rights Courts in 2000, which have the power to hear
and rule on cases of gross human rights violations.

Since their inception, however, only three tribunals – which will be
discussed below – have been held at these courts. The most recent
tribunal was held in 2005. As such, in practice the Human Rights
Courts have ceased to function, while formally they continue to exist.
The Indonesian National Human Rights Commission (*Komisi Nasional
Hak Asasi Manusia*, henceforth Komnas HAM) has continued to conduct preliminary investigations with a view of bringing these to the
Human Rights Courts. Similarly, the Attorney General's office continues
to reserve a part of its annual budget for the prosecution of gross human

---

[1] Some historians have challenged the temporal focus on crimes committed during
Suharto's New Order period. They argue that the record of extreme violence in
Indonesia can be traced back to the thirteenth century (see Linton 2006).

rights violations even if it has been reluctant to do so. This raises the question what the role is of the Human Rights Courts in contemporary Indonesian state and society.

In exploring this question, my analysis in this chapter will draw on the work of Daniel S. Lev on Indonesian law and society. While Lev's work did not specifically address the Human Rights Courts, his focus on the interconnectedness of law (Lev 2000d: 3) is highly relevant to examine the position of the Human Rights Courts. In particular, I will use Lev's concept of legal culture as an analytical tool to understand the politics of the Human Rights Courts and, by extension, to interrogate the role of these courts in Indonesia today. Lev's conceptualisation of legal culture was based on Friedman's work on legal culture, which he explored from the 1960s. Friedman defined legal culture as 'the ideas, values, attitudes, and opinions people in society hold, with regard to law and the legal system' (Friedman 1994: 118). Legal culture thus describes public attitudes to law, which also serve as the source of law: it determines the impact of legal norms on society (Merry 2010: 47).

Lev distinguished two related components of legal culture that are, as I will argue, particularly useful in understanding the role of these courts in contemporary Indonesian state and society. The first element is procedural legal values that act as a means of social regulation and conflict management. These are, in turn, the cultural basis of the legal system.[2] The second element is substantive legal values, which refers to the fundamental assumption about the distribution of resources in a society and their use as well as social rights and wrongs. These assumptions change over time, as societies themselves change (Lev 1972b: 247).

In this chapter, following a historical background of how the Human Rights Courts came into being, the first part of the discussion will focus on the Courts' enabling law, which correlates with the procedural element of legal culture. This will be followed by a discussion of the three tribunals that have been held at the Human Rights Courts since their inception. In this section, I will pay particular attention to the legal proceedings in the courts. This is in order to explore the substantive element of legal culture, tracing the dominant legal values in the legal process. Taking inspiration from Lev's social–political analysis of law and paying attention to power relations and contestations as a lens to

---

[2] Lev defines "legal system" as formal processes that constitute formal institutions together with the informal processes surrounding them. Central institutions of a legal system are bureaucracies, including the courts (Lev 1972b, 246–247).

examine legal institutions and the law, I argue that while the emergence of the Human Rights Courts signals a shift in the procedural element of legal culture they have not changed legal values consistent with human rights principles embedded in law. In fact, since their inception the Human Rights Courts have served to embed impunity for the security forces, rather than breaking this cycle.

Historical Background

The establishment of Indonesia's Human Rights Courts cannot be separated from the immediate period following the end of authoritarianism and the legal and political reforms that followed. Suharto's New Order was notorious for its systematic violation of human rights. The security forces played a key role in repression and in general escaped accountability for their actions, leading to a culture of impunity (McGregor and Setiawan 2019).

The violence that marked the end of the Suharto regime once more highlighted the dominance of the security forces during the authoritarian regime. In May 1998, security forces opened fire on student protestors in Jakarta, killing four and injuring nearly 700 in what is known as the Trisakti killings. In Jakarta, as well as in Medan and Solo, violent outbreaks resulted in the destruction of property, loss of lives and sexual violence particularly targeted at Chinese Indonesians. The involvement of the military in both the attack on the students and in the May 1998 violence brought it into further disrepute. The military responded by rescinding its political role (*dwifungsi*) in September 1998.

The role of the security forces in the violation of human rights influenced reform demands of Indonesia's legal system. International pressure for this should be seen in the context of other countries transitioning from authoritarian rule in the 1980s and 1990s, while domestic pressure placed this demand more broadly in the context of political change. While there certainly was a domestic push for human rights reform, a specific human rights agenda was absent. This was because of the fragmentation of the *reformasi* movement and its focus on the ousting of Suharto from power (McGregor and Setiawan 2019). Nonetheless, the Indonesian government developed a new human rights framework relatively quickly.

In November 1998, the *Majelis Permusyawaratan Rakyat* (MPR, People's Consultative Assembly) passed Decree XVII/MPR/1998 on human rights. The foundation of legislative reform related to human rights in the post-authoritarian era, this Decree includes many civil and political, as well as economic, social and cultural rights. It also explicitly states that the promotion and protection of human rights is the primary responsibility of the state.[3]

This Decree was the precursor to Law 39 of 1999 on Human Rights that was enacted the following year. This Law includes a wide range of human rights provisions and stipulates that all international human rights law ratified by Indonesia becomes national law.[4] It also strengthened the status and mandate of Indonesia's National Human Rights Commission (*Komisi Nasional Hak Asasi Manusia*, henceforth Komnas HAM).[5]

The Law on Human Rights was followed by Government Regulation 1/1999 on the Human Rights Courts to address cases of gross human rights violations (*pelanggaran hak asasi manusia yang berat*). This Regulation designated Komnas HAM as the sole preliminary investigator in cases where gross human rights violations were suspected.[6] The Regulation was in place until the enactment of Law 26 of 2000 on the Human Rights Courts, which will be discussed in detail below.

In addition to the enactment of these new laws, in 2000 the second round of amendments to the 1945 Constitution saw the inclusion of Chapter XA on human rights. These provisions were modelled on the Universal Declaration of Human Rights (UDHR) (Lindsey 2008: 29) and include a wide range of human rights guarantees. More controversial was the prohibition on retroactive application of legislation,[7] of which some observers argued potentially (see below) could cause problems when prosecuting gross human rights crimes that occurred in the past. Taken together, the new laws represented the establishment of a solid legal framework for the protection of human rights in Indonesia. The reforms[8] were indicative of an increase of procedural legal values in which Indonesia displayed a growing adherence to international norms.

---

[3] Decree XVII/MPR/1998, Article 1.
[4] Law 39/1999, Article 7(2).
[5] Law 39/1999, Chapter VII.
[6] Government Regulation 1/1999, Article 10(1).
[7] 1945 Constitution, Article 28I(1).
[8] In addition to these laws, in 2004, the Law on the Truth and Reconciliation Commission (Law 27/2004) was passed, providing for a non-judicial avenue to resolve past human rights abuses. The Constitutional Court cancelled this Law in 2006.

Law 26/2000 on the Human Rights Courts

The second round of constitutional amendments saw the inclusion of a bill of rights that draws on international law. To further realise these rights, a few months later the Law on the Human Rights Courts was enacted. This Law provides for the establishment of courts that have the authority to hear and rule on cases of gross human rights violations.[9] The enactment of this Law, however, eventuated earlier than anticipated: a provision in the 1999 Human Rights Law had envisaged the establishment of the Human Rights Courts by 2003.[10] The fast-tracking of this Law served to pre-empt a proposed international tribunal to try Indonesian officials for crimes committed in the lead up to and following the 1999 independence referendum for East Timor[11] (Linton 2006: 207; Cammack 2016: 191). This seems to suggest that, from the earliest stages, the Human Rights Courts came into existence because of political considerations rather than a genuine attempt to generate change. This resonates with Lev's observations on the politics of courts and that institutions of the law are 'fundamentally derivative, founded on political power conditioned by social and economic influence' (Lev 2007c: 236).

Article 5 of Law 26/2000 provides that the Human Rights Courts have the authority to hear and rule on cases of gross human rights violations perpetrated by an Indonesian citizen outside the territorial boundaries of the Republic of Indonesia. This limitation is inconsistent with international law, as it does not provide for universal jurisdiction of persons suspected of crimes found in Indonesian territory. International principles state that suspects in such cases should be able to be extradited to another state that is willing or able to prosecute them. Indonesia is obliged to adhere to principles of universal jurisdiction as a state party to the Geneva Conventions of 1949, as well as the Convention against Torture and Other Cruel, Inhuman, or Degrading Treatment or Punishment (CAT). Universal jurisdiction serves to avoid impunity and to prevent those who committed serious crimes from finding protection in other countries.

Article 7 stipulates that the Human Rights Courts have jurisdiction to prosecute two categories of crimes as gross violations of human rights;

---

[9] Law 26/2000, Article 4.
[10] Law 39/1999, Article 104.
[11] Although increasingly referred to as Timor-Leste, a reflection of the state's official name (República Democrática de Timor-Leste), in this chapter I use the name 'East Timor' as this can be used consistently.

the crime of genocide (*genosida*) and crimes against humanity (*kejahatan terhadap kemanusiaan*). There is also a provision for command responsibility, which explicitly applies to civilians as well as to the military and police.[12] The elucidation of the Law states that its provisions have been based on the Rome Statute of the International Criminal Court (henceforth Rome Statute), to which Indonesia is not yet a state party. The use of this Statute for the Human Rights Courts Law reflects a global context in which there was more attention for questions of justice in post-authoritarian states and accountability for core human rights crimes. However, the Law did not exactly replicate the jurisdiction of the International Criminal Court (ICC) as it omitted two other crimes identified in the Rome Statute, namely war crimes and the crime of aggression.[13] The omission of one of Indonesia's most pressing human rights concerns – war crimes in internal armed conflict – was not an accident (Linton 2006: 211).

While the Law's definition of genocide is consistent with international principles, ancillary crimes for genocide – such as conspiracy to commit genocide, direct and public incitement to commit genocide, attempts to commit genocide and complicity in genocide – have been excluded. It has been argued that the inclusion of ancillary crimes is necessary to ensure investigation and prosecution at the earliest possible moment (Amnesty International 2001). At the same time, it has been suggested that these ancillary crimes may be able to be prosecuted under various aspects of criminal responsibility in the Code of Criminal Procedure (KUHAP) (Linton 2006: 212).

The Law's provisions on crimes against humanity are inconsistent in a number of ways with international law. While the general definition of the crime has been adapted from the Rome Statute, the provision on crimes against humanity requires a 'widespread or systematic attack with the knowledge that the said attack was directly targeted at the civilian population'.[14] This suggests that there should be an armed conflict and may be interpreted that there is no crime against humanity unless there was a direct (armed) attack on the civilian population. This may rule out frequent and systematic attacks on the population as well as serious forms of discrimination, which may amount to persecution. As such, the

---

[12] Law 26/2000, Article 42.
[13] Rome Statute, Article 5(1).
[14] Law 26/2000, Article 9.

burden of proof for the prosecution has been made very difficult (Linton 2006: 213).

Other provisions in the Law are also problematic from the perspective of international law. The Law's elaboration on extermination,[15] for instance, presents a narrow reading of this crime that had been rejected during the drafting of the Rome Statute. Enslavement[16] in the Human Rights Courts Law fails to include the trafficking of persons, while the definition of torture[17] is also limited. Only when torture is committed as part of a 'broad or systematic direct attack on the civilian population' may it be prosecuted as a crime against humanity. An additional element of crimes against humanity in the Rome Statute, on 'other inhumane acts of a similar character intentionally causing great suffering, or serious injury to body or to mental or physical health',[18] is missing from the Law on the Human Rights Courts. These limitations in fact raise the threshold of crimes, diminishing the likelihood of conviction. As such, these narrow definitions could lead to impunity.

The penal provisions in the Law on the Human Rights Courts include jail sentences of at least ten and at most twenty-five years for the crime of genocide. Life imprisonment and the death penalty may also be imposed. These punishments also apply to a number of crimes against humanity namely killing, extermination, deportation or forcible relocation, deprivation of liberty and apartheid.[19] Those found guilty of enslavement and torture are subject to a minimum of five or maximum of fifteen years imprisonment.[20] Sexual violence, persecution and enforced disappearance are punishable by a minimum imprisonment of ten, and maximum of twenty, years.[21] The Law does not provide guidance to the grounds to distinguish between maximum and minimal custodial sentences. Moreover, while the penalties are consistent with the provisions of the Rome Statute, the death penalty is at odds with international efforts to abolish capital punishment.

The Law on the Human Rights Courts provides for the establishment of two types of courts. First, the permanent human rights courts for violations that occurred after the Law on the Human Rights Courts was

---

[15] Law 26/2000, Article 9(b).
[16] Law 26/2000, Article 9(c).
[17] Law 26/2000, Article 9(f).
[18] Rome Statute, Article 7(1)(k).
[19] Law 26/2000, Article 37.
[20] Law 26/2000, Articles 38 and 39.
[21] Law 26/2000, Article 40(1).

passed.[22] The Law stipulates that permanent courts are established in Central Jakarta, Surabaya, Medan and Makassar, each covering various provinces.[23] To date, the only permanent court has been in Makassar, where the tribunal for Abepura (discussed in detail below) was held. In addition to the permanent courts, the Law provides for the establishment of ad hoc courts, for cases that occurred before 2000.[24] Two tribunals (East Timor and Tanjung Priok, see below) were held at the ad hoc courts in Jakarta. The ad hoc tribunals illustrate that while the principle of non-retroactivity is enshrined in the 1945 Constitution[25] (as discussed in the previous section), in practice principles of international law provide for the investigation, prosecution and punishment of crimes that at the time that they were committed were criminal acts recognised by the community of nations.

Komnas HAM plays a key role in the process of bringing cases of gross human rights violations to court. The Law designates the Commission as the sole body to conduct a preliminary investigation (*penyelidikan*) into a case where it suspects that gross human rights violations have taken place.[26] It has been argued that Komnas HAM's role should not limit the ability of prosecutors to conduct such investigations. By restricting this task to one body, there are indications that this contradicts the UN Guidelines on the Role of Prosecutors (Amnesty International 2001). Komnas HAM's designation as preliminary investigator has displeased the Attorney General's office (Setiawan 2013, 2016), an illustration of the deep historical roots of institutional rivalry between the prosecution and other judicial institutions in Indonesia (Lev 1965b: 173).

When Komnas HAM opens a preliminary investigation, it may include external members in its investigation team (for instance, NGO representatives).[27] If Komnas HAM is of the opinion that there is sufficient preliminary evidence of gross human rights violations, it forwards the findings to the Attorney General[28] who may then decide whether or not to proceed with an investigation (*penyidikan*).[29] Concerns have been raised regarding the position of the Attorney General as a State Minister, which

---

[22] Law 26/2000, Article 2.
[23] Law 26/2000, Article 45(1).
[24] Law 26/2000, Article 43(1).
[25] 1945 Constitution, Article 28I.
[26] Law 26/2000, Article 18(1).
[27] Law 26/2000, Article 18(2).
[28] Law 26/2000, Article 20(1).
[29] Law 26/2000, Article 21(1).

may subject the decision to open an investigation to political considerations (Amnesty International 2001).

Similar to Komnas HAM, the Attorney General can appoint ad hoc investigators from both government and society,[30] who are sworn in.[31] The Law does not make clear whether the Attorney General automatically needs to follow-up with an investigation. This appears to be contingent on whether it is of the opinion that the result of the preliminary investigation is complete.[32] Investigations must be completed within ninety days[33] and then, if the Attorney General's investigation finds evidence of severe human rights violations, brought to the Human Rights Courts. For crimes that took place before the enactment of the Law, an ad hoc court must be established. Ad hoc courts require parliamentary approval and are formally established via presidential decree.[34] This procedure has made the process of establishing ad hoc courts vulnerable to political considerations (Setiawan 2016).

The Law stipulates that a panel of five judges hears each case, three of which are non-career or ad hoc judges.[35] The President, on the recommendation of the Chairperson of the Supreme Court, appoints these judges to the Human Rights Courts.[36] In the case of an appeal to the Supreme Court, the President on the recommendation of the People's Representative Assembly (*Dewan Perwakilan Rakyat*, DPR) appoints ad hoc judges.[37] Ad hoc judges need to meet a number of criteria, including that they 'must have knowledge about and concern for the field of human rights'.[38] Ad hoc judges are appointed for a term of five years that may be

---

[30] Law 26/2000, Article 21(3).

[31] Law 26/2000, Article 21(4). The requirement for investigators to be sworn in does not apply to preliminary investigators. This has on various occasions provided the Attorney General's office with a reason to reject Komnas HAM's findings (see Setiawan 2013 and 2016).

[32] Article 20(3) of the Law on the Human Rights Courts stipulates that if the Attorney General believes the results are incomplete, it must return them to the preliminary investigator (Komnas HAM). The Commission then must deliver the requested information within thirty days. Human rights organisations have commented that these time frames, while supposedly included to ensure the swift processing of these cases, are too rigid considering the complexity of the subject matter (Amnesty International 2001).

[33] Law 26/2000, Article 22(1).

[34] Law 26/2000, Article 43(2).

[35] Law 26/2000, Article 27(2).

[36] Law 26/2000, Article 28(1).

[37] Law 26/2000, Article 33(4).

[38] Law 26/2000, Article 29. Interestingly, the requirements for ad hoc judges in the Human Rights Courts do not include a stipulation that they must not be members of political

renewed once.[39] The same applies to ad hoc judges in other specialised courts. However, a tenure of five years is inconsistent with international guidelines that recommend a long and non-renewable term of office to ensure an independent and impartial tribunal (Amnesty International 2001).

The appointment of ad hoc judges for the Human Rights Courts lacks public consultation and participation of an independent, non-political body. While this is also a concern for the appointment of ad hoc judges to other courts, it should be pointed out that by comparison provisions regarding the appointment process in the Law on the Human Rights Courts are particularly minimal. Specific government regulations were issued for the appointment of ad hoc judges to the Industrial Relations Courts[40] and the Fisheries Courts.[41] These include provisions on who may propose candidate judges and outline the selection process including administrative requirements and the written test that candidates must complete. The lack of clear guidelines pertaining to the selection of ad hoc judges for the Human Rights Courts makes this process even less transparent, potentially having a detrimental impact on the appointment of appropriate candidates and thereby the independency of the courts.

Provisions regarding the protection of witnesses and victims are also problematic. Under Article 34, the Law determines that witnesses and victims have the right to physical and psychological protection from any threats, intimidation and violence that may be directed towards them. This protection is by Law the task of the security apparatus.[42] While this is common, it should be recognised that the security forces are likely to be implicated in the crimes that are heard at the courts. The providing of witness and victim protection is essential for any court investigating human rights violations. Without adequate protections witnesses may not come forward, thereby further jeopardising the trials and ultimately justice.

The establishment of the Human Rights Courts is an important step forward in a country that 'provides a textbook example of the direct link

---

parties, as is the case for ad hoc judges in other specialised courts such as the Fisheries Courts and the Anti-Corruption Courts.

[39] Law 26/2000, Article 28(3).

[40] Government Regulation 41/2004 on the Procedure for the Appointment of Ad Hoc Judges to the Industrial Relations Court and Ad Hoc Judges for the Supreme Court.

[41] Government Regulation 24/2006 on the Procedure of the Appointment and Dismissal of Ad Hoc Judges for the Fisheries Courts.

[42] Law 26/2000, Article 34(2).

between impunity for atrocities going back over decades and perpetual cycles of violence' (Linton 2006: 201). However, the Law is limited in scope and by design any attempts to prosecute cases are at the mercy of political considerations rather than objective criteria. This indicates that while the establishment of the Human Rights Courts has changed the procedural legal values that inform legal culture, a close reading of the Law shows that these values also remained contested. In considering procedural legal values it is thus necessary to differentiate between the broader objectives of laws and regulations in place and their specific provisions, which may show that these oppose one another. The following sections will analyse the cases that have been brought to the Human Rights Courts, paying attention to the social and political ideas that inform substantive legal behaviour.

East Timor

The fall of Suharto saw increased international scrutiny of the Indonesian occupation of East Timor (1975–1999). In January 1999 President B. J. Habibie, who had succeeded Suharto, announced a referendum regarding special autonomy for East Timor to be held on 30 August of that year. Following this announcement, a systematic campaign of violence and terror was directed against those who rejected special autonomy. The perpetrators of this violence were voluntary militias, which were recruited and armed by the Indonesian military (*Tentara Nasional Indonesia*, TNI). The violence escalated further after it was announced that East Timorese had voted overwhelmingly in favour of independence. It has been estimated that 1,400 civilians were killed, 250,000 were forcibly displaced, and 70 per cent of infrastructure was destroyed (Cammack 2016: 193).

There was international condemnation of the violence perpetrated in East Timor, and this led the Indonesian government to devise ways to minimise this criticism. Of primary concern was to convince the international community that Indonesia would be able to bring this case to justice. Komnas HAM was asked to conduct a preliminary investigation into gross human rights crimes in East Timor. In September 1999, Komnas HAM established the *Komisi Penyelidik Pelanggaran HAM Timor Timur* (Investigatory Commission on Human Rights Violations in East Timor or KPP HAM TimTim).[43] The KPP HAM was mandated

---

[43] Decree of the Chair of Komnas HAM 770/TUA/IX/99.

to gather facts, data and other information on the violations of human rights in East Timor since 1999, investigate the degree of involvement of the state apparatus and compile the findings of the inquiry as preliminary evidence for the investigation and prosecution in a Human Rights Court.

Albert Hasibuan, Chair of the KPP HAM, stated that while there were some problems during the investigation – including intimidation and harassment of investigators – the military proved largely willing to cooperate with the investigation. He attributed this to the TNI being largely unaware of the potential consequences of the investigation (Setiawan 2013: 50). The cooperative stance may have also been informed by an effort from the TNI to regain control over the situation and prevent the case from being heard at an international tribunal (Cammack 2016: 195). This was a plausible outcome because, at the same time that Komnas HAM was conducting its investigation, a UN-mandated Commission was conducting a separate inquiry. This Commission came to similar conclusions as the KPP HAM. Within the United Nations, there was significant scepticism whether Indonesia would be able to prosecute the perpetrators. However, it was decided that national courts should be given priority.

The KPP HAM concluded that the Indonesian authorities were responsible for the gross human rights violations that took place between January and October 1999. This included mass murder, persecution, forced disappearances, gender-based violence and the forced movement of civilians. It found evidence that the military, police and civil administration were involved in the creation, support, training and arming of militias that were largely responsible for the violence. The Commission added that the violence was not the result of the inability of the security forces to protect civilians, but a direct result of a 'conscious and planned Indonesian effort to terrorise East Timorese independence supporters' (Cammack 2016: 195).

When Komnas HAM's report was published, it caused quite a stir. The report's detail was widely praised, which included a list of those members of the TNI and government that were primarily responsible for the atrocities committed. The KPP HAM recommended the Attorney General's office to further investigate more than 100 individuals including the four highest-ranking members of the Indonesian armed forces. This included General Wiranto, who as Commander of the TNI carried ultimate responsibility (Cohen 2003: 17).[44] Wiranto was subsequently

---

[44] Other high-ranking members of the Indonesian armed forces identified in the report were Lieutenant General Johny Lumintang (deputy commander of the armed forces), Major

removed as Coordinating Minister of Politics, Law and Security from the Wahid Cabinet (Setiawan 2013: 51).

The Attorney General's office responded to the Komnas HAM report by forming a team of fifteen prosecutors. They were mandated to investigate five incidents, rather than abuses that occurred throughout 1999. After this investigation, prosecutors charged eighteen defendants, who were prosecuted in twelve trials, with crimes against humanity for acts of murder or assault as part of a systematic attack directed against a civilian population. The defendants were members of the TNI (ranging from the rank of major general to sub-district army officers), the Indonesian police, civilian officials and one militia commander. All were charged for acts committed by subordinates based on command responsibility (Cammack 2016: 199).

The ad hoc tribunal for East Timor was established by way of Presidential Decree 53 of 2001.[45] Trials were held between 2002 and 2003. There was minimal support for the proceedings, which was illustrated by ad hoc judges not being paid for their work for up to nine months (Kompas 2002). Prosecutors barely consulted with the KPP HAM and used little of the documentary evidence gathered by this Commission. In fact, when the indictments were made public it was evident that the Attorney General's office had constructed a case that was fundamentally different from the findings of the KPP HAM (Cohen 2003: 19). Among others, the KPP HAM distinguished between more occurrences and patterns of crimes, applied a wider timeframe and identified more alleged perpetrators.[46]

In so doing, the prosecution in the East Timor tribunal failed to produce sufficient accusative evidence, although this was readily available. The prosecution was also flawed in that it did not present an account of the violence that was sufficient to justify convictions. In fact, most of the evidence presented was favourable to the defence (Cohen 2003: 13–15). Cammack has attributed this to the prosecutors' unwillingness to charge active military commanders. Prosecutors systematically talked down defendants' contribution to the crimes or presented other

---

General Zacky Anwar Makarim (director of the intelligence service of the Indonesian army) and Major General (retd.) H. R. Garnadi (vice chairperson of the Task Force for the Popular Consultation on Special Autonomy of East Timor).

[45] This presidential decree also provided for the establishment of an ad hoc tribunal for Tanjung Priok.

[46] For a detailed overview of the discrepancies between the findings of the KPP HAM and those of the Attorney General's office, see Cohen 2003: 20.

justifications. Very little testimony from East Timorese victims was presented, which was favourable to the defendants. The prosecutors also demonstrated little understanding of basic legal concepts, for instance, in failing to recognise that a conviction under the command responsibility provision requires evidence of the commission of crimes by subordinates. Overall, prosecutors' arguments largely reinforced the central claims of the defence that the violence had occurred as a result of opposing political factions. As such, the defendants were found not guilty of crimes against humanity (Cammack 2016: 200–202, 207).

Of the eighteen defendants, twelve were acquitted and six were convicted. In four convictions, the sentences handed down were lower than the minimum stipulated in the Law on the Human Rights Courts. In the case of Adam Damiri, who was the most senior military officer to be brought to trial, the prosecutor asked for the defendant to be released. However, the court found that Damiri failed to prevent certain crimes and handed down a sentence of three years. All convictions were subsequently overturned on appeal (see Table 13.1). The legal process at the Human Rights Courts thus illustrates that there is a gap between procedural and substantive legal values.

Cammack's analysis of the verdicts shows that there is no clear explanation for the different outcomes. He argues that the pattern of convictions (or acquittals) cannot be explained based on the strength of the evidence alone and that the different verdicts resulted primarily from the composition of the panels of judges. For all trials, there was a pool of twenty-three judges, eighteen of whom served on more than one trial. Of these judges, the majority voted consistently to acquit or convict, suggesting that the composition of panels determined the outcome of the trial (Cammack 2016: 208).

In the judgments, the discussion of law was 'uniformly simplistic and imprecise' (Cammack 2016: 209). For instance, the systematic elements of crimes against humanity were equated to the existence of a pattern or similar actions. The judgments did not discuss definitions of crimes against humanity, even if they recognised that civilians were the target of collective violence. In general, there was a disregard of the severity of the crimes committed in East Timor (Cammack 2016: 224).

In the handful of cases that resulted in a conviction, judges credited the testimony of East Timorese witnesses, while discounting that of members of the security forces (Cammack 2016: 212–213). The convictions that were secured were also remarkable considering

Table 13.1 *Charges, sentences and appeals at Indonesia's Human Rights Courts*

Trial	Defendant	Charge	Sentence	Appeal
East Timor				
I	Timbul Silaen	10 years, 6 months	Acquitted	Upheld
II	Abilio Jose Soares	10 years, 6 months	3 years	3 years (High Court) Acquitted (Supreme Court)
III	Herman Sedyono	10 years	Acquitted	Upheld
	Liliek Kushadianto	10 years, 6 months	Acquitted	Upheld
	Ahmad Syamsudin	10 years	Acquitted	Upheld
	Sugito	10 years	Acquitted	Upheld
	Gatot Subiyaktoro	10 years, 3 months	Acquitted	Upheld
IV	Asep Kuswani	10 years	Acquitted	Upheld
	Adios Salova	10 years	Acquitted	Upheld
	Leoneto Martins	10 years	Acquitted	Upheld
V	Endar Priyanto	10 years	Acquitted	Upheld
VI	Soedjarwo	10 years	5 years	Acquitted
VII	Hulman Gultom	10 years	3 years	Acquitted
VIII	Eurico Guterres	10 years	10 years	5 years (High Court) Acquitted (Supreme Court)
IX	Adam Damiri	Release	3 years	Acquitted
X	Tono Suratman	10 years	Acquitted	Upheld
XI	M. Noer Muis	10 years	5 years	Acquitted
XII	Yayat Sudrajat	10 years	Acquitted	Upheld
Tanjung Priok				
I	Sutrisno Mascung	10 years	3 years	Acquitted
	Asrori	2 years	Acquitted	Upheld
	Siswoyo	2 years	Acquitted	Upheld
	Abdul Halim	2 years	Acquitted	Upheld

Table 13.1 (*cont.*)

Trial	Defendant	Charge	Sentence	Appeal
	Zulfatah	2 years	Acquitted	Upheld
	Sumitro	2 years	Acquitted	Upheld
	Sofyan Hadi	2 years	Acquitted	Upheld
	Prayogi	2 years	Acquitted	Upheld
	Winarko	2 years	Acquitted	Upheld
	Idrus	2 years	Acquitted	Upheld
	Mushon	2 years	Acquitted	Upheld
II	Rudolf Butar Butar	10 years	10 years	Acquitted
III	Pranowo	5 years	Acquitted	Upheld
IV	Sriyanto	10 years	Acquitted	Upheld
Abepura				
I	Johny Wainal Usman	10 years	Acquitted	-
II	Daud Sihombing	10 years	Acquitted	-

Compiled from Cohen 2003; ELSAM 2004; International Crimes Database (www
.internationalcrimesdatabase.org) and KontraS (www.kontras.org/data/Matrix%
20Putusan%20Pengadilan%20HAM%20di%20Indonesia.htm).

the close attention the military paid to the trial, including their
physical presence in the courtroom, thereby also placing considerable
pressure on witnesses. Judges appeared to be largely aware that
convictions would most likely not lead to punishment. Despite this,
some remained committed to delivering an independent verdict
(Cammack 2016: 223).

Despite the commitment of some judges, the ad hoc Human
Rights Court for East Timor has been widely and justly criticised
for acquitting a majority of those who were brought to trial. In its
verdicts, the Courts reproduced the 'civil war' narrative put forward
by the defendants and the Indonesian authorities (Drexler 2010:
56). The influence of this narrative, together with weak prosecution,
meant that the military and political elites could evade responsibility for their role in the violence. As such, procedural legal values
did not trigger a change in what Lev has referred to as substantial
legal value or new meanings of right and wrong. This pattern would
be repeated in other cases heard by the Human Rights Courts.

Tanjung Priok

While the establishment of the East Timor tribunal was strongly influenced by international scrutiny, the Tanjung Priok tribunal was largely the consequence of domestic pressures. Religious sentiments, and particularly the rise of political Islam, played an important role in this development. Islamic organisations started to form political parties and started advocating justice for the Tanjung Priok killings because most of those victimised were Muslim (McGregor and Setiawan 2019).

The Tanjung Priok killings took place in September 1984. Local military officers arrested a number of Islamic activists, arguing that they had invited preachers that were critical towards government policies. These activists and preachers were concerned with the drafting of a new law that required all social and religious organisations to adopt the state ideology *Pancasila* as their sole foundation.[47] The arrests caused anger among the local community and hundreds of demonstrators took to the streets. Security forces then opened fire on the protestors. It remains unclear how many people were killed, with some estimates putting this as high as 400 deaths (Sulistiyanto 2007: 77; McGregor and Setiawan 2019).

The combination of increased attention for human rights abuses that occurred under the Suharto regime, the resurgence of political Islam, and coalitions between released political prisoners of Tanjung Priok and human rights organisations led to significant pressure on the authorities to address the matter. In September 1998, a parliamentary team was set up to establish the truth about the killings. Victims' groups, supported by human rights organisations, started to voice more strongly their desire for their case to be heard in court (Sulistiyanto 2007: 79).

In December 1998, Komnas HAM announced that it had nearly finalised collecting information on the killings, in which it particularly focused on the roles of Benny Moerdani (at the time Chief of the Armed Forces) and Try Sutrisno (at the time Commander of Jakarta's Military Command). In March 1999, Komnas HAM publicised its recommendation for the case to be heard through the courts. It should be noted that the Commission arrived at this conclusion without establishing a separate investigatory committee. In addition, Komnas HAM announced this well before it established the KPP HAM for East Timor. That a tribunal was then held for East Timor first generated a sense of unfairness among

---

[47] Law 3/1985 on Political Parties and Functional Groups. This Law replaced Law 3/1975.

those who advocated for the Tanjung Priok case (Sulistiyanto 2007: 79–81).

In February 2000, Komnas HAM established an investigatory commission for Tanjung Priok (*Komisi Penyelidikan Pelanggaran Hak Asasi Manusia Tanjung Priok* or KPP HAM Tanjung Priok). Komnas HAM heard about ninety witnesses, including Moerdani and Sutrisno. They denied giving orders to shoot the demonstrators and argued that the killings occurred because of fighting among the protestors (Sulistiyanto 2007: 82). This largely mirrors the argument put forward in the East Timor trials by the defendants that the violence was the result of a horizontal conflict, rather than one in which the state bore responsibility.

In June 2000, Komnas HAM announced that it had not found evidence of mass killings and that the military had been forced to shoot the protestors as the crowd was uncontrollable. The report thus did not recommend any further legal process. At the same time it urged the government to conduct further investigations and to ask for forgiveness from the public, as well as offer rehabilitation and compensation to the victims and their families. The weak report was attributed by former Komnas HAM member Asmara Nababan to the strong representation of members in the KPP HAM with a background in the security forces (Setiawan 2013: 52). This outcome was deeply disappointing for victims and human rights organisations, while Islamic parties in parliament rejected the report.

In response, President Aburrahman Wahid ordered the Attorney General's office to undertake a further report in July 2000, while Komnas HAM also set up a second investigation team. In this investigation, new forensic evidence gathered through the exhumation of graves indicated that the number killed was much higher than estimated by the military. In addition, it was evident that people were killed as they were shot or due to other violence perpetrated by the military. In October 2000 Komnas HAM stated that twenty-three people, including Moerdani and Sutrisno, were suspected of gross human rights violations in Tanjung Priok and recommended for them to be tried at an ad hoc Human Rights Court. In early 2001, the Attorney General's office set up a team to deal with the Tanjung Priok investigation. The ad hoc court for Tanjung Priok was established simultaneously with that of East Timor by way of Presidential Decree 53/2001 (Sulistiyanto 2007: 83).[48]

---

[48] This decree was later in the year replaced by Presidential Decree 96/2001. This new decree specified the location and time frame of the cases, which earlier had been omitted.

However, there were significant delays in the appointment of ad hoc judges (Kompas 2003), and proceedings in the tribunal for Tanjung Priok did not commence until 2003. In the meantime, senior members of the military led by Try Sutrisno negotiated an *islah*, or form of Islamic reconciliation, with a select number of victims. Sutrisno presented the *islah* as an approach that was more acceptable in a religious (and specifically Islamic) community. The invocation of these cultural arguments, however, served to shield the military from prosecution. As a result of the *islah* agreements and the compensation received by some victims, they subsequently changed or withdrew their testimonies (McGregor and Setiawan 2019).

Prosecutors indicted fourteen defendants. They all argued that they were not guilty of crimes against humanity. Instead, they stated that the killings were the result of the protestors clashing, leaving the military with no choice but to open fire. Only two defendants were convicted, with their sentences overturned on appeal (see Table 13.1). As in the East Timor tribunals, the limited amount of convictions was the result of weak indictments by the prosecution that failed to include the systematic and widespread elements of the crimes. Command responsibility was also overlooked in the indictments, while prosecutors also did not use much of the evidence gathered by Komnas HAM thereby weakening its argument. The legal process was also undermined by intimidation by the security forces, with KOPASSUS (Special Forces) officers attending the hearings (Sulistiyanto 2007: 85–87). The role of the military in undermining legal processes in Indonesia follows a historical pattern (Lev 1972b: 271–272; Lev 2007c: 242). Taken together, the Tanjung Priok tribunal illustrates that procedural legal values mean very little when the military was involved.

Abepura

The first – and so far, only – tribunal held in the permanent Human Rights Courts is that of Abepura. Being the first, this tribunal sets a precedent for potential future proceedings. The Abepura tribunal is also significant because it dealt with human rights violations in Papua, where the security forces remain largely unaccountable for their actions.

The tribunal concerns the events that started on 7 December 2000, when 300 people armed with traditional weapons attacked the police station near the market in Abepura, Papua. One police officer and two members of the Police Mobile Brigade (Brimob) were killed, while several shops were burned. The police suspected that the attack was conducted by highlanders and retaliated by attacking student dormitories (mainly highlanders) and attacked the sleeping students. The police detained ninety, of whom some were tortured and three were killed (Chauvel 2003: 12).

In response to the Abepura killings, Komnas HAM established an investigation commission (*Komisi Penyelidik Pelanggaran Hak Asasi Manusia Papua/Irian Jaya* or KPP HAM Papua/Irian Jaya) in accordance with the 2000 Law on the Human Rights Courts. This was a major step towards addressing cases of torture and summary killings in Papua (Hernawan 2016: 83). The process was obstructed by a lack of cooperation by the police and the intimidation of witnesses. When Komnas HAM's team arrived in Papua, the local office of the Ministry of Law and Human Rights sent an official letter that the investigation was illegal, advising the local police not to cooperate. Local police intimidated witnesses who gave testimony to the Commission. When Komnas HAM published its findings in May 2001, the National Chief of Police accused the Commission of being biased (Human Rights Watch 2001: 21).

The report concluded that there was strong evidence of gross human rights violations, including arbitrary detention, restrictions on freedom of movement, persecution based on gender, race and religion, as well as torture and extrajudicial executions. The report identified twenty-four members of the police and Brimob as possible suspects, including senior officers. It recommended for the events in Abepura to be investigated further by the Attorney General's office with a view of bringing them to trial in a Human Rights Court (Amnesty International 2002: 13–14).

In 2004, proceedings started at the permanent Human Rights Courts in Makassar. The prosecutor only charged two persons out of the twenty-four identified as responsible by Komnas HAM. This weakened the prosecution, as it made it more difficult to prove a chain of command across Papua that affected the violence and identify the facilities in different locations that were used to conduct the operation (ELSAM 2004: 20–21). Both defendants were charged for crimes against humanity including murder, persecution, deprivation of liberty and torture. They were also charged for acts committed by their subordinates based on command responsibility. A significant flaw in the prosecutor's indictment was that while it showed the widespread element of the violations, it did not address the systematic nature of this violence. In fact, the prosecutor failed to define what it understood by 'systematic'. The omission is problematic because the systematic aspect is necessary to secure a conviction. In ignoring the relationship between the events in Abepura and Indonesian policies on Papua, the prosecutor overlooked the major cause of human rights violations in this area (ELSAM 2004: 17–19).

During the proceedings it became evident that the panel of judges largely lacked an understanding of human rights law. Their knowledge of international law on gross human rights violations was also minimal. The weak indictment may have led judges to be largely unresponsive towards the extraordinary nature of the crimes (Dewi, Niemann and Triatmodjo 2017: 45). The defendants denied having perpetrated, or being responsible for, the gross violation of human rights. Rather, they argued that the violations committed were the result of an attack by Papuans against the Indonesian nation. The statement of one of the defendants, Daud Sihombing, illustrates this:

> If there were gross violations of human rights in the manner in which the Abepura case was dealt with, this was not [at the hands of] the police but the attackers themselves (*si penyerang itu sendiri*), as the police never committed any attack against anyone. [...] Their attack was truly widespread and was prepared and planned beforehand conceptually and systematically [...] The police only chased and arrested as part of a *hot pursuit*. [...] I should not be brought to this hearing and prosecuted for gross human rights violations, but I should receive an award from the state and be named a national hero. Because I have sacrificed [myself] to protect many people who are threatened and treated by the Papua Merdeka separatists (ELSAM 2004: 24).

Sihombing's statement uses both the widespread and systematic elements of gross human rights violations, accusing the Papuan population of having committed these crimes. The defendant thus used the arguments that the events in Abepura were a horizontal conflict and that the security forces did not perpetrate gross human rights violations. It is suggested that if transgressions occurred, this was because the security forces were left with no other choice. Defendants in the Tanjung Priok and East Timor tribunals had also used this line of argument successfully.

In referring to 'separatists', Sihombing framed the event as a threat to the unity of the Indonesian state – a trope that throughout history has been used by military and political elites to justify mass violence (McGregor and Setiawan 2019). In portraying victims as subversives, the discourse in effect dehumanises them: as threats to the Indonesian nation, they are unworthy of protection from the law. This process of dehumanisation is powerful and has been systematically used towards Papuans. One witness recalled that when he was beaten in detention a police officer said, 'your mother eats pig and you have the brains of a pig! Even with your college degree you won't get a job. You Papuans are stupid; stupid and yet you think you can be independent' (Human Rights Watch 2001: 17).

The effect of this was evident when the Court delivered its judgment. Both defendants were acquitted (see Table 13.1) and victims' claims for compensation, which were brought forward in a simultaneous class action, were also dismissed (Feith 2006). While there were weaknesses in the indictment of the prosecution, the Court failed to address the evidence of human rights violations presented. Therefore, in its decision the Human Rights Court put forward that when human rights violations were used as an instrument of government policy, human rights principles – as guaranteed by both international and national law – were irrelevant.

Conclusions

When the Human Rights Courts were established, there was some hope that these courts would hold perpetrators of gross human rights crimes to account. Yet, these Courts have led to few prosecutions and even fewer convictions. With no cases heard in the past thirteen years, it seems safe to say that Indonesia's Human Rights Courts exist only in name.

There are a number of interrelated reasons why the Human Rights Courts have failed to meet expectations. First, institutional rivalry between Komnas HAM and the prosecutorial services together with the political role of the Attorney General has led to very few cases being pursued by the Attorney General's office. Only three tribunals were held at the Courts, while many of Komnas HAM's preliminary investigations have been rejected (Setiawan 2013, 2016).[49] Second, in the cases that did proceed to the Courts, the prosecution has left much to be desired. Indictments have been weak, and much of the evidence gathered by Komnas HAM was not taken into account, making it more difficult to secure a conviction. Third, in all three tribunals the security forces actively interfered with the legal process through their physical presence during the proceedings. An independent judicial process was therefore difficult to ensure. The presence of the military also illustrates how the

---

[49] This is not to argue that Komnas HAM's investigations have been faultless – in fact, there is ample scope for improvement of the Commission's investigations. However, the main stumbling block in bringing cases of gross human rights violations to court is the Attorney General's office.

security forces used the Human Rights Court to regain influence and power that had been curtailed in the early *reformasi* period. Fourth, in the three tribunals discussed – for all their differences in time, place and scope – the presiding judges showed limited understanding of the case before them and the legal principles that applied. The Courts disregarded the severity of the crimes that took place and reinforced the narratives put forward by defendants that the violence that took place was a result of horizontal conflicts. This shows that while there appeared to be a greater awareness of international human rights law among legal drafters, the consistent implementation of these norms by judges left much to be desired.

In this chapter, I have used Lev's concept of legal culture as an analytical tool to explore what the role is of the Human Rights Courts in Indonesia today. The elements of procedural and substantial legal values provide a lens through which it is possible to assess the politics of the Human Rights Courts. Procedural legal values refer to the increase of formal law in the area of human rights and the creation of the Human Rights Courts. This resurgence of the importance of legal norms and institutions in the post-authoritarian era served to break with the past, both symbolically and practically. However, this chapter has shown that a close reading of the Law on the Human Rights Courts reveals how these new values were also contested.

The increase in procedural legal values did not translate in a change of substantial legal values. The three tribunals held at the Human Rights Courts show that what was considered 'right' and 'wrong' was not determined by the human rights values recognised in law, but by political power plays that ultimately served to protect members of the security forces from being held to account. In acquiescing to political values, the Human Rights Courts answer to 'a question of convenience unconnected with what is right' (Lev 1972b: 301). The Human Rights Courts have served to embed impunity for the security forces and rendered judicial culture subservient to military imperatives, rather than legal process.

Inevitably, this leaves us with the question of how to ensure that the Human Rights Courts will set historical records straight and hold perpetrators of gross human rights crimes accountable. In answering this question, I once again turn to Lev who wrote that in thinking about how to create a functioning legal system, we first need to understand how this system 'was destroyed and what forces counted most in reducing it to rubble' (Lev 2007c: 237). As this chapter has shown, the Human Rights Courts are based on a Law that still leaves much to be desired. A much larger challenge is the politics that affects the functioning of the Courts. This is illustrated by a reluctant and weak prosecution that is unwilling to follow up on the reports of Komnas HAM, interference from the security forces and a general lack of understanding of human rights laws and the severity of the crimes heard at the Courts. The task of fundamentally reforming the Human Rights Court, and by extension Indonesia's human rights framework, in order to break the cycle of impunity is immense. This will require much more than legal and political change alone and relies upon deep reform in which human rights norms and processes are taken seriously.

14

The Industrial Relations Court

Challenges for Labour Rights

SURYA TJANDRA[*]

Calls for the establishment of a special court to deal with industrial relations issues arose because of government interference in the previous mechanism for settling industrial disputes. One benefit of the establishment of such a court is that it would provide the opportunity to develop greater legal certainty (see Assegaf, this volume). It would do this by ensuring that labour dispute settlement would not be directly controlled by the executive branches of government, reducing the political influence that had plagued labour law practices in Indonesia. Another benefit would be having a clear and accessible history of court decisions in order to establish precedent. This would provide the opportunity for a self-sustaining labour law system to develop, in which matters involving labour relations are handled independently and fairly (see also Cooney and Mitchell 2002: 254).

This proposal has faced challenges in its implementation. In 2004, Indonesia's Industrial Relations Court (*Pengadilan Hubungan Industrial*) (hereafter 'the Court') was established as a special court within the scope of the general courts. It has seen major challenges to its operations from the beginning, both from within the system and from without. These challenges include ongoing internal problems related to the generally high levels of corruption within the Indonesian judicial system; the problems related to the technical competence and legal integrity of career judges, ad hoc judges and registrars; and external problems including the workers' lack of competence in civil litigation procedures and thus access to the court's litigation processes. Together these problems have led to declining public confidence in the performance of the Court; a situation which has

---

[*] This chapter is adapted from part of a chapter of the author's PhD thesis. All copies of newspaper articles and sources are on file with the author. He would like to thank Melissa Crouch for her assistance in the editing process.

a greater adverse effect on employees and trade unions than on employers. The Court needs to be reformed, for example, by turning it into an autonomous special court, a recommendation that has been put forward by several ad hoc judges from union circles (see Tjandra 2014). Such progressive reforms, however, would require strong political commitment both from the judiciary and government; both of which appear currently to be mired in the past.

The Establishment of the Court

The term 'special court' refers not only to the specialized focus – namely, labour disputes in labour relations – but also to the special composition of the panel of judges in this particular court, and the use of special procedures (see Crouch, this volume). The judging panel of the Court comprises one ordinary judge (a career judge) and two ad hoc judges (so-called expert judges, sourced from within union and employers' circles, respectively). It also has special procedures including the waiving of case fees for certain cases, as well as strict time limits for court hearings (a maximum of fifty working days in the Court) and a restriction on appeals in certain types of dispute (*Tempo Interaktif* 2006).

During the establishment phase of the Court, candidates for ad hoc judges were nominated by the employers' organization(s) and trade unions, for consideration first by the Ministry of Manpower, and then by the Supreme Court; with the latter responsible for assessing the nominees' credentials with respect to relevant legal knowledge and technical skills. The Supreme Court was then also responsible for training the ad hoc judges, finalizing the selection process and submitting the names of the accepted ad hoc judges to the President for formal appointment. The Supreme Court was also responsible for preparing the career judges who were to be assigned to the Court. This remains the process for selection today.

The Court should have commenced operations one year after its enactment.[1] After some delay, on 14 January 2006, the Court began operation and the ad hoc judges were symbolically 'inaugurated' by the President. The courts were to be established in thirty-three District Courts in provincial capitals throughout Indonesia. A total of 155 ad

---

[1] Article 126 of Law No. 2/2004. Hereinafter, unless otherwise stated, all articles referred to are articles from Law No. 2/2004.

hoc judges were appointed for the courts in the provincial capitals, and an additional four ad hoc judges at the Supreme Court.

The new Law No. 2/2004 on Industrial Relations replaced previous laws and annulled the existing labour dispute settlement system. The Court is authorized to examine, adjudicate and decide on 'industrial relations dispute' cases. These disputes are defined as

> a difference of opinion resulting in a dispute between employers or an association of employers with workers/labourers or trade unions due to a disagreement on rights, conflicting interests, a dispute over termination of employment, or a dispute among trade unions within one company (art. 1(1)).

The Court has authority over four types of labour disputes, namely disputes over rights; over interests, over termination of employment, and among worker/labour unions within a company (art. 2). Before a case can be brought, the parties concerned are required to attempt a bipartite (two-party) negotiation between worker and employer (art. 3(1)). This negotiation must be completed within thirty days. If no resolution can be obtained, the judges will decide whether to accept or reject a case. If bipartite negotiation fails, one or both parties are required to register their dispute with the Regional Manpower Office at the district level, including providing the minutes of their bipartite negotiation as evidence. After receiving the written complaint, the Manpower Office is required to offer both parties the option of a settlement through either conciliation (through a private institution) or arbitration (through a private institution with the authority to make final and binding decisions) (art. 4(3)). The parties have seven days in which to select either conciliation or arbitration, after which time, if a decision has not been reached, the Manpower Office will refer the dispute to mediation (by a government institution).

Labour disputes may be settled in different ways, depending on the type of dispute in question. The first and second type of disputes (disputes over interest, and disputes among the trade unions in one company) may be settled through mediation, conciliation or arbitration. The third type of dispute, disputes over termination of employment, may be settled through either mediation or conciliation; while the last type, dispute over rights, may only be settled through mediation. In each dispute, the mediator, conciliator or arbiter must complete their duties within thirty working days after receiving the transfer of responsibility for settlement of the dispute.

When an industrial relations dispute can be settled through mediation, a collective agreement is drawn up and signed by the parties involved, witnessed by the mediator, and registered at the Court in. If no agreement can be reached through mediation, the mediator will issue a written recommendation, and the parties are required to provide a written answer to the mediator within ten working days after receiving the recommendation, to indicate whether they accept or reject it. If one of both of the parties fail to provide their answer within the allotted time period, this is taken as a rejection of the written recommendation, and either of the parties may then file to continue with settlement of the dispute through the Court (art. 14(1)).

The Court then is authorized to examine and make a decision at different stages in the dispute settlement process, depending on the type of dispute in question. For cases involving disputes over rights and disputes over termination of employment, the Court is the deciding authority at the first stage of the process; while for cases involving conflicts of interest and disputes among the worker/labour unions in a company, the Court may be the deciding authority at both the first and final levels of the process (art. 56). The judges must take into account all relevant laws, existing agreements, customs and justice in reaching a verdict.

The procedural law that applies is the Civil Procedural Law, which is also used in the courts of general jurisdiction (art. 57). For lawsuits worth not more than Rp. 150 million in compensation, there will be no case fee. One strength of the dispute settlement process is the right of unions and employers' organizations to act as attorneys to represent their members during litigation at the Court (art. 87). Another important new development is the composition of the panel of judges at the Court, comprising the single career judge and two ad hoc judges as nominated by the employers' association and trade unions, respectively. The term of office of the ad hoc judges is five years, following which they may be reappointed for another five years.

Advocates of Law No. 2/2004 claim that the Law can provide a 'fast, precise, fair and cheap' labour dispute settlement mechanism. Yet this raises key questions such as does the system work in practice? How do we understand the practice of Indonesia's new labour dispute settlement mechanism, with the Court as the core; and its impact upon labour? How do labour groups respond to this system?

The Appointment of Judges to the Court

Both unions and employers' organizations have special roles in the Industrial Relations Court system: in particular, they have the right to propose candidates to selection as ad hoc judges. In practice, however, proposing candidates to be ad hoc judges simply required a piece of paper from the union or employers' organization, stating that the organization supported the person concerned in their application to become an ad hoc judge at the Court. It was only at the subsequent stages of the application process – the administrative selection by the Ministry of Manpower and the testing of legal knowledge by the Supreme Court, that the candidates were assessed in a more impartial manner. These latter two stages of (relatively) independent assessment, in combination with the doctrine of impartiality of judges as emphasized by the Supreme Court, may go some way to explaining the relative detachment of ad hoc judges from the unions which had originally nominated them.

Despite concerns from certain observers that some unions might not be able to nominate candidates as ad hoc judges (see Fenwick et al. 2002), currently any union which has met its legal requirement to be a union and has been registered as a union in the Regional Manpower Office, is officially able to nominate a candidate – regardless of the union's background, number of members, level (regional or central organization), location of their domicile or other variables. The selection committees, both within the Ministry of Manpower and within the Supreme Court, have demonstrated their willingness to select ad hoc judges from a wide variety of different unions and backgrounds.

Most ad hoc judges from union circles were people who were already well known to the unions; either former union officials, or legal advocacy practitioners for the unions; or NGO activists and academics who supported the unions. With such backgrounds, many of these ad hoc judges, particularly with the support of the Trade Union Rights Centre, have been active in pushing for Court reforms, including through the judgements they make, and through activities designed to advance the judicial system. Such efforts, however, have not led to significant reforms, due to structural obstacles from within the judiciary itself.

Unions have the power to request the removal of the ad hoc judge they originally proposed, by requesting the court to 'honourably discharge' the particular judge. This power has only been exercised once (Fajerman 2011: 17). Even in cases where unions may request that a judge be removed, this may not be implemented as the Supreme Court has the final authority as to whether to discharge the judge.

The impartiality of ad hoc judges is a point of particular concern in this system. During the twenty-one-day training and selection process for ad hoc judges at the Supreme Court, the principle of impartiality is the most emphasized issue. The judges are told that from the moment they are appointed and begin to work for the Court, they must 'take off their clothes' as union's or employers' representatives and become totally independent and free from any intervention from their organizations. Ad hoc judges from both union and employer circles stated this in interviews and emphasized that there was no obligation whatsoever for them to continue serving either the unions or the employers' organizations which had nominated them.[2] One ad hoc judge from union circles, for example, said: 'I understand the union would expect us to work for their interests, but I am bound by the principle of impartiality. At the time we serve as judges, we have to take off our labour status'.

At the start of their appointment as judges, most ad hoc judges from union circles are concerned about this requirement. They feel they must take the side of the workers, although they recognize their obligation to be impartial. This issue appears to be less of a concern for ad hoc judges from employer circles, who often appear happy to remain more tightly associated with their employers' organization. They gather regularly at annual 'development conferences' in order to ensure their 'maintenance' as their employers' representatives at the Court.[3] Despite the inherent problems with respect to the position of the ad hoc judges, the system is nonetheless fairer than not having the ad hoc judges at all.

Start-up Issues and Wage Delays

In May 2006, the ad hoc judges began examining cases. However, the presidential decree on allowances and other rights for ad hoc judges in the Court was not released until 7 December 2006. The disbursement of the state budget for honorary payments for ad hoc judges was not issued until around two years later, in 2008. This means that for over two years after Court operations commenced, ad hoc judges were required to work

[2] Interview with various ad hoc judges from union and employer circles, at the Court Jakarta, March 2006, just after the appointment ceremony at the Court Jakarta.
[3] 2006 Activity Plan of the Industrial Relation Permanent Committee of the Indonesian Chamber of Commerce and Industry', undated, presented by Hasanudin Rahman of Apindo, August 2008.

without payment. The lack of payment led several ad hoc judges to threaten to conduct public action if they were not paid soon, including to go on strike by refusing to attend court hearings in the Court Tanjung Pinang, Riau Islands, causing delays to court hearings.[4] One problem was that a partial budget for the infrastructure development of the Court had already been disbursed while the budget for the salaries of the ad hoc judges was in limbo. This budget included funds for an official vehicle for the chief justices of the district courts, *ex officio* chief justice of the Court, who were able to enjoy their new cars soon after the Court operations began in May 2006.

For the ad hoc judges who came from employer circles, this discrepancy in disbursement of funds was not usually a significant hardship, as most retained their previous paid positions while acting as judges part-time. But for ad hoc judges from labour unions, the ongoing lack of funds posed a serious problem, as many had quit their previous jobs to become ad hoc judges full-time. As reasons for choosing a full-time role, some cited their new position as a 'noble responsibility' or a 'calling to fulfil their duties',[5] while for others, becoming a judge was an opportunity to upgrade their social status and position in society. One ad hoc judge in the Court Jakarta, for example, prior to his appointment as a judge, worked as a 'barefoot lawyer' at the legal aid office in the Jakarta District Court, with no certainty of income.[6] For him, becoming a judge significantly raised his income and his social position in the eyes of his neighbours and colleagues, and he felt proud when people called him 'Pak Hakim' ('Mister Judge').

Once working in the position full-time, most ad hoc judges were highly dependent on the salaries they were entitled to: Rp. 3,750,000 per month for ad hoc judges at the district level, and Rp. 7,500,000 per month for ad hoc judges at the Supreme Court level. This amount was relatively small, and less than the salaries some ad hoc judges received in their jobs before joining the Court; particularly those from employer circles. Several chose to resign after a couple of years of working with the Court. This led to a shortage of ad hoc judges from employer circles in some regions. In response, after five years of Court operations, in 2011 the President raised the salaries of ad hoc judges at the Court to Rp. 5,5 million/month, and those at the Supreme Court to Rp. 10 million/month. These new salaries

---

[4] *Batam Pos*, 23 November 2006, on file with author.
[5] Interview with Saut Manalu, ad hoc judge at the Court Jakarta, June 2008.
[6] Interview with Tri Endro, ad hoc judge at the Court Jakarta, June 2008.

were available immediately by newly recruited ad hoc judges, but not by the original cohort. In January 2013, a new salary scheme was implemented, with ad hoc judges at the Court receiving Rp. 17.5 million/month, and those at the Supreme Court receiving Rp. 25 million/month, regardless of whether they were new or earlier recruits. As explained by one ad hoc judge from union circles, these significant increases of salaries encouraged many people to apply for the position of ad hoc judges at the Court.[7]

The salaries received by the ad hoc judges still required a deduction of 15 per cent income tax. This was controversial, given the existing government regulation which ruled that 'state officials' were exempt from income taxes (which were covered by the government as the employer). Ad hoc judges were concerned that they were not recognized as 'state officials' by the government, despite the fact that they were appointed by the President with presidential decrees published in the State Gazette, as per normal procedures for 'state officials.' Indeed, the ad hoc judges at the Supreme Court even held the right to stay at 'the official apartment for state officials' in Kemayoran region, Jakarta. Some ad hoc judges, particularly from union circles but also from employer circles, brought the issue to the attention of the Tax Offices in their regions, as well as to the Ministry of Finance in Jakarta, arguing that they should be exempt from taxes and treated as full 'state officials.' These efforts failed: in late 2010, the Minister of Finance issued a letter stating that ad hoc judges were not 'state officials' and thus not exempt from taxes. The letter did not provide any explanation.

During their early days as ad hoc judges at the Court while waiting for payment, many judges survived through their incomes from side jobs or other activities. Some ad hoc judges, for example, ran small shops at home, while others worked part-time as human resources consultants at the companies where they had previously worked. One common side job was the position of resource person for training workshops about Court procedures. Such training was held frequently by companies in the Court's early days and was referred to by ad hoc judges as 'socialization,' in reference to the formal activities of the Supreme Court during the early stages of Court operations.

These 'socialization' activities were preferred, by some ad hoc judges, to their primary task of ruling on disputes – as the training tasks were

---

[7] Personal communication with Joko Ismono, ad hoc judge at the Court Surabaya, September 2013.

straightforward and therefore relatively 'easy money', requiring only that the trainer explain the contents of the law. The financial returns were reasonable: for a two-hour presentation, focusing mostly on normative parts of the Law, ad hoc judges at the district level could expect to be paid around Rp. 6 million; almost double their monthly Court salaries, while career judges, especially those from the Supreme Court, could expect up to around Rp. 8–10 million per session.

Such opportunities for side incomes, however, could be problematic, for several reasons. First, these opportunities were distributed inequitably among the ad hoc judges, with those from big cities such as Jakarta or Surabaya receiving higher income than those from smaller, less industrial cities. Second, despite the claims from organizations that the 'socialization' and training were focused on legal issues, it is doubtful that the companies' motives were purely related to capacity building. Instead, they may have been interested in influencing judges, and the important question emerged as to whether the ad hoc judges and career judges recruited by companies to run their training would be able to maintain their impartiality in future cases involving those companies, or would they then feel obliged to the company.

The difficulties encountered in the recruitment of ad hoc judges were mirrored by similar challenges in recruiting career judges (Fajerman 2011: 16–18). The career judges applying for the positions were of questionable quality – often recruited from mid-level law faculties in Indonesia, while the best graduates instead chose careers as lawyers or in private business. The report also noted that for the most recent recruitment of ad hoc judges, so few applicants were put forward from employer circles that the Ministry of Manpower and the Supreme Court were required to *lower* the recruitment standards for employer-nominated candidates. Despite this, only eleven candidates were appointed from twenty-three applicants. Overall there was a shortage of judges in the Courts, with only eight of the country's thirty-three district-level Courts having an adequate quota of both career and ad hoc judges. Similarly, at the Supreme Court level there were only eight ad hoc judges available, who were expected to deal with over 400 cases a year. As another example, the Court in Jakarta had only four career judges to deal with over thirty new cases per month (which would add to the burden of the ongoing cases). The report further observed that many career judges were reluctant to be appointed to the Court, 'due to the highly sensitive nature of labour disputes, frequent demonstrations outside of the courtroom and the (often) inconvenient distance between the IRC and the District Court.' (Fajerman 2011: 18).

In sum, it is clear that when the Court commenced operations in 2006, the operational infrastructure was not fully prepared. This situation was exacerbated by the lack of communication between the Ministry of Manpower, which had drafted the law, and the Supreme Court, whose duty it was to run the court. This lack of preparedness led to several problems, most critically the delaying of payment of salaries for ad hoc judges; the uncertainty surrounding the status of ad hoc judges as 'state officials' (or not) and the consequences with regard to tax exemption; and the lack of clarity or consistency around working hours. Together these issues had a negative impact on the performance of the ad hoc judges, and thus on the performance of the Court as an institution. Fortunately, after five years of operation, the Court was subject to a number of changes with the goal of improving the courts' effectiveness, including regular and higher salary payments for the ad hoc judges; and revisions to other administrative issues.

The Operation of the Court

The Court has encountered many challenges. For example, in the transition period from the old to the new system, thousands of cases were put on hold after the old mechanism was dissolved and the Court was not yet operational. There is also confusion, inconsistency and uncertainty in the procedural laws that apply, and problems in the sanctions judges impose. Although the court has the specific power under the law to issue an injunction to order an employer to pay the wage of the labourer, injunctions are rarely issued. This is because, instead of relying on the Law, judges rely on the Herzeine Inlandsch Reglement (HIR), which is understood to imply that the courts do not recognize injunctions. This renders certain provisions of the Law unworkable and in need of revision.

In new cases being handled by the Court, disputes over termination of employment are the most frequent. Very few disputes over interests, or disputes over rights, were submitted to the Court; and not a single dispute among trade unions. By far most cases (90 per cent) were submitted by workers. In the first four years of its existence (2006–9), the majority of cases were brought by workers and/or unions, rather than by employers, and the Court's Jakarta and Bandung received most claims. The most active Court outside Java was the Medan Court, while the most inactive were the Papua Court and the Banjarmasin Court. Despite the increasing number of cases brought to the Court in some regions, such as Jakarta and Bandung, in general the trend was for the number of cases to be decreasing – even in Courts based in areas with large numbers of workers and industries (and, presumably, disputes), such as Semarang, Serang and Makassar. Here I consider two issues: the fact that cases are technically free but have hidden expenses; and the issue of time limits and delays that affect the resolution of labour disputes.

'The Case Is Free, but Costly'

In lawsuits worth less than Rp. 150 million, the applicant is not subject to payment of any expenses, including execution expenses. If a lawsuit is worth more than Rp. 150 million, it is subject to payment of certain expenses. Problems arise in practice, however, because for lawsuits worth more than Rp. 150 million, the actual amount of expenses to be paid was not set forth expressly in the Law; leading to ambiguity and frequent examples of discrimination. According to the Technical Instructions for the Implementation of Law No. 2/2004, issued by the Supreme Court, the amount is to be stipulated by the Chief Justice of the Court (*ex officio* the Chief Justice of the District Court), and this instruction has often led to differences in interpretation among Courts in different regions. Problems also arose for cases worth less than Rp. 150 million. Although these are supposed to be exempt from fees, field observations indicate that in practice, fees are being imposed unlawfully on the person filing the case, varying from Rp. 1 million to at least Rp. 1.5 million. One lawyer from a law firm in Jakarta claimed that he was forced to pay case fees of Rp. 1.8 million for one labour case handled by himself (although the case was worth less than Rp. 150 million), simply because he represented an employer.[8]

One strategy often used by union officials is to split a case into several lawsuits, with each lawsuit not exceeding the maximum value allowed for exemption from case fees. The problem is that then these lawsuits are distributed among different panels of judges, and there is the risk that the judgements may differ from one panel to another.[9] There are no data available to indicate how often this approach is actually adopted in the Court, but one ad hoc judge at the Court Jakarta claimed it occurred

---

[8] Interview with a lawyer from RSD Law Firm on 28 September 2006.
[9] Interview with union advocate Timboel Siregar, July 2007.

'quite often', and one union official said that he always used the strategy in cases involving many workers (where the amount exceeds the limit of Rp. 150 million). This official claimed that since 2006, he had filed lawsuits using this strategy for about twenty cases, to various Courts; and he claimed that many other union officials, as well as employers in mass dismissal cases, often used similar strategies.[10] Some ad hoc judges, especially those from busy Courts like Jakarta, have labelled these strategies as 'cheating'; and have attempted to deal with such practices by holding regular meetings between panels of judges to coordinate their approach and avoid inconsistencies in their judgements for split cases.[11] Interestingly, in some Courts with relatively few cases to adjudicate, for example, Court Yogyakarta, the strategy of splitting cases seems to be well liked by ad hoc judges who even suggest that the plaintiffs split their case.[12] One reason for this may be that the ad hoc judges get extra income for each case they handle; receiving Rp. 250,000 in 'case support' ('tunjangan perkara').

The regulation of fees for civil cases in Indonesia state that the listing of the case in the case registry may only occur if the parties have paid a sum of money to cover registration fees, summoning fees and fees for notification to the parties.[13] The article does not, however, mention a specific amount for case fees nor a sanction imposed on parties committing case fees manipulation. As specifically ruled for the Court, and as further conveyed by the Supreme Court Junior Chairman for Civil Law, the state had provided funds amounting to Rp. 7.5 million for each industrial relation dispute case submitted to and examined by the Court (*Hukumonline* 2006c). In practice, however, various additional fees needed to be paid by the parties, such as fees for the legalization of the power of attorney and legalization of evidence (the official amount being Rp. 11,000), and several other 'unofficial' charges such as 'folder fees' (for folders for the case documents), 'typing fees' (charge for typing the decisions), 'electricity fees' (for typing the decision at home), 'copying fees' (for the copying of decisions when asked by parties), fees for 'delivering briefs to the Supreme Court', and other non-specific fees.

The total figure for unofficial fees varies highly between cases, and depends on who the litigants are, and who handles the case. If, for

---

[10] Personal communication with Timboel Siregar, August 2008.
[11] Interview with Junaedi, ad hoc judge at the Court Jakarta, July 2007.
[12] Interview with ad hoc judge at Court Yogyakarta. The Court Yogyakarta receives only some five cases every year.
[13] Article 121 (4) of the HIR or Article 145 (4) RBg.

example, the case was filed by a worker and was handled by the worker him/herself personally, or if he/she was accompanied by a union official, the unofficial fees would be relatively small, or even zero. However, for cases filed by employers, especially if handled by professional lawyers, higher unofficial fees were likely imposed. As one professional lawyer at the Court explained, the substitute registrars were the primary drivers of this practice. According to a substitute registrar at the Court Jakarta,[14] no unofficial fees were imposed for duties such as legalization. However, for some cases, the registrar admitted that fees were allowed, insofar as parties paid them 'voluntarily'. In his own explanation: 'to help cover the operational costs of the court.' These remarks were made as part of a complaint about the lack of attention to the new court from the District Court, with the registrar giving examples that the ad hoc judges' room still had no air conditioner.

For some parties, especially workers, the establishment of Courts in provincial capitals is a major handicap requiring long travel and high travel costs. This is obviously burdensome, especially when compared to the previous dispute settlement mechanism under the P4P/D, which was free and was always held near the parties' own domiciles. As one union official observed, 'Although the case fee is free, bringing cases to the Court is costly and burdensome, especially for workers.'[15]

Time Limits and Delays

The Court must settle an industrial relations dispute within fifty working days after the date of the first court session; while the Supreme Court must settle the case within thirty working days. Almost all the parties involved with the Court, however, report much more time for a case to reach a final decision, both at the Court and, in particular, the Supreme Court. In an evaluation of the Court's performance, the Chairman of Apindo, Sofyan Wanandi, blamed the large number of cases at the Court, observing that this will 'create conflicts between employers and unions, and may create a mess [in the system].'[16] In contrast, Junior Chairperson of the Special Civil Cases of the Supreme Court, Kaddir Mappong, blamed the law itself, which he said added an additional burden of cases to the already overloaded Supreme Court (Hukumonline 2007).

[14] Interview with Asri Tajudin, substitute registrar at the Court in Jakarta, September 2006.
[15] Interview with Indra Munaswar, August 2008.
[16] Kompas, 6 February 2008, on file with author.

He claimed that the 30 days requirement of case-handling at the Supreme Court is impossible. Even for the commercial court, which gave us 60 days, we could not reach decisions on time'. To resolve this problem, Mappong suggested an amendment of Law No. 2/2004 to extend the time limit, which he claimed would be more realistic for the court.

Further investigations into the situation at the Courts and the Supreme Court indicated that case handling at the district court level was relatively on schedule (approximately thirty days per case), but that it was at the Supreme Court that cases tended to take very long. This was due to time delays in internal case administration within the Supreme Court itself. A conservative estimation suggested that it would take at least eight months for one case to go through the full process, from registration to decision, in the Supreme Court. Such an amount of time was considered normal at the Supreme Court, and despite efforts to cut time and accelerate the process, there appeared to be little that Supreme Court judges could do to avoid the delays, as they involved established stages; the same stages as other cases in the Supreme Court.[17] Some union activists claimed that in many cases, the time needed at the Supreme Court was even longer than eight months (see Munaswar 2008).

But even at the Court of first instance there are delays. A substitute registrar must produce a copy of the judgement within fourteen working days after it is signed. The registrar of the district court must dispatch the copy to the parties within seven working days after receipt of the judgement. In practice, as noted by one union activist (Munaswar 2008), two months after a judgement has been read, it has often still not been signed by the judges – sometimes because the chair of the panel is too busy with his duties as a career judge.[18] As Munaswar has noted,

> This situation is detrimental to workers, because it hampers the time needed in order to prepare for cassation or a counter memory cassation. If you encounter this problem, then the only way to resolve it quickly is to ask for 'good service' from the substitute registrar, of course with some money, in order to get a photocopy of the unsigned judgment, to be able to draft the cassation document.

---

[17] Interview with Fauzan, an ad hoc judge at the Supreme Court from union circles, May 2009.

[18] Ad hoc judges cannot sign the judgement, as according to the guidelines, the chair of the panel of judges is required to sign the form first.

The problems with time delays continue once an appeal is made. The Indonesian judiciary is notorious for lengthy processes (see Pompe 2005), and the Industrial Relations Court is no exception.

Challenges for the Court

In this section I focus more specifically on the role of the judge. I first consider the tensions between career and ad hoc judges, and issues of perceived and real bias. I then explain the nature of corruption within the judiciary, a problem consistent with Lev's findings more generally.

The Potential for Judicial Bias

As mentioned above, some ad hoc judges in the Court are appointed by employers and others by unions. The bench then consists of some career judges and some ad hoc judges. Like in all specialized courts with a mixed bench, there are inevitably tensions that arise between career and ad hoc judges.

There is a risk of bias by career judges against labour disputes. One career judge in the Court Tanjung Pinang, for instance, confided that he believed that unlike civil lawsuits, lawsuits at the Court were 'not real',[19] since the disputes were about rights and interests, which, according to him, were 'vaguer' than regular damage claims. Another career judge in the Court Jakarta stated that handling Court cases was a burden for him, with his work becoming 'more intensive' but with 'less incentive.' He compared his work at the Court to his other work at the Corruption Court and the Commercial Court (both special courts like the Court); at the latter two courts, he could obtain additional income for additional work, to the value of more than Rp. 10 million above his regular salary.[20] This situation has apparently reduced the interest of career judges in pursuing Court work, and acts as a greater disincentive than 'the highly sensitive nature of labour disputes' (see Fajerman 2011: 17). This may also explain the observation that most of the work required to draft judgements at the Court is handled not by the career judges but by the ad hoc judges.

---

[19] Statements from career judge Ratmoho, in 'Labour Judges Workshop', Batam, 26 November 2006.

[20] Interview with Heru Pramono, career judge at the Court Jakarta, November 2008.

Further, some career judges disapprove of the use of ad hoc judges more broadly because they are perceived to be an intrusion in the general court system. Some career judges referred to ad hoc judges using insulting nicknames, such as 'contract judge'. While ad hoc judges have become a more frequent feature with the growth of specialized courts in Indonesia, these tensions remain.

Problems of Judicial Corruption

While ad hoc judges face a range of structural challenges, the most concerning one is probably the issue of corruption within the Court, an issue which directly affects the performance and the existence of the new institution. According to one union official from Karawang, West Java province, corruption is typically seen in cases related to disputes over interests, and in cases of collective dismissal, which involve large amounts of money. The union official claimed that he was once approached by an ad hoc judge (from employer circles) in the Court Bandung who asked him to provide some money for the judges in return for a promise to help the workers win the lawsuit. The union official said that he was very worried, as the consequences of losing the case would be serious for the workers involved, because the case was related to the annual wage increases in the company. 'We wanted to give the [requested] money, for the sake of our members, and the risk was too high of losing the case. The problem was that our union did not have money for such purpose.' The union officials were therefore unable to give the money to the judge, 'But I've told the [ad hoc] judge that later if we win the case, we would not forget about her and her colleagues [the panel of judges].' In the end, the official and his union did win the case, and the court decided to award a wage increase of 14.8 per cent, 4.8 per cent higher than the employer had originally accepted. The union then gave the ad hoc judge an amount of money, which the union official believed would be divided among the members of the panel of judges. 'It was not really a bribery', the union official rationalized, 'as we only gave them our expression of gratitude.'

Various union activists have reported similar corrupt practices, although few are made public. One exception was a case involving a cement factory, PT Semen Kupang, in East Nusa Tenggara, which gained widespread media attention. During the case, union officials claimed that one of the ad hoc judges at the Supreme Court, Arief Sudjito, had accepted a bribe of Rp. 2 billion from the company, and claimed that they had lost their case after failing to give the judge a requested 'handling fee' of Rp. 300 million. The union admitted their involvement in the bribery, that they could only afford Rp. 150 million, and that this was the figure that had been handed to the ad hoc judge. The union said they had been approached by the ad hoc judge who had advised that if the union wanted to win the case, they needed to give him the other half of the 'handling fee'; the judge told the union that he had been offered Rp. 2 billion by the company to find in its favour. After losing the case, the union officials said that the ad hoc judge returned the union's money. 'We suspect the judge had [also] received a bribe from the company Semen Kupang,' the union leader was quoted in the media (Liputan 6 2010). The company denied the allegation (*Koran Tempo* 2010a), while the ad hoc judge in question was later investigated and monitored by the Judicial Commission (*Koran Tempo* 2010a). Although the Supreme Court said they would investigate this judge for a possible violation of ethics, and they had questioned the union officials (*Kontan* 2010b), no follow-ups were reported, and the judge, Arief Sudjito, continued to work without any penalty.

The name Arief Sudjito appeared a year later in conjunction with a corruption claim involving another ad hoc judge. Imas Dianasari, an ad hoc judge from employer circles at the Court Bandung, West Java, was arrested on 30 June 2011 while taking a bribe, along with a lawyer representing the company PT Onamba Indonesia. The case was dealt with by the Indonesian Eradication Commission (*Komisi Pemberantasan Korupsi*, KPK). Imas Dianasari claimed that she had contacts who assisted with corrupt activities, including contacts in both the Court and the Supreme Court. Importantly, she named ad hoc judge Arief Sudjito as her contact at the Supreme Court who helped prepare the cases she handled in the Court Bandung which went to appeal. In response to these allegations, the KPK summoned Sudjito for interrogation as a witness (*Detik News* 2011c). He denied the allegations claiming that he only knew ad hoc judge Dianasari because they were both ad hoc judges at the Court. 'It is normal that we know each other from work,' he explained. According to several union officials who were often involved with cases at the Court Bandung, ad hoc judge Imas Dianasari was widely known for corrupt practices. 'We could feel it, but it is also very difficult to prove,' said one union official, while mentioning several 'big cases' handled by ad hoc judge Dianasari he had lost in the Court Bandung.[21]

---

[21] Personal communication with Saepul Tavip, union leader, July 2011.

Ad hoc judge Dianasari was later suspended by the President; however, ad hoc judge Sudjito continued to work.

The above and similar reports suggest that the so-called 'court mafia' (*mafia peradilan*), common and widespread in other courts in Indonesia, has also infiltrated the Court. Some complainants compare the situation to that of the commercial court, which they consider has 'committed suicide'; such is the level of acute corruption taking place there.[22] Given this reputation, the number of people willing to use the commercial court for case settlements has been decreasing; people are unwilling to deal with the court's inefficiency and corruption (see also Pompe 2004). It is particularly interesting, and perhaps ironic, that the commercial court was the source of 'inspiration' for legislators when they established the Court.[23]

Ad hoc Judges as Reformers from Within

Despite at least one instance of a corruption case involving an ad hoc judge from union circles (as discussed above), the performance of the ad hoc judges has been reported as relatively sound, with respect to both their judicial integrity and their level of knowledge and skills. Their roles are arguably crucial for the future of the Court, and for efforts to reform the judiciary to help it become more effective at resolving labour disputes. If this is the case, then efforts to remove their role may lead to additional problems for the Court.

In comparison to their counterparts in other special courts established in Indonesia, union-nominated judges at the Court have some unique characteristics. Most are from trade union backgrounds and have had previous experiences with labour advocacy. Thus, most bring with them some form of idealism, to 'defend workers' rights'. In a meeting of ad hoc judges from various regions organized by the Trade Union Rights Centre on 7–9 April 2006 in Jakarta, just a few months after their appointment, ad hoc judges from union circles generally reported that being an ad hoc judge at the Court was a 'challenge'; a new 'mandate'; and

---

[22] Interview with Muhamad Hafidz, August 2010; a union official who had filed several judicial reviews against Bankruptcy Law No. 37/2004, for constitutional violation of labour rights.

[23] Interview with Indra Munaswar, July 2006; a member of the 'Tim Kecil' (Small Team) of union leaders involved in the formulation of the new labour bills in 2002–4 (Suryomenggolo, 2008).

a 'new stage' in the struggle for workers – with the option to work 'from within'.

The ad hoc judges from union circles also expressed pride at being chosen for what they considered to be an 'honourable job', with great responsibility. However, there was also some concern at being 'new people' in the system, which they perceived to carry a risk of being easily 'forced' to go along with existing systems and customs in the court. Some ad hoc judges voiced concern about the many points of confusion at the start of the Court's operations, including the overdue salaries. There was in particular concern about the widespread corruption practices in the judiciary. They were also worried about their perceived unofficial duty to 'side with the workers', while at the same time needing to be impartial as judges. Nonetheless, many expressed hopes of being able to learn and exchange knowledge on the subject of labour law, and some even showed interest in pursuing further studies in the field. They mentioned the need to have solid networks among the ad hoc judges, including some kind of 'information centre' along with 'supporting systems', to help them to support each other and work properly. All these sentiments were nurtured during the series of workshops that followed and will be discussed further below.

While working within the Court system, many ad hoc judges from union circles continue their contact with unions, albeit informally. One ad hoc judge from union circles in Pekan Baru, for example, explained that although she was no longer registered as an official of her union, she continued to attend regular meetings with her former colleagues, mainly to discuss cases and to provide input if they wanted to file a case to the Court. The judge commented: 'I have to do that, since many of my colleagues are unfamiliar with processes at the Court. And it is important that they will not be misled by the mediator, who seems to scare workers not to bring cases to the Court.' In this way, she justified her continued contact with the union, despite her awareness of the requirement for judges to be impartial. Another ad hoc judge, from Palembang, justified his continued contact with unions by referring to the non-permanent nature of his work as an ad hoc judge. 'When I finish my term, it is likely that I go back to my own union. So, it is important to maintain my communication with them.'

Where ad hoc judges from union circles maintain contact with unions, this was at their own initiative. The unions, even those that had nominated the ad hoc judges, seemed disinclined to take the initiative and left it up to the ad hoc judges to decide what they would do. This led to disappointment on the part of some ad hoc judges. One ad hoc judge from Medan complained that his union seemed disinterested in his work, since there had never been any effort to contact him. 'We need to be watched by unions, otherwise we could become a 'wild ball' [bola liar] in the court,' he said, referring to the notorious corruption problem in the judiciary, which, he believed, had started to infect the Court as well.

In order to provide support for the ad hoc judges from union circles, a series of training workshops has been held in Jakarta annually since 2006, and it is likely to continue. The main organizer has been the TURC, but the trainings were usually facilitated by two ad hoc judges chosen by the ad hoc judges' collective itself – normally one judge from the district Court, and one from the Supreme Court. Selected ad hoc judges from union circles from various Courts across Indonesia are invited. The subjects discussed include recent developments and issues in the Court, including those related to court administration (undue salaries, tax, facilities and the like), and issues arising from actual cases handled by the Court. The ad hoc judges are also asked to bring their recent verdicts to be shared and discussed with other ad hoc judges, and in this manner, they often obtain new perspectives and insights. Since ad hoc judges at the Supreme Court sometimes came to the training workshops as well, an exchange of ideas between the two levels within the judiciary can take place, which provides an opportunity to address differences among Courts and between the district Courts and the Supreme Court. Later on, the ad hoc judges participating in the training also drafted an academic paper on proposed reforms for the Court and amendments to Law No. 2/2004 (Tjandra 2014).

The training coincided with several positive breakthroughs in Court practices, with the initiatives driven largely by the ad hoc judges from union circles. One of the most important of these was an increased sensitivity to labour perspectives, which were mentioned by members of the panel of judges before passing judgement. This resulted in a range of notable judgements, including those regarding 'dwangsom' discussed earlier; and efforts to relax some of the procedural laws in order to increase access for ordinary workers. The increased sensitivity to labour issues also led to initiatives uncommon in Indonesian judicial procedures – such as 'dissenting opinions.' Some judges even sent a 'petition letter' to the President of Indonesia regarding the overdue salaries for ad hoc judges. This letter generated concern among some career judges at the Court, who stated that it was a 'direct attack' on the 'harmonious' environment of the courts[24].

On another occasion, the same innovative ad hoc judges who sent the petition letter also submitted a petition to the Chief Justice of the Supreme Court, regarding 'improvement of the Court's performance'. This letter summarized their evaluation of the Court's performance in the first year after it commenced operation and included suggestions for reforms. More recently, these same ad hoc judges drafted amendments to Law No. 2/2004, including various reforms, which they considered would make the Court more effective. These included ensuring the burden of proof lies with those most capable of finding the resources to present the evidence (employers, rather than workers); the establishment of a special chamber for labour disputes at the Supreme Court; the empowerment of the Court of Appeal at the provincial level, to become he final instance; the revision of the complicated procedural mechanism in the Court; the establishment of Court in industrial dense areas; and the appointment of full-time career judges to the Court.

All these recommended amendments were based on the judges' own experience of real problems faced by the Court during its daily work; which, combined with their expertise in the field, gave the judges' recommendations credibility and quality. It remains to be seen whether the government and the judiciary (the Supreme Court) will support the recommendations. According to the Indonesian government's Legislative Program 2012, parliamentary discussions about the recommendations were to be conducted during 2012. However, parliament ended up not discussing the document or associated issues during 2012, citing that it was caught up with other 'urgent' matters, and the deliberations about amendments to Law No. 2/2004 were postponed until 2015 at the earliest. This indicates a lack of political will and attention to issues of justice in labour law, from both the executive and the legislature. As with the judiciary, as reflected in the speech of the Chief Justice of the Supreme Court, Bagir Manan,[25] the political will to resolve the problems has not been as strong as hoped. In this situation, removing ad hoc judges from the system would arguably only cause new problems, rather than resolve the existing problems.

---

[24] Noted by Eko Pristiwantoro, ad hoc judge at the Court Semarang.
[25] See *Varia Peradilan* (No. 263, October 2007), photo copy in possession of the author.

Conclusion

The establishment of special courts and tribunals, with workers' representation has been an approach taken first by European and then by other countries worldwide, to overcome some of the problems found within ordinary courts (Ramm 1986: 270), Problems special courts intend to address include the resentment harboured by some groups towards the 'spirit' or aims of labour legislation; the inaccessibility of legal processes to most workers; the class bias of many career judges; the lack of experience by the judiciary in labour issues; and the burdensome cost, delays and formalities normally found in ordinary courts. Addressing these issues formed a large part of the motivation behind the establishment of the Industrial Relations Court (Court) in Indonesia as well. However, once established as a special court within the scope of general court, the Court in Indonesia has found itself in a difficult position since the beginning of its existence. Issues such as conceptual inadequacy and the obscurity of some of the provisions in Law No. 2/2004, the problematic relationship between the Court and the district court it is a part of, and corruption from the lowest level of substitute registrar at the District Court right through to the ad hoc judge at the Supreme Court, have all combined to increase the challenges for the disputing parties – particularly workers – in their efforts to maintain confidence in the court and resolve their disputes adequately.

There have been some efforts, particularly from ad hoc judges from union circles, to be sensitive to labour needs; and to try to optimize dispute resolution within the Court, as originally intended. Examples do exist of Court practices and case decisions that represent fresh interpretations and the courage to maintain integrity. These include the decision about *dwangsom* (daily fine), the initiative to maximize pretrial hearings in order to explain to litigants the administrative requirements of lawsuits, and thus reducing the risk of annulment of lawsuits based on small errors during submission, and the efforts to reduce corruption in the court by preventing any person from taking case documents home to type the decisions. As discussed, many of these efforts were challenging, as the existing judiciary apparatus, which saw the changes as an attack on the 'internal harmony' of the judiciary, and may have often held an unconscious bias against, or a sense of superiority over, the non-permanent judges, did not support most initiatives.

Any positive, creative initiatives and proposals have also been overshadowed by the structural problems, which continue to plague the

Indonesian judiciary in general, and the Court in particular. Inconsistencies and sometimes obscurity in the court's practices, low levels of technical knowledge and legal integrity of both career and ad hoc judges as well as the court's registrars, and the lack of competence of workers and labour unions to conduct litigation, have all contributed to the declining confidence in the court. Further ongoing problems include the long duration of the process before a verdict is reached, when a quick resolution is so crucial in labour disputes. The tendency of the Supreme Court to act merely as a guardian of procedural law has also contributed to the growing distrust and disappointment in the Court among workers. The absence of an effective enforcement mechanism has moreover encouraged unethical employers to ignore the court's decisions, knowing that they are unlikely to face negative consequences. The existence of ad hoc judges, particularly those from union circle, may provide the foundation for future reforms of the Court. For this to happen, strong political commitment will be required from both the judiciary and the government, and this may arguably be unlikely in the near future.

Just as courts cannot work well when they are overwhelmed with cases, courts cannot function properly without the confidence of the parties who are using them to resolve conflicts. Thus, perception plays a very important role in the success of the court system: courts must not only be able to perform their main duties – conflict resolution, social control and lawmaking; they must also be perceived to be doing so (Shapiro 1981). The case of the Industrial Relations Court in Indonesia is a story about Indonesia's effort to channel labour disputes into a legal mechanism, and while labour dispute resolution is much needed, to date these efforts have tended to fail. The Court still operates in Indonesia, but until reforms are tackled to ensure consistently fair and effective outcomes, the Court will be as unlikely to elicit confidence in the system as any other court in Indonesia today (cf. Bedner 2009).

15

The Media

Megaspectacles and Transparency in the Courts

ROSS TAPSELL AND SITA DEWI

Imagine you are incorrectly arrested for murder in Indonesia. Being a murder trial, there is significant interest in your case. Your legal team has prepared its defence and gives you the option to allow for cameras in the courtroom to record the trial live, or to ask the judge to make the court 'closed' and ban live television coverage. The decision is not easy. At the heart of any responsible legal culture is transparency. An 'open' court allows for scrutiny of court processes and judges' decisions. The very purpose of media as a 'Fourth Estate' is to comment on and criticise other 'Estates' like the judiciary. Alternatively, televising court proceedings may risk producing sensationalist coverage, misrepresent the case and encourage judges to make decisions based largely on public pressure.

For the purposes of understanding Indonesia's legal culture, perhaps what is interesting here is to ask what factors would lead to your ultimate decision in answering the above question. Does your decision rest on the level of trust (or lack thereof) you place on Indonesia's criminal courts? Or is the predominant factor your prevailing view of Indonesia's media? What worries you most in influencing the outcome of your case: sensationalist and partisan media coverage or a judicial system tainted by corrupt lawyers and judges, or elite power networks in the judicial and media spheres?

If you found it difficult to make a decision, you are not alone. Indonesia's government, media and courts have been struggling with this predicament since the fall of Suharto. There has been no clear-cut agenda explaining how journalists should cover courts, let alone strict rules on whether cameras should be allowed in courtrooms in Indonesia. With the exception of trials involving children and sexual crimes, court cases must be 'open' (terbuka) to the media in Indonesia. But how one defines 'open' and how one defines 'the media' changes accordingly. In some cases, an 'open' court means open for anyone to enter, including journalists, photographers and cameras, including even live broadcasting not only nationwide, but on the Internet too, which means 'open' internationally. In other cases, an 'open' court allows for the public, including print and online journalists, to attend the court and report on the case, but no television cameras or photography. In some rare cases, journalists are ushered into a special room where a camera records the case and they watch the internal feed on a television screen.

Indonesia is a civil law system and so does not have trial by jury. This means that the influence of the media concerns judges (not a jury). How decisions get made around media coverage is also unclear. Legally, the chief judge makes the final decision, but as we shall see, there are a number of other important players, such as the Press Council, the Indonesian Broadcasting Commission, other legal bodies, politicians, even the president, who can all influence the chief judge in determining what defines an 'open' court.

At the heart of Dan Lev's work was the intertwining of law and politics: 'legal systems are politically derivative and cannot be understood apart from political structures, interests, ideology and the conflicts they incur' (Lev, 2000d: 3). Of course, Lev was writing in a time largely before the Internet, and certainly before the recent advances in digital technologies. Lev's writings do not focus significantly on the role of the media in shaping political and legal cultures in Indonesia, perhaps because under Suharto a muzzled mainstream media often played the role of an extension of the State. However, Lev's arguments on how legal culture calls attention to *values* [his italics] relating to law and legal processes remains highly useful. In this chapter we discern how the media and legal cultures are intertwined, discussing briefly the New Order period through to *reformasi,* before turning to more recent examples involving the high-profile courtroom 'megaspectacles'. The case study we undertake here is the issue of television cameras in courtrooms. As we shall see, the debate around live television broadcasting of trials exemplifies the link between law, politics and the media in contemporary Indonesia. The concept of an 'open' and 'transparent' court, and the way in which individuals and institutions interfere with this process, exemplifies much about how the media can influence the judiciary. Yet television cameras are only part of the 'media', and at a time where media technologies are rapidly advancing in the so-called 'digital era', court reporting is taking a very different shape. Understanding responses to new media technologies such as online streaming and social media discourse is crucial in understanding Indonesia's contemporary legal culture.

Court Reporting in Indonesia: An Overview

At the heart of Lev's writing is a concern for power; who has power, how is power mediated and who is vying (and who ultimately dominates) the resources of power (Crouch 2018). Central to political power struggles in contemporary Indonesia is the media. What is the role of the media in shaping Indonesia's legal culture? Who or what influences the way in which trials are covered, and how they are covered? Since the mid-2000s, media owners have become more wealthy, more politically powerful and more dynastic (Tapsell 2017). At the same, new forms of individual communication platforms such as social media and blogs have allowed for citizens' voices to become more prominent in the public sphere. To understand the important changes in media and legal culture in Indonesia, in this section we examine the intertwining of court reporting under the New Order authoritarian regime, before turning to the important reforms in the legal and media sectors throughout Indonesia's democratic transition.

The New Order

The Suharto regime (1965–98) used both the media and judiciary (and often concurrently) to manipulate political events. Reporting of trials was regulated by the Information Ministry through licensing and by co-opting the journalists' associations. National broadcasters were obliged to air compulsory news programmes which largely regurgitated government statements about court cases. Technically, Indonesian laws regulating the judiciary were designed to uphold principles of 'open' justice (Faiz, n.d.; 3).[1] In criminal cases, defendants could request a public trial. Article 153 (3) of the 1981 Criminal Procedure Law stipulates that '*for the purposes of questioning, the presiding judge will open hearing session and declare the trial open for public except for cases of public decency and juvenile trials*'. Using this law, Suharto set up a number of 'show trials' to silence critics and used the media to reverberate this message to citizens (Bourchier 1982; ICAC 1994; Jurriëns 2011).

But coverage of trials did not always have the effect that the regime wished. Among the most publicised trials of the era was that of Sawito

---

[1] Public trial is regulated by Article 19 of the Judicial Authority Law, Article 153 (3) of the Criminal Procedure Law, Article 40 of Supreme Court Law and Article 40 of Constitutional Court Law.

Kartowibowo, a middle-aged man and a former employee of the Agriculture Department. In 1977, the Suharto government announced that Sawito was charged with subversion, a criminal charge worthy of a maximum penalty of death by firing squad. The accusation was based on a document containing an alleged coup plan endorsed by several influential people. However, only Sawito, arguably the least known person in the document, had become the main defendant for the trial. Bourchier (1982: 101) argues that the trial of Sawito was 'demonstrative' and used by the Suharto government as a 'warning for anti-government groups'. But Suharto's aim to set up the affair as a 'show trial' backfired as the man who was supposed to be framed as a threat to the state attracted sympathy from the public (Bourchier 1982: 119). Furthermore, the Sawito affair revealed the 'lack of confidence' of the general public in the Suharto administration at the time (Bourchier 1982: 110).

During Suharto's authoritarian regime, the legal system was used as an instrument to extend the regime's power and control. However, the relations between the regime and the judiciary did not always reflect the relations between the regime and the public. The regime could manipulate the legal system to serve its best interests and achieve its desired legal outcome. However, despite strict controls over the mainstream media, shaping media coverage did not always achieve its desired aims. The public could still interpret political events and subsequent legal trials in their own particular way.

Links between the media and judiciary tell us more about the *desires* of the New Order regime rather than its ability to influence the public sphere. As Lev (1987) has shown, legal aid institute *LBH Masyarakat* used the media to gain a wider profile of its cases which pushed for legal reform under Suharto, which led to a space to contest the regime in some meaningful ways. Tempo's 1994 banning by the Suharto government is an example of the courts being used to uphold media restrictions. The government cancelled *Tempo's* license, but in 1995 the Jakarta State Administrative Court overturned the government's decision. The Ministry of Information appealed, and in 1996 the Supreme court found in favour of the government rather than the magazine. The banning was to stand (Mille 1999). The intertwining of the media and judicial process benefited the regime greatly, and led to a close collaboration between State actors in achieving the desired aims of the regime, in both the trial decision itself, and the reporting and representation of it.

Reformasi

The collapse of Suharto's presidency transformed Indonesia. Democratic transition, coupled with new media technologies, provided a far greater degree of freedom in the media and judicial spheres. Lev argued that when Suharto resigned his presidency under pressure in May of 1998 'one of the loudest and most insistent demands that ensued was for legal reform' (Lev 2005c: 3). This legal reform included calls for a free and independent media. The 1999 Press Law has been described as the 'jewel in the crown of *reformasi*' (Steele 2012). A few years later, the previously draconian Ministry of Information was closed down by President Abdurrahman Wahid. Reflecting on this decision in 2006, Wahid said: 'With that kind of Ministry, the government meddles into the affairs of the society and I don't like it. Under Suharto the Ministry was a kind of police over us' (Tapsell 2014: 69). For television and radio content, the Indonesian Broadcasting Commission or *Komisi Penyiaran Indonesia* (hereafter KPI) regulates the frequencies and provides advice to the industry, and occasional fines for misuse of broadcasting guidelines. The new 2002 Broadcasting Law provided a legal framework and protection for media practitioners to justify their right to cover court cases deemed newsworthy. Thus, one of the biggest challenges for legal practitioners in the post-*reformasi* period was adapting to a public sphere that could now freely comment on and criticise judicial institutions. But perhaps the biggest shift was that the newly independent media could enter courtrooms and broadcast trials live on free-to-air television.

As a result of this shift, twenty-first-century Indonesian politics became centred around numerous high-profile court cases that captured media and public attention. In 2002, the Indonesian public experienced for the first time a live television broadcast of a high-profile trial, in which former president Habibie testified in a corruption case surrounding misappropriation of non-budgetary funds totalling tens of billions of Indonesian Rupiah channelled to the State Logistics Agency (*Badan Urusan Logistik*, or Bulog). The 'Buloggate' scandal was among the biggest corruption scandals in the immediate post-Suharto years (Crouch 2010).[2] The case occurred under the new President Megawati Soekarnoputri (2001–4), who had become president a year earlier

---

[2] The Buloggate scandal, which first broke in 2000, revolves around misappropriation of tens of billions of rupiah managed by a foundation that managed Bulog's pension funds, Yanatera. The scandal led to the impeachment of President Abdurrahman Wahid, or Gus Dur.

following the impeachment of Habibie's successor, Abdurrahman Wahid, who was implicated in the scandal and ultimately led to his impeachment. The press reported that Suharto's Golkar Party had channelled tens of billions of rupiah from Bulog to its 1999 election campaign (McCoy 2005: 501). The scandal also implicated Golkar Party chairperson Akbar Tanjung, who allegedly received a substantial portion of the funds. The Buloggate corruption scandal was covered extensively by both local and foreign media, but it was private TV station Surya Citra Televisi's (SCTV) live broadcasting of a teleconference hearing of former president B. J. Habibie, who was residing in Germany at the time, that was most significant. The TV station rolled out promotional teasers and advertised their coverage in daily newspapers, claiming to be the first in the world to do a cross-country teleconference hearing (Siregar 2002). On 2 July 2002, SCTV's exclusive broadcast of the teleconference hearing occurred from 2.30 pm to 7 pm. During the live broadcast of the teleconference hearing, the editorial team also invited two guest experts to the studio to discuss the trial. Not only did the public watch the unprecedented spectacle, they were also able to engage with the process via interactive channels including messaging and email services (Siregar 2002). The trial generated over 2,000 responses from the public through messaging and email services (Liputan6 2002; Siregar 2002).

Given the success of the Habibie teleconference broadcast, during the mid-2000s, it was unsurprising that other television stations began to broadcast live other high-profile trials. These included a corruption trial of former state secretary Akbar Tanjung and a murder trial of Suharto's youngest son 'Tommy' for the killing of judge Syafiuddin Kartasasmita. Democratic transition has provided a greater degree of freedom in the media and judicial spheres that would have been unimaginable a few years earlier, and international observers pointed to these trials, and the media's robust reportage of them, as a sign of Indonesia's increasingly open and transparent legal and media spheres.

Democratic Consolidation

By the late 2000s, media coverage of Jakarta-based trials linked to political machinations was a feature of Indonesia's democracy. The institution central to these cases was the Corruption Eradication Commission (*Komisi Pemberantasan Korupsi*, or KPK). A 2009 murder trial saw former KPK Commissioner Antasari Azhar sentenced to twenty years in prison (see Butt 2011b). Antasari was found guilty of ordering the murder of businessman Nasruddin Zulkarnaen, the husband of a golf caddy, with whom Antasari allegedly had a sexual affair. As an anti-graft agency leader, Antasari was known for his bold decisions in examining cases involving influential figures, including those connected to then-president Susilo Bambang Yudhoyono.

The Antasari trial was covered extensively by the media from the first session to the final verdict. This coverage was ground-breaking in media reporting not only about broadcasting live from the courtroom, but due to its 'extension' of the trial coverage. Key people surrounding the case became sought after by the media for interviews. This included Rhani Juliani, the young female golf caddy who was at the centre of the scandal and a key witness in the case. For weeks after the news broke, Rhani was nowhere to be found. The media hunted down Rhani to her family home and workplace on the outskirts of Jakarta. Any clues of her existence were deemed worthy of reporting. She eventually appeared in public in a highly anticipated press conference. Antasari's wife and the wife of Williardi Wizar, a senior police officer, regularly gave interviews to newspapers, tabloids and TV stations to defend their husbands. The panel of judges handed down a guilty verdict despite allegations that the accused was 'framed'. As a Commissioner of the KPK he had made a lot of enemies. In 2016, President Joko Widodo granted Antasari clemency after they had served seven and a half years in prison.

In 2008, a similar high-profile case involving KPK commissioners Bibit Samad Rianto and Chandra Muhammad Hamzah occurred. They were charged for allegedly abusing their authority as KPK commissioners to issue and revoke travel bans, a charge which was later found to be based on forged documents. Bibit and Chandra, who were suspended as KPK commissioners following the arrest, subsequently challenged the article on which their expected dismissal was predicated on to the Constitutional Court, arguing that it con-travened their constitutional right to the presumption of innocence (Butt 2011a: 386). Both cases were heavily politicised (Butt 2011a: 386) and both were fervently covered in the Indonesian media. The Constitutional Court's proceedings, one of which revealed a plot to frame Bibit and Chandra in wire-tapped conversations between corruption suspects and senior law enforcement officials, were broadcast live.

Central to the way this trial was 'covered' in the public sphere was the role of social media, in particular Facebook. By 2009, Facebook had over

12 million users, and quickly became one of the most visited websites in Indonesia. Facebook's potential as an interlocutor for power relations was evident in the 'cicak v buaya' case. Here, the small cicak [gecko] was the Corruption Eradication Commission [or KPK] up against the might of the notoriously corrupt police, represented as the buaya [crocodile]. As Baker (2015: 117) has explained, the police are 'not just an instrument of civilian policy. Like the military, they wield enormous coercive power, making them a political force to be reckoned with.' A furore erupted when the police arrested two KPK officials. In this case, the story was initially driven by mainstream media platforms, but citizens turned to social media to encourage greater criticism of the police. One such Facebook page included *Gerakan 1,000,000 Facebookers Dukung Chandra Hamzah & Bibit Samad Riyanto* (movement of 1,000,000 Facebookers supporting Chandra Hamzah and Bibit Samad Riyanto) which surpassed its goal of one million members, while citizens widely shared YouTube videos and other online symbols of the *cicak* and *buaya*. In early December 2009, largely due to public pressure (which also included street rallies organised via social media platforms) charges against Bibit and Chandra were dropped.

The significance of social media activism is summed up by key government advisor Dewi Fortuna Anwar, who listed 'the rise of civil society' as one of the seven key achievements of the Yudhoyono Presidency (2004–14). Fortuna Anwar has identified how citizens use information and communications technology to generate support from the public for major causes. Fortuna Anwar cited the '*Cicak v Buaya*' as an example of this civil society online action. While this case was instinctively a reactive attempt to manipulate the outcome a legal battle, it resonated deeply with everyday Indonesians because it exemplified the corruption and injustice inherent in Indonesia's sociopolitical context (Molaei 2015: 104).

As the Bibit and Chandra case showed us, public reaction has the ability to influence media discourse and pressure judicial authorities to make certain decisions, such as dropping charges. While in this instance such pressure worked in favour of a just outcome, in other cases this may not necessarily be the case. That is, public pressure in court cases may lead to illiberal outcomes. In many ways, the legal system has not changed very much under Suharto (see earlier sections of this book), but the way it operates is driven much more by contestations not only between elites and the judiciary, but by the general public as played out through media coverage. The rise of social media as a central aspect of urban Indonesian public discourse heralds a new age of populist, media-driven decision-making at the centre of power struggles (see Tapsell 2017). The judiciary is not exempt from the impact of these new technologies.

Courtroom 'Megaspectacles' and the Digital Era

In the mid-2000s, the arrival of digital forms of media production heralded the beginning of the 'convergence era' in media in Indonesia (Tapsell 2014). Media convergence means the merging of traditionally separate media platforms such as print, television, radio and online into the one media conglomerate. The arrival of social media site Facebook (established 2004) and Twitter (2006) in Indonesia also led to a shift in the way citizens consumed – and produced – news and information.

In this environment, a certain story such as a criminal trial can *transcend* all media platforms, providing 'wall-to-wall' coverage in print, television, radio and online and social media news and commentaries. The use of twenty-four-hour rolling news coverage, including live television broadcasts from the courtroom, has been described as 'megaspectacles' (Kellner 2012). A 'megaspectacle' is defined as coverage which is more than simply media interest in an event itself – but rather reflects a media culture that puts contemporary dreams, nightmares, fantasies and values on display. Well-known international courtroom megaspectacles include the O. J. Simpson trial in the United States in the mid-1990s, and more recently South African athlete Oscar Pistorious's murder trial in 2014. Indonesia received a taste of this megaspectacle trial coverage from the Australian media during the Schappelle Corby drug trials in Bali in 2004, where the narrative of the innocent white female caught up in Southeast Asia's crowded, unruly legal system represented a prominent Australian cultural tradition of the 'little girl lost'. Unlike in their own country, Australian journalists were able to film inside the courtroom and broadcast live back to Australia. A total of 1.7 million viewers tuned to the live coverage of the verdict on the Nine and Seven networks in Australia (Tapsell 2014). But in Indonesia the trial received little coverage. Given the Jakarta-centric nature of Indonesia's mainstream media coverage and production, it is of no surprise that Indonesia's two megaspectacle trials of the digital era so far both involved Indonesians in the capital.

The Jessica Wongso Trial

Twenty-seven-year-old Jessica Wongso faced trial after the sudden death of her friend Mirna Salihin on 6 January 2016, and became Indonesia's most famous murder case of the digital era, transcending media platforms from 'traditional' print and television media to the vast array of online news, views and social media commentaries. Salihin's death was believed to have been caused by someone placing cyanide in her Vietnamese iced coffee. The coffee was ordered by Wongso before Salihin arrived. As the case unfolded, it was believed that Wongso held a grudge against the victim and plotted her murder.

The motives based around deceit and jealousy meant Indonesian television stations had a storyline reminiscent of popular television soap operas known as 'Sinetron'. Wongso was believed to have been motivated by anger over her own failed relationship, and jealous of Salihin's own happy relationship. In some reports, a theory was posited that Wongso was romantically interested in Salihin (Rahmah 2016). The murder scene location in a trendy café in one of Jakarta's largest and most prestigious malls frequently visited by the middle and upper class was also significant in raising interest. The court heard that the victim died from cyanide placed in her coffee, a unique murder which titillated viewers' interest. Finally, the fact that no cameras in the café filmed Wongso placing cyanide in the coffee (and toxicology and forensics experts testifying in the trial doubted the theory) meant there was no solid evidence of the definitive cause of the victim's death. This led to a great 'water cooler' discussion: 'Do you think she did it?'

Indonesia's mainstream media spared no expense in deploying resources for this 'trial of the century'. A designated satellite news gathering team was despatched to the Central Jakarta District Court. There, the team would set up a makeshift studio as a backdrop for on-site interviews with sources, including witnesses, experts, even the chief judge himself. A Kompas TV reporter assigned to cover the trial said:

> The planning will be discussed in editorial meeting one or two days prior to the hearing session. [The planning] includes which sources will be interviewed, such as witnesses or experts being questioned. Sometimes we contacted the sources and made an appointment, but most of the time the negotiation [with the sources] took place on site.[3]

---

[3] Frisca Clarissa, email correspondence, 17 October 2017.

On-site reporters would answer questions raised by news anchors from the studio, superimposed on the screen. The coverage included court-room scenes regularly replayed, as well as consistent footage of key figures entering and exiting the courtroom. Another regular feature employed by television stations throughout the Jessica Wongso trial was the use of visual and audio gimmicks accompanying the trial broadcast. Such gimmicks included pre-produced 'teasers' of what was to come next, and regular 'breaking news' segments. A final element was pseudo-experts with no effective links to the case but who were deemed relevant to discuss the case. These included a so-called 'micro-expression specialist' interviewed to discuss Wongso's psychological state during the verdict readout. The specialist offered her analysis based on observations of the TV footage of the oral testimony of Wongso. Other interviewees not directly linked to the trial included criminologists, toxicologists and the victim's relatives.

National television broadcasters provided uninterrupted, 'gavel-to-gavel coverage' of the trial proceedings from June 15 until the verdict ruling on October 27. The trial became the most watched show of the year, with TV ratings of the trial beating those of major political events such as cabinet reshuffles or presidential speeches. Three major twenty-four-hour television stations broadcast the trial extensively and enjoyed a surge in TV ratings every time they aired the trial live (KompasTV, TvOne and iNews). TV audience share of KompasTV rose to average 5.64 per cent throughout the trial broadcasting from 2.06 per cent before the trial started (Hanifan 2016). The verdict ruling topped social media's list of trending topics on the day it was read out (Batubara 2016b). Humorous and cynical memes surrounding the case also circulated rapidly on the social media, reflecting differing public opinions on the matter. The Indonesian Broadcasting Commission issued warning letters for the three television stations named above for violating the principle of the presumption of innocence and for excessive broadcasting of the trial.

The panel of judges found Wongso guilty of plotting the murder and sentenced her to twenty years in prison. Many observers believed the sensationalist coverage impacted on the decision. Ronald Lumbuun, former Supreme Court District Judge from 2006–16, believed the Jessica Wongso case was an exception to the usual cases because the chief judge allowed himself to be interviewed on television throughout the case, and that 'the lesson needs to be about teaching judges how to handle television cameras and how to behave', rather than to 'enjoy' being interviewed on television.[4] Lumbuun said: 'Trials should remain open to the media. It is a way for the public to control the judges. Otherwise judges have absolute power. The media can affect the behaviour of the judges to make a fairer trial'.[5] In other countries, a *sub judice* rule exists, which prohibits conduct or comment which could prejudice ongoing judicial processes. In Indonesia, which does not have a jury system, this law is not in place. There exist, however, various Codes of Ethics for judges, although there seems little by way of enforcement if these Codes are broken.

The case of Jessica Wongso shows that Indonesia's media no longer solely saw courtroom megaspectacles as trials linked to the political machinations of elites. There was no suggestion that Wongso had any political connections nor was the murder of Salihin politically motivated. Rather, the Wongso trial succeeded as a courtroom megaspectacle because, first, it was a trial based in Jakarta, where mainstream media have their head offices and where the majority of Indonesia's news originates. Around 60 per cent of Indonesian television audience comes from Jakarta. Second, the victim and murder suspect were both young females, which linked to popular Indonesian soap programmes of jealous, evil female characters who committed crimes against other unsuspecting female victims. Wongso may indeed have murdered Salihin, but much of the coverage did not provide the defendant with the opportunity to be innocent until proven guilty, and many aspects of its coverage breached Article 5 (1) section of the Press Law, which states that 'the national press is obliged to report news or opinions based on the principle of the presumption of innocence'. The Wongso trial megaspectacle took 'gavel-to-gavel coverage' to new heights, and would have an immediate effect on how the media would report Indonesia's next political megaspectacle trial, one defined not by a 'Sinetron' wicked feminine figure but defined by one which centred around elite political machinations.

The Ahok Blasphemy Trial

In 2017, the trial of Jakarta Governor Basuki Tjahaja Purnama (known as Ahok) is significant in understanding the shifting nature of media and legal culture in Indonesia. In September 2016, Ahok was named a suspect

---

[4] Lumbuun personal telephone interview, January 2018.
[5] Lumbuun, personal communication, Jakarta, 2018.

(and later arrested) for making a blasphemous speech against Islam, insinuating that politicians often use Koranic verses to manipulate or fool voters and thus deter them from voting for him, a Christian of Chinese descent.[6] On three occasions between November and February, millions of Indonesian Muslims protested in central Jakarta thoroughfares to demand Ahok's arrest – the biggest series of street protest in post-Suharto Indonesia.

On 4 November 2016, television stations live broadcast the first mass rally in Jakarta. But on 10 November, the Indonesian Television Journalists Association met with the Press Council (and a few other interested parties) in Bali and decided that future 'anti-Ahok' rallies should not be broadcast live. Press Council Chairman Imam Wahyudi, who was at the meeting, justified the decision by saying: 'Journalism is not CCTV. The process of gatekeeping and editorial policies is central to journalism'.[7] Sure enough, at the second mass rally in Jakarta on 2 December 2017, television stations only minimally reported on the event, and did not provide live coverage.

Once it was clear Ahok would face trial, there was considerable debate and discussion over how the media should cover the trial. President Jokowi stated that he wanted the trial to be televised for the purposes of 'transparency' (*The Jakarta Post* 2016a). Ahok also hoped that his trial could be held publicly and broadcasted by television stations. He was quoted in the media as saying: 'I'm expecting an open trial. I hope that the media will broadcast the trial just like Jessica's [Mirna's] case,' he said (*Detik.com* 2016). Indonesia's leading newsmagazine *Tempo* exemplified the difficulties in this decision in mid-November 2016, arguing on the one hand: 'although the police chief pledges an open trial just like the murder case of defendant Jessica Kumala Wongso, they must guarantee the process is free from intervention'. But in the next sentence it asked rhetorically: 'When the trial is held openly, can the judges be trusted not to make a decision pragmatically?' (*Tempo* 2016).

On 9 December 2016, four days prior to the first trial session, the Indonesian Broadcasting Commission, the Press Council and the Indonesian Television Journalists Association held a meeting to discuss the reporting of the trial (Laksono 2017). The meeting was attended by a diverse range of sectors of Indonesia's society, including the Minister of Communication and Information, the Jakarta Police

---

[6] On the history and use of the blasphemy law in Indonesia, see Crouch (2014) and Crouch (2012a).

[7] Imam Wahyudi, personal interview, Jakarta, January 2018.

chief, chief editors of major TV stations, representatives of the North Jakarta District Court, the Information Commission, the Judicial Commission, major Muslim organisations such as Nahdlatul Ulama and Muhammadiyah, as well as academics and public figures. The forum eventually agreed on 'selective' reporting of the Ahok trial. In the aftermath of sensationalist coverage of the Jessica Wongso trial, authorities and experts believed live and rolling news coverage had the potential to exacerbate already lingering racial and religious divides simmering in the country. Broadcasting Commissioner Mayong Laksono, who was at the meeting, wrote that rather than an attempt to undermine democratic values, 'selective' trial coverage was needed to uphold journalistic principles (Laksono 2017: 19).

How did they argue this legally? Despite ambiguous interpretation on what constitutes an 'open' public trial, article 159 (1) of the Criminal Law Procedures (KUHAP) states that 'witnesses who are being questioned should be summoned separately and each testimony should not be heard by other witnesses'. Authorities cited this article as the basis for a camera ban in courtrooms but, in reality, the decision was based more around the potential for violence and conflict. Mayong Laksono said: 'It was about SARA [acronym for suku, agama, ras, antar-golongan]. We must be on extra alert. We must protect the nation after our bad experience in the 2014 election where there was "red TV" and "blue TV". We were worried that Ahok trial would be similar'.[8] Laksono's depiction of 'red' and 'blue' TV in Indonesia comes from the increased partisan reporting of politics from Indonesian television stations, shaped largely by direction from media owners who have links to political parties (Tapsell 2017). The 2014 election was a clear case of one twenty-four-hour news station supporting Jokowi (MetroTV), while another clearly supported Prabowo (TvOne).

Put simply, it was believed that Indonesian television stations could not be trusted to report on the trial of a prominent politician accurately and fairly, and as such their access was restricted on the grounds that it was better for societal harmony. This is in stark contrast to the earlier political trials of Indonesia's post-*reformasi* media coverage, where television cameras were seen as positive influencers on the country's increasingly open and transparent courtrooms. Clearly, policymakers in Indonesia had reduced trust in the independence and professionalism of their mainstream media companies. The panel of judges hearing the Ahok trial accepted the recommendations and decided to ban live

---

[8] Laksono, personal interview with author, Jakarta, 2017.

broadcasting from the courtroom during most sessions. Cameras were allowed during indictment, plea and verdict sessions. Due to security and capacity concerns, the North Jakarta District Court decided to set up the trial at an auditorium at the Agriculture Ministry office in South Jakarta. Due to the same concerns, Ahok was moved from the Cipinang Penitentiary in East Jakarta to the Mobile Brigade headquarters in Depok, West Java. There, reporters were allowed into the court gallery to follow the sessions, but they were not allowed to bring in television cameras.

The details of the case still received significant media coverage in Indonesia. Because cameras were banned, media companies needed a reporter inside the courtroom to make notes and write narratives for another reporter on standby outside ready to do live reporting. One CNN Indonesia online and television reporter explained his professional practice in this way:

> We had three different teams to cover the trial. The first team consists of a reporter who stayed in the court gallery to write down facts unveiled in the proceeding without recording. He/she will report it to the second team, which was on standby outside the courtroom. The second team, or the big team, consists of the satellite newsgathering team. The third team was tasked to cover pro and anti-Ahok rallies outside the Ministry of Agriculture compound (Istiarto Sigit, personal online communication 2017).

However, because cameras were not allowed in courtrooms, television coverage of the case focused around the heavy security measures needed to separate rallies held by pro- and anti-Ahok camps throughout the trial. Protestors were regularly interviewed in front of barricades and heavily armoured police, and a sense of tension outside the court was regularly conveyed. Thus, television focused more on the happenings *outside* the court rather than the specific details of what was going on *inside* it. In the case of Ahok's blasphemy trial, there was little evidence that television media was providing a 'Fourth Estate' to provide democratic checks and balances on the Indonesian judiciary. Furthermore, the court's decision to ban live courtroom broadcasting upset some within the general public, as well as some in Ahok's legal team, who were optimistic that live courtroom broadcasting would benefit his defence.

Despite (or because of) the courtroom ban, television broadcasters still used similar approaches undertaken during the Wongso trial: pre-produced visual and audio gimmicks, and talk shows with perceived 'relevant' sources and experts. And despite the live camera ban for most of the trial, television and still cameras still captured some significant moments on the two occasions when they were allowed to film and take pictures. At the first hearing, a picture of gloomy Ahok being consoled by a woman wearing an Islamic headscarf (identified as Ahok's adoptive sister) circulated on the social media, with pro-Ahok netizens emphasising the former governor's pro-Muslim stance having been brought up among Muslims in an Islamic environment. During the first hearing, a tearful Ahok read out his plea of not guilty, emphasising his pro-Muslim stance and lack of intention of hurting Muslims. This part of the trial also took social media by storm, with hashtags like #SidangAhok (Ahok trial) and #KamiAhok or #KamiBersamaAhok (we are Ahok or we are with Ahok) trending on Twitter and Facebook (Batubara 2016a).

What does the Ahok trial tell us about the intertwining of media, politics and law in Indonesia? First, it shows that Indonesian authorities worry about the way in which media owners with political interests shape coverage of the courts, and do not trust them to do so fairly. Overall, there is a belief that a significant threat to judicial independence is not only corruption and political pressure, but in fact is public opinion. Second, authorities believe that the media will deliberately or inadvertently create ethnic and religious tensions if they freely or sensationally cover the trial, and that citizens on social media will be incited and enraged and potentially create an atmosphere of violence. Third, they did not believe the media was a crucial actor in making the court more transparent, and they did believe that judges would be better making decisions without the television cameras rolling. In short, in one of Indonesia's most important trials in its post-*reformasi* period, Indonesian authorities (and many of its citizens) believed that their media was more of a hindrance than a watchdog for democracy and judicial integrity.

Conclusion: The Media and Indonesia's Legal Culture

In assessing the role of the media in shaping Indonesia's legal culture, research conducted for this chapter posits two central arguments. The first conclusion is that the Indonesian media has produced highly sensationalist coverage of court cases, in some cases megaspectacles, whereby a political and/or criminal trial became the biggest media event of the year. The pattern of coverage is based around gaining higher audiences through rolling, twenty-four-hour coverage and sensationalist, gripping 'breaking news' reporting of the so-called 'twists and turns' of courtroom arguments, introduction of witnesses as 'new characters' with alternate versions of events, and ultimately a suspenseful 'countdown' to the verdict. The professional practice of journalists in this scenario is to try to find new angles or testimonies to add to the 'breaking news'. In this case, TV reporters and news anchors often play a pseudo-private detective role, conducting 'investigations' by interviewing 'relevant' individuals who had something to say about the case.

Tensions, conflicts, motives and differing opinions unveiled outside the courtroom became part of the trial coverage. TV reporters would then pursue these angles and discussions ensued during talk shows or current affairs programmes. However, key actors (such as defendants, witnesses and family members) were not passive participants. Often, they actively used the media to convey their points of view. Live courtroom broadcasting has transformed into what Indonesian Broadcasting commissioner Mayong Laksono called a 'public theatre' (Laksono 2017: 17). New social media forms of commentary and images have meant a more engaged public, but an arguably more partisan and fervent commentariat online, shaped by media representation of the court itself. As we saw in the case of Corby and Salihin, the consequences of 'live' reporting for television meant that audience assessment of trials is enslaved to images, or 'moving hieroglyphics' and 'imagespeak', where the repetition of images take on a symbolic, and not just literal, meaning.

It is clear that sensationalist, emotive, entertainment-driven reporting interferes with principles of a fair trial and the presumption of innocence, rather than acting as a 'watchdog' in making sure that the judiciary is functioning in a fair and legally correct manner. Of course, few of Indonesia's journalists have significant legal training or education in law. Faced with a mainstream media that values entertainment over the principles of a fair trial, authorities have felt the need to reduce media coverage of the judicial system. But is this the right approach? Ahok's sentence of two years' imprisonment was unexpected, because the prosecution had argued for a two-year suspended sentence. The independence of the judges may have been reduced if they were not the focus of extensive media (including television) coverage. Thus, the culture of Indonesia's free, rambunctious but ratings-centric media has led to a reduction of its role as 'watchdog' of the country's judicial system.

A second conclusion is that the courts and media remain heavily intertwined in shaping Indonesia's legal culture post-Suharto. As we have heard, under Suharto the power rested with the authoritarian government, who shaped significant legal cases and much of the mainstream media coverage in ways they saw fit. In the post-*reformasi* era, courtroom and the media have both been sites of conflict between Indonesia's elite, or 'oligarchs'. As Jeffrey Winters argues, conflict and debate arises in Indonesia's media predominantly due to 'clashes between oligarchic personalities or political groups that own them' (Winters 2013). Because the dominant source of these conflicts is owners' financial and political interests, the power of oligarchs to frame debate and discussion in the public sphere is evident.

The courts, too, are places where oligarchs battle out conflicting financial and political interests, and decisions in particular are said to be framed around which oligarch has access to the Attorney General's department. It is no surprise that both the court cases and the media coverage of trial megaspectacles are in Jakarta, where these power contests play out and where the owners base their media offices. *Reformasi* significantly transformed two pillars of democracy in Indonesia: the press and judiciary, but the power over how decisions are made in these institutions has moved from New Order government to that of elite actors in politics and media power strata.

This is not to say that Indonesia's judiciary and media are the same as they were in the New Order, nor that oligarchs always get their way when looking to influence these institutions. But in the digital era, authorities seemingly do not see the media as an institution that is of assistance to a more transparent judiciary. This includes mainstream media owned by oligarchs, but is also true of the way in which citizens engage with legal cases on social media and online commentaries. Increasingly, digital media is seen as a space which divides and enrages society rather than one which supports democratic institutions. Of course, in the long-term Indonesia must strengthen its media and journalism practice to report on court proceedings and the judiciary with greater independence and professionalism. In the short-term, the question facing legal and media culture in the archipelago will be: is Indonesia's notoriously corrupt legal culture best served by a media kept at arms-length? Or is a media which inspires both transparency and partisan, politically driven vitriol ultimately a better alternative?

Worth considering here is what or who is a trial 'for'? Is it for the defendant, the victim, the public, the state, or something else? In most Western democracies, trials are largely framed for defendants – to enable them to defend themselves against criminal allegations, which is important given that they face criminal sanctions. But the victim and the general public also have an interest. The victim and the public will often want to see justice done. In Indonesia, the trial seems far less 'for' the defendant than in the West; judges regularly ask defendants questions to 'trip' them up, for example, and media often report with a verdict already established or at least implied. Perhaps the uncertain area around who the trial is 'for' in Indonesia is one of the sources of the lack of policy and legal direction in media coverage around trials.

16

Lev on the Links between Legal Evolution, Political Change and Activism

FRANK W. MUNGER

Daniel Lev's legacy of scholarship remains the starting point for the best writing about Indonesia's courts. Lev is the starting point only in part because he was one of the first Western scholars to study Indonesia's modern legal system. More importantly, Lev is revered because his approach set future research on a productive path that avoided all too frequent snares including mistaken assumptions about legal development and reliance on theory developed to explain law in the European tradition. This collection of contemporary studies of Indonesia's courts amply demonstrates that Lev continues to enrich decisions about what to study, where to look and how to go about learning from fieldwork.

Among other lessons, Lev's studies of courts showed that multiple points of entry may be required to understand their functions and dependence on political authority. Thus, Lev's deep understanding of the courts and law combined knowledge gained from the perspectives of judges, legal advocates (of many descriptions), litigants, journalists and the media, politicians, activists and others, as well as familiarity with the society in which his informants lived and intimate knowledge of local history. This book is a continuation of that labor, Lev's avocation, pursuing penetrating description and illuminating detail about particular courts and related organizations in a complex system. The authors' own methods of research follow Lev's advice, incorporating the perspectives of actors within and outside the courts who constitute the court system but are simultaneously integrated within multiple social relationships and Indonesia's hierarchies of power and authority. Lev led the way to a vibrant, productive and coherent, if complex, field of research that continues to examine the contemporary courts and their political context.

When Lev began his work, political science and sociolegal studies of courts in developing countries typically focused on the fate of familiar-seeming legal institutions under unfamiliar conditions. Lev perceived clearly, and well ahead of many of his contemporaries, the precise ways in which the rule of law, the foundation for courts, had emerged in European political history, following a path of political conflict, compromise and contingent achievement that bore little relationship to later theorizing about the universal qualities of rule of law or the functions of courts. As Melissa Crouch tells us in her introduction, Lev was skeptical of theories of legal development, which he characterized as a source of "grand myths" – generalizations that obscure critical details, details that distinguish one court from another and comprise what is often referred to as "culture." Lev's prescription: examine the foundations of Indonesian legal experience through "deep research." Lev's research, in contrast to studies by Western scholars who sometimes failed to put aside assumptions about the functions or form of legal institutions and often eschewed field work, involved close observation of the motivations, work routines, decision making and interconnections among the actors who shaped the courts' structure, character and importance. Among the important perspectives he studied, he included those of actors who sought change or subverted it. As Crouch notes, to some degree Lev anticipated the "cultural turn" in sociolegal studies that marked rediscovery of the agency of individuals and groups in constructing the society in which they live. His research gave concrete meaning to the courts and legal development from the perspectives of those whose actions construct them.

Indonesia may have been the perfect case study for such a grounded approach. Indonesia is a supremely complex society, as different from Europe and North America as could be imagined – in its geography, religious diversity and ethnic hierarchy, and it was influenced by many globalizations before Europeans appeared on the scene, mostly notably from China, India and cultures migrating from neighboring countries in Southeast Asia. Indonesia's fractured political structure and multi-layered courts present every challenge imaginable and few familiar reference points for a scholar trained in Western political or sociological theory attempting to understand legal development.

Lev was well aware that Western legal ideals and institutions could have strong appeal in Indonesia and elsewhere. Law was employed by the powerful to legitimate their power, control subordinates and regulate globalizing markets, while limiting its influence beyond these functions. Law appealed to those who lacked power and sought accountability from those who had it and wider opportunities for themselves. The point was, Lev emphasized, that "foreign ideas, in Asia as in Europe or anywhere else, take hold only when they make sense domestically and are adapted to domestic purposes" (Lev 2000d: 6).

Chapters in this collection represent the full range of Lev's own diverse interests and approaches to studying courts, but they share a common theme – and explicit focus on Lev's concept of legal culture, exploiting the complexity of Lev's conceptualization and the relationship of culture to specific contexts. Lev initially defined the term broadly, following Lawrence Friedman's study of generational shifts in values and resulting shifts in litigation and legal remedies. Lev came to use the term in a different way in his own research, at times rejecting use of the term (in its broadest, societal values, sense). Rather, Lev used the term culture to refer to the orientation (not unlike Bourdieu's 1977 term *habitus*) of situated actors who both instantiate and create the character of institutions. Motivations, perceptions and possibilities for action are linked to a role in the system that defines and shapes the functions of courts – a judge, a litigant, a legal advocate, a journalist or an influential political figure – and, in turn, are derived from experience in that role but also from broader social environments organized by religion, politics, social class or social movements. The authors of the chapters in this volume capture this complexity in revealing ways showing us how Indonesia's legal system matches its fragmented politics. Over more than half a century, Indonesia's rulers and legislatures have established courts at different times that have become embedded in the complex political and social environments. For example, Rifqi Assegaf's chapter on the Indonesian Supreme Court describes the embedding of the Court in existing modes of legal thought and politics in ways that pushed its judges toward accepting a limited mission, that of dispute resolution, while avoiding the more risky mission of policymaking. Assegaf's description of the culture of the Supreme Court may be contrasted with Theunis Roux's examination of the Constitutional Court, a court that initially assumed a bold policymaking role reflecting institutional independence and a very different judicial culture. At the same time, the authors' descriptions of cultural variation share a theme found in Lev's understanding of Indonesian judicial culture, corruption, having roots in Indonesia's continuing political realities that are structured by oligarchy and military power. Lev's concept of culture, like that of the New Institutionalists', assumes that both institutions and their social and political environments are responsible for "creating the lenses through which actors view the world and the very categories of structure, action and thought" (Powell and DiMaggio 1991: 12–13). Indonesia's political institutions continue to undermine the independence and power of its courts, allowing a more self-serving, entrepreneurial judicial culture to survive.

Unlike the new institutionalists, Lev had a keen interest in actual politics and political change. I want to underscore two points that should not be lost in the richness of this volume or its wealth of detail about Indonesia's contemporary court system. First, like the authors, Lev sought to understand legal development by studying the micropolitics of courts and related sites of legal action in a context of ongoing political change. The studies in this volume examine the results of attempts to reform the courts following the democratic opening in the 1990s. Mechanisms of political and legal change form an important element of the background and motivation for the research. But Lev himself had more to say about conditions under which political change occurs and when it could succeed that are worth remembering because they may provide a fruitful additional perspective on these chapters. The second theme of Lev's work and life I want to underscore is their relationship to activism. Lev's interests were never far from the possibilities for political change and his admiration for advocates for a more just distribution of power, constitutionalism and an impartial rule of law.

Lev as Comparativist: Class Structure and Political Change

Knowledge of the unique circumstances of European legal development made Lev a cautious comparativist. Nevertheless, the social and political conflict that drove legal development in Europe not only reinforced his interest in political change but also offered a template for understanding the influence of class and the distribution of power on the courts and rule of law evolving under very different conditions. In an essay addressing the comparative study of constitutionalism (1993), Lev underscored the importance of constitutionalism, that is, establishing written or unwritten limits on rulers, as a basis for a rule of law. Legal rules must count over and above decisions made by religious orders or customary rulers or military commanders. Lev asserts that rules of this type begin to count as a result of political demand. In turn, Lev viewed that demand as arising from "fundamental changes ... in class structure," more specifically formation of a middle class.[1] Here and elsewhere in his writings, Lev observes that pressure for rule of law by an emerging middle class has become a global pattern. By implication, the struggles of an emerging middle class to establish a government that respects rules lies at the core

---

[1] Pressure for change has been "the peculiar ideological haven of the middle class that could not claim an inherently legitimate right to govern but were dissatisfied with their lack of regular access to and influence over those who did govern" (1993: 141).

of legal development. Conversely, enduring power structures that resist such a change through force or by establishing rules that serve the powerful alone explains its failures. In the transition to postcolonial status, conditions have seldom favored democracy movements which have given way in most cases to the enduring power of traditional elites, oligarchs or the military – groups that are often allied or overlapping. Rule of law may be established but not rule of law that limits the power of rulers.

In this essay, written two decades into his career, Lev describes not only the historical grounding for his interest in political change but also his research methods. Political contentions over the status of law, he says,

> are local matters, fed by local issues, interests, values and historical circumstance, the outcomes [of which] ... are comprehensible essential only in local terms. [P]olitical compromises worked out historically, the tacit social and economic agreement made along the way, the play of local habit and values and cultural assumptions, the ways in which change proceeds, are all taken for granted at home but are unfathomable away. Without an understanding of the conflicts that go on in state and society, and between the two, of the ways in which power is generated and authority actually exercised, of the values and ideologies that inform political structure and behavior, we cannot comprehend constitutionalist (or any other) movements as they have evolved. (Lev 1993: 141)

Motivation for Lev's continuing interest in the role of lawyers defending the rule of law is found in the further observation that pressure for development of a rule of law is typically aligned with social movements that attempt to broaden and generalize the appeal of such protections.[2]

Like Lev, the authors in this collection engage political change and possibilities for further change in important ways, but examination of the history of political change, its key players and possibilities for changing the course of legal development in the future remain unfinished work. In some chapters, Indonesia's political past and present is essential background (for example, Pascoe's excellent discussion of district courts or Bedner and Wiratraman's updated examination of the administrative courts), while other chapters address the means and outcome of reform efforts directly (for example, illuminating chapters on the Anti-corruption Courts, Human Rights Courts and Constitutional Courts,

---

[2] He also notes the important connection between such movements and the concept of human rights. Lacking an indigenous ideology similar to European law's grounding in natural rights, human rights, and the conditions under which they become meaningful, serve a similar purpose.

each of which has experienced the penetration of politics into promising beginnings and attempts to encourage actors with a new orientation toward the function of law and the courts). These chapters invite more direct examination, in the spirit of Lev's own work, of the possibilities for further change and where pressure for change would have to be directed. Characteristically, Lev would also encourage special attention to the question: Who is likely to take up the struggle and the conditions under which the outcome might be different?

Lev and Legal Activists

My admiration for Daniel Lev's work as scholar grew from my first encounter with him while I was serving as General Editor of the *Law & Society Review* in 1993, overseeing publication of a symposium (organized by David Engel, Jane Collier and Barabara Yngvesson) titled *Law and Society in Southeast Asia* – one of the first collections of sociolegal scholarship on Southeast Asia to appear anywhere. Dan Lev (1994) wrote the Foreword. Dan drew attention not only to Southeast Asia's diversity and promise for comparative study but to the role of law in its politics. The subject matter is, he said, "a moving object" and the "uses of law . . . for getting anything done legitimately in Southeast Asian states are all contested and undergoing change . . . [set off by] economic transformations, social upheaval, ideological battles over the very shape of the state and its relationship to society" (at 414). Soon after, I had the opportunity to spend extended periods of time with members of a network of human rights lawyers and activists in Thailand, and I was quickly hooked, in much the same way Lev must have been drawn to study the roles of lawyers and courts in political change in Indonesia. During my first years of fieldwork in this new environment, I encountered Lev's influence in an entirely different way through a chance meeting with one of his former graduate students turned grassroots activist, a career transition mentored by Lev and likely inspired by the political spark that contributed to Lev's own interest in political transitions, his romance with fieldwork and his friendships with activists in Indonesia.

I have described Lev's essay on the roots of constitutionalism in Europe, in which he observed that establishing rule-based limits on the powerful has been associated with social movements and, therefore, with activism directed against autocratic regimes. The conditions under which pressure for political inclusion and governmental restraint succeeded in European countries were complex but provided support for Lev's class and social movement-based theory of legal evolution (for a similar argument, see Tilly 1990; for additional complexity, see Vu 2010). Lev's interest in advocates for rule of law in Indonesia is likely to have had still deeper roots and greater importance than can be explained by his knowledge of Western history alone. Lev studied the careers of lawyers who resisted Soekarno's efforts to undermine the rule of law in a pathbreaking working paper on legal aid in Indonesia, written in 1987 (Lev 1987). An early working paper described the founding of the Legal Services Institute (LBH) by outspoken lawyer Adnan Buyung Nasution with the support of PERADIN, the first association of Indonesian lawyers. Together, LBH and PERADIN became a bulwark of rule of law advocacy, promoting litigation challenging Indonesia's autocratic rulers and training generations of rule of law advocates notwithstanding the considerable risk of reprisal by powerful rulers. Nasution, lawyers who followed him, and the support provided by LBH and PERADIN played a part in the parallel history of Indonesian courts through the work of legal advocates who brought cases to the courts. Many were also outspoken public advocates for court reform. Lev's later writing on "cause lawyers" included comparison of lawyer-activists among Indonesian and Malaysian lawyers who, in spite of quite different constitutional systems and political conditions, have played functionally similar roles in creating and defending a "law-state" (Lev 1998). Lev's analysis of cause lawyers has continuing relevance. It would be valuable to understand, for example, the nature and source of the commitment to the rule of law among the relatively independent investigators and prosecutors working for the Indonesian Anti-corruption Commission [KPK], described by Simon Butt in his chapter on the Anti-corruption Courts. Further research might reveal whether their successful prosecutions and resilience in the face of political resistance results from self-selection among recruits or principles of bureaucratic independence (or both), findings that could guide future reforms.

Lev's last work, published posthumously, is a biography of Yap Thiam Hien, a Peranakan (Indonesian Chinese) lawyer of great courage and principle, and a personal friend whom Lev greatly admired (2010). Benedict Anderson, in his introduction to the biography, speculates about the sources of Lev's attraction to activism. Lev's career as a scholar began in the 1950s during a period of global reordering and hope for liberal change. His graduate school mentor was himself a passionate sympathizer with the Indonesian nationalist cause and friend of its leaders, adding to the romance of fieldwork there and the excitement of Indonesia's revolutionary uprising and democratic opening in 1955. For Lev, Anderson writes, law was not a matter of statutes and decisions but became "a social, economic and political institution" (Anderson 2011:6). Indonesia's revolution in the 1950s was followed, of course, by Soekarno's rise and abrogation of a liberal constitution, the starting point, perhaps, of Lev's career-long interest in the efforts to restore a meaningful rule of law. Nasution's outspoken defense of the rule of law and Yap's outrage at abuses by the government were likely to have been part of what drew Lev's attention and mirrored his own reasons for his deep lifelong interest in the progress of legal development in Indonesia. Not coincidentally, many of the authors contributing to this volume have been activists in their own right, and thus are likely to have found in Lev a true mentor – a kindred spirit as well as a deeply informed scholar – for research about the evolution, functions and possible futures of Indonesia's court system.

~

Epilogue

FRITZ EDWARD SIREGAR

This book brings together a distinguished group of scholars who are experts in their field. The authors are leading scholars in Indonesia and globally. It is a great challenge to write about the development of various courts of Indonesia. Dan S. Lev's work is critical to Indonesian scholarship, and this volume pays tribute to his important work. Dan is a pioneer of social-political legal studies in Indonesia. Lawyers tend to think that the law is autonomous, in contrast to political science scholars who often view law and regulations as entirely the end product of political relations. Dan applied political science to the legal field by analysing legal institutions and the law through attention to power relations. Dan also observed relations between legal institutions and practitioners. He was of the view that the legal system could be understood through its institutions, profession and basic concepts. The autonomy of legal institutions and the legal profession is critical to protect from political influence.

The court system in Indonesia is complex and is deserving of greater study. The creation of a court may be because of political decisions, but social culture, legal autonomy and its context determines whether there is support for the court. Dan's vast contribution to the role of political relations, economic development and social culture enables us to understand the development of these various courts and the extent to which they have broad political and social support.

As an academic first at the University of Indonesia and now at Indonesia Jentera Law School, I believe this volume will be useful for students and scholars in Indonesia. Many of Dan Lev's works and library are held at the Dan S. Lev Library at Jentera Law School, Jakarta, Indonesia. But this is the first volume that views the creation of various courts through a sociolegal view similar to Dan Lev. Further, as a Commissioner of the Election Supervision Agency, Bawaslu, an independent accountability agency, I believe that the perspective this volume offers on courts in Indonesia will be welcomed by the government, non-government agencies and policymakers. This volume begins an important task of studying trends in the Indonesian court system over time, and will be welcomed by students, scholars, policymakers and other agencies seeking to understand court reform in comparative contexts more broadly.

List of Institutions

Badan Pengawas Pemilihan Umum, (Bawaslu)	General Election Supervisory Body
Komisi Nasional Hak Asasi Manusia (Komnas HAM)	National Human Rights Commission
Komisi Keberantasan Korupsi (KPK)	Anti-corruption Commission
Komisi Yudisial (KY)	Judicial Commission
Komisi Perlindungan Anak Indonesia (KPAI)	Indonesian Commission for the Protection of Children
Komisi Pemilihan Umum (KPU)	General Election Commission
Mahkamah Agung (MA)	Supreme Court
Mahkamah Konstitusi (MK)	Constitutional Court
Pemeriksaan Gugatan Sederhana	Small Claims Court
Pengadilan Anak	Juvenile Court
Pengadilan Hak Asasi Manusia	Human Rights Court
Pengadilan Militer	Military Court
Pengadilan Niaga	Commercial Court
Pengadilan Pajak	Tax Court
Pengadilan Hubungan Industrial	Industrial Relations Court
Pengadilan Perikanan	Fisheries Court
Pengadilan Tata Usaha Negara (PTUN)	Administrative Courts
Pengadilan Tindak Pidana Korupsi (Pengadilan Tipikor)	Anti-corruption Courts
Peraturan Mahkamah Agung (PERMA)	Regulation of the Supreme Court
Tentara Nasional Indonesia, (TNI)	Indonesian National Army

List of Indonesian Terms

adat	customary law
dwifungsi	dual role of the military in politics
fitnah	calumny
genosida	genocide
hak uji materiil	judicial review
jaksa	public prosecutor
kejahatan terhadap kemanusiaan	crimes against humanity
Kitab Undang-Undang Hukum Acara Pidana (KUHAP)	Criminal Procedure Code
musyawarah	judges' internal deliberations
partisipasi kriminal (parmin)	participation in crime
pelanggaran hak asasi manusia yang berat	gross human rights violations
pencemaran	slander
pengayoman	guardianship
peninjauan kembali	special review/reconsideration
penyidikan	investigation
praperadilan	pretrial hearings
surat edaran	circular letter
tokoh-tokoh masyarakat	respected community leader/public figure
yurispudensi tetap	a repeated Supreme Court decision on a particular legal issue

BIBLIOGRAPHY

Abdurrasyid, H. P. 2001. *Dari Cilampeni Ke New York Mengikuti Hati Nurani*. Jakarta: Pustaka Sinar Harapan.

AC Nielsen. 2001. *Survey Report on Citizens' Perceptions of the Indonesian Justice Sector, Preliminary Findings and Recommendations*. Jakarta: The Asia Foundation.

ADB. 2006. *Anti-Corruption Policies in Asia and the Pacific: Progress in Legal and Institutional Reform in 25 Countries*. Manila: Asian Development Bank and OECD.

Afandi, F. 2013. 'Diskresi Kepolisian Republik Indonesia Resort Malang Kota', *Arena Hukum* 6(3): 379–393.

Afandi, F. 2015. 'Problematika pelaksanaan diversi dalam penyidikan pidana dengan pelaku anak di kepolisian resort malang', *Arena Hukum* 8(1): 19–34.

Agung, W. 2009. 'Perkara di Court Tanjung Pinang Makin Sepi', in Tjandra, S. (ed.), *Hakim Ad hoc Menggugat: Catatan Kritis Pengadilan Hubungan Industrial*. Jakarta: TURC.

AJNN. 2017. 'Kapolres Sabang ajak Duel Kasi Pidum Kejari Sabang', 23 May. Available at: www.ajnn.net/news/kapolres-ajak-duel-kasi-pidum-kejari-sabang/index.html.

Aktual. 2017. 'Jumlah Putusan Perkara MA Menurun Dibanding Tahun Lalu', 28 December. Available at: www.aktual.com/jumlah-putusan-perkara-ma-menurun-dibanding-tahun-lalu/.

Alim, H. 2010. 'Mahkumjakpol', *Kompas*, 18 May. Available at: https://gagasanhukum.wordpress.com/tag/mahkamah-agung/.

Amaliyah et al. 2015. *Realitas Penjara Indonesia: Survei Kualitas Layanan Pemasyarakatan*. Jakarta: Center of Detention Studies.

Amanda, P. K. 2014. 'Juvenile Sex Offender Rehabilitation: How the US Approach Can Help Indonesia Satisfy Its Commitment to Restorative Justice Principles', *Indonesia Law Review* 7(1): 86–115.

Ambarita, D. D. 2012. 'Vonis Bebas Pengadilan Tipikor: 14 Terdakwa Divonis Bebas Dalam 4 Hari', *Tribune News*, 10 January. Available at: www.tribunnews.com/nasional/2012/01/10/14-terdakwa-divonis-bebas-dalam-4-hari.

Amnesty International. 2001. *Amnesty International's Comments on the Law on Human Rights Courts (Law No. 26/2000)*. AI Index: ASA 21/005/2001. Available at: www.refworld.org/docid/3c29def1a.html.

Amnesty International. 2002. *Indonesia: Impunity and Human Rights Violations in Papua*. AI Index: ASA 21/010/2002. Available at: https://reliefweb.int/report/indonesia/indonesia-impunity-and-human-rights-violations-papua.

Anderson, Benedict. 2011. 'Foreword', in Lev, D. S. (ed.), *No Concessions: The Life of Yap Thiem Hien, Indonesian Human Rights Lawyer*. Seattle, WA: University of Washington Press.

Anggara, N. E. and Hernowo, A. A. 2016. *Studi Implementasi Penanganan Anak di Pengadilan berdasarkan UU SPPA*. Jakarta: Institute for Criminal Justice Reform.

Antlov, H. 2013. 'Village Leaders and the New Order', in Antlov, H. and Cederroth, S. (eds.), Leadership on Java: Gentle Hints, Authoritarian Rule. Routledge.

Antons, C. 2011. 'The Intellectual Property Jurisdiction of the Indonesian Commercial Court', in Antons, Christoph (eds.), *The Enforcement of Intellectual Property Rights: Comparative Perspectives from the Asia-Pacific Region*. The Hague: Kluwer Law International, pp. 363–382.

Arinanto, S. 2018. 'Desperately Reforming Legal System', *The Jakarta Post*, 22 May.

Aritonang, M. S. 2012. 'Govt Considers Shutting Down Corruption Courts in Regions', *The Jakarta Post*, 21 August. Available at: www.thejakartapost.com/news/2012/08/21/govt-considers-shutting-down-corruption-courts-regions.html.

Armytage, L. (ed.) 2009. *Searching for Success in Judicial Reform: Voices from the Asia Pacific Experience*. Oxford: Oxford University Press.

Arsil. 2010. *Sekelumit Masalah Pengadilan Khusus*. Jakarta: Lembaga Kajian dan Advokasi untuk Independensi Peradilan (LeIP).

Arsil, Hertanto, H., Farihah, L. and Mahkamah Agung, P. 2016. *Pengurangan Arus Perkara ke Mahkamah Agung*. Jakarta. Available at: from http://leip.or.id/wp-content/uploads/2017/05/Kertas-Kebijakan-Pengurangan-Arus-Perkara-ke-MA_Final-versi-PDF.pdf.

Arsil, K. 2018. 'Inkonsistensi Sikap MA dalam Perkara Narkotika', *Hukumonline*, 2 February. Available at: www.hukumonline.com/berita/baca/lt5a73e81c17a51/inkonsistensi-sikap-ma-dalam-perkara-narkotika/.

ASEAN Law Association. 2005. *Legal Systems in ASEAN: Indonesia*. Available at: www.aseanlawassociation.org/legal-indonesia.html.

Aspinall, E. 2018. *Twenty Years of Indonesian Democracy: How Many More?*. Available at: www.newmandala.org/20-years-reformasi/.

Aspinall, E. 2016. 'The New Nationalism in Indonesia', *Asia & the Pacific Policy Studies* 3(1): 72.

Assegaf, I. 2002. 'Legends of the Fall: An Institutional Analysis of Indonesian Law Enforcement Agencies Combating Corruption', in Lindsey, T. and Dick, H. W. (eds.), *Corruption in Asia: Rethinking the Governance Paradigm*. Leichhardt: Federation Press.

Assegaf, R. S. 2004. 'Perubahan UU Bidang Peradilan: Momentum Pembaruan yang Disia-siakan', *Dictum* 2: 95.

Assegaf, R. S. 2007. 'Judicial Reform in Indonesia, 1998–2006', in Sakumoto, N. and Juwana, H. (eds.), *Reforming Laws and Institutions in Indonesia: An Assessment*. Chiba: Institute of Developing Economies (IDE)/Japan External Trade Organization (JETRO).

Assegaf, R. 2015. 'Pretrial Hearings: Who Will Fix the Mess?' *Indonesia at Melbourne*, 7 July. Available at: http://indonesiaatmelbourne.unimelb.edu.au/pretrial-hearings-who-will-fix-the-mess.

Assegaf, R.S. 2018a, '20 years of judicial reform: mission not yet accomplished' (*Indonesia at Melbourne*, 2 May) http://indonesiaatmelbourne.unimelb.edu.au/20-years-of-judicial-reform-mission-not-accomplished.

Assegaf, R.S., 2018b 'Sentencing Guidance in Indonesia's Criminal Code Reform Bill: For Whose Benefit?' 19(1) Australian Journal of Asian Law 1 https://papers.ssrn.com/sol3/Delivery.cfm/SSRN_ID3239777_code1807995 .pdf?abstractid=3239777&mirid=1

Assegaf, R. S. Forthcoming. 'Injustice and Inconsistency: Sentencing Minor Property Offences Post Supreme Court Regulation 2 of 2012'. Jakarta.

Austin, G. 1999. *Working a Democratic Constitution: A History of the Indian Experience*. New Delhi: Oxford University Press.

A'yun, R. Q. 2014. 'The Problems of Expert Witness in Criminal Law', *Indonesia Law Review* 4(3): 340–357.

Badan Diklat Kejaksaan. 2016. 'Ceramah Pimpinan Ketua Umum Persatuan Jaksa Indonesia' (Speech of the Indonesian Prosecutor's Association) 25 October. Available at: https://badiklatkejaksaan.net/ceramah-pimpinan-ketua-umum-persatuan-jaksa-indonesia/.

Badan Pusat Statistik. 2013. *Survei Sosial Ekonomi Nasional (SUSENAS)*. Jakarta: Badan Pusat Statisk.

Baker, J. 2015. 'Professionalism without Reform: The Security Sector under Yudhoyono', in Aspinall, E., Mietzner, M. and Tomsa, D. (eds.), *The Yudhoyono Presidency: Indonesia's Decade of Stability and Stagnation*. Singapore: Institute of Southeast Asian Studies, pp. 114–135.

BAPPENAS. 2003. *White Paper on Employment*. Jakarta: Bappenas.

BAPPENAS. 2014. *Rancangan Awal Rencana Pembangunan Jangka Menengah Nasional 2015-2019, Buku I Agenda Pembangunan Nasional*. Jakarta: Badan Perencanaan Pembangunan Nasional.

BAPPENAS. 2016. 'Perkembangan UMKM Dan Koperasi', *Warta KUMKM* 5(1). Jakarta: Badan Perencanaan Pembangunan Nasional.

Batserin, L. 2009. 'Hukum Acara Court dan Pengalaman Aktual Hakim Ad hoc Court Manado', in Tjandra, S. (ed.), *Hakim Ad hoc Menggugat: Catatan Kritis Pengadilan Hubungan Industrial*. Jakarta: TURC, pp. 27–43.

Batubara, H. 2016a. 'Ahok jadi tersangka, hashtag #KamiAhok trending topic di Twitter', *Detik News*, November 16. Available at: https://news.detik.com/berita/d-3346565/ahok-jadi-tersangka-hashtag-kamiahok-trending-topic-di-twitter.

Batubara, H. 2016b. 'Sidang putusan Jessica Kumala Wongso jadi topik utama di jagat raya', *Detik News*, October 27. Available at: https://news.detik.com/berita/d-3330893/sidang-putusan-jessica-kumala-wongso-jadi-topik-utama-di-jagat-maya.

Bedner, A. 2001. *Administrative Courts in Indonesia: A Socio-Legal Study*. The Hague: Kluwer Law International.

Bedner, A. 2008. 'Rebuilding the Judiciary in Indonesia: The Special Courts Strategy', *Yuridika* 23(3): 230–253.

Bedner, A. 2009. '"Shopping Forums": Administrative Courts in Indonesia', in Harding, A. and Nicholson, P. (eds.), *New Courts in Asia*. Oxford: Hart Publishing, pp. 167–180.

Bedner, A. 2010. 'An Elementary Approach to the Rule of Law', *The Hague Journal on the Rule of Law* 2(1): 48–74.

Bedner, A. 2013. 'Indonesian Legal Scholarship and Jurisprudence as an Obstacle for Transplanting Legal Institutions', *Hague Journal on the Rule of Law* 5(2): 253–273.

Bedner, A. 2016. 'Autonomy of law in Indonesia', *Recht der Werkelijkheid* 37: 10–36.

Bedner, A. 2018. 'Ombudspersons in Developing Countries: The Case of Indonesia', in Hertogh, M. and Kirkham R. (eds.), *Research Handbook on the Ombudsman*. Cheltenham: Edward Elgar Publishing, pp. 167–187.

Bedner, A. and Huis, S. C. van. 2010. 'Plurality of Marriage Law and Marriage Registration for Muslims in Indonesia: A Plea for Pragmatism', *Utrecht Law Review* 6(2): 175–191.

Bell, G. 2017. 'Indonesia's Weak State Courts and Weak Law Fare Poorly in a Pluralist Commercial World', in Bell, G. (ed.), *Pluralism, Transnationalism and Culture in Asian Law: A Book in Honour of M. B. Hooker*. Singapore: ISEAS, pp. 116–150.

Benda-Beckmann, K. von. 2009. 'Balancing Islam, Adat and the State: Comparing Islamic and Civil Courts in Indonesia', in Benda-Beckmann, F. von, Benda-Beckmann, K. von and Griffiths, A. M. O. (eds.), *The Power of Law in a Transnational World: Anthropological Enquiries*. New York: Berghahn Books, pp. 216–235.

Benda-Beckmann, F. von. and Benda-Beckmann, K. von. 2011. 'Myths and Stereotypes about Adat Law: A Reassessment of Van Vollenhoven in the Light of Current Struggles over Adat law in Indonesia', *Bijdragen tot de Taal-, Land en Volkenkunde* 167(2/3): 167–195.

Bergoglio, M. I. 2003. 'Argentina: The Effects of Democratic Institutionalization', in Friedman, L. M. and Perez-Perdomo, R. (eds.), *Legal Culture in the Age of Globalization: Latin America and Latin Europe*. Stanford: Stanford University Press.

Berita Satu. 2011a. 'Hakim Syarifuddin Diduga Terlibat Dalam 30 Vonis Bebas Koruptor', 3 June. Available at: http://sp.beritasatu.com/home/hakim-syarifud din-diduga-terlibat-dalam-30-vonis-bebas-koruptor/7494.

Berita Satu. 2011b. 'Syarifuddin Protes Kasusnya Melebar', 8 June. Available at: http://sp.beritasatu.com/home/syarifuddin-protes-kasusnya-melebar/ 7612.

Berita Satu. 2015. 'Petinggi Polda Maluku ancam tembak Jaksa', 1 July. Available at: www.beritasatu.com/hukum/287332-petinggi-polda-maluku-ancam-tembak-prosecutor.html.

Boey, K. Y. 2016. 'Trikomsel Move Shuts out Singapore Bondholders', *Reuters*, 11 February. Available at: www.reuters.com/article/trikomsel-oke-debt-bonds/ trikomsel-move-shuts-out-singapore-bondholders-idUSL3N15Q150.

Boulton, A. J. 2002. *The Future Structure of Industrial Relations in Indonesia: Some Issues and Challenges*. Jakarta: International Labour Organization.

Bourchier, D. 1982. *Dynamics of Dissent in Indonesia: Sawito and the Phantom Coup*. Ithaca, NY: Cornell Modern Indonesia Project.

Bourchier, D. 1999. 'Magic Memos, Collusion and Judges with Attitude: Notes on the Politics of Law in Contemporary Indonesia', in Jayasuriya, K. (ed.), *Law, Capitalism and Power in Asia*. London: Routledge.

Bourdieu, P. 1977. *Outline of a Theory of Practice*. Cambridge: Cambridge University Press.

Bowen, J. R. 2003. *Islam, Law and Equality in Indonesia*. Cambridge: Cambridge University Press.

Brata, R. A. 2014. *Why Did Anticorruption Fail? A Study of Anticorruption Policy Implementation Failure in Indonesia*. Charlotte, NC: Information Age Publishing.

Brewer-Carías, A. R. 2013. *Constitutional Courts as Positive Legislators: A Comparative Law Study*. Cambridge: Cambridge University Press.

Bruinessen, M. van. 1995. 'Shari'a Court, Tarekat and Pesantren: Religious Institutions in the Banten Sultanate', *Archipel: Études Interdisciplinaires Sur Le Monde Insulindien* 50: 165–200.

Bruinessen, M. van. 1996. 'Islamic State or State Islam? Fifty Years of State-Islam Relations in Indonesia', in Wessel, I. (ed.), *Indonesien am Ende des 20. Jahrhunderts: Analysen zu 50 Jahren unabhängiger Entwicklung: Deutsche in Indonesien*. Hamburg: Abera Verlag Meyer & Co., pp. 31–58.

Burns, J. J. 1980. 'Civil Courts and the Development of Commercial Relations: The Case of North Sumatra', *Law & Society Review* 15(2): 347–368.

Burns, P. 2004. *The Leiden Legacy: Concepts of Law in Indonesia*. Leiden: KITLV Press.

Butt, S. 1999. 'Polygamy and Mixed Marriage in Indonesia: The Application of the Marriage Law', in Lindsey, T. (ed.), *Indonesia: Law and Society*. Sydney: Federation Press, pp. 122–144.

Butt, S. 2008. 'Indonesian Terrorism Law and Criminal Process', *Islam, Syari'ah and Governance Background Paper Series*. Melbourne: ARC Federation Fellowship, The University of Melbourne.

Butt, S. 2011a. 'Anti-Corruption Reform in Indonesia: An Obituary?', *Bulletin of Indonesian Economic Studies* 47(3): 381–394.

Butt, S. 2011b. 'Corruption, Law, Politics and Frame-Ups: The Plot to Dismantle Indonesia's Anti-Corruption Commission', *Harvard Asia Pacific Review* 11(2).

Butt, S. 2012. *Corruption and Law in Indonesia*. London, New York: Routledge.

Butt, S. 2013. 'Freedom of Information Law and Its Application in Indonesia: A Preliminary Assessment', *Asian Journal of Comparative Law* 8(1): 1–42.

Butt, S. 2015a. *The Constitutional Court and Democracy in Indonesia*. Leiden: Brill Nijhoff.

Butt, S. 2015b. 'The Rule of Law and Anti-Corruption Reforms under Yudhoyono: The Rise of the KPK and the Constitutional Court', in Aspinall, E., Mietzner, M. and Tomsa, D. (eds.), *The Yudhoyono Presidency: Indonesia's Decade of Stability and Stagnation*. Singapore: ISEAS Publishing, pp. 175–195.

Butt, S. 2018. 'Judicial Reasoning and Review in the Indonesian Supreme Court', *Asian Journal of Law and Society*, pp. 1–31.

Butt, S., Dixon, R. and Crouch, M. 2016. 'Special Issue: The First Decade of Indonesia's Constitutional Court', *Australian Journal of Asian Law* 16(2): 1–7.

Butt, S. and Lindsey, T. 2011. 'Judicial Mafia: The Courts and State Illegality Indonesia', in Aspinall, E. and van Klinken, G. (eds.), *The State and Illegality in Indonesia*. Leiden: KITLV Press.

Butt, S. and Lindsey, T. 2012. *The Constitution of Indonesia: A Contextual Analysis*. Oxford: Hart Publishing.

Butt, S. and Lindsey, T. 2018. *Indonesian Law*. Oxford: Oxford University Press.

Butt, S. and Parsons, N. 2014. 'Judicial Review and the Supreme Court in Indonesia: A New Space for Law?', *Indonesia* 97: 55–85.

Butt, S. and Schutte, S. 2014. 'Assessing Judicial Performance in Indonesia: The Court for Corruption Crimes', *Crime, Law and Social Change* 62(5): 603–619.

Cammack, M. 2007. 'The Indonesian Islamic Judiciary', in Feener, M. and Cammack, M. (eds.), *Islamic Law in Contemporary Indonesia: Ideas and Institutions*. Cambridge: Harvard University Press, pp. 146–169.

Cammack, M. 2010. 'Indonesia's Human Rights Court', in Harding, A. and Nicholson, P. (eds.), *New Courts in Asia*. London: Routledge.

Cammack, M. 2016. 'Crimes against Humanity in East Timor', in Sellars, K. (ed.), *Trials of International Crimes in Asia*. Cambridge: Cambridge University Press, pp. 191–225.

Cammack, M., Bedner, A. and Huis, S. C. van. 2015. 'Democracy, Human Rights, and Islamic Family Law in Post-Soeharto Indonesia', *New Middle Eastern Studies* 5: 1–24.

Cammack, M., Young, L. A. and Heaton, T. 1996. 'Legislating Social Change in an Islamic Society: Indonesia's Marriage Law', *The American Journal of Comparative Law* 44(1): 45–73.

Carrillo, J. 2011. 'To Influence, Shape, and Globalize: Popular Legal Culture and Law' in Gordon, R. W. and Horwitz, M. J. (eds.), Law, Society, and History: Themes in the Legal Sociology and Legal History of Lawrence M. Friedman. Cambridge University Press.

Chandra, S. 2016. *Labour Law and Development in Indonesia*. PhD thesis, University of Leiden. Available at: https://openaccess.leidenuniv.nl/handle/1887/37576.

Chauvel, R. 2003. *Essays on West Papua Volume Two*. Clayton: Monash Asia Institute/Monash University Press.

Chazawi, A. 2011. *Lembaga Peninjauan Kembali (PK) Perkara Pidana: Penegakan Hukum dalam Penyimpangan Praktik dan Peradilan Sesat*. Jakarta: Sinar Grafika.

Churchill, G. 1992. *The Development of the Legal Information Systems in Indonesia: Problems and Progress to Date*. Leiden: Van Vollenhoven Institute No 92/1.

Churchill, G. 2000. 'Indonesian Bankruptcy Reforms: A Chronological Overview', in Lindsey, T. (ed.), *Indonesia, Bankruptcy, Law Reform and the Commercial Court*. Sydney: Desert Pea Press, Appendix I.

Clancy, K. et al. 1981. 'Sentence Decision-Making: The Logic of Sentence Decisions and the Extent and Sources of Sentence Disparity', *The Journal of Criminal Law & Criminology* 72(2): 524.

CNN Indonesia. 2016. 'Mensos Targetkan 2018 Tak Ada Anak di Penjara Dewasa', 15 August. Available at: www.cnnindonesia.com/nasional/20160815070803–12-151351/mensos-targetkan-2018-tak-ada-anak-di-penjara-dewasa.

Cochrane, J. 2018. 'Top Indonesian Official, Long Seen as Untouchable, Gets Prison for Graft', *New York Times*, 24 April. Available at: www.nytimes.com/2018/04/24/world/asia/indonesia-setya-novanto-corruption.html.

Cohen, D. 2003. 'Intended to Fail: The Trials Before the Ad Hoc Human Rights Courts in Jakarta', *International Center for Transitional Justice Occasional Paper Series*. Available at: www.ictj.org/sites/default/files/ICTJ-Indonesia-Rights-Court-2003-English.pdf.

Colmey, J. and Liebhold, D. 1999. 'Suharto Inc: The Family Firm', *BBC News*, 24 May. Available at: http://news.bbc.co.uk/2/hi/business/3567745.stm.

Cooney, S. and Mitchel, R. 2002. 'Labour Law and Labour Market Regulation in East Asian States: Problems and Issues for Comparative Inquiry', in Cooney et al. (eds.), *Law and Labor Market Regulation in East Asia*. Routledge.

Córdova, E. 1984. *Industrial Relations in Latin America*. New York: Praeger.

Cotterrell, R. 1983. 'The Sociological Concept of Law', *Journal of Law and Society* 10: 241–55.

Cotterrell, R. 1995. *Law's Community: Legal Theory in Sociological Perspective.* New York: Oxford University Press.

Cotterrell, R. 1997. 'The Concept of Legal Culture', in Nelken, D. (ed.), *Comparing Legal Cultures.* Aldershot: Dartmouth, pp. 13–32.

Cotterell, R. 2004. 'Law in Culture', *Ratio Juris* 17(1): 1–14.

Cotterell, R. 2006. *Law, Culture and Society: Legal Ideas in the Mirror of Social Theory.* Aldershot: Ashgate.

Cotterell, R. 2006. 'Comparative Law and Legal Culture', in Reimann, M. and Zimmerman, R. (eds.), *The Oxford Handbook of Comparative Law.* Oxford: Oxford University Press, pp. 710–737.

Cribb, R. 2005. 'Circles of Esteem, Standard Works, and Euphoric Couplets: Dynamics of Academic Life in Indonesian Studies', *Critical Asian Studies* 37(2): 289–304.

Crouch, H. 2010. *Political Reform in Indonesia after Suharto.* Singapore: ISEAS Publishing.

Crouch, M. 2007. 'The Yogyakarta Local Ombudsman: Promoting Good Governance through Local Support', *Asian Journal of Comparative Law* 2(1): 219–246.

Crouch, M. 2008. 'Indonesia's National & Local Ombudsman Reforms', in Lindsey T. (ed.), *Indonesia: Law and Society* (2nd edn). Sydney: Federation Press, ISEAS, pp. 382–406.

Crouch, M. 2009. 'Religious Regulations in Indonesia: Failing Vulnerable Groups', *Review of Indonesian and Malaysian Affairs* 43(2): 53–103.

Crouch, M. 2011. 'Cause Lawyering, the Legal Profession and the Courts in Indonesia: The Bar Association Controversy', *LawASIA Journal*: 63–86.

Crouch, M. 2012a. 'The Indonesian Blasphemy Case: Affirming the Legality of the Blasphemy Law', *Oxford Journal of Law and Religion* 1(2): 514–518.

Crouch, M. 2012b. 'Judicial Review and Religious Freedom: The Case of Indonesian Ahmadis', *Sydney Law Review* 34(3)(September): 545–572.

Crouch, M. 2012c. 'No Concessions: The Life of Yap Thiam Hien, Indonesian Human Rights Lawyer', *Australian Journal of Asian Law* 13(1): 1–4.

Crouch, M. 2013. 'Asian Legal Transplants and Lessons on the Rule of Law: National Human Rights Commissions in Indonesia and Myanmar', *Hague Journal of the Rule of Law* 5(2): 146–177.

Crouch, M. 2014. *Law and Religion in Indonesia: Conflict and the Courts in West Java.* London, New York: Routledge.

Crouch, M. 2016a. 'Islamic Law and Society in Southeast Asia', in Emon, A. M. and Ahmed, R. (eds.), *The Oxford Handbook on Islamic Law.* New York: Oxford University Press, pp. 1–25.

Crouch, M. 2016b. 'Constitutionalism, Islam and the Practise of Religious Deference: The Case of the Indonesian Constitutional Court', *Australian Journal of Asian Law* 16(2): 1–15.

Crouch, M. 2017a. 'The Expansion of Emergency Powers: Social Conflict and the Military in Indonesia', *Asian Studies Review* 41(3): 459–475.

Crouch, M. 2017b. 'Negotiating Legal Pluralism in Court: Fatwa and the Crime of Blasphemy in Indonesia', in Bell, G. (ed.), *Pluralism, Transnationalism and Culture in Asia: A Book in Honour of M B Hooker*. Singapore: ISEAS, pp. 231–257.

Crouch, M. 2018. 'Religion, Constitutionalism and Inequality: Perspectives from Asia', *Asian Journal of Comparative Law* 13(2): 233–243.

Crouch, M. (forthcoming) 'Constitution-making and Public Participation in Southeast Asia', in Landau, D. and Lerner, H. (eds.), *Constitution-Making*. Cheltenham: Edward Elgar.

Crouch, M. and Missbach, A. 2013. 'The Criminalisation of People Smuggling: The Dynamics of Judicial Discretion in Indonesia', *Australian Journal of Asian Law* 14(2): 1–19.

Dakolias, M. 1995. 'A Strategy for Judicial Reform: The Experience in Latin America', *Virginia Journal of International Law* 36: 167.

Danubrata, E. 2015. 'Bakrie Telecom debt ploy exposes new foreign investor pitfall in Indonesia', *Reuters*, 19 February. Available at: www.reuters.com/article/us-bakrie-telecom-debt/bakrie-telecom-debt-ploy-exposes-new-foreign-investor-pitfall-in-indonesia-idUSKBN0LM2EN20150219.

Davidson, J. S. 2007. 'Politics-as-usual on Trial: Regional Anti-corruption Campaigns in Indonesia', *The Pacific Review* 20(1): 75–99.

Davies, P. H. J., 2001. 'Spies as Informants: Triangulation and the Interpretation of Elite Interview Data in the Study of the Intelligence and Security Services', *Politics* 21(1): 73.

Davies, S. G. and Robson, J. 2016. 'Juvenile (in)Justice: Children in Conflict with the Law in Indonesia', *Asia-Pacific Journal on Human Rights and the Law* 17: 119–147.

Dermawan, M. K. et al. 2007. *Analisis Situasi Anak yang Berhadapan dengan Hukum di Indonesia*. Indonesia: UNICEF and Pusat Kajian Kriminolog.

Detik News. 2011a. 'Pengadilan Tipikor Daerah, Kebijakan Setengah Hati', 7 November. Available at: https://news.detik.com/berita/1761492/pengadilan-tipikor-daerah-kebijakan-setengah-hati.

Detik News. 2011b. 'Gelapkan Uang Hasil Pailit, Dua Kurator Terancam 15 Tahun Bui', 19 December. Available at: https://news.detik.com/berita/d-1795073/gelap kan-uang-hasil-pailit-dua-kurator-terancam-15-tahun-bui.

Detik News. 2011c. 'Akui kenal Imas hakim Arif Sudjito bantah jadi perantara' 18 July at https://news.detik.com/berita/1683711/akui-kenal-imas-hakim-arif-sudjito-bantah-jadi-perantara.

Detik News. 2015. 'Cara 'Kreatif' Bakrie Telecom Bereskan Utang Triliunan Rupiah', 20 February. Available at: https://finance.detik.com/bursa-dan-valas/d-2838363/cara-kreatif-bakrie-telecom-bereskan-utang-triliunan-rupiah.

Detik News. 2016a. 'Sidang Putusan Jessica Kumala Wongso jadi topik utama di jagat maya', 27 October. Available at: https://news.detik.com/berita/d-3330893/sidang-putusan-jessica-kumala-wongso-jadi-topik-utama-di-jagat-maya.

Detik News. 2016b. 'Kisah Ahok Jessica Wongso dan siding Terbuka', 19 November. Available at: https://news.detik.com/berita/d-3349144/kisah-ahok-jessica-wongso-dan-sidang-terbuka.

Detik News. 2017. 'Kunjungan Kerja ke Belanda-Spanyol, Ketua MA: Belajar Sistem Kamar', 1 March. Available at: https://news.detik.com/berita/3434987/kunjungan-kerja-ke-belanda-spanyol-ketua-ma-belajar-sistem-kamar.

Dewi, F. A. 2015. 'Yudhoyono's Legacy: An Insider's View', in Aspinall, E., Mietzner, M. and Tomsa, D. (eds.), *The Yudhoyono Presidency: Indonesia's Decade of Stability and Stagnation*. Singapore: ISEAS, pp. 22–36.

Dewi, I. 2016. *Penegakan Hukum Tindak Pidana Perikanan*. Jakarta: Pusat Penelitian Badan Keahlian DPR RI & Dian Rakyat.

Dewi, Y. T. N., Niemann G. R. and Triatmodjo, M. 2017. 'Indonesia's Human Rights Court: Need for Reform', *Asia-Pacific Journal on Human Rights and the Law* 18: 38–47.

DGC (Directorate General of Corrections) 2018. *Sistem Database Pemasyarakatan*. Available at: http://smslap.ditjenpas.go.id/public/arl/current/monthly/kanwil/all/year/2018/month/1/page/50 (accessed on 9 May 2018).

Dias, J. P. 2016. 'The Transition to a Democratic Portuguese Judicial System: (Delaying) Changes in the Legal Culture', *International Journal of Law in Context* 12(1): 24.

Dick, H. and Butt, S. 2013. *Is Indonesia as Corrupt as Most People Believe and Is It Getting Worse?*, Melbourne: Centre for Indonesian Law, Islam and Society Policy Papers. Available at: https://law.unimelb.edu.au/__data/assets/pdf_file/0010/1547821/CILISPolicyPaper3-Dick_Butt_finalforweb2.pdf.

Djafar, W. and Abidin, Z. 2014. *Repressing Expression: Case Study of Blocking and Filtering of Internet Content and Criminalization of Internet Users in Indonesia*. Jakarta: Institute for Policy Research and Advocacy.

Djamin, A. 1995. *Awaloedin Djamin Pengalaman Seorang Perwira Polri*. Jakarta: Pustaka Sinar Harapan.

Djamin, A., Ratta, I. K., Gunawan, I. G. P. and Wulan, G. A. 2006. *Sejarah perkembangan kepolisian di Indonesia : dari zaman kuno sampai sekarang*. Jakarta: Yayasan Brata Bhakti.

Domingo, P. and Denney L. 2013. *The Political Economy of Pre-Trial Detention*. Overseas Development Institute.

Doorn-Harder, P. van 2007. 'Reconsidering Authority: Indonesian Fiqh Texts about Women', in Feener, M. and Cammack, M. E. (eds.), *Islamic Law in Contemporary Indonesia: Ideas and Institutions*. Cambridge: Harvard University Press, pp. 27–43.

Dressel, B. and Inoue, T. 2018. *Megapolitical Cases before the Constitutional Court of Indonesia since 2004: An Empirical Exploration.* Unpublished paper. The 2nd Indonesian Constitutional Court International Symposium, Yogyakarta.

Drexler, E. 2010. 'The Failure of International Justice in East Timor and Indonesia', in Hinton, A. L., *Transitional Justice: Global Mechanisms and Local Realities after Genocide and Mass Violence.* New Brunswick: Rutgers University Press.

Eddyono, S. W., Sriyana, S. H., Wiryawan, S. M., Wagiman, W. and Djafar, W. 2012. *Potret Penahanan Pra-Persidangan di Indonesia: Studi tentang Kebijakan Penahanan Pra-Persidangan dalam Teori dan Praktek* (M. Yasin, ed.), Jakarta: Institute for Criminal Justice Reform.

El-Awa, M. S. 1982. *Punishment in Islamic Law.* Indianapolis: American Trust Publications.

ELSAM (Lembaga Studi dan Advokasi Masyarakat). 2004. *Laporan Pemantauan Pengadilan Hak Asasi Manusia Kasus Abepura. Perkara Johny Wainal Usman dan Daud Sihombing.* Jakarta: ELSAM Centre of Research and Advocacy Archival Centre.

Emont, J., 'As Shariah Experiment Becomes a Model, Indonesia's Secular Face Slips', *The New York Times,* 12 January 2007. Available at: www.nytimes.com/2017/01/12/world/asia/indonesia-sharia-law-aceh.html

Engel, D. M. 2010. 'The Uses of Legal Culture in Contemporary Socio-Legal Studies: A Response to Sally Engle Merry', *Journal of Comparative Law* 5(2): 59–65.

Engel, D. M. and Yngvesson, B. 1984. 'Mapping Difficult Terrain "Legal Culture," "Legal Consciousness," and Other Hazards for the Intrepid Explorer', *Law and Policy* 6: 299–307.

Ewick, P. and Silbey, S. 1992. 'Conformity, Contestation and Resistance: An Account of Legal Consciousness,' *New England Law Review* 26: 731.

Fachruddin, I. 2004. *Pengawasan Peradilan Administrasi Terhadap Tindakan Pemerintah,* Bandung: Alumni.

Faivovich, E. F. 2003. 'Law and Legal Culture in Chile, 1974–1999', in Friedman, L. M. and Perez-Perdomo, R. (eds.), Legal Culture in the Age of Globalization: Latin America and Latin Europe. Stanford: Stanford University Press.

Faiz, P. M. *Keterbukaan informasi persidangan [Judicial information openness].* Jakarta: ELSAM Centre of Research and Advocacy Archival Centre.

Fajerman, M. 2011. *Report: Training Needs Assessment for Court Judges.* Jakarta: ILO Office.

Fajriando, H. 2016. 'Masalah hukum implementasi pemenuhan hak atas layanan bantuan hukum bagi masyarakat miskin', *Jurnal Penelitian HAM* 7(2): 125–140.

Falaakh, M. F. 2014. 'Legalitas Prosecutor Agung', in Falaakh, M. F. et al. (eds.), *Konsisten Mengawal Konstitusi.* Jakarta: Komisi Hukum Nasional, pp. 427–429.

Fauzan. 2009. 'Perbedaan Lingkup Kewenangan Kasasi dan Peninjauan Kembali Perkara Court', in Tjandra, S. (ed.), *Hakim Ad hoc Menggugat: Catatan Kritis Pengadilan Hubungan Industrial.* Jakarta: TURC, pp. 93–101.

Fauzi, M. L. 2013. 'Women in Local Politics: The Bylaw on Prostitution in Bantul', in *Regime Change, Democracy and Islam: The Case of Indonesia.* Leiden: Universiteit Leiden, p. 110.

Fealy, G. 2017. 'Bigger than Ahok', *Indonesia at Melbourne,* 7 December. Available at: http://indonesiaatmelbourne.unimelb.edu.au/bigger-than-ahok-explaining-jakartas-2-december-mass-rally.

Federspiel, H. M. 1998. 'Islamic Values, Law and Expectations in Contemporary Indonesia', *Islamic Law and Society* 5(1): 90–117.

Feener, R. M. 2010. *Muslim Legal Thought in Modern Indonesia.* Cambridge: Cambridge University Press.

Feener, R. M. 2014. *Sharia and Social Engineering: The Implementation of Islamic Law in Contemporary Aceh, Indonesia.* Oxford: Oxford University Press.

Feith, A. 2006. 'Justice for Papuans?', *Inside Indonesia* 87. Available at: www .insideindonesia.org/justice-for-papuans.

Fenwick, C., Lindsey, T. and Arnold, L. 2002. *Labour Dispute and Settlement Reform in Indonesia: A Guide to the Policy and Legal Issues Raised by the Industrial Disputes Settlement Bill.* Jakarta: ILO.

Fenwick, S. 2008. 'Measuring Up? Indonesia's Anti-Corruption Commission and the New Corruption Agenda', in Lindsey, T. (ed.), *Indonesia: Law and Society* (2nd edn). Sydney: The Federation Press.

Ferrarese, M. R. 1997. 'An Entrepreneurial Conception of the Law: The American Model through Italian Eyes', in Nelken, D. (ed.), *Comparing Legal Cultures.* London: Routledge.

Firmanto, D., Purnomo, W. A. and Faiz, A. 2017. 'Building the Case against KPK', *Tempo English Edition.*

Fiss, O. M. 1992. 'The Right Degree of Independence', in Stotzky, I. P. (ed.), *Transition to Democracy in Latin America: The Role of the Judiciary.* Boulder, CO: Westview Press.

Fitzpatrick, D. 2008. 'Culture, Ideology and Human Rights: The Case of Indonesia's Code of Criminal Procedure', in Lindsey, T. (ed.), *Indonesia: Law and Society* (2nd edn). Sydney: The Federation Press.

Foussard, C. and Giulia, M. 2016. *Addressing Juvenile Justice Priorities in the Asia-Pacific Region.* Belgium: International Juvenile Justice Observatory.

Ford, M. 2007. *Evaluation of Project Legal Protection for Trade Unionists in Indonesia.* Bonn: DGB Bildungswerk.

Fraksi TNI Polri. 2002. *Tanggapan atas Usul Rancangan Undang-Undang Usul Inisiatif tentang Perikanan.* Jakarta: Fraksi TNI Polri.

Friedman, L. M. 1969. 'Legal Culture and Social Development', *Law and Society Review* 4: 29–44.

Friedman, L. M. 1975. *The Legal System: A Social Science Perspective*. New York: Russel Sage Foundation.

Friedman, L. M. 1977. *Law and Society: An Introduction* (Prentice-Hall Foundation Sociology Series). London: Pearson College Division.

Friedman, L. 1985. *Total Justice*. Russell Sage Foundation.

Friedman, L. M. 1994. 'Is There a Modern Legal Culture?', *Ratio Juris* 7(2): 117–131.

Friedman, L. M. 1997. 'The Concept of a Legal Culture: A Reply', in Nelken, D. (ed.), *Comparing Legal Cultures*. Aldershot: Dartmouth, pp. 33–40.

Friedman, L. M. 2006. 'The Place of Legal Culture in the Sociology of Law', in Freeman, M. (ed.), *Law and Sociology*. Oxford: Oxford University Press.

Gabrillin, A. 2016. 'Divonis Untuk Dua Kasus Berbeda, Hukuman Nazaruddin Jadi 13 Tahun Penjara', *Kompas.com*, 16 June. Available at: http://nasional.kompas.com/read/2016/06/16/07530431/divonis.untuk.dua.kasus.berbeda.huku man.nazaruddin.jadi.13.tahun.penjara.

Gatra. 2012a. 'Tergelincir Aset Budel Pailit', 11 January. Available at: http://arsip.gatra.com/2012–01-07/majalah/artikel.php?id=150869.

Gatra. 2012b. 'Intervensi Berlabel Pengawasan', 14 March. Available at: http://arsip.gatra.com/2012–03-14/majalah/artikel.php?id=151350.

Geertz, C. 1964. 'Ideology as a Cultural System', in Apter, D. (ed.), *Ideology and Discontent*. New York: Free Press.

Geertz, C. 1971. 'Thick Description: Toward an Interpretive Theory of Culture', in *The Interpretation of Cultures*. New York: Basic Books.

Geertz, C. 1976. *The Religion of Java*. Chicago: University of Chicago Press.

Geertz, C. 1983. 'Local Knowledge: Fact and Law in Comparative Perspective', in *Local Knowledge: Further Essays in Interpretive Anthropology*. New York: Basic Books.

Goodpaster, G. 2000. 'Indonesian Bankruptcy: The Case of the Phantom Creditors', *Australian Journal of Asian Law* 2(2): 217–218.

Goodpaster, G. 2002. 'Reflections on Corruption in Indonesia', in Lindsey, T. and Dick, H. W. (eds.), *Corruption in Asia: Rethinking the Governance Paradigm*. Sydney: The Federation Press.

Grodeland, A. B. and Miller, W. L. 2015. *European Legal Cultures in Transition*. Cambridge University Press.

Halim, H. 2016. 'Suryadharma Gets 6 Years for Haj Scam', *Jakarta Post*, 12 January. Available at: www.thejakartapost.com/news/2016/01/12/suryadharma-gets-6-years-haj-scam.html.

Halliday, T. C. and Carruthers, B. G. 2009. *Bankrupt: Global Lawmaking and Systemic Financial Crisis*. Stanford: Stanford University Press.

Hammergren, L. 2007. *Envisioning Reform: Improving Judicial Performance in Latin America*. University Park, PA: Pennsylvania State University Press.

Hamzah, A. 1984. *Korupsi Di Indonesia: Masalah Dan Pemecahannya*. Jakarta: Gramedia.

Hanartani, M. M. (n.d.), *UU No. 2 tahun 2004 tentang Penyelesaian Perselisihan Hubungan Industrial*. Jakarta: Departemen Tenaga Kerja.

Hanstein, T. 2002. *Islamisches Recht und Nationales Recht: Eine Untersuchung zum Einfluß des Islamischen Rechts auf die Entwicklung des Modernen Familienrechts am Beispiel Indonesiens*. Frankfurt am Main: Peter Lang.

Harahap, M. Y. 2007. *Pembahasan Permasalahan dan Penerapan KUHAP (Penyidikan dan Penuntutan)*. Jakarta: Sinar Grafika.

Harkrisnowo, H., Hikmahanto, Juwana and Yu Un, Oppusunggu. 2018. *Law and Justice in a Globalized World*. London: Routledge.

Harman, B. 2017. 'DPR Apresiasi Berkurangnya Tunggakan Perkara di MA', *Netralnews*, 15 March. Available at: www.netralnews.com/news/nasional/read/1584/dprapresiasiberkurangnyatunggakanperkaradima.

Hawkins, K. (1992) 'The Use of Legal Discretion: Perspectives from Law and Social Science' in Hawkins, K. (ed.), The Uses of Discretion. Oxford: Clarendon Press.

He, W. F. 1994. 'The Methodology of Comparative Study of Legal Cultures', *Asia Pacific Law Review* 3: 37–44.

Hendrianto, S. 2013. *The Indonesian Constitutional Court at a Tipping Point*. Available at: www.iconnectblog.com/2013/10/the-indonesian-constitutional-court-at-a-tipping-point/.

Hendrianto, S. 2018. *Law and Politics of Constitutional Courts: Indonesia and the Search for Judicial Heroes*. London: Routledge.

Hepple, B. (ed.) 1986. *The Making of Labour Law in Europe: A Comparative Study of Nine Countries Up To 1945*. London: Mansell Publishing Ltd.

Herdiyanto, E. and Achmad Z. A. 2013. 'Kebijakan mediasi penal pada kasus pencurian di kepolisian Surakarta', *Jurnal Masalah-Masalah Hukum* 42(2): 244–250.

Herlambang, P. W. 2014. *Press Freedom, Law and Politics in Indonesia: A Socio-Legal Study*. PhD thesis, University of Leiden. Available at: https://openaccess.leidenuniv.nl/handle/1887/30106.

Hernawan, B. 2016. 'Torture as Theatre in Papua', *International Journal of Conflict and Violence* 10(1): 77–92.

Hirschi, T. 2017. *Causes of Delinquency*. London: Routledge.

Hisyam, M. 2001. *Caught between Three Fires: The Javanese Pangulu under the Dutch Colonial Administration, 1882–1942*. Jakarta: INIS.

Hockey, J. and James, A. 1993. *Growing Up and Growing Old: Ageing and Dependency in the Life Course*. London: Sage.

Hoff, J. 1999. *Indonesian Bankruptcy Law*. Jakarta: PT Tata Nusa.

Holmes, S. 2004. 'Judicial Independence as Ambiguous Reality and Insidious Illusion', in Dworkin, R. (ed.), *From Liberal Values to Democratic Transition: Essays in Honour of János Kis*. Budapest: Central European University Press, pp. 3–14.

Honna, J., 2010. 'The Legacy of New Order Military in Local Politics: West, Central and East Java', in Aspinall, E. and Fealy, G. (eds.), *Soeharto's New Order and Its Legacy*. ANU E Press.

Hooker, M. B. 2008. *Indonesian Syariah: Defining a National School of Islamic Law*. ISEAS Publishing.

Hooker, M. B. and Lindsey, T. 2002. 'Public Faces of "Syarī'ah" in Contemporary Indonesia: Towards a National "Mażhab"?', *The Australian Journal of Asian Law* 4(3): 259–294.

Horowitz, D. L. 1994. 'The Qur'an and the Common Law: Islamic Law Reform and the Theory of Legal Change', *American Journal of Comparative Law* 42(2): 233–293.

Horowitz, D. L. 1994. 'The Qur'an and the Common Law: Islamic Law Reform and the Theory of Legal Change (Part II)', *American Journal of Comparative Law* 42 (3): 543–580.

Horowitz, D. L. 2013. *Constitutional Change and Democracy in Indonesia*. Cambridge: Cambridge University Press.

Hosen, N. 2005. 'Religion and the Indonesian Constitution: A Recent Debate', *Journal of Southeast Asian Studies* 36(3): 419–440.

Hosen, N. 2017. 'The Indonesian Courts: From Non-Independence to Independence without Accountability', in Lee, H. P. and Pittard, M. (eds.), *Asia-Pacific Judiciaries: Independence, Impartiality and Integrity*. Cambridge: Cambridge University Press.

Huis, S. C. V. 2015. *Islamic Courts and Women's Divorce Rights in Indonesia: The Cases of Cianjur and Bulukumba*. PhD thesis, University of Leiden. Available at: https://openaccess.leidenuniv.nl/handle/1887/35081.

Huis, S. C. van and Wirastri, T. D. 2012. 'Muslim Marriage Registration in Indonesia: Revised Marriage Registration Laws Cannot Overcome Compliance Flaws', *Australian Journal of Asian Law* 13(1): 1–17.

Hukumonline. 2000a. 'Kuasa Hukum Kreditur Davomas Minta Cek Ulang Kreditur Fiktif', 11 September. Available at: www.hukumonline.com/berita/baca/hol587/kuasa-hukum-kreditur-davomas-minta-cek-ulang-kreditur-fiktif-.

Hukumonline. 2000b. 'Hari ini Nasib Davomas Ditentukan', 12 September. Available at: www.hukumonline.com/berita/baca/hol588/hari-ini-nasib-davomas-ditentukan.

Hukumonline. 2001. 'Kontroversi di Pengadilan Niaga I Fadel Pailit, Panca Overseas Lolos', 31 December. Available at: www.hukumonline.com/berita/

baca/hol4490/font-size1-colorff0000bkontroversi-di-pengadilan-niaga-ibfontbr–fadel-pailit-panca-overseas-lolos.

Hukumonline. 2002a. 'Lucas Ikut Deklarasikan Ikatan Kurator dan Pengurus Indonesia', 12 March. Available at: www.hukumonline.com/berita/baca/ hol5062/lucas-ikut-deklarasikan-ikatan-kurator-dan-pengurus-indonesia.

Hukumonline. 2002b. 'IKAPI Gugat Kepengurusan AKPI', 6 June. Available at: www.hukumonline.com/berita/baca/hol5724/ikapi-gugat-kepengurusan-akpi.

Hukumonline. 2002c. 'Pengawasan Tingkah Laku Kurator Akan Diperketat', 12 December. Available at: www.hukumonline.com/berita/baca/hol7062/penga wasan-tingkah-laku-kurator-akan-diperketat.

Hukumonline. 2003. 'Perseteruan Dua Organisasi Kurator: Gugatan Ditolak', 7 March. Available at: www.hukumonline.com/berita/baca/hol7577/font-size1-colorff0000bperseteruan-dua-organisasi-kuratorbfontbrgugatan-ditolak-.

Hukumonline. 2004. 'UU Kepailitan Belum Memberikan Solusi Mengungkap Kreditor Fiktif', 9 December. Available at: www.hukumonline.com/berita/ baca/hol11712/uu-kepailitan-belum-memberikan-solusi-mengungkap-kredi tor-fiktif.

Hukumonline. 2006a. 'Banyak Kendala, Pembentukan Pengadilan Perikanan Tertunda', 20 April. Available at: www.hukumonline.com/berita/ baca/hol14738/banyak-kendala-pembentukan-pengadilan-perikanan-tertunda.

Hukumonline. 2006b, 'MA: Biaya Perkara Bukan Pungli' 16 August. Available at: www.hukumonline.com/berita/baca/hol15325/ma-biaya-perkara-bukan-pungli.

Hukumonline 2007. 'Jelang dua tahun PHI kelemahan hukum acara disorot' 24 September. Available at: www.hukumonline.com/berita/baca/hol17656/ jelang-dua-tahun-phi-kelemahan-hukum-acara-disorot/.

Hukumonline. 2009a. 'Pengadilan Perikanan belum Efektif', 19 February. Available at: www.hukumonline.com/berita/baca/hol21242/pengadilan-perikanan-belum-efektif.

Hukumonline. 2009b. 'Era Keterbukaan Penjatuhan Sanksi bagi Hakim Nakal', 27 December. Available at: www.hukumonline.com/berita/baca/ lt4b3732ae228d1/era-keterbukaan-penjatuhan-sanksi-bagi-hakim-nakal.

Hukumonline. 2010a. 'MA Tantang ICW Uji Data Vonis Kasus Korupsi', 17 September. Available at: www.hukumonline.com/berita/baca/ lt4c938a1a6089b/ma-tantang-icw-uji-data-vonis-kasus-korupsi.

Hukumonline. 2010b. 'MA Ingin Tambah Jumlah Hakim Agung', 23 November. Available at: www.hukumonline.com/berita/baca/lt4cebece0e522c/ma-ingin-tambah-jumlah-hakim-agung/.

Hukumonline. 2011a. 'Peminat Minim, KY Seleksi Seadanya', 18 March. Available at: www.hukumonline.com/berita/baca/lt4d83634e2f981/peminat-minim-ky-siap-seleksi-seadanya.

Hukumonline. 2011b. 'KPK Tangkap Kurator dan Hakim', 2 June. Available at: www.hukumonline.com/berita/baca/lt4de6eec63a231/kpk-tangkap-kurator-dan-hakim.

Hukumonline. 2011c. 'Tak Ada Upaya Hukum untuk Fee Kurator', 7 November. Available at: www.hukumonline.com/berita/baca/lt4eb7715162988/tak-ada-upaya-hukum-untuk-fee-kurator.

Hukumonline. 2011d. 'Kurator Puguh Mengaku Akrab dengan Hakim Syarifuddin', 22 November. Available at: www.hukumonline.com/berita/baca/lt4ecb5ab498853/kurator-puguh-mengaku-akrab-dengan-hakim-syarifuddin.

Hukumonline. 2012a. 'Mahkumjakpol 'Dihidupkan' Kembali', 10 January. Available at: www.hukumonline.com/berita/baca/lt4f0c18d3d394c/mahkumjak pol-dihidupkan-kembali.

Hukumonline. 2012b. 'Mekanisme Pemilihan Ketua MA Rawan Dipolitisasi', 31 January. Available at: www.hukumonline.com/berita/baca/lt4f28065fd1a37/mekanisme-pemilihan-ketua-ma-rawan-dipolitisasi.

Hukumonline. 2012c. 'ICW: 84 Hakim Tipikor Dinilai Bermasalah', 29 August. Hukumonline 2017. 'Ketua MK Yakin Patrialis Bertindak Sendiri', 7 February. Available at: www.hukumonline.com/berita/baca/lt58997963cf66b/ketua-mk-yakin-patrialis-bertindak-sendiri.

Hukumonline. 2012d. 'Permintaan Mundur Bentuk Hukuman Bagi Yamanie', 19 November. Available at: www.hukumonline.com/berita/baca/lt50aa5c ded9bf5/permintaan-mundur-bentuk-hukuman-bagi-yamanie.

Hukumonline. 2012e. 'Achmad Yamanie Dipecat', 11 December. Available at: www .hukumonline.com/berita/baca/lt50c73771ae803/achmad-yamanie-dipecat.

Hukumonline. 2013a. 'Telkomsel Tolak Bayar Fee Kurator', 12 February. Available at: www.hukumonline.com/berita/baca/lt511a4f8336870/telkomsel-tolak-bayar-fee-kurator.

Hukumonline. 2013b. 'Aturan Penyadapan, Memangkas KPK', 21 March. Available at: www.hukumonline.com/berita/baca/lt514abdf2afade/aturan-penyadapan–memangkas-kpk.

Hukumonline. 2013c. 'Hakim Kasus Telkomsel Didemosi', 15 April. Available at: www.hukumonline.com/berita/baca/lt516be2b65367b/hakim-kasus-telkomsel-didemosi.

Hukumonline. 2013d. 'Ini Alasan MA Hukum Hakim Kasus Telkomsel', 19 April. Available at: www.hukumonline.com/berita/baca/lt51714d36e1da3/ini-alasan-ma-hukum-hakim-kasus-telkomsel.

Hukumonline. 2013e. 'Pengacara Minta MA Kabulkan PK Telkomsel', 23 April. Available at: www.hukumonline.com/berita/baca/lt5175ed7737d36/pengacara minta-ma-kabulkan-pk-telkomsel.

Hukumonline. 2013f. 'Kurator Ajukan Judicial Review Aturan Fee Kurator', 14 July. Available at: www.hukumonline.com/berita/baca/lt51e1f6b8a04d8/kura tor-ajukan-judicial-review-aturan-fee-kurator.

Hukumonline. 2013g. 'Uji Materi Kedua Imbalan Kurator', 17 August. Available at: www.hukumonline.com/berita/baca/lt520f6b25cbfe3/uji-materi-kedua-imbalan-kurator.

Hukumonline. 2013h. 'Inilah Pertimbangan PK MA atas Fee Kurator Telkomsel', 25 September. Available at: www.hukumonline.com/berita/baca/lt5242422eb837b/inilah-pertimbangan-pk-ma-atas-fee-kurator-telkomsel.

Hukumonline. 2013i. 'Eks Kurator Telkomsel Lawan PK Mahkamah Agung', 1 October. Available at: www.hukumonline.com/berita/baca/lt524a20f7d90c4/eks-kurator-telkomsel-lawan-pk-mahkamah-agung.

Hukumonline. 2013j. 'MA Perberat Vonis Angie', 21 November. Available at: www.staging.hukumonline.info/berita/baca/lt528db36e825e2/ma-perberat-vonis-angie.

Hukumonline. 2014a. 'MA Kabulkan Uji Materi Aturan Fee Kurator', 6 January. Available at: www.hukumonline.com/berita/baca/lt52ca9cdd95f10/ma-kabulkan-uji-materi-aturan-fee-kurator.

Hukumonline. 2014b. 'Kisah Kontroversial Permen Fee Kurator', 24 January. Available at: www.hukumonline.com/berita/baca/lt52e232cf06594/kisah-kontroversial-permen-ifee-i-kurator.

Hukumonline. 2014c. 'Dilaporkan ke Polisi, Eks Kurator Kymco Minta Perlindungan AKPI', 29 January. Available at: www.hukumonline.com/berita/baca/lt52e871a8ae562/dilaporkan-ke-polisi–eks-kurator-kymco-minta-perlindungan-akpi.

Hukumonline. 2014d. 'ICW: Hakim Terima Suap Harus Diproses Hukum', 5 March. Available at: www.hukumonline.com/berita/baca/lt531754de70973/icw–hakim-terima-suap-harus-diproses-hukum.

Hukumonline. 2014e. 'Kurator Ditangkap, Bahayakan Profesi Kurator', 6 April. Available at: www.hukumonline.com/berita/baca/lt53410c26b362c/kurator-ditangkap–bahayakan-profesi-kurator.

Hukumonline. 2014f. 'Hak Imunitas Advokat "Menyelamatkan" Ricardo Simanjutak', 6 May. Available at: www.hukumonline.com/berita/baca/lt5368dc043d6db/hak-imunitas-advokat-menyelamatkan-ricardo-simanjutak.

Hukumonline. 2014g. 'ICJR Apresiasi Terbitnya Perma Diversi Peradilan Anak', 12 August. Available at: www.hukumonline.com/berita/baca/lt53ea34c25d2f8/icjr-apresiasi-terbitnya-perma-diversi-peradilan-anak.

Hukumonline. 2014h. 'Kekuasaan Kehakiman Satu Atap, Anggaran MA Membengkak', 4 September. Available at: www.hukumonline.com/berita/baca/hol11087/kekuasaan-kehakiman-satu-atap-anggaran-ma-membengkak.

Hukumonline. 2014i. 'Tuntut Kesejahteraan Diperhatikan, Jaksa Akan Mogok Sidang Sehari', 9 September. Available at: www.hukumonline.com/berita/baca/lt540ed4fd4f2ff/tuntut-kesejahteraan-diperhatikan–prosecutor-akan-mogok-sidang-sehari.

Hukumonline. 2015a. 'MA Lolos dari Gugatan PMH Tiga Advokat', 26 May. Available at: www.hukumonline.com/berita/baca/lt556435f13ffb3/ma-lolos-dari-gugatan-pmh-tiga-advokat.

Hukumonline. 2015b. 'MA Jatuhkan Saksi untuk Ketua Kamar Pengawasan', 28 May. Available at: www.hukumonline.com/berita/baca/lt5566cc8ad082a/ma-jatuhkan-sanksi-untuk-ketua-kamar-pengawasan.

Hukumonline. 2015c. 'Ikah Tolak Pembentukan Pengadilan Pertananhan', 27 August. Available at: www.hukumonline.com/berita/baca/lt55dec169c305f/ikahi-tolak-pembentukan-pengadilan-pertanahan.

Hukumonline. 2016a. 'Pertama Kalinya, KY Rekrut Hakim Ad Hoc Tipikor Pada MA', 29 January. Available at: www.hukumonline.com/berita/baca/lt56a94b3aa937e/pertama-kalinya–ky-rekrut-hakim-ad-hoc-tipikor-pada-ma.

Hukumonline. 2016b. 'Jadi Tersangka Pemalsuan Keterangan, 3 Kurator Ajukan Praperadilan', 22 June. Available at: www.hukumonline.com/berita/baca/lt576a56a4db1e1/jadi-tersangka-pemalsuan-keterangan–3-kurator-ajukan-praperadilan.

Hukumonline. 2016c. 'Kisah Upaya Kriminalisasi Dua Pengurus oleh Pihak Berutang', 16 August. Available at: www.hukumonline.com/berita/baca/lt57b2e55126cea/kisah-upaya-kriminalisasi-dua-pengurus-oleh-pihak-berutang.

Hukumonline. 2016a. 'Presiden Jokowi Puji Kerja Mahkamah Agung', 16 August. Available at: www.hukumonline.com/berita/baca/lt57b296661c254/presiden-jokowi-puji-kerja-mahkamah-agung.

Hukumonline. 2016b. 'RUU Jabatan Hakim Evaluasi Kinerja Hakim Agung Potensial Langgar Independensi', 24 December. Available at: www.hukumonline.com/berita/baca/lt585e32fd9589c/evaluasi-kinerja-hakim-agung-potensial-langgar-independensi.

Hukumonline. 2016c. 'SK Menkumham terkait Kepengurusan- DPP PPP Diperdebatkan', 18 February. Available at: www.hukumonline.com/berita/baca/lt56c595b3a553d/sk-menkumham-terkait-kepengurusan-dpp-ppp-diperdebatkan.

Hukumonline. 2016d. 'Urgensi Pengadilan Pertanahan Menurut Kajian MA', 17 July. Available at: www.hukumonline.com/berita/baca/lt578aeb03d4514/urgensi-pengadilan-pertanahan-menurut-kajian-ma.

Hukumonline. 2017a. 'Pendaftaran Calon Hakim Agung 2017 Sepi Peminat', 19 March. Available at: www.hukumonline.com/berita/baca/lt58cd58d9ae765/pendaftaran-calon-hakim-agung-2017-sepi-peminat.

Hukumonline. 2017b. 'Reklamasi: Putusan PTUN Mestinya Jadi Momentum Bagi Pemerintah', 21 March. Available at: www.hukumonline.com/berita/baca/lt58d0fb36e7a1a/putusan-ptun-mestinya-jadi-momentum-bagi-pemerintah.

Hukumonline. 2017c. 'Lantik Pimpinan DPD 2017–2019, Sikap MA Dinilai Mengecewakan', 5 April. Available at: www.hukumonline.com/berita/baca/

lt58e4a8a1a0667/lantik-pimpinan-dpd-2017–2019–sikap-ma-dinilai-mengecewakan.

Hukumonline. 2017d. 'Mengurai Status Hakim: Dilema 'Wakil Tuhan' sebagai Pejabat Negara', 6 June. Available at: www.hukumonline.com/berita/baca/lt593588044e278/dilema-wakil-tuhan-sebagai-pejabat-negara.

Hukumonline. 2018a. 'Laptah MA 2017: Tahun 2017, Kontribusi MA Terhadap Negara Capai Rp18 Triliun', 1 March. Available at: www.hukumonline.com/berita/baca/lt5a98448c18c1d/tahun-2017–kontribusi-ma-terhadap-negara-capai-rp18-triliun.

Hukumonline. 2018b, 'Potret Ketua MA dari Masa ke Masa', 19 August. Available at: www.hukumonline.com/berita/baca/lt5b79032a55b70/potret-ketua-ma-dari-masa-ke-masa.

Hukumonline. 2018c. 'Putusan-Putusan Pengadilan Terbaru Terkait Lingkungan Hidup yang Layak Diketahui', 11 January. Available at: www.hukumonline .com/berita/baca/lt5a5756a4b9428/putusan-putusan-pengadilan-terbaru-terkait-lingkungan-hidup-yang-layak-diketahui.

Human Rights Watch. 2001. *Violence and Political Impasse in Papua.* Available at: www.hrw.org/reports/2001/papua/PAPUA0701.pdf.

Human Rights Watch. 2010. *World Report 2010.* USA: Human Rights Watch.

Hurst, W. 2014. 'Indonesia's Courts of Industrial Relations: Context, Structure, and a Look at Surabaya Cases', *Indonesia* 97: 29–54.

Hutabarat, R., Isnur, M. and Tobing, T. 2012. *Memudarnya Batas Kejahatan dan Penegakan Hukum (Situasi Pelanggaran Hak Anak dalam Peradilan Pidana).* Jakarta: Lembaga Bantuan Hukum Jakarta.

Idema, H. A. 1938. *Leerboek Landraad-Strafprocesrecht in zaken van Misdrijf.* Leiden: E. J. Brill.

IMF/Netherlands Program. 2005. *Legal and Judicial Reform in Indonesia 2000–2004 External Evaluation Final Report.* Available at: www.imf.org/en/Publications/Policy-Papers/Issues/2016/12/31/IMF-Netherlands-Program-Legal-and-Judicial-Report-in-Indonesia-2000–2004-External-PP3866.

Indonesia Corruption Watch (ICW). 2001. *Menyingkap Tabir Mafia Peradilan (Hasil Monitoring Peradilan ICW).* Jakarta: Indonesia Corruption Watch.

Indonesia Corruption Watch (ICW). 2009a. *Hakim Karir Juara Bebaskan Terdakwa Korupsi.* Available at: http://antikorupsi.org/docs/bahanrili sputusanbebaspengadilanumumsemesterI20095agustus2009.pdf.

Indonesia Corruption Watch (ICW). 2009b. *Pengadilan Umum: "kuburan" Pemberantasan Korupsi.* Available at: https://antikorupsi.org/id/news/pengadi lan-umum-kuburan-pemberantasan-korupsi.

Indonesia Corruption Watch (ICW). 2013. *Awas (Calon) Koruptor Jadi Hakim Ad Hoc Tipikor!.* Available at: https://antikorupsi.org/id/news/awas-calon-korup tor-jadi-hakim-ad-hoc-tipikor.

Indonesia Corruption Watch (ICW). 2014. *Studi atas Disparitas Putusan Pemidanaan Perkara Tindak Pidana Korupsi.* Jakarta: Indonesia Corruption Watch.

Indonesia Corruption Watch (ICW). 2015. *Calon Hakim AD Hoc Tipikor 2015 Tak Ada Satupun Yang Layak,* 13 November. Available at: www.antikorupsi.org/id/ news/calon-hakim-ad-hoc-tipikor-2015-tak-ada-satupun-yang-layak.

Indonesia Corruption Watch (ICW). 2018. *Catatan Pemantauan Perkara Korupsi Yang Divonis Oleh Pengadilan Selama 2017: Vonis Pengadilan Untungkan Koruptor.* Available at: https://antikorupsi.org/sites/default/files/tren_voni s_icw_2017.pdf.

Indonesia Investments. 2018. 'Corruption in Indonesia: DPR the Most Corrupt Government Institution', 28 January. Available at: www.indonesia-investments .com/id/news/news-columns/corruption-in-indonesia-dpr-the-most-corrupt-government-institution/item7667.

Indonesian Judicial Reform Forum. 2017. *Capaian, Tantangan dan Rekomendasi Pembaruan Peradilan.* Indonesian Judicial Reform Forum.

Indrayana, D. 2008. *Indonesian Constitutional Reform 1999–2002: An Evaluation of Constitution-making in Transition.* Jakarta: Kompas.

Indrayana, D. 2018. 'Successful Justice Sector Collaboration: A Prerequisite for a Healthy Australia-Indonesia Relationship', in Lindsey, T. and McRae, D. (eds.), *Strangers Next Door? Indonesia and Australia in the Asian Century.* Oxford: Hart Publishing.

Inilah. 2011. 'MA Setuju Rentut Dihapus' 21 January 2011 available at https://m.inilah .com/news/detail/1166692/ma-setuju-rentut-dihapus.

International Centre Against Censorship. 1994. *The Press under Siege: Censorship in Indonesia.* ICAC Article 19.

International Financial Law Review. 2013. 'Telkomsel Highlights Indonesia's Bankruptcy Shortcoming', 24 April. Available at: www.iflr.com/Article/ 3196298/Telkomsel-highlights-Indonesias-bankruptcy-shortcomings.html.

Irianto, et al. 2017. *Problematika Hakim Dalam Ranah Hukum, Pengadilan, Dan Masyarakat Di Indonesia: Studi Sosio-Legal.* Jakarta: Komisi Yudisial Republik Indonesia.

Ismawati, S. 2013. 'Upaya perlindungan hak asasi manusia dalam pembinaan narapidana anak (studi di lembaga pemasyarakatan klas II B anak Pontianak)', *Jurnal Masalah-Masalah Hukum* 42(3): 405–415.

Isnaeni, Hendri F. 2017. 'Teror Terhadap Pemburu Koruptor' 11 April, Historia, https://historia.id/modern/articles/teror-terhadap-pemburu-koruptor-vxGVo

Jamaludin et al. 2008. *Efektivitas Mekanisme Mediasi, Pengadilan Hubungan Industrial, dan Pengawasan Ketenagakerjaan untuk Memberikan Perlindungan Hukum terhadap Buruh.* Surabaya: Forum Pendamping Buruh Nasional Wilayah Timur.

Jorg, N., Field, S. A., and Brants, C. 1995 'Are Inquisitorial and Adversarial Systems Converging?' in Harding, C. and others (eds.), *Criminal Justice in Europe: A Comparative Study*. Oxford: Clarendon Press.

Jpnn.com. 2011. 'KPK Tangkap Basah Hakim Pengadilan Niaga', 2 June. Available at: www.jpnn.com/news/kpk-tangkap-basah-hakim-pengadilan-niaga.

Judicial Sector Support Project. 2015. *Penerapan Sistem Kamar pada Mahkamah Agung*. Judicial Sector Support Project.

Jumadi, R. J. 2013. 'Implementasi diversi terhadap anak yang berhadapan dengan hukum (studi kasus di pulau lombok)', *Jurnal Masalah-Masalah Hukum* 42(2): 274–281.

Junquiera, E. B. 2003. 'Brazil: The Road of Conflict Bound for Total Justice', in Friedman, L. M. and Perez-Perdomo, R. (eds.), *Legal Culture in the Age of Globalization: Latin America and Latin Europe*. Stanford: Stanford University Press.

Jurriëns, E. 2011. '"Radio Active": The Creation of Media-literate Audiences in Post-Suharto Indonesia', in Sen, K. and Hill. D. T. (eds.), *Politics and the Media in Twenty-First Century Indonesia: Decade of Democracy*. London and New York: Routledge.

Jusuf, M. 2014. *Hukum Public Prosecution Service: Eksistensi Public Prosecution Service sebagai Pengacara Negara dalam Perkara Perdata dan Tata Usaha Negara*. Surabaya: Penerbit Laksbang Justitia.

Juwana, H. 2014. 'Courts in Indonesia: A Mix of Western and Local Character', in Yeh, J. R. and Chang, W. C., *Asian Courts in Context*. Cambridge: Cambridge University Press.

Kadafi, B. 2016a. 'Revitalizing Indonesian Civil Justice', *The Jakarta Post*, 29 March, p. 7.

Kadafi, B. 2016b. 'Paket Kebijakan Reformasi Hukum Jokowi', *Koran Tempo*, 20 October. Available at: https://kolom.tempo.co/read/1001118/paket-kebija kan-reformasi-hukum-jokowi.

Kadafi, B. 2017. 'Masyarakat dan Sengkteta Usahanya', *Hukumonline*, 13 September. Available at: www.hukumonline.com/berita/baca/ lt59b8d6b52211e/masyarakat-dan-sengketa-usahanya-oleh–binziad-kadafi.

Kahin, A. 1999. Rebellion to integration: West Sumatra and the Indonesian Polity, 1926-1998. Amsterdam: Amsterdam University Press.

Kahn-Freund, O. 1981. *Labour Law and Politics in the Weimar Republic*. Oxford: Basil Blackwell.

Kammen, D. A. and Chandra, S. 2010. *A Tour of Duty: Changing Patterns of Military Politics in Indonesian in the 1990s*. Singapore: Equinox Publishing.

Kantor Berita Politik. 2017. 'Kejaksaan Ungguli KPK Berantas Korupsi', 1 June. Available at: http://politik.rmol.co/read/2017/06/01/293732/Kejaksaan-Ungguli-KPK-Berantas-Korupsi.

Kata data. 2016. *Produksi Ikan Tangkap di Indonesia 2000–2004*. Available at: https://databoks.katadata.co.id/datapublish/2016/08/08/produksi-ikan-tang kap-indonesia-2000–2014.

Katz, J. S. and Katz, R. S. 1975. 'The New Indonesian Marriage Law: A Mirror of Indonesia's Political, Cultural, and Legal Systems', *The American Journal of Comparative Law* 23(4): 653–681.

Katz, J. S. and Katz, R. S. 1978. 'Legislating Social Change in a Developing Country: The New Indonesian Marriage Law Revisited', *American Journal of Comparative Law* 26: 309–320.

KBR. 2018. 'Ini Laporan Lengkap Hasil Kerja Pansus Angket DPR Terhadap KPK', 14 February. Available at: http://kbr.id/nasional/02-2018/ini_laporan_lengka p_hasil_kerja_pansus_angket_dpr_terhadap_kpk/95056.html.

Kellner, D. 2012. 'Megaspectacle: The O.J. Simpson Murder Trial', in Kellner, D. (ed.), *Media Spectacle*. London: Routledge, pp. 93–125.

Kelompok Kerja Mahkamah Agung Tata Cara Penyelesaian Gugatan Sederhana. 2015. *Naskah Akademik Tata Cara Penyelesaian Gugatan Sederhana*. Jakarta: Mahkamah Agung RI.

Kelsen, H. 1928. 'La Garantie Juridictionnelle de la Constitution', *Revue du Droit Public et de la Science Politique en France et à l'étranger* 45: 197–257.

Ketua KPK ragukan kualitas Pengadilan Tipikor daerah, *Antara*, 25 April 2012.

Keyaksaan Agung. 2016. *Laporan Tahunan Public Prosecution Service Republik Indonesia 2015*. Jakarta: Kejaksaan Agung.

Khopiatuziadah. 2017. 'Evaluasi Pengadilan Perikanan dalam Penegakan Hukum di bidang Perikanan', *Jurnal Legislasi* 4(1): 17–28.

Knierbein, S., and Hou, J. 2017. 'City Unsilenced: Spatial Grounds of Radical Democratization', in Knierbein, S. and Hou J. (eds.), *City Unsilenced: Urban Resistance and Public Space in the Age of Shrinking Democracy*. London: Routledge.

Komisi Kejaksaan. 2013. Laporan Penelitian Biaya Penanganan Perkara Tindak Pidana Umum Kejaksaan Republik Indonesia, Tim Peneliti Komisi Kejaksaan RI, Jakarta.

Komisi Yudisial Republik Indonesia. 2017. *Etika dan Budaya Hukum dalam Peradilan*. Jakarta: Sekretariat Jenderal Komisi Yudisial Republik Indonesia.

Kompas. 2002. 'Tokoh Hak Asasi Manusia Prihatin atas Kondisi Hakim HAM', 14 November. (n.p).

Kompas. 2003. 'Hakim Ad Hoc HAM pada MA Belum Juga Ditetapkan', 24 January. (n.p.).

Kompas. 2010. 'Ada Satgas, Mafia Tiarap?', 8 January. Available at: https://tekno .kompas.com/read/2010/01/08/1733040/ada.satgas.mafia.tiarap.

Kompas. 2011. 'Puguh Akui Uang untuk Syarifuddin', 15 June. Available at: https://nasional.kompas.com/read/2011/06/15/02260359/puguh.akui.uang.untuk .syarifuddin.

Kompas. 2012a. 'KPK Diminta Pantau Pemilihan Ketua MA', 8 February. Available at: https://sains.kompas.com/read/2012/02/08/10211746/kpk.diminta.pantau.pemilihan.ketua.ma.

Kompas. 2012b. 'Pengadilan Tipikor: Empat Hakim Di Semarang Diduga Langgar Kode Etik', 19 June. Available at: https://nasional.kompas.com/read/2012/06/19/02054754/Empat.Hakim.di.Semarang.Diduga.Langgar.Kode.Etik.

Kompas. 2012c. 'Suap Instruksi Wali Kota', 26 June. Available at: https://nasional.kompas.com/read/2012/06/26/02360962/suap.instruksi.wali.kota.

Kompas. 2012d. 'Hakim Syarifuddin Divonis Empat Tahun Penjara,' 29 February, available online at: https://nasional.kompas.com/read/2012/02/28/13401220/Hakim.Syarifuddin.Divonis.Empat.Tahun.Penjara.

Kompas. 2014. 'Hak Politik Luthfi Hasan Ishaaq Dicabut, Hukumannya Diperberat Jadi 18 Tahun', 16 September. Available at: http://nasional.kompas.com/read/2014/09/16/06315561/Hak.Politik.Luthfi.Hasan.Ishaaq.Dicabut.Hukumannya.Diperberat.Jadi.18.Tahun.

Kompas. 2015. 'Kejaksaan Ibarat "Tukang Pos" dan "Kena Getah" Polisi', 21 September. Available at: https://nasional.kompas.com/read/2015/09/21/08510391/Kejaksaan.Ibarat.Tukang.Pos.

Kompas. 2016a. 'Idrus Marham Bantah Pihaknya Main Suap Saat Kasasi Sengketa Golkar', 8 August. Available at: https://nasional.kompas.com/read/2016/08/08/11274671/idrus.marham.bantah.pihaknya.main.suap.saat.kasasi.sengketa.golkar.

Kompas. 2016b. 'Petani Kendeng Menang di MA Lawan PT Semen Indonesia', 12 October. Available at: https://nasional.kompas.com/read/2016/10/12/09164211/petani.kendeng.menang.di.ma.lawan.pt.semen.indonesia.

Kompas. 2016c. 'Komisioner KY: Banyak Rekomendasi Sanksi Hakim "Nakal" Ditolak MA', 17 December. https://nasional.kompas.com/read/2016/12/17/20262581/komisioner.ky.banyak.rekomendasi.sanksi.hakim.nakal.ditolak.ma.

Kompas. 2016d. 'MA Terbitkan Perma Pidana Korporasi, Ini Respons KPK', 28 December. https://nasional.kompas.com/read/2016/12/28/22185771/ma.terbitkan.perma.pidana.korporasi.ini.respons.kpk.

Kompas. 2016e. 'Jaksa Agung Ancam Pecat Jaksa yang Tak Patuhi Instruksi Jokowi', 20 July. Available at: https://nasional.kompas.com/read/2016/07/20/13210581/prosecutor.agung.ancam.pecat.prosecutor.yang.tak.patuhi.instruksi.jokowi.

Kompas. 2016f. 'Jaksa Agung: Meski MK nyatakan Tak bisa, Kami Tetap Ajukan PK.,' 6 June. Available at: https://nasional.kompas.com/read/2016/06/06/19043121/prosecutor.agung.meski.mk.nyatakan.tak.bisa.kami.tetap.ajukan.pk.

Kompas. 2017. 'Survei Kompas: Citra TNI Naik Hingga 94 Persen, Citra DPR Terendah', 21 October. Available at: https://nasional.kompas.com/read/2017/10/21/07122651/survei-kompas-citra-tni-naik-hingga-94-persen-citra-dpr-terendah.

Kompas. 2018a. 'MA Keluarkan Peraturan untuk Sederhanakan Format Putusan Kasasi', 12 January. Available at: https://nasional.kompas.com/read/2018/01/12/17260431/ma-keluarkan-peraturan-untuk-sederhanakan-format-putusan-kasasi.

Kompas. 2018b. 'Petinggi Freeport and Hakim di Papua Dilaporkan ke KPK', 12 February. Available at: https://nasional.kompas.com/read/2018/02/12/14551811/petinggi-freeport-dan-hakim-di-papua-dilaporkan-ke-kpk.

Kontan. 2010. 'MA telusuri kasus suap hakim hubungan industrial' 7 May at https://nasional.kontan.co.id/news/ma-telusuri-kasus-suap-hakim-hubungan-industri-1.

Kontan. 2017. 'Polisi thangkap 3 kurator perkara pailit bumi asih', 19 May. Available at: https://nasional.kontan.co.id/news/polisi-tangkap-3-kurator-per kara-pailit-bumi-asih.

Kontan. 2018. 'Jadi tersangka KPK, ini jejak Lucas di berbagai kasus besar', 9 October. Available at: https://nasional.kontan.co.id/news/jadi-tersangka-kpk-ini-jejak-lucas-di-berbagai-kasus-besar.

Koran Tempo. 2010a. 'Direktur Utama Semen Kupang bantah lakukan suap', 5 May at https://nasional.tempo.co/read/245737/direktur-utama-pabrik-semen-kupang-bantah-lakukan-suap/full&;view=ok.

Krisnawati, D. 2012. 'Law Enforcement Preparedness for the Implementation of Indonesia's Law on Juvenile Justice System', *Mimbar Hukum* 25(3): 477–488.

Kumparan. 2017a. 'MA Kritik Peran Pengadilan Perikanan Belum Efektif, Apa Kata KKP?', 11 December. Available at: https://kumparan.com/@kumparan bisnis/ma-kritik-peran-pengadilan-perikanan-belum-efektif-apa-kata-kkp.

Kumparan. 2017b. 'Menteri Susi Tenggelamkan 317 Kapal Asing Pencuri Ikan Selama Menjabat', 26 July. Available at: https://kumparan.com/@kumparan news/menteri-susi-tenggelamkan-317-kapal-asing-pencuri-ikan-selama-menjabat.

Kurkchiyan, M. 2010. 'Comparing Legal Cultures: Three Models of Court for Small Civil Cases', *Journal of Comparative Law* 5: 169–194.

Kurkchiyan, M. 2012. 'Comparing Legal Cultures: Three Models of Court for Small Civil Cases', in Nelken, D. (ed.), *Using Legal Culture*. London: Wildy, Simmons and Hill.

Kusuma, E. F. 2016. 'Buwas Ingin Ada Peradilan Khusus Nark Seperti Pengadilan Tipikor', *Detik.com*, 19 April. Available at: https://news.detik.com/berita/d-3191869/buwas-ingin-ada-peradilan-khusus-narkoba-seperti-pengadilan-tipikor.

Kusumaningrum, S. 2012. 'Reforming Indonesia's Juvenile Justice System: Lost Cause or Worth the Investment?', *The Indonesian Journal of Leadership, Policy and World Affairs Strategic Review*. Available at: www.sr-indonesia.com/in-the-journal/view/reforming-indonesia-s-juvenile-justice-system-lost-cause-or-worth-the-investment.

Laksono, M. S. 2017. 'Pelajaran dari sidang Ahok: Larangan liputan langsung dan ancaman kebebasan pers [Lesson Learned from Ahok Trial: Ban on Live Courtroom Broadcasting and Threat against Press Freedom]', *Penyiaran Kita*. Jakarta: Komisi Penyiaran Indonesia Pusat.

Langer, M., Tanenhaus, D. S. and Zimring, F. E. (eds.) 2015. *Juvenile Justice in Global Perspective*. New York: New York University Press.

Leechaianan, Y. and Longmire, D. R. 2013. 'The Use of the Death Penalty for Drug Trafficking in the United States, Singapore, Malaysia, Indonesia and Thailand: A Comparative Legal Analysis', *Laws* 2(2): 115–149.

Legal and Constitutional Affairs References Committee. 2012. *Detention of Indonesian Minors in Australia*. Available at: www.aph.gov.au/Parliamentary_Business/Committees/Senate/Legal_and_Constitutional_Affairs/Completed_inquiries/2010–13/indonesianminors/index.

LEIP. 2018. *Judicial Sector Support Program*, Available at: http://leip.or.id/judicial-sector-support-program-jssp/.

Lembaga Kajian dan Advokasi untuk Independensi Peradilan. 2010. *Pembatasan Perkara: Strategi Mendorong Peradilan Cepat, Murah, Efisien dan Berkualitas*. Jakarta: Lembaga Kajian dan Advokasi untuk Independensi Peradilan.

Lembaga Kajian dan Advokasi untuk Independensi Peradilan. 2010. *Konsep Ideal Peradilan Indonesia: Menciptakan Kesatuan Hukum & Meningkatkan Akses Masyarakat Pada Keadilan*. Jakarta: Lembaga Kajian dan Advokasi untuk Independensi Peradilan.

Lev, D. S. 1958. *A Bibliography of Indonesian Government Documents and Selected Indonesian Writings on Government in the Cornell University Library Data Paper No. 31*. Ithaca, NY: Southeast Asia Program, Cornell University.

Lev, D. S. 1962. 'The Supreme Court and Adat Inheritance Law in Indonesia', *American Journal of Comparative Law* 11(2): 205–224.

Lev, D. S. 1965a. 'The Lady and the Banyan Tree: Civil-Law Change in Indonesia', *The American Journal of Comparative Law* 14(2): 282–307.

Lev, D. S. 1965b. 'The Politics of Judicial Development in Indonesia', *Comparative Studies in Society and History* 7: 173–202.

Lev, D. S. 1966. *The Transition to Guided Democracy*. Ithaca, NY: Cornell Modern Indonesia Project.

Lev, D. S. 1972a. *Islamic Courts in Indonesia: A Study in the Political Bases of Legal Institutions*. Berkley: University of California Press.

Lev, D. S. 1972b. 'Judicial Institutions and Legal Culture in Indonesia', in Holt, C. (ed.), *Culture and Politics in Indonesia*. Ithaca, NY: Cornell University Press, pp. 246–281.

Lev, D. S. 1973a. *Bush Lawyers in Indonesia: Stratification, Representation and Brokerage Working Paper No. 1*. Berkeley: UC Law and Society Program.

Lev, D. S. 1973b. 'Judicial Unification in Post-Colonial Indonesia', *Indonesia* 16: 1–39.

Lev, D. S. 1976. 'The Origins of the Indonesian Advocacy', *Indonesia* 21: 135–169.

Lev, D. S. 1978. 'Judicial Authority and the Struggle for an Indonesian Rechtsstaat', *Law and Society Review* 13: 37–71.

Lev, D. S. 1985. 'Colonial Law and the Genesis of the Indonesian State', *Indonesia* 40: 57–74.

Lev, D. S. 1987. Legal Aid in Indonesia. Working Paper No 44. Southeast Asian Studies, Monash University.

Lev, D. S. 1990. 'Human Rights NGOs in Indonesia and Malaysia', in Welch, C. E. and Leary, V. (eds.), *Asian Perspectives on Human Rights*. Boulder, CO: Westview Press.

Lev, D. S. 1992. *Lawyers as Outsiders: Advocacy Versus the State in Indonesia, Working Paper No 2 (November)*. London: University of London, School of Oriental and African Studies.

Lev, D. S. 1993. 'Social Movements, Constitutionalism, and Human Rights', in Greenberg, D., Katz, S. N., Oliviero, L. B. and Wheatley, S. C. (eds.), *Constitutionalism, Democracy, and the Transformation of the Modern World*. London and New York: Oxford University Press. pp 139–150.

Lev, D. S. 1994 'Law & Society in Southeast Asia: Forward', *Law & Society Review* 28(3): 413–415.

Lev, D. S. 1996. 'Between State and Society: Professional Lawyers and Reform in Indonesia', in Lev, D. S. and McVey, R. (eds.), *Making Indonesia*. Ithaca, NY: Cornell Southeast Asia Program Publications.

Lev, D. S. 1998 'Lawyers' Causes in Indonesia and Malaysia', in Sarat, A. and Scheingold, S. (eds.), *Cause Lawyering: Political Commitments and Professional Responsibilities*. Oxford: Oxford University Press.

Lev, D. S. 1999. 'The Criminal Regime: Criminal Process in Indonesia', in Rafael, V. (ed.), *Figures of Criminality in Indonesia, the Philippines, and Colonial Vietnam*. Ithaca, NY: Cornell Southeast Asia Program Publications.

Lev, D. S. 2000a. 'Between State and Society: Professional Lawyers and Reform in Indonesia', in Lev, D. S. (ed.), *Legal Evolution and Political Authority in Indonesia: Selected Essays*. The Hague: Kluwer Law International.

Lev, D. S. 2000b. 'Comments on the Course of Legal Reform in Modern Indonesia', in Lindsey, T. (ed.), *Indonesia: Bankruptcy, Law Reform, and the Commercial Court*. Sydney: Desert Pea Press.

Lev, D. S. 2000c. 'Introduction', in Lev, D. S. (ed.), *Legal Evolution and Political Authority in Indonesia: Selected Essays*. The Hague: Kluwer Law International.

Lev, D. S. 2000d. *Legal Evolution and Political Authority in Indonesia: Selected Essays*. The Hague: Kluwer Law International.

Lev, D. S. 2000e. 'The Law and the Banyan Tree: Civil-Law Change in Indonesia', in Lev, D. S. (ed.), *Legal Evolution and Political Authority in Indonesia: Selected Essays*. The Hague: Kluwer Law International.

Lev, D. S. 2000f. 'The Politics of Judicial Development in Indonesia', in Lev, D. S. (ed.), *Legal Evolution and Political Authority in Indonesia: Selected Essays*. The Hague: Kluwer Law International.

Lev, D. S. 2000g. 'The Supreme Court and Adat Inheritance Law in Indonesia', in Lev, D. S. (ed.), *Legal Evolution and Political Authority in Indonesia: Selected Essays*. The Hague: Kluwer Law International.

Lev, D. S. 2005a. 'Comments on the Judicial Reform Program in Indonesia', *Current Developments in Monetary and Financial Law*: 1–4.

Lev, D. S. 2005b. 'Conceptual Filters and Obfuscation in the Study of Indonesian Politics', *Asian Studies Review* 29(4): 345–356.

Lev, D. S. 2005c. 'Forward', in Pompe, S. (ed.), *The Indonesian Supreme Court: A Study of Institutional Collapse*. Ithaca, NY: Cornell University Press.

Lev, D. S. 2007a. 'A Tale of Two Legal Professions: Lawyers and State in Malaysia and Indonesia', in Alford, W. (ed.), *Raising the Bar: The Emerging Legal Profession in East Asia*. Cambridge: Harvard University Press.

Lev, D. S. 2007b. 'Judicial Institutions and Legal Culture in Indonesia', in Holt, C. (ed.), *Culture and Politics in Indonesia*. Singapore: Equinox Publishing, pp. 246–318.

Lev, D. S. 2007c. 'State and Law Reform in Indonesia', in Lindsey, T. (ed.), *Law Reform in Developing and Transitional States*. New York: Routledge.

Lev, D. S. 2008. 'Between State and Society: Professional Lawyers and Reform in Indonesia', in Lindsey, T. (ed.), *Indonesia: Law and Society*. Sydney: The Federation Press.

Lev, D. S. 2009. *The Transition to Guided Democracy: Indonesian Politics, 1957–59*. Singapore: Equinox Publishing.

Lev, D. S. 2011. *No Concessions: The Life of Yap Thiam Hien, Indonesian Human Rights Lawyer*. Seattle, WA: University of Washington Press.

Lev, D. S. and McVey, R. (eds.) 1996. *Making Indonesia*. Ithaca, NY: Cornell Southeast Asia Program Publications.

Liddle, R. W. 1996. 'The Islamic Turn in Indonesia: A Political Explanation', *Journal of Asian Studies* 55(3): 613–634.

Lilleker, D. G., 2003. 'Interviewing the Political Elite: Navigating a Potential Minefield' *Politics* 23: 207.

Lindsey, T. 1998. 'The IMF and Insolvency Law Reform in Indonesia', *Bulletin of Indonesian Economic Studies* 34(3): 119–124.

Lindsey, T. (ed.) 2000. *Indonesia: Bankruptcy, Law Reform and the Commercial Court*. Sydney: Desert Pea Press.

Lindsey, T. 2008. 'Constitutional Reform in Indonesia: Muddling towards Democracy', in Lindsey, T. (ed.), *Indonesia Law and Society*. Sydney: The Federation Press, pp. 23–47.

Lindsey, T. and Crouch, M. (2013). 'Cause Lawyers in Indonesia: A House Divided', *Wisconsin International Law Journal* 31(3): 620–645.

Lindsey, T. and Nicholson, P. 2016. *Drugs Law and Legal Practice in Southeast Asia: Indonesia, Singapore and Vietnam*. London: Hart Publishing.

Lindsey, T., and Santosa, M. A. 2008. 'The Trajectory of Law Reform in Indonesia' in Lindsey, T. (ed.), *Indonesia: Law and Society* (2nd edn). Sydney: Federation Press.

Lindsey, T. and Taylor, V. 2000. 'Rethinking Indonesian Insolvency Reform: Contexts and Frameworks', in Lindsey, T. (ed.), *Indonesia: Bankruptcy, Law Reform & the Commercial Court: Comparative Perspectives on Insolvency Law and Policy*. Sydney: Desert Pea Press, pp. 2–14.

Linnan, D. 2008. 'Commercial Law Enforcement in Indonesia: The Manulife Case', in Lindsey, T. (ed.), *Indonesia: Law & Society*. Sydney: Federation Press, pp. 596–619.

Linnan, D. 2010. 'Reading the Tea Leaves in the Indonesian Commercial Court: A Cautionary Tale, But for Whom?', in Harding, A. and Nicholson, P. (eds.,) *New Courts in Asia*. London: Routledge, pp. 56–79.

Linton, S. 2006. 'Accounting for Atrocities in Indonesia', *Singapore Year Book of International Law* 10: 199–231.

Liputan 6, 2010. 'Puluhan buruh Semen Kupang demo di MA', 28 April. Available at: www.liputan6.com/news/read/274673/puluhan-buruh-semen-kupang-demo-di-ma.

Liputan 6, SCTV. 2002. 'Sore ini, Habibie akan bersaksi dari Jerman', July 2. Available at: http://news.liputan6.com/read/37052/sore-ini-habibie-akan-bersaksi-dari-jerman.

Litbang Mahkamah Agung. 2010. *Kedudukan dan Relevansi Yurisprudensi untuk Mengurangi Disparitas Putusan Pengadilan: Laporan Penelitian*. Jakarta: Mahkamah Agung.

Loebis, A. B. 1974. *Pengadilan Negeri Jakarta in Action*. Selbstverl.

Lolo, F. T. A. 2008. *The Prosecutorial Corruption during the New Order Regime Case Study: The Prosecution Service of the Republic Indonesia*. Unpublished PhD thesis, University of Auckland Law School.

Lubis, H. 2016. *Penerapan Pidana Pasal 102 Undang-Undang Perikanan*. Available at: https://nuecoreligioncenter.blogspot.com/2016/05/penerapan-pidana-pasal-102-uu-perikanan_18.html.

Lubis, N. A. F. 1994. *Islamic Justice in Transition: A Socio-Legal Study of the Agama Court Judges in Indonesia*. Los Angeles: University of California Press.

Mahkamah Agung. 2010. *Cetak Biru Pembaharuan Peradilan 2010–2035*. Jakarta: Mahkamah Agung. [Judicial Reform Blue Print 2010–2035].

Mahkamah Agung. 2014. *Laporan Tahunan Direktorat Jenderal Badan Peradilan Umum Tahun 2013*, Direktorat Jenderal Badan Peradilan Umum.

Mahkamah Agung. 2015. *Laporan Tahunan Direktorat Jenderal Badan Peradilan Umum Tahun 2014*, Direktorat Jenderal Badan Peradilan Umum.

Mahkamah Agung. 2016. *Laporan Tahunan Direktorat Jenderal Badan Peradilan Umum Tahun 2015*, Direktorat Jenderal Badan Peradilan Umum.

Mahkamah Agung. 2017. *Laporan Tahunan Direktorat Jenderal Badan Peradilan Umum Tahun 2016*, Direktorat Jenderal Badan Peradilan Umum.

Mahkamah Agung. 2018. *Laporan Tahunan Direktorat Jenderal Badan Peradilan Umum Tahun 2017*, Direktorat Jenderal Badan Peradilan Umum.

Mahkamah Agung. 2018a. *Sistem Informasi Administrasi Perkara Mahkamah Agung RI*. Available at: http://kepaniteraan.mahkamahagung.go.id/perkara.

Mahkamah Agung, Pusat Studi Hukum & Kebijakan Indonesia (PSHK) & LeIP. 2010. *Cetak Biru Pembaruan Peradilan 2010-2035*. Jakarta: Mahkamah Agung RI.

Mahkamah Agung, Pusat Studi Hukum & Kebijakan Indonesia (PSHK) & LeIP. 2015. *Buku Saku Gugatan Sederhana*. Jakarta: Mahkamah Agung RI.

Mahkamah Agung, Pusat Studi Hukum & Kebijakan Indonesia (PSHK) & LeIP. 2018. *Laporan Tahunan Mahkamah Agung RI 2017*. Jakarta: Mahkamah Agung RI.

Mahy, P. 2013. 'The Evolution of Company Law in Indonesia: An Exploration of Legal Innovation and Stagnation', *American Journal of Comparative Law* 61: 377–432.

Manan, A. 2008. *Aneka Masalah Hukum Perdata Islam di Indonesia*. Jakarta: Kencana.

Manan, A. 2006. *Reformasi Hukum Islam di Indonesia*. Jakarta: Raja Grafindo Persada.

Mann, T. 2015. 'Q&A: Todung Mulya Lubis on judicial reform' (*Indonesia at Melbourne*, 25 August 2015). Available at: http://indonesiaatmelbourne.unimelb.edu.au/justice-sector-reform-mulya-lubis/

MaPPI FHUI. 2015. *Laporan Pemantauan Kejaksaan*. Jakarta: MaPPI FHUI.

Massier, A. 2008. *The Voice of the Law in Transition: Indonesian Jurists and Their Languages, 1915-2000*. Leiden: KITLV University Press.

McCloskey, R. G. 2005. *The American Supreme Court*. Chicago: University of Chicago Press.

McCoy, M. 2005. 'The Media in Democratic Transitions: Institutionalising Uncertainty in Post-Suharto Indonesia'. Unpublished PhD thesis, Northwestern University.

McGregor, K. and Ken Setiawan. 2019. 'Shifting from International to "Indonesian" Justice Measures: Two Decades of Addressing Past Human Rights Violations', *Journal of Contemporary Asia* 1–25.

McLaughlin, K. and Perdana, A. 2010. *Conflict and Dispute Resolution in Indonesia: Information from the 2006 Governance and Decentralisation Survey*. Jakarta: Indonesian Social Development Paper No. 16.

McLeod, R. 2000. 'Soeharto's Indonesia: A Better Class of Corruption', *Agenda* 7(2): 99–112.

McRae, D. 2012. 'A Key Domino? Indonesia's Death Penalty Politics.' Sydney: Lowy Institute for International Policy. Available at: https://archive.lowyinstitute.org/sites/default/files/mcrae_a_key_domino_web-1_0.pdf.

Merry, S. E. 2006. *Human Rights and Gender Violence: Translating International Law into Local Justice.* Chicago: University of Chicago Press.

Merry, S. E. 2010. 'What Is Legal Culture: An Anthropological Perspective', *Journal of Comparative Law* 5(2): 40–58.

Meuwese, S. 2003. *Kids Behind Bars.* Amsterdam: Defence for Children International.

Mezey, N. 2001. 'Law as Culture', *Yale Journal of Law and the Humanities* 13: 35–67.

Mietzner, M. 2010. 'Political Conflict Resolution and Democratic Consolidation in Indonesia: The Role of the Constitutional Court', *Journal of East Asian Studies* 10(3): 397–424.

Mietzner, M. 2011. 'The Political Marginalisation of the Military in Indonesia', in *The Political Resurgence of the Military in Southeast Asia: Conflict and Leadership.* Abingdon: Routledge.

Mietzner, M. 2018. 'Fighting Illiberalism with Illiberalism: Islamist Populism and Democratic Deconsolidation in Indonesia', *Pacific Affairs* 91: 261–282.

Millie, J. 1999. 'The Tempo case: Indonesia's press laws, the *Pengadilan Tata Usaha Negara* and the Indonesian *negara hokum*', in Lindsey, T. (ed.), *Indonesia; Law and Society.* Sydney: Federation Press, pp. 269–278.

Ministry of Women's Empowerment and Child Protection/ Kementerian Pemberdayaan Perempuan dan Perlindungan Anak. 2015. *Profil Anak Indonesia.* Jakarta: KPPPA.

Mitchell, O., Cochran, J., Mears, D. and Bales, W. 2017. 'The Effectiveness of Prison for Reducing Drug Offender Recidivism: A Regression Discontinuity Analysis', *Journal of Experimental Criminology* 13: 1–27.

Miyazawa, S. 1997. 'For the Liberal Transformation of Japanese Legal Culture: A Review of the Recent Scholarship and Practice', *Zeitschrift für Japanisches Recht* 4: 101–115.

Mizuno, K. 2005. 'The Rise of Labor Movements and the Evolution of the Indonesian System of Industrial Relations: A Case Study', *The Developing Economies*, XLIII (1): 190–211.

Moeljo Mangoenprawiro, D. 1999. *Kiat Andi Muhammad Ghalib Memeriksa KKN Soeharto.* Jakarta: Raga Mukti.

Mohr, R. 2007. 'Local Court Reforms and "Global" Law', *Utrecht Law Review* 3(1): 41–59.

Molaei, H. 2015. 'Discursive Opportunity Structure and the Contribution of Social Media to the Success of Social Movements in Indonesia', *Information, Communication and Society* 18(1): 94–108.

Morgan, B. and Halliday, S. 2013. 'I Fought the Law and the Law Won? Legal Consciousness and the Critical Imagination', *Current Legal Problems* 66: 1–32.

Morn, F. and Toro, M. 1990. 'The Legal Culture and Legal System in Post-Franco Spain', *International Journal of Comparative and Applied Criminal Justice* 14(2): 211–223.

Movanita, A. N. K. 2015. 'Hukuman Anas Urbaningrum Jadi 14 Tahun, Bayar Rp 57 M, Dan Hak Dipilih Dicabut', Kompas.com, 8 June. Available at: http://nasional.kom pas.com/read/2015/06/08/20072581/Hukuman.Anas.Urbaningrum.Jadi.14.Tahun .Bayar.Rp.57.M.dan.Hak.Dipilih.Dicabut.

Movanita, A. N. K. 2017. 'Ini Daftar Mereka Yang Disebut Terima Uang Proyek E-KTP', Kompas, 9 March. Available at: http://nasional.kompas .com/read/2017/03/09/16182831/ini.daftar.mereka.yang.disebut.terima.uang .proyek.e-ktp.

Movanita, A. N. K. 2017. '51 Anggota Komisi II DPR 2009–2014 Dapat Kucuran Dana Proyek E-KTP', Kompas, 9 March. Available at: http://nasional.kompas.com/read/ 2017/03/09/14362681/51.anggota.komisi.ii.dpr.2009–2014.dapat.kucuran.dana .proyek.e-ktp.

Mulya Lubis, T. 2003. *In Search of Human Rights: Legal-Political Dilemmas of Indonesia's New Order 1966-1990*. Jakarta: PT Gramedia Pustaka Utama.

Mulyadi, L. 2005. *Pengadilan Anak di Indoneia. Teori, Praktek dan Permasalahannya*. Bandung: Mandar Maju.

Munaswar, I. 2008. 'Trend dan Perkembangan Court: Antara Kenyataan dan Harapan', paper presented at *Labour Law Practitioners Conference*, Jakarta, 2–5 March.

Muradi. 2014. *Politics and Governance in Indonesia: The Police in the Era Reformasi*. New York: Routledge.

Na'īm, A. A. A. 2002. *Islamic Family Law in a Changing World: A Global Resource Book*. London: Zed Books.

Nader, L. (ed.) 1969. *Law in Culture and Society*. Berkeley: University of California Press.

Naibaho, N. 2011. 'Human Trafficking in Indonesia: Law Enforcement Problems', *Indonesia Law Review* 1: 83–99.

Nardi, D. 2018. *Embedded Judicial Autonomy: How NGOs and Public Opinion Influence Indonesia's Constitutional Court*. PhD thesis, University of Michigan. Available at: https://deepblue.lib.umich.edu/bitstream/handle/2027.42/144040/dnardi_1.pdf? sequence=1&;isAllowed=y.

Nasution, A. B. 2004. *Pergulatan tanpa henti / Adnan Buyung Nasution; Dirumahkan Soekarno, dipecat Soeharto*. Ramadhan, K. H. and Pane, N. eds., Jakarta: Aksara Karunia.

Nelken, D. 1995. 'Disclosing/Invoking Legal Culture: An Introduction', *Social and Legal Studies* 4(4): 435–452.

Nelken, D. 2001. 'Towards a Sociology of Legal Adaptation' in Nelken, D. and Feest, J. (eds.), *Adapting Legal Cultures*. Oxford: Hart Publishing.

Nelken, D. 2003. 'Legal Cultures', in Sarat, A. (ed.), *The Blackwell Companion to Law and Society*. Malden: Blackwell Publishing.

Nelken, D. 2004. 'Using the Concept of Legal Culture', *Australian Journal of Legal Philosophy* 29: 1–26.

Nelken, D. 2011. 'Why Compare Criminal Justice', in Bosworth, M. and Hoyle, C. (eds.), *What is Criminology?* Oxford: Oxford University Press.

Nelken, D. 2014. 'Thinking about Legal Culture', *Asian Journal of Law and Society* 1(2): 255–274.

Nelken, D. 2016. 'Comparative Legal Research and Legal Culture: Facts, Approaches, and Values', *Annual Review of Law and Social Science* 12: 45–62.

Nicholson, D., 2009. *Environmental Dispute Resolution in Indonesia*. Leiden: KITLV Press.

Nicholson, P. and Harding, A. (eds.) 2010. *New Courts in Asia*. London: Routledge.

Nonet, P. and Selznick, P. 2009. *Toward Responsive Law: Law and Society in Transition*. Piscataway, NJ: Transaction Publishers.

Nurlaelawati, E. 2010. *Modernization, Tradition and Identity: The Kompilasi Hukum Islam and Legal Practice in the Indonesian Religious Courts*. Amsterdam: Amsterdam University Press.

Nurlaelawati, E. and Abdurrahman, R. 2012. 'The Training, Appointment, and Supervision of Islamic Judges in Indonesia', *Pacific Rim Law and Policy Journal* 21: 43–64.

O'Shaughnessy, K. 2009. *Gender, State and Social Power in Contemporary Indonesia: Divorce and Marriage Law*. London: Routledge.

Ombudsman. 2018. *Laporan Tahunan 2017*. Jakarta: Ombudsman Republik Indonesia.

Osei-Kufour, P. 2010. 'Does Institutionalising Decentralisation Work? Rethinking Agency, Institutions and Authority in Local Governance', PhD thesis, Development and Economic Studies, University of Bradford.

Otto, J. M. 1992. *Conflicts between Citizens and the State in Indonesia: The Development of Administrative Jurisdiction*. Leiden: Van Vollenhoven Institute, Working Paper no. 1.

Otto, J. M. 2002. 'Towards an Analytical Framework: Real Legal Certainty and Its Explanatory Factors', in Chen, J., Li, Y. and Jan Michiel Otto, J. M. (eds.), *Implementation of Law in the Poeple's Republic of China*. The Hague: Kluwer Law International.

Otto, J. M. 2010. 'Sharia and National Law in Indonesia', in Otto, J. M. (ed.), *Sharia Incorporated: A Comparative Overview of the Legal Systems of Twelve Muslim Countries in Past and Present*. Leiden: Leiden University Press, pp. 433–490.

Parwito. 2012. 'Pengadilan Tipikor Semarang Bebaskan Penyuap Bupati Kendal' *Suara Merdeka*, 12 June. Available at: www.merdeka.com/peristiwa/pengadilan-tipikor-semarang-bebaskan-penyuap-bupati-kendal.html.

Pascoe, D. 2014. 'Clemency in Southeast Asian Death Penalty Cases' 1 CILIS Policy Papers https://law.unimelb.edu.au/__data/assets/pdf_file/0003/1547094/ALC-CILISPolicyPaper_Pascoe_web2.pdf.

Pascoe, D. 2017. 'Researching the Death Penalty in Closed or Partially-Closed Criminal Justice Systems', in Bosworth, M., Hoyle, C. and Zedner, L. (eds.), *Changing Contours of Criminal Justice*. Oxford: Oxford University Press.

Pascoe, D. 2017a. 'Legal Dilemmas in Releasing Indonesia's Political Prisoners', *Indonesia Law Review* 7(3): 313.

Pascoe, D. 2017b. 'On "Elite" Interviewing in Semi-Secretive Jurisdictions' (Oxford Centre for Criminology Blog, 8 May 2017). Available at: www.law.ox.ac.uk/centres-institutes/centre-criminology/blog/2017/05/%E2%80%98elite%E2%80%99-interviewing-semi-secretive-jurisdictions.

Pascoe, D. 2019. *Last Chance for Life: Clemency in Southeast Asian Death Penalty Cases*. Oxford: Oxford University Press.

Pearson, Z. 2001. 'An International Human Rights Approach to Corruption', in Larmour, P. and Wolanin, N. (eds.), *Corruption and Anti-Corruption*. Canberra: Asia Pacific Press.

Pemberton, J. 1999. 'Open Secrets: Excerpts from Conversations with a Javanese Lawyer, and a Comment', in Rafael, V. and Mrazek, R. (eds.), *Figures of Criminality in Indonesia, the Philippines and Colonial Vietnam*. Ithaca, NY: Cornell University Press.

Perry, N. 2006. 'Daniel Lev; Scholar, Friend of Indonesia', *Seattle Times*, 1 August. Available at: http://old.seattletimes.com/html/obituaries/2003166510_levobit01m.html.

PN Kota Cirebon. *Sosialisasi Gugatan Sederhana Di Bank BRI Cabang Cirebon.* Available at: www.pn-kotacirebon.go.id/berita-sosialisasi-gugatan-sederhana-di-bank-bri-cabang-cirebon.html. Accessed 11 June 2018.

PN Rengat. *PN Rengat Terima 30 Gugatan Sederhana Dari BRI*. Available at: http://pn-rengat-terima-30-gugatan-sederhana-dari-bri.html. Accessed 11 June 2018.

Polri & KKN. 2004. Jakarta: Kemitraan-Partnership for Governance Reform in Indonesia.

Pompe, S. 1996. *The Indonesian Supreme Court: Fifty Years of Judicial Development*. Phd thesis, Universiteit Leiden.

Pompe, S. 2004. 'Indonesian Courts Create Unemployment', *The Jakarta Post*, 26 January.

Pompe, S. 2005. *The Indonesian Supreme Court: a Study of Institutional Collapse*. Ithaca, NY: Cornell University Press.

Pompe, S. 2012. 'In Memoriam, Daniel S. Lev (1933–2006)', *Indonesia* 93: 197–207.

Powell, W. W. and DiMaggio, P. J. 1991. *The New Institutionalism in Organizational Analysis*. Chicago: The University of Chicago Press.

Pratiwi, C., Yulita, C. Fauzi, Purnamawati, S. and Nasima, I. 2016. *Penjelasan Hukum (Restatement): Asas-Asas Umum Pemerintahan yang Baik (AUPB)*. Jakarta: JSSP, CILC and LEIP.

Prins, J. 1951. 'Adat Law and Muslim Religious Law in Modern Indonesia: An Introduction', *The World of Islam* 1(4): 283–300.

PTUN Jakarta. 2015a. Statistik Perkara Pengadilan Tahun 1991–1995. Available at: https://ptun-jakarta.go.id/?statistik=statistik-perkara-april-2015.

PTUN Jakarta. 2015b. Statistik Perkara Pengadilan Tahun 1996–2000. Available at: https://ptun-jakarta.go.id/?statistik=statistik-perkara-pengadilan-tahun-1996–2000.

PTUN Jakarta. 2018. Register [number of cases 2004–2018]. Available at: https://putusan.mahkamahagung.go.id/pengadilan/ptun-jakarta/periode/register/.

PTUN Yogyakarta. 2018. Register [number of cases 1998–2018]. Available at: https://putusan.mahkamahagung.go.id/pengadilan/ptun-yogyakarta/periode/register.

Public Prosecution Service (PPS) 1985. *Lima Windu Sejarah Public Prosecution Service 1945–1985*. Jakarta: Panitia Penyusunan dan Penyempurnaan Sejarah, Public Prosecution Service Republik Indonesia.

Purniati. 2002. *Analisa Situasi Sistem Peradilan Pidana Anak di Indonesia*. Jakarta: UNICEF.

Purwati, A. and Alam, A. S. 2015. 'Diversi sebagai wujud kebijakan pemidanaan sistem peradilan pidana anak di Indonesia', *De Jure* 7(2): 179–190.

Pusat Data Statistik dan Informasi. 2009. 'Maritime and Fisheries Affairs Figures 2009', *Kementrian Kelautan dan Perikanan*.

Pusat Data Statistik dan Informasi. 2015. 'Maritime and Fisheries Affairs 2015', *Kementrian Kelautan dan Perikanan*. Available at: http://statistik.kkp.go.id/sidatik-dev/Publikasi/src/kpda2015.pdf.

PUSKAPA. 2014. *Practice of Detention as the Last Resort & for the Minimum Necessary Period: A Study on Pre-Trial and Pre-Sentence Situations in the Juvenile Justice System in Indonesia*. Unpublished.

PUSKAPA. 2018. *Bappenas Meeting Series: Policy Brief*. Unpublished.

Raffles, T. S. 1817. *The History of Java: In Two Volumes. With a Map and Plates*. London: Black, Parbury & Allen.

Rahmadi, T. 2016. 'Sistem Kamar Dalam Mahkamah Agung: Upaya Membangun Kesatuan Hukum', *Web MA*, 24 June. Available at: www.mahkamahagung.go.id/id/artikel/2141/sistem-kamar-dalam-mahkamah-agung-upaya-memban gun-kesatuan-hukum-profdrtakdir-rahmadi-sh-llm.

Rahmi, N. 2014. 'Divonis Seumur Hidup, Akil Akan Banding Sampai Ke Surga', *Hukumonline*, 1 July. Available at: www.hukumonline.com/berita/baca/lt53b1e d116ed6a/divonis-seumur-hidup–akil-akan-banding-sampai-ke-surga.

Rajab, U. S. 2003. *Kedudukan dan Fungsi Polisi Republik Indonesia Dalam Sistem Ketatanegaraan (berdasarkan UUD 1945)* (Cet. 1). Bandung: Utomo.

Rajah, J. 2012. *Authoritarian Rule of Law: Legislation, Discourse and Legitimacy in Singapore*. New York: Cambridge University Press.

Ramm, T. 1986. 'Laissez-faire and State Protection of Workers', in Hepple, B. (ed.), *The Making of Labour Law in Europe: A Comparative Study of Nine Countries Up To 1945*. London: Mansell Publishing Ltd., pp. 73–113.

Ramseyer, J. M. 2010. 'Comparative Litigation Rates', *Harvard John M. Olin Discussion Paper Series* 681.

Rastika, I. 2012. 'Hakim Syarifuddin Divonis Empat Tahun Penjara', *Kompas*, 29 February. Available at: https://nasional.kompas.com/read/2012/02/28/13401220/Hakim.Syarifuddin.Divonis.Empat.Tahun.Penjara.

Rastika, I. 2013. 'Zulkarnaen Djabar Divonis 15 Tahun Penjara', *Kompas*, 30 May. Available at: http://nasional.kompas.com/read/2013/05/30/20290254/Zulkarnaen.Djabar.Divonis.15.Tahun.Penjara.

Ravensbergen, S. 2018. *Courtrooms of Conflict; Criminal Law, Local Elites and Legal Pluralities in Colonial Java*. PhD Thesis, Leiden University. Available at: https://openaccess.leidenuniv.nl/handle/1887/61039

Rayanti, D. 2016. 'Kejar Peringkat 40 Kemudahan Berusaha, Ini yang Dilakukan Pemerintah', *Detik.com*, 11 April. Available at: https://finance.detik.com/berita-ekonomi-bisnis/d-3184838/kejar-peringkat-40-kemudahan-berusaha-ini-yang-dilakukan-pemerintah.

Rentel, A. D., 1998. 'Clash of Civilizations? Cultural Differences in the Development and Interpretation of International Law,' *American Society of International Law Proceedings* 92: 232.

Republika. 2012. *Over Crowded di Lapas/ Rutan, Sampai Kapan? (Bagian 1)*. Available at: www.republika.co.id/berita/jurnalisme-warga/wacana/14/08/13/na6zjo-over-crowded-di-lapasrutan-sampai-kapan-bagian-1.

Rigon, A. 2015. 'Unequal Relations in the Governance of the World Social Forum Process: An Analysis of the Practices of the Nairobi Forum', *Interface* 7(2): 75.

Riles, A. 2005. 'A New Agenda for the Cultural Study of Law: Taking on the Technicalities', *Buffalo Law Review* 53: 973–1033.

Ritonga, R., Pujalaksana, N., Solemanto, S. and Ginting, S. 2003. *Singgih Memoar Seorang Prosecutor Agung*. Jakarta: PT. Quaulquita Communication.

Rokhani, E. 2008. 'Inter-union Conflict in Three Indonesian Factories', *Labour and Management in Development Journal* 9: 1–10.

Rosen, L. 2008. *Law and Culture: An Invitation*. Princeton: Princeton University Press.

Roux. T. 2013. *The Politics of Principle: The First South African Constitutional Court, 1995–2005*. Cambridge: Cambridge University Press.

Roux, T. 2018. *The Politico-Legal Dynamics of Judicial Review: A Comparative Analysis*. New York: Cambridge University Press.

Roux, T. 2018. 'Indonesia's Judicial Review Regime in Comparative Perspective', *Constitutional Review Journal*.

Roux, T. and Siregar, F. 2016. 'Trajectories of Curial Power: The Rise, Fall and Partial Rehabilitation of the Indonesian Constitutional Court', *Australian Journal of Asian Law* 17: 1–21.

Sahardjo., S. H. 1963. *Pohon Beringin Pengajoman Hukum Pantjasila*. Jakarta: Fakultas Hukum Universitas Indonesia.

Sahbani, A. 2016. 'Lima Pengadilan Ini Terbanyak Tangani Gugatan Sederhana', *Hukumonline*, 13 September. Available at: www.hukumonline.com/berita/baca/lt57d7d504a0587/lima-pengadilan-ini-terbanyak-tangani-gugatan-sederhana.

Salim, T. 2015. 'Govt forms another anti-illegal fishing task force', *The Jakarta Post*, 4 June. Available at: www.thejakartapost.com/news/2015/06/04/govt-forms-another-anti-illegal-fishing-task-force.html.

Saputra, A. 2016. 'PK Ditolak, Mantan Kepala SKK Migas Rudi Rubiandini Tetap Dibui 7 Tahun', *Detik News*, 19 April. Available at: http://news.detik.com/berita/3191187/pk-ditolak-mantan-kepala-skk-migas-rudi-rubiandini-tetap-dibui-7-tahun.

Saragih, B. B. T. 2015. 'Hadi's Pre-Trial Victory a "Disaster" for KPK', *Jakarta Post*, 26 May. Available at: www.thejakartapost.com/news/2015/05/26/hadi-s-pre trial-victory-a-disaster-kpk.html.

Sarat, A. and Kearns, T. R. 2000. 'The Cultural Lives of Law', in *Law in the Domains of Culture*. Ann Arbor: University of Michigan Press.

Satrio, A. 2018. 'Constitutional Retrogression in Indonesia under President Joko Widodo's Government: What Can the Constitutional Court Do?', *Constitutional Review* 2.

Satuan Tugas Pemberantasan Mafia Hukum. 2010. *Mafia Hukum: Modus Operandi, Akar Permasalahan dan Strategi Penanggulangan*. Indonesia: Satuan Tugas Pemberantasan Mafia Hukum.

Schröeder-van Waes, M. and K. O. Sidharta. 2004. 'Upholding Indonesian Bankruptcy Legislation', in Chatib Basri, M. and van der Eng, P. (eds.), *Business in Indonesia, New Challenges, Old Problems*. Singapore: Institute of South East Asian Studies, pp. 191–203.

Schubert, B., Rusyidi, B., Pratiwi, A. and Halim, M. A. 2015. *Rapid Assessment of the Child Social Welfare Program (PKSA)*. Jakarta: UNICEF.

Schwartz, J. 2005. 'Pot and Prejudice: Australian Coverage of the Corby Saga', *Metro Magazine* 145: 138–143.

Sen, A. 2004. 'How Does Culture Matter', in Raq, V. and Walton, M. (eds.), *Culture and Public Action*. Stanford: Stanford University Press.

Setiawan, K. 2013. *Promoting Human Rights. National Human Rights Commissions in Indonesia and Malaysia*. Leiden: Leiden University Press.

Setiawan, K. 2016. 'From Hope to Disillusion: The Paradox of Komnas HAM, the Indonesian National Human Rights Commission', *Bijdragen tot de Taal-, Land- en Volkenkunde* 172(1): 1–32.

Shapiro, M. 1981. *Courts: A Comparative and Political Analysis*. Chicago: University of Chicago Press.

Siems, M. 2014. *Comparative Law*. Cambridge: Cambridge University Press.

Silbey, S. S. 2005. 'After Legal Consciousness', *Annual Review of Law and Social Science* 1: 323–368.

Silbey, S. S. 2010. 'Legal Culture and Cultures of Legality', in Hall, J., Grindstaff, L. and Lo, M. (eds.), *Handbook of Cultural Sociology*. London and New York: Routledge.

Silverstein, G. 2008. 'Singapore: The Exception That Proves Rules Matter', in Ginsburg, T. and Moustafa, T. (eds.), *Rule by Law: The Politics of Courts in Authoritarian Regimes*. Cambridge: Cambridge University Press, pp. 73–101.

Simanjuntak, R. S. 2009. 'Potret Buram Pelaksanaan Eksekusi di Indonesia', *Hukumonline*, 3 April.

Sindonews. 2017. 'Penghuni Lapas Di Indonesia Didominasi Napi Kasus Narkoba Rabu', 17 May. Available at: https://nasional.sindonews.com/read/1205976/13/penghuni-lapas-di-indonesia-didominasi-napi-kasus-narkoba-1495035513.

Siregar, F. E. 2016. *Indonesian Constitutional Politics: 2003–2013*. PhD thesis, University of New South Wales. Available at: http://unsworks.unsw.edu.au/fapi/datastream/unsworks:40210/SOURCE02?view=true.

Siregar, L. 2002. 'Sinetron keadilan' *Pantau*, 2 September. Available at: www.pantau.or.id/?/=d/212.

Soepomo, I. 1994. *Hukum Perburuhan Bidang Hubungan Kerja*. Jakarta: Djambatan.

Soepomo, R. 1997. *Sistem Hukum Di Indonesia Sebelum Perang Dunia II* (15th ed.). Jakarta: PT Pradnya Paramita.

Steele, J. 2012. 'The Making of the 1999 Indonesian Press Law', *Indonesia* 94: 1–22.

Steele, S. 1999. 'The New Law on Bankruptcy in Indonesia: Towards a Modern Corporate Bankruptcy Regime?', *Melbourne University Law Review* 5: 144–160.

Stockmann, P. 2007. *The New Indonesian Constitutional Court: A Study into its Beginnings and First Years of Work*. Hanns Seidel Foundation.

Subdirektorat Statistik Demografi. 2013. *Proyeksi Penduduk Indonesia 2010–2035*. Indonesia: Badan Pusat Statistik.

Sukmana, Y. 2015. 'Kecewa Berat, Menteri Susi Minta Pemerintah Tutup Pengadilan Perikanan Ambon', *Kompas*, 14 September. Available at: https://ekonomi.kompas.com/read/2015/09/14/160246826/Kecewa.Berat.Menteri.Susi.Minta.Pmerintah.Tutup.Pengadilan.Perikanan.Ambon.

Sulistiyanto, P. 2007. 'Politics of Justice and Reconciliation in Post-Suharto Indonesia', *Journal of Contemporary Asia* 37(1): 73–94.

Sumner, C. and Lindsey, T. 2010. *Courting Reform: Indonesia's Islamic Courts and Justice for the Poor*. Sydney: Lowy Institute for International Policy.

Sunarti, T. et al. 2017. *Optimalisasi Pelaksanaan Eksekusi Pidana Denda dikaitkan pasal 102 Undang-Undang no 31 Tahun 2004 Tentang Perikanan*. Jakarta: Miswar (Anggota IKAPI).

Sundhaussen, U. 1986. *Politik Militer Indonesia 1945–1967 Menuju Dwi Fungsi ABRI.* Jakarta: Lembaga Penelitian, Pendidikan dan Penerangan Ekonomi dan Sosial LP3ES.

Surabaya Pagi. 2013. 'DPR Usul Hakim Agung Diuji Lima Tahunan', 11 September. Available at: www.surabayapagi.com/read/104877/2013/09/11/DPR_Usul_Hakim_Agung_Diuji_Lima_Tahunan.html.

Surya Online. 2012. 'Hakim Tipikor Surabaya Bebaskan 19 Koruptor', 17 September. Available at: http://surabaya.tribunnews.com/2012/07/27/hakim-dame-bebas kan-tujuh-perkara-korupsi.

Suryomenggolo, J. 2004. 'Dinamika Perumusan UU Ketenagakerjaan dan UU Penyelesaian Perselisihan Hubungan Industrial: Apa, Siapa, dan Bagaimana?', *Laporan Studi TURC.* Jakarta: TURC.

Suyudi, A. 2004. *An Inquiry to Indonesian Judicial Decision-making Behaviour on Bankruptcy Cases (1998–2002), a Jurimetrical Analysis*, paper presented at the 4th Forum for Asian Insolvency Reform (FAIR), New Delhi, 3–5 November 2004.

Suyudi, A., Nugroho, E. and Nurbayanti, H. S. 2003. *Analisis Hukum Kepailitan Indonesia: Kepailitan di Negeri Pailit.*, Jakarta: Pusat Studi Hukum & Kebijakan (PSHK).

Syukur, F. A. and Bagshaw, D. M. 2015. 'Victim-offender Mediation with Youth Offenders in Indonesia', *Conflict Resolution Quarterly* 32(4): 389–410.

Tabalujan, B. S. 2002. 'Why Indonesian Corporate Governance Failed – Conjectures Concerning Legal Culture', *Columbia Journal of Asian Law* 15(2): 141–171.

Tahyar, B. 2010. The Politics of Indonesia's Pengadilan Tipikor. In P. Nicholson & A. Harding (Eds.), *New Courts in Asia*, Routledge, pp. 279–298.

Tahyar, B. H. 2012. *Patrimonialism, Power and the Politics of Judicial Reform in Post-Soeharto Indonesia: an Institutional Analysis.* PhD thesis, University of London.

Tapsell, R. 2014. *By-Lines, Balibo, Bali Bombings: Australian Journalists in Indonesia.* Melbourne: Australian Scholarly Publishing.

Tapsell, R. 2017. *Media Power in Indonesia: Oligarchs, Citizens and the Digital Revolution.* Maryland: Rowman and Littlefield International.

Tempo. 2011. 'Kurator Puguh Wirawan Divonis 3,5 Tahun Penjara', 1 November. Available at: https://nasional.tempo.co/read/364264/kurator-puguh-wirawan-divonis-35-tahun-penjara.

Tempo. 2012. 'Hybrid Judges', 3 September.

Tempo. 2016. 'Terima Suap OC Kaligis Hakim PTUN Medan Divonis 2 Tahun Bui', 27 January. Available at: https://nasional.tempo.co/read/739770/terima-suap-oc-kaligis-hakim-ptun-medan-divonis-2-tahun-bui.

Tempo. 2016. 'Lessons from Ahok case', 21 November. Available at: https://en.tempo.co/read/news/2016/11/21/080821751/Lesson-from-Ahoks-Case.

Tempo Interaktif 2006. 'Ketua MA Resmikan 33 Pengadilan Hubungan Industrial', 14 January. Available at: https://nasional.tempo.co/read/72305/ketua-ma-resmi kan-33-pengadilan-hubungan-industrial.

The Asia Foundation. 2001. *Survey Report on Citizens' Perceptions of the Indonesian Justice Sector. Preliminary Findings and Recommendations.* Jakarta: The Asia Foundation.

The Jakarta Post. 2001. 'Adi Andojo Resigns from the Anti-Corruption Team', 28 March. Available at: www.accessmylibrary.com/article-1G1-72410845/adi-andojo-resigns-anti.html.

The Jakarta Post. 2012. 'Govt Considers Shutting down Corruption Courts in Regions', 21 August.

The Jakarta Post. 2015. 'Former Makassar Mayor Wins Pre-Trial Court Decision,' 12 May. Available at: www.thejakartapost.com/news/2015/05/12/former-makas sar-mayor-wins-pretrial-court-decision.html.

The Jakarta Post. 2016a. 'Court Sends Jero Wacik to Four Years in Prison for Corruption', 9 February. Available at: www.thejakartapost.com/news/2016/02/ 09/court-sends-jero-wacik-four-years-prison-corruption.html.

The Jakarta Post. 2016b. 'Ahok case expose to be televised: police chief', 11 June. Available at: www.thejakartapost.com/news/2016/11/06/ahoks-case-expose-to-be-televised-police-chief.html.

The Liang Gie. 1995. *Pertumbuhan Pemerintahan Daerah di Negara Republik Indonesia* Vol 3. Liberty.

The World Bank. 2002. *Initiatives in Legal and Judicial Reform.* Washington: The World Bank.

The World Bank. 2015. *Doing Business 2016: Measuring Regulatory Quality and Efficiency, Indonesia.* Washington: The World Bank.

The World Bank. 2017. *Doing Business 2017: Equal Opportunity for All.* Washington: The World Bank.

Thio, L. 2012. 'Between Apology and Apogee, Autochthony: The Rule of Law Beyond the Rules of Law in Singapore', *Singapore Journal of Legal Studies*: 269–297.

Thompson, E. P. 1975. *Whigs and Hunters: The Origin of the Black Act.* New York: Pantheon Books.

Tilly, Charles. 1990. *Coercion, Capital and European States: AD 990–1992.* Cambridge, MA: Blackwell.

Tjandra, S. 2004. 'Sekadar Bekerja? Analisis UU No.2 tahun 2004 tentang Penyelesaian Perselisihan Hubungan Industrial: Perspektif Serikat Buruh', TURC Discussion Paper. Jakarta: TURC.

Tjandra, S. 2007. 'The Court in Indonesia, Quo Vadis? Some Notes from the Courtroom'; an article presented at the Conference on Current Issues in Indonesian Law: In Honour of Professor Daniel S. Lev, University of Washington School of Law in Collaboration with the University of Indonesia, Faculty of Law, Seattle, 27–28 February 2007.

Tjandra, S. 2010. 'Imprisoning Employers?', *The Jakarta Post*, 16 January. Available at: www.thejakartapost.com/news/2010/01/15/imprisoning-employers.html.

Tjandra, S. (ed.) 2014. *Catatan Akademik RUU Pengadilan Perburuhan*. Jakarta: TURC.

Tjandra, S. 2016. *Labour Law and Development in Indonesia*. Leiden: Leiden University Press.

Tjandra, S. and Pangaribuan, M. (eds.) 2007. *Kompilasi Putusan Pengadilan Hubungan Industrial Terseleksi: 2006–2007*. Jakarta: TURC.

Tjandra, S. and Suryomenggolo, J. (eds.) 2006. *Makin Terang Bagi Kami: Belajar Hukum Perburuhan*. Jakarta: TURC.

Topsfield, J. and Rompies, K., 'Australian Embassy Bomber's Role in Jakarta Attacks Exposes Jail Weaknesses', *The Sydney Morning Herald*, 4 March 2016. Available at: www.smh.com.au/world/australian-embassy-bombers-role-in-jakarta-attacks-exposes-jail-weaknesses-20160304-gnad11.html

Tresna, R. 1955. *Komentar HIR* (13th ed.). Jakarta: PT Pradnya Paramita.

Turan, A., Gunawan, I. P., Triharjoko, S. and Rochaedi, D. 2000. *Jenderal Polisi RS Soekanto Bapak Kepolisian Negara Republik Indonesia*. Jakarta: Karya Jaya, YBB Polri Pusat.

Tyson, A. D. 2010. *Decentralization and Adat Revivalism in Indonesia: The Politics of Becoming Indigenous*. New York: Routledge.

Uhlenbeck, E. M. 1978. Studies in Javanese Morphology. Martinus Nijhoff.

Unger, R. 1976. *Law in Modern Society*. New York: Free Press.

UNICEF. 2004. *Indonesia: Establishing a Child-Sensitive Juvenile Justice System in Indonesia*. Available at: www.un.org/ruleoflaw/blog/document/establishing-a-child-sensitive-juvenile-justice-system-in-indonesia.

USAID. 2007. *Bankruptcy Study on Asset Recovery by the Center for Legal Studies*. Jakarta: USAID.

USAID 2010. *Indonesia Anticorruption and Commercial Court Enhancement (In-ACCE) Project, Final Report*. Jakarta: USAID.

USAID. 2015. *Changes for Justice Project, Final Report*, Jakarta: USAID.

Van Hoecke, M. and Warrington, M. 1998. 'Legal Cultures, Legal Paradigms and Legal Doctrine: Towards a New Model for Comparative Law', *The International and Comparative Law Quarterly* 47(3): 495–536.

Van Welzenis, I. 2016. *Country-Level Summaries of Diversion and Other Alternative Measures for Children in Conflict with the Law in East Asian and Pacific Island Countries*. UNICEF.

Velde, J. J. van 1928. *De Godsdienstige Rechtspraak in Nederlandsch-Indië: Staatsrechtelijk Beschouwd*. Phd thesis, Universiteit Leiden. Leiden: Drukkerij A. Vros.

Viva. 2010. 'Definisi Mafia Hukum Menurut Satgas', 8 January. Available at: www.viva.co.id/berita/nasional/119677-definisi-mafia-hukum-menurut-satgas.

Vollenhoven, C. Van. 1931. *Het Adatrecht van Nederlandsch-Indië: 2*. Leiden: Brill.

Vriend, K. 2016. *Avoiding a Full Criminal Trial: Fair Trial Rights, Diversions and Shortcuts in Dutch and International Criminal Proceedings*. Springer.

Vu, Tuong. 2010 'Studying the State through State Formation', *World Politics* 62 (1): 148–175.

Wagner, B. B. and Jacobs, L. G. 2008. 'Retooling Law Enforcement to Investigate and Prosecute Entrenched Corruption: Key Criminal Procedure Reforms for Indonesia and Other Nations', *University of Pennsylvania Journal of International Economic Law* 30(1): 183–265.

Weber, M. 1968. *Economy and Society*. Berkeley: University of California Press.

Wee, V. 2012. 'The Politicization of Women's Bodies in Indonesia: Sexual Scripts as Charters for Action', in Helie, A. and Hoodfar, H. (eds.), *Sexuality in Muslim Contexts: Restrictions and Resistance*. London and New York: Zed Books.

Welker, M. 2014. *Enacting the Corporation: An American Mining Firm in Post-Authoritarian Indonesia*. Berkeley: University of California Press.

Wessels, B. 1999. *Business and Bankruptcy Law in the Netherlands: Selected Essays*. The Hague: Kluwer Law International.

Widayati, L. S. 2012. 'Rehabilitasi Narapidana Dalam Overcrowded Lembaga Pemasyarakatan', *Jurnal Negara Hukum* 3(2): 201–226.

Wilson, J. Q. 1989. *Bureaucracy: What Government Agencies Do and Why They Do It*. New York: Basic Books.

Winters, J. 2013. 'Oligarchy and Democracy in Indonesia', *Indonesia* 96: 11–33.

Wiratraman, H. 2014. *Press Freedom, Law and Politics in Indonesia: A Socio-Legal Study*. Leiden: Leiden University Press.

Wiratraman, H., Pratiwi, C., Herlambang, U. and Jebabu, A. 2017. *Studi Sosio-Legal: Asas-Asas Umum Pemerintahan yang Baik (AUPB)*. Jakarta: JSSP, CILC and LEIP.

Wisnubroto, A. 1997. *Hakim dan Peradilan di Indonesia dalam Beberapa Askes Kajian*. Yogyakarta: Universitas Atma Jaya Yogyakarta.

Wiwoho, B. 2017. 'Kejakgung Berencanan Bentuk Kembali Direktorat Pelanggaran HAM', *CNN Indonesia*, 13 April. Available at: www.cnnindonesia.com/nasional/20170412230149-12-207157/kejagung-berencana-bentuk-kembali-direktorat-pelanggaran-ham.

Yahya, I. D. 2004. *Mengadili Menteri Memeriksa Perwira Prosecutor Agung Soeprapto dan Penegakan Hukum di Indonesia Periode 1950–1959*. Jakarta: PT. Gramedia Pustaka Utama.

Yanow, D. and Schwartz-Shea, P. (eds.) 2006. *Interpretation and Method: Empirical Research Methods and the Interpretive Turn*. London: ME Sharpe.

Zikry, I., Ardhan, A. and Tiara, A. E. 2016. Prapenuntutan Sekarang, Ratusan Ribu Perkara Disimpan, Puluhan Ribu Perkara Hilang (Vol. 1). Available at: http://mappifhui.org/wp-content/uploads/2016/12/Prapenuntutan-Sekarang-Ratusan-Ribu-Perkara-Disimpan-Puluhan-Ribu-Perkara-Hilang.pdf.

Zoelva, H. 2013. 'Aspek Konstitutionalitas Pengadilan Khusus di Indonesia', in Hermansyah, et al (eds.), Putih Hitam Pengadilan Khusus. Jakarta: Komisi Yudisial.

Laws

General Elucidation of Law No 31/2004

Government Regulation No 24/2006 on the procedures for recruitment and dismissal of ad hoc judges for the fisheries court, art 3(g)-(h)

Government Regulation in lieu of Law No. 1/1998 on the Amendment of the Bankruptcy Law

Herziene Inlandsch Reglement. Staatsblaad No. 44/1941.

Keputusan Menteri Kelautan dan Perikanan No: Kep. 18/Men/2002 tentang Rencana Strategis Pembangunan Kelautan dan Perikanan tahun 2001 – 2004.

Kitab Undang-Undang Hukum Perdata/Indonesian Civil Code (Burgerlijk Wetboek/BW). Staatsblaad No. 23/1847.

Kitab Undang-Undang Hukum Pidana/Indonesian Criminal Code (Wetboek van Strafrecht). Staatsblaad No. 732/1915.

Law No. 7/1970 on the Judiciary

Law No. 8/1981 on Criminal Procedural Law (KUHAP).

Law No. 14/1985 on the Supreme Court

Law No. 3/1997 on Children's Criminal Court

Law No. 4/1998 on Ratification of Government Regulation In Lieu of Law No. 1 of 199

Law No. 30/2002 on the Corruption Eradication Commission

Law No. 5/2004 on the Supreme Court

Law No. 37/2004 on Bankruptcy and Suspension of Payments

Law No. 31/2004 on Fisheries

Law No. 11/2008 on Information and Electronic Transaction

Law No. 46/2009 on the Anti-Corruption Court

Law No. 3/2009 on the Supreme Court

Law No. 35/2009 on Narcotics

Law No. 45/2009 on the Amendment of Law No 21/2004 on Fisheries, art 73(2) and (3)

Law No. 48/2009 on the Basic Provisions of Judicial Power

Law No. 12/2011 on Legislation

Law No. 16/2011 on Legal Aid

Law No. 11/2012 on the Juvenile Justice System

Law No. 18/2013 on the Prevention and Eradication of Forest Destruction

Law No. 23/2014 on Local Government

Law No. 7/2017 on Elections

Ministry of Social Affairs Regulation No. 15/2014 on Standards for Social Welfare Institution for Children in Conflict with the Law (Permensos 15/2014)

Minister of Justice Decree No. M.09-HT.05.10.Tahun 1998

Minister of Law and Human Rights Regulation No. 1/2013 re Guidelines for the Honorarium of Receivers and Administrators

Minister of Law and Human Rights Regulation No. 11/2016 on Guidelines for the Honorarium of Receivers and Administrators

Minister of Law and Human Rights Regulation No. 2/2017 on the Revision of Regulation of the Minister of Law and Human Rights No. 11/2016

Minister of Law and Human Rights Decree No. M.HH-01.AH.06.06 Tahun 2014 on the Joint Committee

Minister of Law and Human Rights Decree No. M.HH-01.AH.06.06 Tahun 2016 on the Joint Committee

Peraturan Kapolri No 21 tahun 2010 tentang Susunan Organisasi dan Tata kerja Satuan Organisasi di Tingkat Maber Polri

Presidential Decree No. 37 of 2009 on the Legal Mafia Eradication Task Force

Presidential Regulation No. 20/2011 on support and other entitlements for the Ad hoc judges of the Industrial Relations Court

Presidential Regulation No. 86/2010 for ad hoc judges of the Anti-Corruption Court

Presidential Regulation No. 87/2010 for ad hoc judges of the Fisheries Court

Presidential Regulation No. 115/2015 on the Task Force on Illegal Fishing

Presidential Regulation No. 79/2017 on Government's 2018 Workplan

Supreme Court letter No. 6/KM/a 6/KM/845/M/A/III/67

Supreme Court letter No. 3/2015

Supreme Court Regulation No. 2/2000 on the Perfection of Presidential Decision No. 71/M/1999

Supreme Court Regulation No. 2/2012

Supreme Court Regulation No. 4/2014

Supreme Court Regulation No. 2/2015 on the Small Claims Mechanism

Supreme Court Regulation No. 3/2017

Supreme Court Regulation No. 13/2016

Supreme Court Circular Letter No. 7/2009

Supreme Court Circular Letter No. 4/2010

Supreme Court Circular Letter No. 7/2012

Supreme Court Circular Letter No. 3/2015

Supreme Court Circular Letter No. 2/2016 on the Improvement of Efficiency and Transparency for Handling Bankruptcy and Suspension of Payments at Court

The 1945 Constitution of the Republic of Indonesia

Court Decisions

Constitutional Court Decision 27/PUU-XI/2013

Constitutional Court Decision 31/PUU-XV/2017

Constitutional Court Decision 33/PUU-XIV/2016

Constitutional Court Decision 48/PUU-IX/2011

Constitutional Court Decision 50/PUU-VI/2008

Commercial Court Decision 05/Pailit/1998/PN.Niaga/Jkt.Pst

Commercial Court Decision 16/Pailit/1998/PN. Niaga/Jkt.Pst

Commercial Court Decision 02/PKPU/2000/PN.JKT.PST

Commercial Court Decision 65/Pailit/2000/PN.JKT.PST

Commercial Court Decision 16/PKPU/2000/PN.JKT.PST

Commercial Court Decision 10/Pailit/2002/PN.Niaga/Jkt.Pst

Commercial Court Decision 13/Pailit/2004/PN.Niaga.Jkt.Pst

Commercial Court of Central Jakarta, Decision 53/Pdt.Sus-PKPU/2013/PN Niaga. Jkt.Pst.

Commercial Court of Central Jakarta, Decision 59/Pdt.Sus-PKPU/2014/PN.Niaga. Jkt.Pst

Commercial Court of Central Jakarta Decision 98/Pdt.Sus-PKPU/2015/PN.Niaga. Jkt.Pst

Court of Appeal Jakarta, Decision. 23/PID/TPK/2012/PT.DKI

District Court of Blora, Decision 4/Pdt.G.S/2016/PN Bla

District Court of Gorontalo, Decision 9/Pdt.G.S/2017/PN Gto

District Court of Palangkaraya, Decision 4/Pdt.G.S/2016/PN Bla

District Court of Banyuwangi, Decision 202/Pid.Sus-PRK/2018/PN Byw

District Court of Ternate, Decision 134/Pid.Sus/2018/PN Tte

District Court of Tarakan, Decision 90/Pid.B/2018/PN Ta

District Court of Palalawan, Decision 08/Pid.B/2012/PN

District Court of Melauboh, Decision 12/Pdt.G/2012/PN.BO

District Court of Central Jakarta, Decision 2081/Pid.B/2011/PN.JKT.PST

Fisheries Court of Ambon, Decision 01/Pid.Sus/PRK/2015/PN.Amb

Fisheries Court of Ambon, Decision 04/Pid.Sus.PRK/2015/PN.Amb

High Court of Ambon, Decision 15/Pid.Sus-PRK/2015/PT.Amb

High Court of Ambon, Decision 33/Pid.sus-Prk/PT.Amb

High Court of Banda Aceh, Decision 50/PDT/2014/PT.BNA

High Court of Riau, Decision 235/Pid.Sus/2012/PTR
Supreme Court Decision 021 K/N/2002
Supreme Court Decision 1266/Pid.Sus/2014
Supreme Court Decision 1127 K/Pid.Sus/2014
Supreme Court Decision 138 PK/Pid.Sus/2013
Supreme Court Decision 203 PK/Pid.Sus/2013
Supreme Court Decision 2184 K/Pid.Sus/2016
Supreme Court Decision 225/PK/Pid.Sus/2011
Supreme Court Decision 2303 K/Pid.Sus/2013
Supreme Court Decision 2671 K/Pid.Sus/2015
Supreme Court Decision 300/Pdt/2010
Supreme Court Decision 340 K/Pid.Sus/2015
Supreme Court Decision 712 K/Pid.Sus/2016
Supreme Court Decision 73 PK/Pid.Sus/2013
Supreme Court Decision 750 K/Pid.Sus/2014
Supreme Court Decision 76 K/Kr/1969
Supreme Court Decision 8 K/N/2004
Supreme Court Decision 822 K/Pid.Sus/2010
Supreme Court Decision 942 K/Pid.Sus/2017
Supreme Court Decision 1824 K/Pid.Sus/2012
Supreme Court Decision 555 K/Pdt.Sus-Pailit/2013
Supreme Court Decision 48 PK/Pdt.Sus-Pailit/2013
Supreme Court Decision 83 PK/Pdt.Sus-Pailit/2015
Supreme Court Decision 167 PK/Pid.Sus/2015

Parliamentary Records

DPR 2018. Risalah Rapat Panitia Kerja (Panja) Komisi III DPR RI dalam rangka Pembahasan Rancangan Undang-Undang tentang Perikanan, DPR, Jakarta.

DPR 2015. Brief Report of Legislative Body Public Hearing with Indonesian Judges Association (IKAHI), 27 August. Jakarta.

DPR 2009. Risalah Rapat Tim Perumus Komisi IV dengan Pemerintah RUU tentang Perikanan, 29 September. Jakarta.

DPR 2004a. Risalah Rapat Panitia Kerja (Panja) Komisi III DPR RI dalam Rangka Pembahasan Rancangan Undang-Undang tentang Perikanan, DPR RI. on 16 July, Jakarta.

DPR 2004b. Risalah Rapat Panitia Kerja (Panja) Komisi III DPR RI dalam Rangka Pembahasan Rancangan Undang-Undang Perikanan, DPR RI, 17 July. Jakarta.

DPR 2004c. Proses Pembahasan RUU tentang Perikanan, Biro Persidangan DPR RI, Jakarta.

DPR 2004d. Risalah Rapat Paripurna DPR RI Pembicaraan Tingkat II/ Pengambilan Keputusan Terhadap Rancangan Undang-Undang Republik Indonesia Tentang Kepailitan dan Penundaan Kewajiban Pembayaran Utang, Jakarta 22 September,

DPR 2002–2004. Risalah Pembahasan Undang-undang Kejaksaan 2002–2004 (Legislative minutes of IPS Law). Jakarta.

Report of Commission IV (2009), Report of Commission IV to the DPR Plenary Assembly to adopt the amended draft on 30 September 2009, Jakarta.

INDEX